REPUTATIONS

Titles in the Reputations series

THOMAS BECKET

Anne Duggan

Professor of Medieval History at King's College London

A member of the Hodder Headline Group
LONDON
Distributed in the United States of America by
Oxford University Press Inc., New York

First published in Great Britain in 2004 by
Arnold, a member of the Hodder Headline Group,
338 Euston Road, London NW1 3BH

http://www.arnoldpublishers.com

Distributed in the United States of America by
Oxford University Press Inc.
198 Madison Avenue, New York, NY10016

The advice and information in this book are believed to be true and
accurate at the date of going to press, but neither the author nor the publisher
can accept any legal responsibility or liability for any errors or omissions.

British Library Cataloguing in Publication Data
A catalogue record for this book is available from the British Library

Library of Congress Cataloging-in-Publication Data
A catalog record for this book is available from the Library of Congress

ISBN 0 340 74137 6 (hb)
ISBN 0 340 74138 4 (pb)

1 2 3 4 5 6 7 8 9 10

Typeset in 10/12 pt Sabon by Charon Tec Pvt. Ltd, Chennai, India
www.charontec.com
Printed and bound in Great Britain by CPI Bath

What do you think about this book? Or any other Arnold title?
Please send your comments to **feedback.arnold@hodder.co.uk**

Contents

General editorial preface

Hero or villain? Charlatan or true prophet? Sinner or saint? The volumes in the Reputations series examine the reputations of some of history's most conspicuous, powerful and influential individuals, considering a range of representations, some of striking incompatibility. The aim is to demonstrate not merely that history is indeed, in Pieter Geyl's phrase, 'argument without end', but that the study even of contradictory conceptions can be fruitful: that the jettisoning of one thesis or presentation leaves behind something of value.

In Iago's self-serving denunciation of it, reputation is 'an idle and most false imposition; oft got without merit, and lost without deserving', but a more generous definition would allow its use as one of the principle currencies of historical understanding. In seeking to analyse the cultivation, creation and deconstruction of reputation, we can understand better the wellsprings of actions, the workings out of competing claims to power, the different purposes of rival ideologies – in short, see more clearly ways in which the past becomes History.

There is a commitment in each volume to showing how understanding of an individual develops (sometimes in uneven and divergent ways), whether in response to fresh evidence, the emergence or waning of dominant ideologies, changing attitudes and preoccupations in the age in which an author writes, or the creation of new historical paradigms. Will Hitler ever seem *quite* the same after the evidence of a recent study revealing the extent of his Jewish connections during the Vienna years? Reassessment of Lenin and Stalin has been given fresh impetus by the collapse of the Soviet Union and the opening of many of its archives; and the end of the Cold War and of its attendant assumptions must alter our views of Eisenhower and Kennedy. How will our perceptions of Elizabeth I change in the presence of a new awareness of 'gendered history'?

There is more to the series than illumination of ways in which recent discoveries or trends have refashioned identities or given recent actions new meaning – though that is an important part. The corresponding aim is to provide readers with a strong sense of the channels and course of debate from the outset: not a Cook's Tour of the historiography, but identification of the key interpretative issues and guidance as to how commentators of different eras and persuasions have tackled them.

Preface

Just this week, as I was preparing this study for the publisher, I received remarkable confirmation of the abiding fascination that Becket's name still inspires, with an invitation to contribute a background piece for a new opera on Henry II and Thomas Becket. Composed by Stephen Barlow, with libretto by Philip Wells, the work is scheduled for performance at Canterbury in autumn 2004. I have not seen the libretto yet, and I have no idea how St Thomas will be presented in this work. Proud prelate, traitor who got what he deserved or victim of Angevin ruthlessness are three of the numerous possibilities that immediately spring to mind, to say nothing of the story of friendship destroyed.

In writing this book I have benefited, as all scholars do, from the labours of others, especially the critical and thought-provoking study by Professor Frank Barlow. Among earlier writers, I should like especially to acknowledge the work of David Knowles, Raymonde Foreville and Beryl Smalley, and, for introducing me to the intricacies of twelfth-century canon law, my late husband, Charles Duggan, to whose memory these pages are dedicated.

Anne J. Duggan
King's College London
27 May 2004

Abbreviations

Annales monastici	*Annales monastici*, ed. H.R. Luard, 5 vols, RS 36 (London, 1864–69)
Anon. I	*Vita sancti Thomae, Cantuariensis archiepiscopi et martyris, sub Rogerii Pontiniacensis monachi nomine olim edita: MTB*, iv, 1–79. 'Roger of Pontigny'
Anon. II	*Vita sancti Thomae, Cantuariensis archiepiscopi et martyris, auctore Anonymous II: MTB*, iv, 80–144. 'The Lambeth Anonymous'
AT	Alan of Tewkesbury, *Vita et Passio S. Thomae martyris, auctore Alano abbate Tewkesberiensi: MTB*, ii, 299–301, 323–52
Barlow, *Becket*	Frank Barlow, *Thomas Becket* (London, 1986)
BIHR	*Bulletin of the Institute of Historical Research* (now *Historical Research*)
Bischofsmord	*Bischofsmord im Mittelalter. Murder of Bishops*, ed. Natalie Fryde and Dirk Reitz (Göttingen, 2003)
BL	British Library
BP	Benedict of Peterborough, *Passio S. Thomae Cantuariensis, auctore Benedicto Petriburgensi abbate: MTB*, ii, 1–19
BP, *Miracula*	Benedict of Peterborough, *Miracula S. Thomae Cantuariensis, auctore Benedicto, abbate Petriburgensi: MTB*, ii, 21–281

Brixius, *Die Mitglieder*	J.M. Brixius, *Die Mitglieder des Kardinalkollegiums von 1130–1181* (Berlin, 1912)
CCSL	*Corpus Christianorum, Series Latina* (Turnhout, 1953–)
CCCM	*Corpus Christianorum, Continuatio Mediaevalis* (Turnhout, 1953–)
CTB	*The Correspondence of Thomas Becket, Archbishop of Canterbury 1162–1170*, ed. and trans. A.J. Duggan, 2 vols, OMT (Oxford, 2000)
Codex	*Codex Iustinianus*: see *Corpus iuris civilis*
Corpus iuris civilis	*Corpus iuris civilis*, ed. Paul Krueger, Theodor Mommsen, Rudolf Schoell, and William Kroll, 3 vols (Berlin, 1905–29; repr. 1954)
Diceto	*Radulfi de Diceto decani Lundoniensis opera historica*, ed. W. Stubbs, 2 vols, RS 68 (London, 1876)
Decretales ineditae	*Decretales ineditae saeculi XII*, ed. and revised S. Chodorow and C. Duggan, Monumenta Iuris Canonici Series B: Corpus Collectionum, 4 (Città del Vaticano, 1982)
Decretum	*Decretum Gratiani; Corpus Iuris Canonici*, ed. E. Friedberg, i (Leipzig, 1879)
Digest	*The Digest of Justinian*. Latin Text ed. by Theodor Mommsen with the aid of Paul Krueger, English translation ed. by Alan Watson, 4 vols (Philadelphia, 1985)
EG	Edward Grim, *Vita S. Thomae, Cantuariensis archiepiscopi et martyris, auctore Edwardo Grim: MTB*, ii, 353–450
English Lawsuits, i, ii	*English Lawsuits from William I to Richard I*, ed. R.C. Van Caenegem, 2 vols, Selden Society, 106–7 (London, 1990–91)

Eyton	R.W. Eyton, *Court, Household, and Itinerary of King Henry II* (London, 1878)
Foreville, *L'Église et la royauté*	Raymonde Foreville, *L'Église et la royauté en Angleterre sous Henri II Plantagenêt* (Paris, 1943)
GC	*Gallia Christiana* (nova), 16 vols (Paris, 1715–1865; repr. Farnborough, 1970)
Gerald of Wales	*Giraldi Cambrensis Opera*, i–iv, ed. J.S. Brewer; v–vii, ed. James F. Dimock; viii, ed. George F. Warner, RS 21 (London, 1861–91)
Gervase	*The Historical Works of Gervase of Canterbury*, ed. W. Stubbs, 2 vols, RS 73 (London, 1879–80)
Gesta regis Henrici secundi	*Gesta regis Henrici secundi Benedicti abbatis*, ed. W. Stubbs, 2 vols, RS 49 (London, 1867)
GFL	*The Letters and Charters of Gilbert Foliot*, ed. A. Morey and C.N.L. Brooke (Cambridge, 1967)
Guernes	Guernes de Pont-Sainte-Maxence, *La Vie de Saint Thomas le Martyr*, ed. E. Walberg (Lund, 1922)
HB	Herbert of Bosham, *Vita S. Thomae, Cantuariensis archiepiscopi et martyris, auctore Herberto de Boseham: MTB*, iii, 155–534
Heads	*The Heads of Religious Houses: England and Wales 940–1216*, ed. D. Knowles, C.N.L. Brooke, and V.C.M. London (Cambridge, 1972)
Howden	Roger of Howden: *Chronica magistri Rogeri de Houedene*, ed. W. Stubbs, 4 vols, RS 51 (London, 1868–71)
Institutes	*Justinian's Institutes*, trans. Peter Birks and Grant McLeod (with the Latin text of Paul Krueger) (Ithaca, New York, 1987); cf. J.A.C. Thomas, *The Institutes of Justinian, Text, Translation and Commentary* (Amsterdam/Oxford, 1975)

JL	P. Jaffé, *Regesta Pontificum Romanorum ad annum 1198*, 2nd edn by S. Loewenfeld, F. Kaltenbrunner and P.W. Ewald, 2 vols (Leipzig, 1885–88)
JS	John of Salisbury, *Vita et Passio S. Thomae martyris, auctore Johanne Saresberiensi: MTB*, ii, 302–22
JS, *Letters*, i, ii	*The Letters of John of Salisbury*, i: *The Early Letters*, ed. and trans. W.J. Millor and H.E. Butler, NMT (London, 1955; reissued, Oxford, 1986); *The Letters of John of Salisbury*, ii: *The Later Letters (1163–1180)*, ed. and trans. W.J. Millor and C.N.L. Brooke, OMT (Oxford, 1979)
Knowles, *Colleagues*	David Knowles, *The Episcopal Colleagues of Archbishop Thomas Becket* (Cambridge, 1951)
Knowles, *Becket*	David Knowles, *Thomas Becket* (Cambridge, 1973)
Liber Pontificalis	*Liber Pontificalis*, ed. L. Duchesne, Bibliothèque des Écoles françaises d'Athènes et de Rome, 2nd Ser., 3, 2nd edn, 3 vols (Paris, 1955–57)
MTB	*Materials for the History of Thomas Becket, Archbishop of Canterbury*, ed. J.C. Robertson and J.B. Sheppard, 7 vols, RS 67 (London, 1875–85)
NCE	*New Catholic Encyclopedia*, 2nd edn (New York, 2002)
Newburgh	William of Newburgh, *Historia rerum Anglicarum*, ed. R.G. Howlett, *Chronicles of the Reigns of Stephen, Henry II, and Richard I*, 4 vols, RS 82 (London, 1884–89), i–ii, 1884–85).
NMT	Nelson's Medieval Texts
OMT	Oxford Medieval Texts

PL	*Patrologiae cursus completus, series latina (Patrologia latina)*, 221 vols, ed. J.P. Migne (Paris, 1841–64)
PR	*Pipe Rolls 5 Henry II–39 Henry II*, Pipe Roll Society (London, 1844–1925): cited by regnal year
PU England	*Papsturkunden in England*, ed. W. Holtzmann, 3 vols, Abhandlungen … Göttingen, phil.-hist. Klasse, i, NS 25 (Berlin, 1930); ii, 3rd Ser., 14–15 (Berlin 1935–36); iii, 3rd Ser., 33 (Göttingen, 1952)
Recueil des historiens	*Recueil des historiens des Gaules et de la France*, ed. M. Bouquet, *et al.* [xiv–xviii, ed. M.-J.-J. Brial], new edn, directed by L. Delisle, 19 vols (Paris, 1869–80)
RS	Rolls Series: *Rerum Britannicarum Medii Aevi Scriptores, Chronicles and Memorials of Great Britain and Ireland during the Middle Ages, published … under the direction of the Master of the Rolls*, 99 vols (London, 1858–96)
Staunton	*The Lives of Thomas Becket*, trans. M. Staunton (Manchester, 2001)
Thomas Becket, ed. Foreville	*Thomas Becket. Actes du colloque international de Sédières 19–24 Août 1973*, ed. Raymonde Foreville (Paris, 1975)
TRHS	*Transactions of the Royal Historical Society*
Warren, *Henry II*	W.L. Warren, *Henry II* (London, 1973)
WC	William of Canterbury, *Vita et passio S. Thomae, auctore Willelmo, monacho Cantuariensi: MTB*, i, 1–136
WC, *Miracula*	William of Canterbury, *Miracula S. Thomae Cantuariensis, auctore Willelmo, monacho Cantuariensi: MTB*, i, 137–546

WF

William FitzStephen, *Vita S. Thomae, Cantuariensis archiepiscopi et martyris, auctore Willelmo filio Stephani: MTB*, iii, 1–154

Zenker, *Die Mitglieder*

Barbara Zenker, *Die Mitglieder des Kardinalkollegiums von 1130 bis 1159* (Diss. Würzburg, 1964)

Introduction

On Saturday, 29 December 2001, Thomas Becket was listed in the *Daily Mail*'s list of the 100 people who deserved commemoration among those who had made Britain 'Great'; and in 2003 Jonathan Freedland made him the centrepiece of the BBC Radio 4 programme *The Long View*, which considered issues of the relationship of Church and State in the context of the appointment of Dr Rowan Williams as archbishop of Canterbury. Later in the same year, the then president Charles Taylor of Liberia attempted to silence the criticisms of the archbishop of Monrovia by reminding him of the fate of Thomas à [*sic*] Becket. This is quite something for a twelfth-century archbishop of Canterbury, whose tenure of office had lasted for less than nine years and whose memory was officially obliterated by royal edict in the sixteenth century. It is highly unlikely that any Canterbury prelate from the last century will be so remembered in 800 years' time. That argues for enduring reputation – or at least notoriety. Becket's name has remained in the folk memory, so that even if the average citizen could not date him or say much about his outlook, character or ideas, many would probably be able to say that he was murdered 'in the cathedral'. The more educated might even know something of T.S. Eliot's thought-provoking *Murder in the Cathedral* (1935) and some would have seen the film *Becket*, which adapted Jean Anouilh's *Becket, ou, L'honneur de Dieu* (1959), with Richard Burton in the title role; and a very small number of enthusiasts for twentieth-century classical music would know Ildebrando Pizzetti's rarely performed opera, *L'Assassinio nella cattedrale*, based on Albert Castelli's translation of Eliot's play.

Stripped down to its bare essentials, the Becket story is a tale of heroic resistance to the point of suffering a bloody and public murder at the hands of what learned contemporaries called 'the public power' – that is, the State. The dramatic ending of his life did more

to publicize his cause than almost anything else. The majority of
those who know his name today may not know why he died, but they
know, vaguely, that he was murdered by four barons from the king's
(Henry II's) court. His reputation, then, is largely founded on his status as heroic victim. Nothing so became him in life as the manner of
his leaving it. But men, even archbishops, can be murdered for many
reasons – not all of them meriting either sympathy or canonization.
As St Augustine of Hippo wrote 1600 years ago, it is the cause (*causa*)
and not the suffering (*poena*) that makes the martyr. Was Becket's
undoubted brutal murder anything more than an act of violence? Did
he provoke it? If he didn't, could he have prevented it? If there was a
cause, what was it, and was it worth it? Those who would defend
Becket's status as heroic victim concentrate on the wider issues of tensions between the Church and the State, and on the justification for
Becket's opposition to measures that in the twelfth century would, it
is argued, have significantly reduced the freedom that the Church,
both locally in England and generally in Latin Christendom, was
coming to enjoy. For those who challenge Becket's reputation as
heroic defender of those freedoms, the argument shifts, either to criticism of those claims or to the narrower focus of Becket's behaviour,
the immediate circumstances and the 'natural' anger of a king whose
honour was grievously affronted by this jumped-up clerk. For them,
also, the construction of the 'martyr' image was a clerical conspiracy.

No one can deny the fact of the 'murder in the cathedral'. It was
witnessed by members of Becket's household and monks from
Canterbury Cathedral Priory, and heard if not seen by ordinary people who had come into the cathedral on the fifth day of Christmas to
hear the monks chanting vespers, the evening service of praise. This
was no back-street clandestine affair. The four conspirators had made
no secret of their identity: indeed they had summoned forces from the
castles of Kent and had attempted to press the citizens of Canterbury
to assist in the seizure of their archbishop in his own palace. The
whole city would have been agog at the events unfolding before its
eyes in the gathering dusk. And when the deed was done, two eye-
witnesses set down what they had seen: William FitzStephen, a highly
educated cleric, who had been one of the archbishop's legal team, and
Edward Grim, an Oxford clerk, who had just been ordained priest by
Thomas and who was severely wounded in an attempt to ward off the
first sword stroke from Reginald FitzUrse. Both were with the archbishop in the north transept and stood by him until the end. Three
other writers were also in the cathedral: John of Salisbury, one of the
most highly regarded writers and thinkers of the century, who had

been a colleague and friend for 15 years; William of Canterbury (one of the monks who had been ordained deacon a few days earlier), who had come down the steps from the choir when the armed men pursued the archbishop into the cathedral; and Benedict, another, probably older monk, usually called 'of Peterborough', because he ended his days as abbot of that great Benedictine monastery. John and William were certainly present, for they acknowledged that they had hidden themselves at the moment of crisis; Benedict's exact location is not certain, but he was almost certainly within earshot.

There are thus five witnesses whose evidence would be admitted in a modern court of law. To these the historian (though perhaps not the lawyer) can add the reports by men who were not there, but who spoke to witnesses and had access to the earliest biographies. Foremost among these is a freelance French writer, Guernes, a cleric from Pont-Sainte-Maxence in the Île-de-France. Spotting a good story, as soon as he heard the news of Becket's assassination he hurried to Canterbury and interviewed as many people as possible – including Becket's sister Mary, whom the king had made abbess of Barking in 1173; but he also made extensive use of the works of Edward Grim and William of Canterbury, whom he would have met; and he consulted Benedict of Peterborough's 'Passion', of which only fragments have been recovered from a later compendium, and also William FitzStephen's biography. From interviews and written evidence he produced his long verse epic, *La Vie de Saint Thomas le Martyr*, whose first 'unpublished' version was stolen by a rival. The second, which survives, was completed in 1174.[1] That this French cleric should have devoted about a year to compiling and writing up the story of the new St Thomas is in itself highly significant: it testifies to the interest that the raw event at Canterbury had generated outside England. Guernes may not rank as an investigative journalist, but his *Vie* is detailed and remarkably accurate, and its language takes us closer to the vernacular world of the Anglo-Norman and French élites than the formal Latin of the other writers. In addition, there are two anonymous Lives. The first, Anonymous I, once attributed to 'Roger of Pontigny', was written *c.* 1175–76[2] by a cleric who claimed to have served the archbishop in exile, and to have been ordained priest by him. The second, Anonymous II, is known as the 'Lambeth Anonymous' because the single surviving manuscript is in the library of Lambeth Palace in London (MS 135), where it precedes a copy of Benedict of Peterborough's Miracles. Even less is known about Lambeth's author,[3] but the *Vita* is very early (*c.* 1172–73), and although less detailed than the others, it has the advantage of reflecting upon the events it describes. Also in the first rank is the monumental *Thomus* by Herbert of Bosham. This Old Testament expert wrote at leisure 15 to 16 years after the murder, which, to his eternal grief, he had not witnessed: but he had been associated with Becket from his days as chancellor and served him devotedly until the end. Despite small disagreements between the accounts, there can, then, be little doubt about what happened – when, where and by whom the blows were struck. To these must be added Master Alan, monk (1174) and prior of Canterbury (1177–86), always called 'of Tewkesbury', because he was abbot of that Benedictine monastery from 1186 to 1202. Although he came late to the Becket story, so to speak, he would have heard echoes of the English crisis during his earlier career as a cleric in Benevento, where the papal Curia was resident for most of the period 1168–70 and where Becket's former clerk, Lombard of Piacenza, was archbishop from 1171 to 1179. It may have been this connexion that brought him to Canterbury in 1174, where he was rapidly promoted to prior. His dedication to the further promotion of Becket's cause produced not only an important supplement (*c.* 1176) to John of Salisbury's *Vita*, which concentrated on events from 1164 to 1169, but the most comprehensive collection of materials, principally letters, relating to the controversy.[4]

Seven authors thus completed their work within four years of Becket's death, and a further two within six, when not only the doings at Canterbury, but the major events of Becket's life were still reasonably fresh in their minds. Their knowledge of the man and of the events varied considerably, however. Grim, William of Canterbury and Benedict had witnessed the murder and its aftermath, but not much else; John of Salisbury, FitzStephen and Herbert of Bosham knew him well, although FitzStephen deemed discretion the better part of valour and did not follow the archbishop into exile. Anon. II claimed to have served him in exile; Guernes had glimpsed him in France, when he was chancellor; and Alan could have known of him only by repute. Anon. I does not disclose himself, but he was probably a cleric, perhaps in London. Although their broad division into secular clergy (John, Grim, FitzStephen, Guernes, Bosham, possibly Anon. I and II) and Canterbury monks (William of Canterbury, Benedict, Alan) provides a degree of contrast in their treatment of the subject, all were interpreting his career in the light of its dramatic ending.

There is no avoiding the fact that they saw Becket the Martyr as God's chosen instrument. Their accounts are full of the rhetoric of sanctity: Thomas is 'holy' (*sanctus*) or 'blessed' (*beatus*), 'Christ's' or 'God's champion' (*athleta Christi/Dei*), and echoes of the Gospels' sacred narrative of the life and death of Christ are interwoven in the texts. The big question is whether the hagiographical imperative – the desire to record the life of a saint – led the biographers to falsify the reality of Becket's life so that the 'real' man and the 'real' issues are either distorted and obscured. Did they, individually and collectively, simply construct a pious myth? One way of attempting to answer that question is to see what is left if the vocabulary of sanctity is stripped out. Unlike most early saints' lives, such a process reveals very substantial narrative accounts, which vary in detail according to their authors' knowledge. Becket's biographers were so close to their subject that they did not need to invent detail to fill out a meagre tale centuries after the event; nor did they invent miraculous events to substantiate the saintly status of their subject. Instead of attempting to ignore the problematical elements in their hero's life, all (except Benedict and Alan, who did not deal with Thomas' early years) confronted the profound disjunction between the early and the late Becket. None of them claimed that Thomas the clerk or Thomas the chancellor or even Thomas the archbishop had been saintly, although all, except John, Benedict and Alan, contrived to find pointers to his later status, either in his private piety or in stories of maternal premonitions or prophetic events in his childhood. The upwardly mobile son of Norman settlers in London, who enjoyed such unsaintly pursuits as feasting and hunting, and who led 700 men and more on campaigns in France, is clearly discernible. Far from discrediting the later saint, these disconcerting realities threw into even sharper focus the mysterious workings of God's providence, for it was He who had made this unlikely choice and wrought the transformation from courtier to bishop.

That so much was written by so many in so short a time is not the least astonishing feature of Becket's story. In addition to these biographies or hagiographies, the historian has one of the largest collections of contemporary letters assembled in the middle ages. Compiled by Alan (later abbot of Tewkesbury) from the mid-1170s, and copied at Cirencester Abbey from a Canterbury original in the early 1180s, it contains just short of 600 items of correspondence (598), arranged in broadly chronological order, and intended to provide an authentic documentary record. The collection is not complete, even so, and there are some chronological displacements, but it provides an invaluable insight into the complexities and intricacies of Thomas Becket's dispute with the king. It also plugs many of the gaps in the biographers' accounts, and enables the construction of an accurate chronology of the years of exile. The 329 letters that constitute

Becket's own correspondence (that is, letters sent to or by him) is now available in a new Latin edition, with full English translation;[5] the letters of John of Salisbury and Peter of Celle are also available in distinguished dual-language editions.[6] This immensely rich vein of material was written during Becket's life and contains important critical material, including the fierce denunciation written in late summer 1166 by Gilbert Foliot;[7] but it is not easy to read. Just as the biographers were writing in a tradition of sacred narrative that fundamentally affected the way they told their story, Becket himself, and his secretaries and correspondents were deeply influenced by the conventions of their time. They, too, relied extensively on biblical allusion to support their arguments and interpret events. The Old and New Testaments formed not just the background to their thought, but the framework within which, or even through which, they saw their contemporary world. Typical of the complex interlacing of biblical image and metaphor, highly valued at the time, is the elaborately constructed letter that Peter of Celle sent to Thomas in late 1169 (*Solicito reuoluens animo* ['Turning over with an anxious mind']). In it, the abbot of Saint-Rémi declared that 'from generation to generation will it be preached that the archbishop of Canterbury, setting himself like a wall for the house of Israel, follows the footprints of the saints of old, as in nakedness he follows Christ hanging naked from the cross'.[8] Uncongenial though such modes of thought may be for many of today's readers, they should not be set aside, either as a kind of mania or as mere rhetorical colouring. It was normal to set current affairs in the context of a universal history, in which good and evil, God and the Devil, were in struggle until the end of time.

As if all that material were not enough, two very large compilations of Miracles attributed to Thomas's intercession were assembled by late 1174;[9] and a series of liturgical offices – the first dating from 1173 – with specially composed readings and chants, show how Thomas the Saint was celebrated throughout the middle ages. And there is more. From nearly every region of Latin Christendom, including Iceland and Sicily, Poland and Hungary, there survives physical evidence of Becket's cult, in church dedications, wall paintings, sculptures and stained glass.[10] That so much was written and preserved is itself a matter for historical comment. What was it about this man and this crisis and this murder that excited so much and such continuing interest?

The problem for the historian is not absence of evidence, but its interpretation. Since most of the written evidence and all the pictorial evidence is generally favourable to its subject, readers since the Reformation have suspected conspiracy and bias. In this regard,

Becket differs little from other historical characters. Unless recorded, actions pass from the historical vision, and the form of the record shapes the history. All records are products of their time; all were written for a purpose; and all were subject to the bias and selective or defective memory of their authors. But the opponent of a cause is not necessarily more reliable than its supporter: evidence can be 'spun' in either direction.

Becket's case is peculiarly difficult, however, not only because of the mass (or morass) of documentation, but because generations of writers and polemicists have read into it the prejudices and preoccupations of their own time. Becket's reputation has oscillated backwards and forwards with the winds of political and religious change.[11] The inscription on the title page of an exhaustive two-volume study on Becket's death and miracles, published in 1898, which described Thomas as 'Now venerated by some as saint and martyr; by others admired as a hero; by some few vilified as a narrow ecclesiastic,'[12] marks only the widest parameters of the historical pendulum.

The accounts of Archbishop Thomas (with one notorious exception, contemporaries never referred to him as 'Archbishop Becket' – it was the murderers who shouted 'Thomas Becketh', with studied contempt) confronting King Henry II at Clarendon and Northampton, or facing his murderers at Canterbury, can be read as courageous defence of the Church or insolent challenge to the lawful power of the crown; as defence of the rights of the clergy, or protection of a clerical privilege that had already outlived its usefulness. Becket thus becomes the courageous hero or the power-hungry and traitorous disturber of the peace. When viewed through the prisms of the English Reformation, the Act of Supremacy, the Thirty-Nine Articles and the 1688 Revolution, the second alternatives were almost inevitable, and they remain so for many of today's readers. In a period when religion has become a private matter, and a single law governs lay and clerical society, and equality and democracy are the catchwords of the age, the details of canon law and the concept of 'freedom of the church' for which Becket struggled, are seen as either petty or wrong-headed, especially since King Henry, imbued with a totally spurious cloak of modernity, is depicted as a precursor of the modern constitutional state. It takes an effort of historical imagination to overcome the cultural barriers that impede understanding of the cause, and of the man who attracted so much admiration for his courageous stand. It is necessary for us to understand both our own biases and the 'otherness' of the time in which Thomas lived. Merely to import the conventions of the present into the world of the past is to subvert the very purpose of historical study.

1

The social climber

Becket's story begins in the heart of the City of London. He was the son of Norman immigrants, the Beckets, who had settled in London and made a good living as merchants in the City. It is hard to place him precisely in his social milieu. He said himself that his origins were modest – that his parents lived blamelessly in the midst of their fellow citizens, but by no means among the lowest. That means not quite the highest either, but as Frank Barlow showed,[1] they owned a substantial house in Cheapside, where the Mercer's Hall now stands. They entertained guests, like Richer de Laigle, who were of baronial rank; and Gilbert Becket had known Archbishop Theobald when they were young men in Normandy. At a time when the overwhelming majority of the English population was not free, the Beckets were both free and Norman; and they belonged to the rapidly rising merchant class in a city that had substantial trade links with continental Europe. It also had the makings of a financial sector: the first employer of the young Thomas was Osbert Huitdeniers (Eightpence), whose name probably denotes his business; and William Cade lent money to King Henry II himself in the late 1150s. They were certainly not poor, by the standards of the day – and Gilbert was respected enough to be chosen as sheriff of the City – but they were not noble. For a boy from his background, advancement beyond the status into which he was born required intelligence, education and the patronage of the great.

Thomas was born on the feast of St Thomas the Apostle (21 December), after whom he was named, very probably in 1120.[2] His biographers transmit prophetic dreams and images of his future greatness – but while they fitted into the pattern of saints' lives – God's purpose revealed at an early stage – it is likely that if there was any truth in them they were no more than the kind of childhood stories that circulate in families. Mothers do have dreams about their children; minor incidents can in retrospect be seen as prophetic.[3] Yet there are some aspects of the childhood stories that ring true. He is said to have had a special attachment to his mother, Matilda, and from her acquired practices of charitable giving and a special devotion to the Virgin Mary.[4] Both claims are certainly possible. Until about the age of six or seven, boys were under the tutelage of their mothers, before joining the male world; and the cult of the Virgin was especially popular in the twelfth century. Her unique status as virgin, mother and queen drew together many disparate elements of contemporary society. Priests, monks and nuns could admire the virginity; mothers could emulate the images of the mother of God; noble women and queens could see themselves reflected in her elevated dignity as the queen of heaven. While the papacy especially encouraged her cult in Rome – where many great churches were dedicated to her honour (S. Maria Maggiore, S. Maria in Trastevere, S. Maria Nuova, etc.) – the Cistercian Order made her its special patroness, and Italian cities were beginning to see her as a kind of queen-substitute, whose powerful patronage could be invoked in times of need. A widely distributed hymn was attributed to Becket's authorship from the late thirteenth century onwards, but that may be no more than pious myth; yet he did invoke the Virgin at the moment of his death. As for his charity: that, too, became a feature of his life as archbishop, when he increased the customary doles established by Archbishop Theobald.[5]

A London merchant's wife, moreover, was likely to be literate, at least in French, which would have been the language of the household; and she would have learned to speak English. Given the evidence of her charity and piety, she would also have known the essential prayers – the Our Father and Hail Mary – as well as the Creed, in their Latin form; and the family would have attended its local parish church for mass on Sundays and the many festivals of the Christian calendar. The cathedral of St Paul's, of course, was within walking distance of their house, where the young Becket could have experienced the liturgical splendour of a great church. And a merchant's wife was likely to have been ambitious for her children. Matilda was said to have been the driving force in his education – again, not surprising if, as seems to have been the case, Thomas was the only son in a family of four. There is no evidence at all about his early education (before the age of ten), but there were plenty of opportunities for a boy to acquire the rudiments of reading and writing in Latin from a neighbourhood cleric or, more formally, in a kind of preparatory school attached to St Paul's itself, or one of the collegiate churches.

When it came to serious study, though, he was sent in about 1130 to the school attached to the monastery of canons regular at Merton, where he must have lived for some years. Little is known about how he fared there, but he retained an attachment to the monastery until the end of his life; and, when he became archbishop, it was from Merton that he summoned a special spiritual adviser in the person of the canon Robert, whom he appointed as chaplain and confessor. There he would have advanced his knowledge of Latin, based on textbooks that had been used since the end of the Roman Empire. From there, he seems to have attended one of the local schools in the City, although it is impossible to establish where or what he studied; it is likely, though, that he learned Latin composition, rhetoric and the discursive skills that would fit him for the world of government and administration. FitzStephen gives a lively – and probably exaggerated – account of the intellectual life of the city schools, where disputation and dialectic flourished. It is more than likely that by the age of 19 or so he was the equivalent of a modern Arts graduate, but one who could debate and argue in accurate Latin, who had learned a store of classical quotations and who had passed through a basic curriculum that comprised the trivium (grammar, rhetoric, logic) and quadrivium (astronomy, arithmetic, geometry and music). The level to which these were studied depended on the schoolmaster, of course; but although the London schools did not acquire the reputation of those in Paris, they should not be disparaged. They might not have reached the intellectual heights of the Petit-Pont or Notre Dame or Saint-Victor, but they could inculcate something of the 'new learning', based on analysis, argument and disputation. An anonymous satire on the consequences of such expertise, which found its way into the *Carmina Burana*, gives a taste of this new brand of learning:

> For students hardly in their prime
> find themselves wise before their time;
> they know it all – impertinence
> replaces plain intelligence. ...
> Now lads of barely a decade
> can graduate – get themselves made
> professors too! And who's to mind
> how blind the blind who lead the blind?
> So fledglings soar upon the wing
> so donkeys play the lute and sing;
> bulls dance about at court like sprites;
> and ploughboys sally forth as knights.[6]

During those teenage years, though, he established a friendship with Richer de Laigle, a minor noble who sometimes stayed at the

Becket house in London. It was in his company that he acquired the skills and tastes of the landed aristocracy, a delight in hunting with dogs and birds, and perhaps some of the manners appropriate to more elevated circles.[7] This acquaintance may also have induced his parents to aspire even higher for their son. It is possible that they hoped he would enter the clerical world, for he was sent in about 1138 to Paris, then one of the two principal centres of higher learning in the Latin West. In its schools young men learned to master the more elaborate Latin that was necessary for the pursuit of an administrative career in the service of a lay or ecclesiastical lord. If they had the time and inclination, they could move on to Theology or Canon and/or Roman Law. Growing numbers of 'Englishmen' pursued such a path, and some rose very high indeed. John of Salisbury spent 12 years in the Parisian schools, making himself one of the best-educated clerks of his generation; this also equipped him for the life of clerical service that had become a pathway to success and fortune.

Thomas of London, as he came to be known, was not in John's league, however. He may not have had John's academic interests or his intellectual powers, and he did not stay more than a couple of years or so in Paris. FitzStephen said that it was the death of his mother that brought his higher education to an abrupt end; and that may, indeed, have been so. There are lingering doubts about his aptitude. Did he drop out because he was not 'up to it' – a failed Paris scholar, Barlow called him[8] – or because of drastically changed home circumstances? Stephen of Rouen ridiculed his Latin;[9] but while he could not have rivalled John of Salisbury, it is unlikely that he would have been recruited into Archbishop Theobald's household if he could not function effectively in the Latin-speaking and Latin-writing world of an archbishop of Canterbury, who assembled around himself one of the most learned households of the twelfth century; and he would not have been promoted by him as a future chancellor of England. John of Salisbury himself later spoke of his oral fluency; and Thomas was to make a name for himself as one of Theobald's emissaries. English clerics had to be bi- if not tri-lingual. The language of the French and English royal courts was French; the language of education, law and the papal court was Latin; and the language of the London citizenry was English and French. His abandonment of the schools in Paris may, however, have been through lack of interest in the subtleties of logic and dialectic which the legacy of Peter Abelard had made so popular. If my reading of his educational achievement in London is correct, he went to Paris, not to pursue the whole Arts curriculum, but to 'cherry pick' the more advanced courses. He had no intention of becoming a scholar like John of Salisbury – Beryl Smalley called him, memorably, 'a scholar *de dimanche*.[10] His merchant background may have propelled him to seek the more immediately useful courses available. He was going to have to earn his living with whatever skills he acquired, and what one may call a 'competent clerkship' may have been the height of his ambition. It is probable, also, that the combination of education at Merton preparatory and London grammar schools was enough to give him the linguistic mastery that was required – and that a sojourn of a year or two in Paris was enough to complete his transformation into an employable commodity.

Since precise dating is difficult, we cannot be sure which masters he heard, apart from the English theologian, Robert 'of Melun', but Paris in the 1130s was buzzing with new intellectual life. It was there that Peter Abelard had made his reputation; it was there that Aristotelian logic – which John of Salisbury called 'the club of Hercules in the hands of pygmies' – and the arts of argument elaborated by Quintilian were incorporated into the study of ancient learning. Depending on the chronology, the young Becket might have caught a glimpse of Abelard in his second period of teaching at Paris (*c.* 1136–40); he might have heard Hugh of St-Victor, who died in 1141; and he would in any case have been exposed to the disputations that became a feature of the new scholastic method.

By the time he left the schools, in late 1141, he was just 21 years old. Given that many students in fact completed their education at that age, he was well enough educated for entry into the service of a nobleman or bishop. He was naturally intelligent, with an excellent memory and a verbal fluency that would have enabled him to hold his own in all but the most demanding academic circles. His first job – and we should call it just that – was as assistant to a relative, Osbert Huitdeniers, who seems to have been a moneylender.[11] If his main occupation was to keep Osbert's accounts, he would have learned some of the skills that would suit him when he became royal chancellor – for the chancellor sat, *ex officio*, at Exchequer. He was probably in minor orders; but that would not have prevented lawful marriage, since marriage was forbidden only to clerics in the subdiaconate and above. But he was lucky. Through the influence of two clerks from Boulogne, Archdeacon Baldwin and Master Eustace,[12] he was presented to Archbishop Theobald, who was always on the lookout for likely talent. In this way, he joined the household of the archbishop of Canterbury – a very good step-up from his mediocre origins – and entered a world very different from the mundane concerns of a moneylender in the City of London.

The mid-twelfth century was a time of opportunity. At the very moment when Becket joined Theobald, another Englishman was being catapulted to the highest rungs in the ecclesiastical ladder. From an equally undistinguished background, Nicholas Breakspear, the son of a clerk in the service of the abbot of St Albans, had been forced to leave England as an impoverished student adventurer. As far as we can tell, he went to Paris where, rather like Becket a generation later, 'he did not prosper', and, still a teenager, he made his way south-east to the Rhone valley. There he joined the schools at Arles, and became a jurist, was ordained and served as a priest in the church of St James in Melgueil, before joining the reformed congregation of Saint-Ruf near Avignon, probably before 1140. There he was elected abbot (after 1143), and he travelled to Catalonia on the abbey's business in 1148, where he was present at the sieges of Muslim Lérida and Tortosa by Christian forces, and established a firm friendship with Count Ramon Berenger IV of Barcelona. When some business took him to the papal Curia at the end of 1148, he was head-hunted by Pope Eugenius III, who appointed him cardinal bishop of Albano (December) and sent him as papal legate to complete the constitutional organization of the Scandinavian Church (1152–54). Scarcely had he completed that mission when he was unanimously elected pope in December 1154 as Adrian IV – the only man of English birth to sit on the papal throne. Nicholas had gone from total obscurity in Abbots Langley (Hertfordshire) to the pinnacle of ecclesiastical power in something like 30 years, the final stages – abbot, cardinal, legate, Pope – being achieved in six; and it was all done through personal accomplishments and a bit of luck.[13]

Thomas Becket's rise displays similar features. Nicholas's success was put down to affability and hard work:

> Because he was handsome of body, smiling of face, prudent
> in words, and swift to carry out instructions, he pleased
> everyone … And since he was of quick mind and ready
> tongue, he made great strides in learning and eloquence
> by regular and careful study.[14]

Becket was even more physically impressive, being over six foot tall, with a slim build and aquiline nose. Like Nicholas, he had a quick brain and a fluent tongue. One of the fullest descriptions has been transmitted from a lost Life written by Robert of Cricklade, prior of

St Frideswide, Oxford (1141–74), by the late thirteenth-century Icelandic Saga:

> At the time when Stephen had become king, the blessed Thomas left school. He was then twenty-two years of age, a slim man of pale countenance and dark hair, with a long nose and regular features. He was gentle of manner and sharp of intellect, and he was easy going and amiable in conversation. He was authoritative in speech, if somewhat stammering. He was so keen in discernment and comprehension that he would always solve difficult questions wisely. His memory was so amazing that whatever he heard of scriptures and legal judgments he was able to cite any time he chose.[15]

Apart from the stammer, the similarities between Thomas Becket and Nicholas Breakspear are almost uncanny – and there is no possibility of contamination between the two sources; the speech impediment may have made Becket particularly careful in his choice of words, and therefore even more effective as a speaker. But he was also a good horseman, a keen hunter with birds and an effective swordsman. The man who joined the ex-abbot Theobald at Canterbury shared more of the tastes of the contemporary knightly world than those of the cloister. There is no doubt that he was a thoroughly secular clerk in his tastes and accomplishments. Attachment to Theobald's household, however, brought him into a very different environment. Not only did he begin to accumulate ecclesiastical benefices, bestowed by a multiplicity of patrons (St Mary le Strand in London, Otford in Kent, and prebends in St Paul's London and Lincoln), which gave him an independent income, but Theobald allowed him to study law in Bologna and Auxerre for a year, before appointing him as archdeacon of Canterbury in late 1154. This last office brought in a substantial revenue of about £100 a year.[16]

There is no reliable evidence about his attendance at the schools in Paris. Apart from Robert of Melun, we cannot be certain which masters he heard or which friends he may have made in the city. Although his relatively short stay in the schools occurred during John of Salisbury's 12-year marathon (1136–48), for example, there is no indication that they encountered one another there; yet the possibility cannot be wholly excluded. By the time he went to Bologna, however, he was a man of substance, with a specific objective – to study 'the laws' – and he would have sought the best teachers. He would have heard the Roman lawyer Bulgarus, one of the 'four masters' whose teaching established Justinian's Corpus of Civil Law as one of the pillars of juristic science; and he would also have heard the canonist Omnebene, later bishop of Verona (1157–85).[17] In that prestigious law school, he may also have met or heard the lectures of Master Albert de Morra, whose curial career took him from cardinal deacon of S. Adriano al Foro (1156–58), to cardinal priest of S. Lorenzo in Lucina (1158–87) and chancellor of the Roman Church (1178–87), to the papacy itself, where he reigned as Pope Gregory VIII for just short of three months in 1187.[18] The fact that Thomas had been educated by the Augustinians at Merton may have established a bond between the two men, for Albert was a canon regular. And we may suggest Bologna as the point of contact with another man who was to be an important support during the years of crisis. This was Master Humbert Crivelli of Milan, another canonist, whose *cursus honorum* reads like every cleric's dream: archdeacon of Bourges, archdeacon of Milan, cardinal priest of S. Lorenzo in Damaso (1182), bishop-elect of Vercelli (1183–84), archbishop of Milan (1185) and finally pope (Urban III, 1185–87).[19] Thomas may not have learned a great deal of law during his time at Bologna, but he saw enough to understand the vital importance of the discipline; he heard some of the best law professors of the century; and he established contact, and possibly friendship, with men who were destined for brilliant careers in the Church.

The importance of such associations should not be underestimated. About ten years after Becket's attendance at Bologna, Stephen of Orléans attended the same schools, and when, some 15 years later, by which time he had become abbot of Ste-Geneviève in Paris (1176–92), he needed to conduct some business in the papal Curia, he invoked the aid of Gratian of Pisa, who had just been elevated to the cardinalate, reminding him that, 'I was your companion in Bulgarus's lecture room.'[20] Bologna in the 1150s and 60s was something like the Harvard Law School today. Its students considered themselves among the élite of their generation; and contacts made there could last a lifetime.

Visits to the papal Curia could be equally beneficial; and Thomas had the good fortune to represent the archbishop of Canterbury there more than once (1149–50, 1150, 1151); and he accompanied Theobald to the important papal council that Pope Eugenius III convened to Reims in 1148. These occasions offered opportunities for Becket – in his early thirties – to meet some of the men who would become very important in the protection of his cause in later years. Most distinguished, perhaps, was Cardinal Hubald, then cardinal priest of S. Prassede (1141–58), who was subsequently cardinal bishop of Ostia and Velletri (1158–81) and dean of the College of Cardinals, and finally pope, as Lucius III (1181–85).[21] But there were three others, almost equally important, whom he almost certainly met at Reims. The first was Cardinal Hyacinth, who was to become the longest-serving member of the papal court, first as cardinal deacon of S. Maria in Cosmedin (1144–91) and then as Pope Celestine III (1191–98);[22] the second was Cardinal Boso, cardinal deacon of SS. Cosma e Damiano (1156–66) and cardinal priest of S. Pudenziana (1166–78);[23] and the third was Cardinal Henry (of Pisa), cardinal priest of SS. Nereo e Achilleo (1151–66), whose presence as a sub-deacon of the papal Curia was attested by John of Salisbury.[24]

Chancellor of England

The man whom Theobald recommended as chancellor to the new King Henry II in late 1154 was, therefore, already experienced in conducting business at the highest levels in the Latin Church: he was a well-regarded clerk in the household of the archbishop of Canterbury; he had met Pope Eugenius III; he had established contacts with a significant number of leading cardinals; and he had had a taste of the highest legal learning then to be had. Theobald's purpose was to insinuate a loyal cleric into the service of the new king – to have his own man at court who could represent his views and, perhaps, moderate the king's policies in respect of the Church.[25] The chancellorship was one of the highest offices in the land. As described by FitzStephen,

> The dignity of the chancellor of England is such that he is considered second to the king in the realm; that he seals his own mandates with the other side of the king's seal [the counter seal], which belongs to his charge; that the king's chapel is in his care and subject to his organization; that he receives and takes care of all the vacant archbishoprics, bishoprics, abbacies, and baronies which fall into the king's hands; that he is present in all the king's counsels and may attend even without a summons; that all documents are sealed by his clerks, keepers of the royal seal, and all matters arranged according to his advice; likewise, if through God's grace the merits of his life allow it, he may, if he wishes, be made archbishop or bishop before he dies. That is why the Chancellorship cannot be bought.[26]

What FitzStephen is describing is one of the major administrative offices of the English state at a moment when the king's government was becoming more bureaucratic and professional than ever before; but he is claiming something more. The phrase 'second to the king' implies that in Becket's time, the chancellorship eclipsed the justiciarship. As to the office, something of its great power can be gauged from FitzStephen's remark that 52 clerks served Thomas the Chancellor in various capacities.[27] Some deputized for him in his strictly ecclesiastical offices; others were employed in the king's administration. Of these, some wrote the royal writs and mandates, which ran the whole complex machine of government, as well as the charters and grants conferred by the king in increasing numbers, and they kept records of that business – early versions, now lost, of what became the Chancery rolls. From surviving royal documents, Bishop was able to identify no fewer than 15 different scribes who worked in the Chancery during Becket's period of office.[28] Still others had key roles in the royal Exchequer. Not only did Becket appoint the chancellor's clerk, predecessor of the chancellor of the Exchequer, who had oversight of the Exchequer's business, but also the chancellor's scribe (the later comptroller of the pipe), who recorded the annual shire accounts on the Chancellor's Roll – the Great Roll of the Pipe. These pipe rolls, which were drawn up annually during the Michaelmas Audit, were one of the most impressive products of English royal administration in the twelfth century.[29] A further group administered the secular wardships and vacant churches. Thomas of London, then, presided over a major department of state (the Chancery) and had *ex officio* a major role in a second (the Exchequer). The 52 clerks constituted the staff; and it was they – mostly unnamed – who carried out the onerous duties, day to day, in much the same way that civil service personnel are responsible for running the departments of modern cabinet ministers.

From one perspective, Theobald's initiative was extremely successful. The youthful Henry (then about 21 years of age) hit it off immediately with the tall cleric who had so many un-clerkly tastes and accomplishments. They became personal friends, and it seems that their closeness, in which the king trusted his chancellor with greater powers than any such officer had ever had in the post-Conquest court, enabled Thomas of London to become, in FitzStephen's words, 'second in the realm after the king'. This short period coincided with Henry's own reconstruction of royal power: systematic visitation of his dominions, systematic imposition of oaths of homage and fealty to all who owed them, and systematic acquisition or destruction of

seigneurial castles that had been constructed without royal licence
during the period of the troubles in Stephen's reign.

This king was young, masterful and energetic. He ruled by force
and fear;[30] and Thomas the Chancellor, who travelled with him
throughout his dominions, became the principal agent of that policy
of recuperation. We can trace his perambulations with the king
through the witness lists of royal charters, where the phrase [*teste*]
Toma cancellario ([witnessed by] Thomas the Chancellor) regularly
headed the lay aristocracy who were present. He was at the king's
side on his visitation of England (1155),[31] Normandy, Touraine,
Anjou and the Limousin (1156–mid-1157),[32] England (mid-
1157–August 1158),[33] Normandy and Toulouse (1159–May 1162).[34]
In his mid-thirties, 15 years older than the 21-year-old Henry, but
arguably at the height of his physical and intellectual powers,
Thomas of London was everywhere seen at the centre of Henry II's
court and therefore associated in the mind of the great with the
king's policies of recuperation, including the failed attempt to sub-
ordinate the county of Toulouse to his lordship. At the time, if
FitzStephen is to be believed – and there is no reason not to accept
his testimony – the pacification of the realm after the 'eighteen years
when Christ and his angels slept', was generally popular and beneficial, although aspects of Becket's role in it would later be held
against him.

Just as his service of Theobald had brought an accumulation of
ecclesiastical benefices, his royal service brought him not only the
fruits of office but an assortment of high-status appointments, clerical and lay: the provostship of Beverley Minster, for example, and
custody of the castles of Eye and Berkhampstead, as well as the
Tower of London. Eye, Berkhampstead and the Tower were major
military and administrative responsibilities: all three had significant
garrisons of knights attached to them – Eye alone was reckoned to
command the service of 120. Chancellor Thomas was therefore equal
in wealth and status to a major baron, and he lived up to the expectations of the rank. Not only did his household rival the establish-
ments of the nobility, it was treated by them as parallel to the king's.
Some nobles, indeed, attached their young sons to Becket's service for
education in his court, and the king himself followed suit, placing his
eldest son Henry, then aged about six, in Becket's charge in 1161.
This was an extraordinary demonstration of the king's regard for his
bourgeois chancellor. Not surprisingly, his patronage was now
sought by all who wanted to influence the king; and many nobles and
knights gave him their personal homage.[35]

During his period of office, not only did his court function as an adjunct to the royal court, where visitors of the highest rank were entertained, the office of chancellor, with the incomes from the secular wardships and ecclesiastical vacancies which it then administered, supported the lavish outlay that such royal hospitality required. An example of this magnificence was the great embassy of 1158, when he negotiated what might have been the marriage of the century, between the infant son of Henry II and the still younger Margaret, daughter of King Louis of France. According to FitzStephen, he took more than 200 horsemen with him – knights, clerics, stewards, sergeants, sons of nobles bearing arms in his service, all splendidly attired; and he himself had 24 changes of dress, as well as silken cloths to be given away as presents. The needs of this travelling court were served by eight wagons: two carried superior English beer, to be distributed to the French; one his chapel (sacred vessels, books and vestments); one his chamber (bed, coverings, chairs); one his bursary; one his kitchen; and 12 packhorses transported the gold and silver plates, cups and platters that would furnish his table.[36] That a man of such relatively humble origins should have adopted so extravagant a style may be read as arrogance; Knowles thought it tasteless for a cleric to cultivate such excessive tastes. But conspicuous display and the bestowal of valuable gifts was an important part of medieval diplomacy. The cavalcade was, and was intended to be, a splendid show – a vivid demonstration of the wealth and magnificence of the English king. 'How marvellous must the English king be, if his chancellor comes thus?'[37] And it was all paid for, no doubt, from the various incomes that passed through the chancellor's hands. When later the king demanded accounts, it was claimed that £30,000 had passed through his hands in seven or eight years – an average of between £3750 and £4285 per annum, when the royal income as recorded in the Exchequer Rolls stood at about £20,000.

Such extravagant display was one thing, but in the following year (1159) the chancellor was deeply involved in King Henry's attempt to establish his lordship over the important county of Toulouse in the right of his wife, duchess of Aquitaine. Not only was a very heavy tax (scutage) imposed on the military tenants of the crown, which included bishops and abbots (although Canterbury was not charged),[38] but Thomas of London led a contingent of 700 knights, and, with the Constable, Henry of Essex, directed a very effective (and bloody) rear-guard action when the king decided to abandon the siege of Toulouse, because his overlord, the king of France, had put himself within the city. When the king withdrew from the conflict after capturing Cahors and other strongholds in the region, Thomas and the Constable remained behind to defend the acquisitions. Not only that, but the Chancellor

> put on hauberk and helmet and captured three heavily fortified castles, which seemed impregnable. He also crossed the Garonne with his troop of soldiers in pursuit of the enemy, and when all this province had been confirmed in obedience to the king, he returned in favour and honour.[39]

Two years later, in 1161, Thomas was on active service again, this time in the war between Henry and Louis in and around the Vexin. In addition to the 700 knights he had led for the Toulouse campaign, FitzStephen records that he had a very substantial force of stipendiary troops, engaged to fight for 40 days: 1200 cavalry and 4000 infantry. Each stipendiary 'knight' was paid three shillings per day for his expenses. But that was not all. 'Although he was a clerk, when Engelram of Trie, a powerful French knight came directly at him, fully armed, his horse under the spur', Thomas fought him, 'with lance couched and horse at the gallop, cast him off his horse and claimed his charger as a prize.' This personal prowess inspired the men under his command:

> And in all the army of the English king, the chancellor's knights were always first, always the most daring, always performed excellently, for he trained, led, and urged them on, the signal to advance or retreat being sounded on the slender trumpets which he had, peculiar to his soldiers, but well known to rest of the army.[40]

Even allowing for some exaggeration on FitzStephen's part, these were extraordinary actions for a man from Cheapside; and they must in some way have reflected Becket's own interests and capacities. One cannot imagine John of Salisbury taking command of a whole division of the royal army and leading it on the battlefield, for example, or defeating a French knight in single combat. Although clerks and knights were accomplished horsemen, the use of knightly arms required additional exercise and training, which probably acquired in the company of Richer de Laigle. For modern historians, this period of Becket's life is the hardest to square with the image of the later saint. There wasn't much that was saintly – or even clerical – about either his magnificent manner of life or his participation in the Toulouse and Vexin campaigns. Medieval warfare involved the infliction of considerable collateral damage on the territories of the enemy. Devastation 'with fire and sword' was the medieval equivalent of 'shock and awe', intended to intimidate the enemy and deprive him of support and supplies from his own land. It was a scorched-earth policy, which destroyed crops and burned down villages. FitzStephen's descriptions of Becket's military engagements would not have dishonoured the later great William Marshal, about whom a vernacular epic was written. Indeed, had Thomas not been a clerk, such exploits could have set him on a similar career path, to secular fame, fortune and marriage to a great heiress. William Marshal ended his days as earl of Pembroke! Thomas enjoyed the splendid clothes, the rich fare and fine wines, and the adulation of the powerful. His closeness to the king meant that the greatest in the land, bishops, nobles, earls, even Archbishop Theobald himself, often had to engage his support for a petition to the king. In September 1160, for example, Theobald had to ask the chancellor to persuade the king to promote Archdeacon Bartholomew to the bishopric of Exeter. That same letter reported that 'common report and rumour seems to indicate that you [and the king] are so strongly of one heart and mind, that in view of such intimate friendship your desires and dislikes must coincide'.[41] This intimacy, which is well attested by FitzStephen, engendered such trust that Henry did not require the presentation of annual accounts – a practice that was to tell against Thomas when he lost the king's favour and Henry could use the absence of accounts to trump up charges of embezzlement in 1164.

If the chancellorship seemed on the face of it to make Thomas an inappropriate archbishop, there were countervailing influences. Here, again, it is William FitzStephen who provides the evidence of the chancellor's personal piety, charity and the encouragement and protection of ecclesiastical interests. Almost certainly as an antidote to the lavish public style of his office, Thomas practised private mortifications. Whether in London or in Canterbury, he submitted himself to penitential whipping, administered by local priests, Ralph, prior of Holy Trinity (London) and Thomas, priest of St Martin's (near Canterbury). This use of the discipline does not appeal to modern sensibilities – to many it is repulsive – but it was widely practised in the twelfth century.[42] It was part of the normal regime of Carthusian monks, for example. He did not allow ecclesiastical vacancies to be extended; he secured the appointment of distinguished Englishmen (his former teacher, Robert of Melun, as bishop of Hereford; William, a monk from St-Martin-des-Champs in Paris, as abbot of Ramsey); he persuaded the king to endow Merton, his old *alma mater*; and on one occasion, at least, he spent the three days preceding Easter at Merton, attending the solemn services of Maundy Thursday, Good Friday and Easter Saturday, and visiting local churches on foot, accompanied by only one attendant.[43] This powerful royal official, then, was not quite so forgetful of his clerical status as his love of display suggests; and the evidence of his personal pieties goes some way towards explaining the claim, transmitted to FitzStephen by his confessor and chaplain (Robert of Merton), that he did not indulge in the promiscuity that was prevalent in court life.[44] Even with that mitigation, the contrast between the chancellor and the archbishop is too great for many historians; not surprisingly, they smell hypocrisy.[45] But Edward Grim, William FitzStephen and Herbert of Bosham did not share that squeamishness. Grim likened his position to that of Joseph in Egypt; William devoted a seventh of his biography (19 out of 142 pages) to Becket's life as chancellor; and Herbert of Bosham unashamedly called him 'magnificent'.[46]

As chancellor, Thomas Becket was certainly riding high in the late 1150s and early 1160s, but the lavish display masked a fundamental weakness in his position, which William FitzStephen illustrated in a very telling anecdote. As king and chancellor were riding through London one winter's day, they saw an old beggar by the wayside, clothed in threadbare rags. 'Wouldn't it be a great piece of charity to give him a thick warm cloak?' said the king. 'Great indeed,' said the chancellor, thinking that the king would give up his. 'You shall have this great alms deed', declared Henry, beginning to pull Becket's fine new scarlet cloak off his back. In the ensuing tussle, Thomas allowed the king to win, and the beggar went off with the chancellor's cloak, scarcely able to believe his luck.[47] This story was recorded to demonstrate the degree of intimacy between king and chancellor – but it also revealed the reality of their relationship. However great the chancellor might appear to be, he was the king's servant; and he was utterly dependent on the king's continued goodwill.[48]

Successor of Augustine

The aged Theobald died after a long illness on 18 April 1161; and Henry determined that Thomas of London, the chancellor, should be his successor. One need not agonize over why. Thomas had served him well as chancellor; as chancellor-archbishop he would be able to serve him even better. Although Gilbert Foliot was later to allege that Becket had not only willingly agreed but had plotted to acquire the chair of St Augustine, virtually all the writers stress his reluctance, which was overcome by an old Curial friend, Henry of Pisa, cardinal priest of SS. Nereo e Achilleo (1151–66), then papal legate in Normandy.[49] Cardinal Henry was an accomplished papal diplomat, *persona grata* to Henry II, whose recognition of Alexander III he had received in July 1160 and whose daughter Eleanor he had baptized in September 1161.[50] There is no good reason to disbelieve the testimony of Becket's biographers, that Thomas had pointed out the possible difficulties and needed persuasion. Among those difficulties were not only his relationship with the king, but also acceptability to the bishops. His chancellorship had been a preparation for secular not spiritual government; and although there were plenty of secular bishops, Canterbury had not, since the Conquest, been filled by a Curialist; nor had the archbishop held secular as well as spiritual office. Moreover, none of them had had the military reputation that Becket had acquired in Toulouse. His credentials for the office were not good, whatever the saintly Theobald had seen in him. To succeed to the chair of Augustine, Theodore, Lanfranc and Anselm was no light matter for a man of faith. Herbert of Bosham, in fact, who was then a member of the chancellor's staff, put into his mouth a declaration of his unworthiness. When the king announced his purpose, Becket said, 'What a religious and saintly man you wish to appoint to so holy a see, and over so renowned and holy a community of monks!'[51]

The formal process of 'election' was put into rapid motion in May 1162. There is no doubt that it was forced through by royal fiat. Popular in any sense of the word it was not. Neither the monks of Christ Church Canterbury, who were the formal electors, nor the English and Welsh bishops, whose spiritual father this Curial clerk would become, were in favour of Becket's candidacy; and there is unlikely to have been support among the nobility or the general population. Three bishops (Hilary of Chichester, Bartholomew of Exeter and Walter of Rochester), accompanied by the justiciar, Richard de Lucy and his brother, Abbot Walter of Battle, were sent to secure the monks' vote. Of the three detailed accounts, Edward Grim's is the best. Paraphrasing the king's writ, the justiciar opened the proceedings in the Chapterhouse, 'You should know that it is the king's will that you should have a free vote, as in the past, in the election of a pastor, but the person so chosen should be capable of the burden, worthy of the honour, and pleasing to the king'; and he added that it would be better for them to choose someone who could protect their Church and be of advantage to them in relations with the king: 'for if someone is chosen who does not please the king, you will be in schism and discord and will experience not refuge but dispersion under such a pastor;

whereas, if you choose one who pleases the king, you will immediately enjoy no small advantage.'[52] The prior took counsel outside with some senior monks and then formally concurred with the king's nomination, and, 'after invoking the Holy Spirit' the chancellor was unanimously elected as pastor and patron.[53] Grim tells only part of the story, however. Herbert of Bosham and the Lambeth Anonymous emphasize that there were serious objections raised against this 'man chained by the military belt' being turned into 'a pastor of sheep'.[54]

A similar process then unfolded on 23 May in the refectory of Westminster Abbey, in what was as much a general council of the realm as a council of bishops and abbots, for the secular nobles were also present. After Prior Wibert announced the canonical election at Canterbury and the bishops who had been present confirmed it, the whole assembly agreed and applauded the election; the young prince gave his approval, and Henry of Winchester sought and was granted discharge from legal liability for the archbishop-elect.[55] Ralph de Diceto (? from Diss in Norfolk), who probably attended as archdeacon of Middlesex, speaks of the election being made *nemine reclamante*, and says that Bishop Henry, as the most senior bishop, announced that it had been made *sine aliqua contradictione*.[56] These statements are no doubt true in so far as they refer to the final outcome. In formal terms, the process was 'canonical' in that the two recognized electoral bodies, the monastic chapter at Canterbury and the bishops of the province, had conducted the election in accordance with the established procedural form, even if it was not, strictly speaking, free; and a unanimous vote was secured. This does not mean, however, that there had been no dissentient murmurings. Foliot's voiced criticism is corroborated by many reports, but he withdrew his opposition and did not disturb the recorded unanimity.[57] Whether this was due to direct threat or recognition that his dissent would be fruitless in the circumstances is hard to establish, but no other source suggests anything like the degree of pressure he later alleged.

There was in fact nothing unusual about this exercise of blatant royal power in ecclesiastical appointments. What is unusual is the detail with which the event was recorded, and the consequences. King Henry got what he wanted; but, as Gilbert Foliot, whose opposition was stifled at the time, later claimed in *Multiplicem*, there was general consternation:

> Many people indeed know how religiously, how
> scrupulously, how canonically, and by what merit of life
> that was secured, and that knowledge is etched deep in

the hearts of good men with what one might call the
sharp stylus of grief.[58]

Why did Thomas of London accept the poisoned chalice? Perhaps
he thought that it would be possible to combine the two offices, as
the king wished. He might have thought that his earlier services, to
say nothing of their friendship, would have made accommodation
possible.

Becket's appointment was an enormous shock. All archbishops of
Canterbury since the Conquest had been monks or canons regular;
and two (Lanfranc and Anselm) had been distinguished scholars
in their own day; Theobald was a highly spiritual ex-abbot of Bec
in Normandy. All, moreover, had been exclusively archbishops of
Canterbury. Although the practice was growing of combining episcopal and secular office (Roger of Salisbury was justiciar; Nigel
of Ely was treasurer, for example), the archbishopric had been
exempted from such profanation. The elevation of Thomas of
London, who had risen no higher then the diaconate in the clerical
hierarchy, and whose very public official life had been characterized
by extravagant display and unswerving devotion to royal interests,
was a scandal. There must have been many long faces around the
high altar in Canterbury Cathedral on 3 June 1162, when the chancellor, who had been ordained priest only the preceding evening,
was consecrated archbishop of St Augustine's see by Bishop Henry
of Winchester.

Borrowing from one another, most chroniclers and biographers
relate a marvellous transformation: 'as soon as he was consecrated,
he became a new man', and, realizing that he could not serve two
masters, he resigned the Chancery. Many modern biographers have
pointed out, however, that the transmutation was not quite as swift as
that, on the evidence of Edward Grim's story that it was only after the
Canterbury monks had remonstrated with him for entering the choir
in secular dress that he adopted the modest black robes of a cleric.[59]
This anecdote has something of the ring of truth about it; but there
may have been another explanation for the delay in laying aside the
grandeur of the chancellorship. Although he had been elected on
23 May and consecrated on 3 June 1162, it was not until early August
that he received the *pallium*, the special mark of metropolitical dignity
that only the pope could confer. Ralph de Diceto recorded that five
envoys, including John aux Bellesmains, treasurer of York, John of
Salisbury and Abbot Adam of Evesham, had been sent to receive the
pallium from Pope Alexander III, recently arrived in Montpellier;[60]

and they were back in England in early August, for Thomas solemnly received the insignia at Canterbury on 10 August.[61]

This was a defining moment in Becket's career. The ordination and consecration had transformed the archdeacon into the bishop, but it was the reception of the *pallium* that made the archbishop into the metropolitan: the consecration conferred the order; the *pallium* conferred the jurisdiction. This simple emblem was the equivalent of a chain of office. Essentially it was a circle of woven white lambs' wool, embroidered with crosses, which was worn over pontifical vestments as a mark both of the wearer's eminence and his subordination to the Holy See. Its heraldic form is still part of the arms of the archbishop of Canterbury. Without the *pallium*, an archbishop could not fully exercise his authority over the bishops in his province; with it, he became part of a chain of authority that linked him directly with the pope. Its importance for Becket should not be underestimated. Before receiving the symbol of his archiepiscopal powers, he took the customary oath of allegiance to the papacy:

> I Thomas archbishop of Canterbury from this moment
> forward shall be faithful and obedient to St Peter and the
> Holy Roman Church and to my lord Pope Alexander
> and his canonical successors. I shall not be party to any
> counsel or deed whereby they lose life or limb or are
> captured through wicked deceit. Their counsel which is
> entrusted to me by them or by letters or by envoy, I shall
> not to their injury knowingly reveal to anyone. I shall be
> a support to keep and defend the Roman papacy and the
> regalia of St Peter, saving our order, against all men.
> When summoned to a council, I shall come, unless
> prevented by some canonical impediment. The legate of
> the Apostolic See – whom I know to be its true legate – I
> shall treat honourably, both in coming and in going, and
> I shall assist him in his needs. I shall visit the Apostolic See
> every three years, either in my own person or through an
> envoy, unless I am absolved by their licence. So help me
> God and these God's holy gospels.[62]

When he took the *pallium* from the high altar in Canterbury Cathedral, then, he accepted a special commission from Alexander III, which bound him by oath to defend the rights of the Apostolic See. This may have been the point at which he decided to resign the chancellorship. Ralph of Diss implies as much by recording the resignation immediately after the ceremony. It was then, after putting on 'the vestment bestowed by God on the high priests [pontifical vestments]', that he decided to withdraw from the business of the court; and he sent the royal seal back to the king in Normandy by the hands of his chancellor, Master Ernulf.

Whether Becket's action was conscientious – a realization that he could not combine the two offices without doing violence to the demands of one of them – or a mark of his arrogance, remains moot. For some (Warren, Barlow, Türk), this was the satanic *Non serviam* – 'I shall not serve' – with which Lucifer, prince of the angels had defied the Almighty. Once settled in the throne of St Augustine, it is argued, the over-promoted son of London merchants saw the opportunity to throw off once and for all the subservience that he had had to manifest, first to Archbishop Theobald and then to King Henry II, to both of whom he owed his promotions. This was nothing less than serial betrayal.[63] Yet there are some significant indications, apart from the possibly biased biographers, that he was conscious of his un-preparedness for the spiritual role that had been thrust upon him. An early letter to Gilbert Foliot, for example, spoke of the 'imperfection [in himself], which we see in many things'.[64]

At the same time, he was well aware of contemporary opinion among the reforming clerics coming out of the schools in Paris or the papal Curia, that it was unbecoming of clergy to serve kings and nobles in a secular capacity. His own friend, John of Salisbury, had written very eloquently about the dignity of the priestly office and the need for the king to have a paid civil service separate from that of the Church. Royal control and exploitation of clerical appointments had been one of John's targets in his 'Statesman's Book' (*Policraticus*), which he had dedicated to Chancellor Thomas in 1159. Nor did these ideas remain in the realm of pious theory. A very intriguing letter from John to an unknown correspondent criticizes his proposal to promote the appointment of a ranking ecclesiastic (perhaps a dean) to some secular office, perhaps itinerant judge, on the grounds that 'No man can serve two masters' (Matt. 6: 24; Luke 16: 13). The implications of the evangelical commonplace were spelled out: 'This man cannot both watch over the interests of the brethren and serve the satellites of the court to win their favour', because '[the satellites of the court] ... oppose the king's authority to every effort of the Church.' Then, in a comment that is eerily prophetic of Becket's later predicament, John added, 'If you act rightly and defend the liberty of the Church, the authority of the king bars the way; whereas if you act ill, the authority of the law of God cries out against you on every side.'[65] It was easier for an archdeacon, who was not even a priest,

than it was for an archbishop of Canterbury, to square his conscience
in supporting the king's authority against the Church's. There may
have been a genuine reluctance to breach the Canterbury exclusion of
public servants on his part: and the memory of some high-profile
cases in which he, as Chancellor, had subordinated ecclesiastical to
royal interests would have warned of conflicts of interest ahead.

One such example was the Battle Abbey case. In that fierce dispute
between the abbot of Battle and the bishop of Chichester in 1157, the
king's case was put by Thomas the Chancellor, then archdeacon of
Canterbury – a case that involved disregarding lawful papal privileges confirming the bishop's authority over the monastery in favour
of monastic charters that were in fact forged. The decision was made
because the king favoured the abbey, whose abbot was Walter de
Lucy, brother of the justiciar, Richard. A new article by Nicholas
Vincent has warned us to be cautious about accepting the details of
the Battle Abbey account of the event, but it is accurate as to general
details. Boiled down to its bare essentials, the case was decided not
by formal judicial procedure but by the will of the king, to which all
parties had to defer.[66] One suspects that Hilary of Chichester's later
coolness towards Becket as archbishop stemmed from their earlier
encounter in the Battle Abbey case, when the chancellor could be seen
as the chief agent of the bishop's humiliating discomfiture. There is
no reason to believe that Henry II would have expected Becket the
chancellor-archbishop to have acted in a manner different from
Becket the chancellor-archdeacon. The crux of the matter was not the
much vaunted friendship between the two men, but the much more
fundamental question of the relationship between master and servant,
king and court official.

Apart from the bishop of Rochester, all English bishops and the
leading Benedictine abbots paid homage to the king before their
respective consecrations. Those who remember the present queen's
coronation, or who have seen the film record made at the time, will
recall that the Anglican archbishops and bishops all knelt individually before the newly crowned queen and, placing their joined hands
in hers, swore an oath, not merely of loyalty (fealty) but of personal
service (homage). The text of the modern oath differs little from its
medieval predecessor, which read,

> I [Thomas, archbishop of Canterbury] become your
> liegeman for life, limb, and all earth honour, to live and
> die for you against all manner of men, saving my order,
> so help me God.

It was not until the bishop or abbot had taken this oath that he was invested with the landed estates that belonged to his church. Those lands were held by military service – Canterbury originally owed the service of 60 knights, but more were enfeoffed, and during Becket's exile, scutage was charged for 84¾ fees.[67] Moreover, prelates held their estates *per baroniam* – that is, by barony. In other words, in so far as they held their territorial estates from the king, bishops and major abbots were bound to perform all the service, military, legal, fiscal and personal, that a member of the lay baronage was required to perform, on pain of deprivation of the estates. Like their secular counterparts, the estates themselves were subject to the feudal incidents of wardship during vacancy. In baronies, generally, the kings admitted male heirs who were of full age to their father's lordships without much trouble on payment of a relief, a kind of entry fee that varied according to the value of the estate and the king's good or ill will. The question of relief was in fact a thorny one throughout the post-Conquest period, as all kings exploited the right to their own advantage. So contentious was the issue that it found a place in Magna Carta, as the barons sought to set reasonable limits to the king's right. Where the heir was under age, the king had the right of wardship of the heir and of any younger children, as well as wardship of the estates. Both were lucrative sources of income, in that the king had the right to arrange the marriages of the children – often for a price, and his agents managed, or rather exploited, the estates to his and their advantage. All profits in excess of the living expenses of the children went to the king.

The same, in effect, *mutatis mutandis*, applied to ecclesiastical estates. On the death of a bishop or abbot, the estates of the now vacant church came into the king's hand, administered by his officers for his advantage. This practice – a consequence of what one may call the feudalization of ecclesiastical estates – led inexorably to the prolongation of vacancies, as kings deferred allowing a new election or making a new appointment as long as possible. Bishops, archbishops and abbots were therefore tightly bound to the crown, and many of them owed their appointment to the king. Gilbert Foliot's sense of scandal at Becket's appointment – by royal fiat – rings rather hollow in this context. For the present discussion, however, it is important to recognize how tight were the ties that bound the Church's leaders to the personal service of the king. The bonds were specifically personal: the oath was an oath of *homage*, a sworn obligation of man to man, which bound the vassal for life. There was, indeed, something like a 'conscience clause' included in the oath taken by ecclesiastics. The phrase 'saving my order' was inserted to protect the cleric from forms of service unbecoming to his clerical status; but the precise meaning of the clause was unclear. It seems to have boiled down to an understanding that clerics need not participate in judgments of the king's court that involved the spilling of blood by mutilation or execution; but how far this exemption worked in practice is difficult to assess, since high-ranking clerics were regularly appointed as royal justices. In Henry I's day, the office of justiciar was held by Bishop Roger of Salisbury, one of a family of royal servants, which included his nephews, Nigel, bishop of Ely and royal treasurer, and Alexander, bishop of Lincoln. There is no doubt that the appointments of Roger and Nigel were primarily administrative; and the incomes of their bishoprics were used to support the king's administration. Modern historians seem to find nothing odd in this arrangement, which seriously compromised the independence of the spiritual office. It is argued in the king's defence that reliance on the Church was a necessary consequence of its monopoly on education. If the king wanted an effective civil service, he had to recruit 'churchmen'. That is true enough, but he did not have to make them bishops.

In Thomas's case, the stark contradiction between the offices of chancellor and archbishop was accentuated by the reception of the *pallium*. The implications of his new oath should not be cast aside as of no moment. King Henry may have seen no conflict of interest between the Crozier and the Seal, but Thomas could not have been unaware of what would be expected of him in the years ahead. If he was being accused of betraying the Church's interests in his earlier tenure of the chancellorship, what greater betrayal might be required in the future? For his new episcopal colleagues, however, the sudden change of direction may have been as surprising as the Canterbury appointment; for members of the king's court, and for the king himself, it was a shocking demonstration of arrogance and ingratitude. Ralph of Diss, the dean of St Paul's, who puts the resignation at the head of a list of 12 numbered causes of dispute between king and archbishop, says that Henry took the action as a personal affront. He knew that the archbishops of Mainz and Cologne were archchancellors, respectively of Germany and Italy, and they saw nothing wrong with holding the pastoral staff in their right hand while in the left they bore the seal either of the empire or of the kingdom.[68]

Would matters have turned out differently if Becket had kept the Great Seal in his left hand? Theobald has been commended for his diplomatic handling of the new King Henry, with the inference that Becket should have adopted the same approach. But Becket's position was very different from his. Not only was Theobald a former abbot of Bec, but he had also been an important supporter of the Angevin cause: he had refused to crown King's Stephen's heir Eustace; he had crowned Henry II; and his venerable age, and indeed his growing ill-health from 1155, made serious confrontation with the young Henry unlikely, especially since four and a half of the first seven years of his reign (1156–mid-1157, 1159–61 inclusive) were spent overseas. Even so, there were indications that a more aggressive policy was being pursued in English ecclesiastical affairs,[69] which lends support to FitzStephen's assertion that the king made his chancellor archbishop of Canterbury in order to facilitate his 'designs against the Church'.[70] When Thomas was pressed to succeed the much respected arch-bishop, he would have been acutely aware of how different his own position was; and he would have realized more than anyone else that there was no place in Henry's service for split loyalty. Theobald the monk had held no office save that of archbishop; Becket was being asked to combine the spiritual with the secular in a manner not seen in the English kingdom. Brushing aside the reality of the situation, Professor Warren thought that 'for the archbishop to have remained chancellor would only have been a piece of make-believe'[71] – implying that Thomas could have retained the title while a deputy carried out the onerous duties of running the department. The administrative chores could certainly have been devolved to a deputy, but not the responsibilities of the office. Was it conceivable that Henry would have tolerated a chancellor-archbishop who did not support his poli-cies? The chancellor was an officer of the court; more than that, in Becket's hands, the chancellorship had outranked the justiciars, Richard de Lucy and Earl Robert of Leicester. It is likely, in fact, that Henry was thinking of the precedent of Bishop Roger of Salisbury (1101–39), who had run Henry I's English administration as a kind of viceroy. If there was a 'make-believe' element in Roger's twin posi-tion, it applied more to the bishopric than to the government office, for he lived a thoroughly secular life, even to the extent of keeping Matilda of Ramsbury as his mistress, and he used his position to accumulate great wealth for himself, while advancing three members of his immediate family to high office.[72]

If Thomas had continued as chancellor-archbishop, the first office would almost certainly have absorbed the second, and the protection of the king's interests would have been the overriding priority of both. Henry wanted the able Becket to collaborate with him in the ecclesi-astical field as he had so effectively in the secular, and the good rela-tions between king and chancellor-archbishop could have lasted only as long as Becket discharged both offices to the king's satisfaction. Such in fact was the evidence of the much-vaunted imperial examples. When Frederick I's able Chancellor Rainald of Dassel was appointed to Cologne in 1159, he became the emperor's principal agent in ecclesiastical affairs and a promoter of the papal schism.[73] The example of Mainz is even more instructive. When the archbishop-elect, Conrad of Wittelsbach, withdrew his allegiance from the imperially supported anti-pope in 1164–65, Frederick had no compunction about replacing him with the more compliant Christian von Buch (1165–83).[74] There is no reason to believe that Henry II would have been any more tolerant of opposition than the emperor; and Thomas had seen Henry's masterful ruthlessness at first hand. Rather than a search for even greater power, then, the resignation of the chancellorship should be seen as a conscientious choice:[75] not the Satanic denial of obedience to God, but Christ's rebuttal of Satan's temptation of earthly dominion:

> And the devil, taking him [Christ] up into an high mountain, shewed unto him all the kingdoms of the world in a moment of time. And the devil said unto him, 'All this power will I give thee, and the glory of them, for that is delivered unto me, and to whomsoever I will I give it. If thou therefore wilt worship me, all shall be thine.' And Jesus answered and said unto him, 'Get thee behind me, Satan, for it is written, "Thou shalt worship the Lord thy God, and him only shalt thou serve." ' (Luke 4: 5–8)

2

The controversial archbishop

So, Thomas of London, now ex-chancellor, was archbishop of Canterbury; and the transition from royal favourite to something approaching public enemy of the state was to be swift and brutal. Gilbert Foliot was to lay all the blame on Becket's own shoulders:

> A man of your prudence should have ensured that the disagreements gradually arising between the kingdom and you did not grow too serious, that the tiny spark did not flare up into so great a fire, to the ruin of many. It was managed differently, and from causes too numerous to list, disagreements were multiplied, indignation was inflamed, and hatred firmly entrenched. (*CTB*, i, no. 109)

Even after resigning the Chancery, Becket should have been able to manage the king. That he did not could only be the consequence of pride. Far from being overawed by the spiritual responsibilities of the primacy, it was alleged, the archbishopric went to his head, and he strove to use the spiritual office to build a new power base from which to overawe the king. Unlikely as this interpretation is, it had some currency in 1164–65. In the course of a complex and ambiguous letter, which pledges support as long as it could remain secret, Bishop Arnulf of Lisieux told Becket that 'some people' thought precisely that: 'that you strove to keep the former habits of the Chancellorship in this dignity too..., no longer do you sit watching the footstool or even the throne, but oversee even the diadem on his head.'[1]

Among recent historians, Warren, Türk and Barlow interpret the first nine months or so as a string of needless confrontations with secular authorities – in Warren's words, a series of 'grand gestures' made to demonstrate his commitment to the archiepiscopal office.[2] But the sequence can be interpreted very differently: not as endeavours to 'out-bishop' the bishops[3] or challenge the king, but as attempts to discharge the normal duties of the archiepiscopal office in an atmosphere of mounting harassment and opposition. On his return to England in January 1163, after an absence of more than four years (August 1158–January 1163), Henry made it clear that Becket was no longer *persona grata*. The moment was graphically recorded by the London chronicler, Ralph de Diceto, the dean of St Paul's. As Thomas advanced to greet the king at Southampton, 'he was admitted to the kiss of peace, but not into the fullness of grace, as the king publicly demonstrated to all who were present, by the manner in which he turned his countenance away from the archbishop'.[4] From that moment, Thomas was a political outcast, and everyone knew it.

Diceto charted 12 steps to disaster, of which the resignation was the first. The second step was Becket's grant of the archdeaconry of Canterbury to Geoffrey Ridel, at the king's vehement insistence. Given that he did what the king wanted, the presence of this compliance as an example of dispute might appear strange. Barlow thought that Becket had sought to keep the office of archdeacon with the archbishopric – a shocking example of pluralism, and that the king had to prise it out of him. Another explanation is more likely, however. Becket had been given the archdeaconry as a mark of Theobald's trust; and it is likely that he intended to pass it on to one of his own loyal staff when he had settled into his new dignity. Henry's insistence that it should go to one of *his*, was a further sign of Becket's disfavour, whose consequences were spelled out in Diceto's steps 3–6, 10 and 12. What links them together – and with the loss of the king's grace – is that all concern challenges to the new archbishop's jurisdiction over the see of Canterbury. Two (4 and 5) were acts of feudal contumacy in which the king connived. In the process of taking legal charge of the Canterbury estates, Becket summoned the lay tenants to pay their due homage to himself as new lord of the fee. One of them, Earl Roger de Clare, who held Tonbridge castle and its appurtenances from the archbishopric for the service of four knights (although only two were acknowledged in 1171), refused his summons (22 July 1163), declaring that he was answerable to the king, rather than to the archbishop;[5] and in another case, an inquest into the secular service owed by lay tenants in Kent found that William de Ros, holder of one and a half knights' fees in the manor of Maidstone, owed the service to the crown rather than to the archbishopric.[6]

Diceto's account of the de Ros affair is illuminating, however. He says that the judgment was *secured* by the justices, implying undue pressure, and comments, 'Thus did hatred for the person [of the archbishop] redound to injury to the Church.' He meant, of course, that the judgment was prejudiced and motivated by the king's loathing for Becket:[7] in other words, Becket could not hope to obtain a fair verdict in a process involving royal officials. The archbishop's secular interests were similarly damaged by the king in the case of the former royal Constable, Henry of Essex. Having been defeated in trial by battle at Windsor (31 March 1163) by Robert of Montfort, on charges of cowardice and treason, the estates Henry held from the crown were duly forfeited; but the king also seized the two knights' fees in Saltwood, including the castle, which belonged to the archbishopric.[8] There is no doubt that Henry was not justified in this action, since forfeited lands should revert to the lords from whom they were held – but his seizure of them was a further demonstration of the withdrawal of his favour. These disputes were not insignificant. The estates amounted to seven and a half knights' fees, together with the castles of Tonbridge and Saltwood, and the homage of an earl, and no lord of an estate could suffer such losses with equanimity. Far from demonstrating Becket's power-hungry troublemaking, these events reveal the way in which the king's *malevolentia* could operate systematically against a person who had lost his grace.

The same was true of Diceto's third conflict: the blessing of Clarembald, the new abbot of St Augustine's Canterbury. Like the dispute between the archbishoprics of Canterbury and York, it had its roots in Lanfranc's post-Conquest settlement of the English Church under his jurisdiction, with the support of William the Conqueror. The exemption of great monasteries from episcopal jurisdiction was a cause of unending friction; and at Canterbury, the close proximity of St Augustine's and the cathedral priory of Holy Trinity (Christ Church) exacerbated the anomaly. Archbishop Theobald had been locked in dispute with Clarembald's predecessor Silvester (1151–61) for six years, and he finally secured the abbot's submission in 1157, against the wishes of Henry II, with the support of two papal mandates.[9] Like Geoffrey Ridel's intrusion into the Canterbury archdeaconry, Clarembald's appointment in 1163 resulted from direct royal intervention, and his resistance to the archbishop's demand for the abbot-elect to make profession to him before conferment of abbatial blessing had the king's support. Henry's agents even promoted his case at the Curia in spring 1164. Becket did in fact secure three successive papal mandates ordering Clarembald's profession (1164, 1165, 1166/67), but all three remained ineffective.[10]

Not listed by Diceto, but equally demonstrative of Henry's cultivation of Becket's adversaries, was his support of Archbishop Roger of York's renewal of the campaign to achieve parity for his archdiocese. This issue was raised not by Becket but by Roger himself, who had petitioned the new Pope Alexander for confirmation of York's privileges in 1161 and 1162,[11] and again at the papal council of Tours in May 1163, where the assembled bishops and abbots were presented with the spectacle of the two English archbishops competing for the honour of sitting at the pope's right hand. Canterbury won; but York renewed the campaign when they were back in England, by having his cross solemnly borne before him as he travelled through the southern province to the council at Westminster in October 1163.

Again, these disputes can be made to reflect badly on the new archbishop,[12] yet they were both ancient, and they were not raised by Becket, but reinvigorated when opportunists saw his weakened position. With the king behind him, neither York nor the abbot of St Augustine's would have made much headway; with the king's enmity, they knew that they would have the king's backing in the papal Curia. As an anonymous messenger, perhaps John of Salisbury, wrote in *c.* May 1164:

> I urge and advise that, no matter what the twisted mind
> of wicked men contrives against your honour, you should
> strive to obtain and keep the king's favour for yourself, as
> far as you can, according to God, because that is best for
> God's Church. I cannot see that you can achieve anything
> worthwhile as long as things remain as they are and
> the king opposes you in everything – especially since the
> Roman Church can receive nothing from you except
> words, and whatever loss it suffers on account of others
> it ascribes to you, because it will not allow you to be
> overthrown at the king's pleasure. (*CTB*, i, no. 29)

Neither of these controversies was of Becket's manufacture and neither could have been avoided without loss to the reputation of Canterbury and its archbishop. If these disputes had not been part of the complex of problems besetting Thomas Becket, it is unlikely that much would have been made of them by historians; it is unlikely, too, that an archbishop of Canterbury would have been censured for doing what he was expected to do. Just as the king himself had set about recovering rights and properties, and tearing down unlicensed castles and insisting on the exercise of his inherited authority, so the new archbishop set about securing his rights and resisting challenges to his authority.

Seisin was a central point in the law of ownership. To prove right, one needed not only written evidence, but proof of occupation. The principle of 'use it or lose it' applied as much to rights and properties as it does to muscle tone. Becket's excommunication of William of Eynsford, one of the prominent knightly tenants of the archbishopric, for the forceful intrusion of a clerk into the church of St Martin at Eynsford, Diceto's sixth example, fits into this pattern of defence and recuperation.[13] The particular issue was commonplace. Every bishop and monastery in England had to defend its rights of patronage against challenge from the heirs of grantors. St Martin's had been given to Christ Church as early as *c.* 1135, when an earlier William entered the monastery, and the patronage passed to Canterbury. The patronage of churches, however – the right to nominate clergy to serve in them – was treated as real property: it could be inherited, exchanged, even divided between multiple heiresses; and the right of jurisdiction over such disputes that arose was contested between royal and ecclesiastical courts. Despite Warren's assertion to the contrary,[14] there is no suggestion here that Becket acted unlawfully in the Eynsford case, since the dispute was determined in Canterbury's favour in 1182,[15] but he incurred the king's wrath, because William claimed to be a tenant of the crown, whose excommunication should have been cleared with the king first. There is no evidence that William was indeed a tenant-in-chief, but his contumacy fits the pattern of the two other disputes in which Canterbury tenants took advantage of Becket's disfavour to repudiate his authority. It is possible to argue that, once the seal had been returned, Henry simply hung Becket out to dry. The former chancellor had outlived his usefulness, and there were many envious 'creatures of the court', like the justiciar, Richard de Lucy, and ambitious royal clerks (Geoffrey Ridel, Richard of Ilchester, John of Oxford and others), who were more than willing to exploit the situation to their own advantage.[16]

Quite independent of questions of Canterbury jurisdiction, however, was Becket's refusal, at the council held at Woodstock in July 1163, to allow the transfer of the so-called sheriffs' aid to the king. For William of Canterbury, this was the second significant cause of estrangement between king and archbishop (the resignation of the chancellorship being the first).[17] The 'aid' was a levy of two shillings per hide, paid by landlords to the county sheriff, independently of whatever was owed to the king. Professor Warren could see no justification in Becket's opposition, which he called 'obtuse and cantankerous', and his refusal to allow the Canterbury estates to pay the money into the king's Exchequer was deemed 'quite improper, for the debate was not about the obligation to pay but to whom it should be paid'.[18] Quite so. Becket was not challenging the payment; he was opposing the arbitrary transfer to royal coffers of a customary good-will payment, which was made to oil the wheels of shrieval administration. As he expressed it, the reason was crystal clear: 'It was not right that what was freely given by himself and others should be counted as royal income';[19] and it is likely that he was voicing the opinion of every baron in England.[20] His opposition, however, was another nail in his coffin.

Where the dean of St Paul's had concentrated on administrative tensions, the lawyer FitzStephen traced the beginning of the estrangement to issues of jurisdiction. Some time between Becket's consecration on 3 June 1162 and mid-1163, a cleric was accused of seducing a girl in Warwickshire and killing her father. Henry wanted the trial to take place in a secular court; Becket had the clerk retained in episcopal custody for trial according to canon law; in a second case, Becket caused a cleric who had stolen a silver chalice from St Mary-le-Bow in London to be tried and degraded in an ecclesiastical court, and, to please the king, branded as a thief;[21] and in a third case (which Diceto listed as his tenth confrontation), Philip of Broi, canon of St Paul's in Bedford, having been acquitted of killing a knight following purgation in the court of the bishop of Lincoln, was prosecuted again by a royal justice, Simon FitzPeter. Philip indignantly refused to undergo a second trial, and heated words were exchanged between them. Simon then complained to King Henry in London (probably in July 1163), who demanded a lay trial. Becket, however, had the clerk arraigned in his own court. There the initial charge of homicide was raised again, but thrown out on the grounds that it had already been decided in an earlier case. Then a subsidiary charge was laid, namely insulting a royal officer. Philip considered the charge beneath his dignity and refused to enter a plea on the charge. Simon's supporters, however, demanded judgment on the matter, and Philip offered to make satisfaction. The bishops decreed that Philip should relinquish his prebend into the king's hands for two years and also present himself 'naked' before Simon 'according to the custom of the land'. The king declared that the judgment was not a true judgment; the bishops maintained that it was, except that they had been more severe on the canon than was appropriate, out of consideration for the king's peace and honour.[22] These three cases left King Henry extremely angry with the archbishop. Whether this was because of righteous indignation or because of his existing displeasure is unclear. Becket's biographers tend to the latter; and the Philip de Broi case is explained by two of them in terms of pre-existing tension between the canon and Simon FitzPeter, since the family of the dead knight had been satisfied with the outcome of the original trial.[23] It is also probable that the king's return to England in January 1163, after an absence of more than four years, led to the raising of many such issues.[24]

Examples of tension between ecclesiastical and secular jurisdiction over crimes committed by the clergy were not new, or confined to Becket's pontificate. While he was still chancellor, one case made the headlines. This was the *cause célèbre* (1154–56) of the accusation launched by Symphorian, chaplain (and nephew) of the late archbishop William of York (d. 1154), that Archdeacon Osbert of Richmond (Yorks) had murdered the archbishop by poisoning the chalice at mass. The case had opened at the end of Stephen's reign, and Henry disputed the Church's jurisdiction over the case when he became king, but, as a letter of Archbishop Theobald recounted to Pope Adrian IV, 'we just and only just succeeded in recalling the case to the judgment of the Church', and that was achieved only 'with much difficulty and by strong pressure, to the indignation of the king and all his nobles'.[25] The matter was a thorny one, especially since a mass of clergy in minor orders (below the subdiaconate) were covered by the immunity; and there was some doubt as to whether the bishops were exercising sufficient authority over them.[26]

Clerical immunity

The core issue in these cases was the clerical claim to immunity from secular trial and punishment, but the question was not provocatively raised by Thomas Becket. Like the problems relating to his lordship of Canterbury, it came with the territory; but, unlike them, the jurisdictional issue had profound implications for the present and future relationship between the English Church and the monarchy. At a council of bishops and abbots held at Westminster Abbey in the wake of the solemn translation of the body of the newly canonized Edward the Confessor, Henry raised the issue of the punishment of 'criminous clerks'. With the advice of those who, in Herbert of Bosham's words, claimed to be expert in both laws (Roman and canon),[27] he proposed a double process, in which accused clerics should be tried in an ecclesiastical court and, if convicted, be degraded and transferred to a secular court for sentence and punishment. In the succeeding debate, the bishops stood together as a fairly solid phalanx, refusing to accede to the king's demands. The episcopate and its legal experts were unanimous in their defence of clerical immunity from secular judgment and punishment. This is important. Thomas was not at the beginning an isolated figure seeking personal aggrandizement by challenging the king's lawful authority in this matter. There was no disagreement between him and the episcopate on the principle of clerical immunity.

Having failed to obtain agreement to the new procedure, the king then required recognition of what he called his royal customs. After consulting the bishops, Thomas agreed that he and his brethren would observe them, *saving their order*. Each prelate was then asked to repeat his undertaking individually, and all gave the same response, except Hilary of Chichester, who substituted *in good faith*. Neither formula satisfied the king, who demanded, but did not obtain, an unreserved acknowledgment. Furious with his public failure to bend the bishops to his will, he left London before dawn on the next day, leaving the episcopate in a quandary.[28] All were anxious to placate the king: some more than others; and Henry found it relatively easy to follow the advice of Bishop Arnulf of Lisieux (who was anxious to get into the king's good graces) in destroying the bishops' unanimity, by approaching individually Roger of York, Gilbert of London, Robert of Lincoln and Hilary of Chichester, whom he judged more amenable to persuasion.[29] At the same time, he encouraged Becket's ecclesiastical adversaries (Roger of York, Clarembald of St Augustine's and possibly Gilbert of London) in their challenges to his authority, even to the extent of asking the pope to make Roger papal legate for England.[30] Simultaneously, he tried his utmost to persuade Pope Alexander III, then in exile in Sens (France), to approve the 'customs of the realm'. Two of his ablest negotiators, this same Arnulf and Richard of Ilchester, recently appointed archdeacon of Poitiers, travelled backwards and forwards between England and France in an attempt to cajole the pope.[31]

Alexander's position was extremely insecure. Elected only four years earlier (September 1159) in a split election, his title was disputed by an imperially supported rival, Victor IV (1159–64), and it had taken considerable diplomacy to obtain the recognition of the kings of France and England, which was secured only in mid-1160. His hold on Rome and the papal states had been shattered by Frederick I's invasion of Italy in 1162, which forced him to flee to the protection of Louis VII in France (1162–mid-1165). In the longer term, Frederick's plans for a re-establishment of direct imperial rule in Italy were to fail (following his defeat at Legnano, 1176), but for the whole of the Becket dispute and its immediate aftermath, the pope's position was precarious in the extreme; and, at the beginning, during his French exile, he was virtually reduced to begging for financial support from the princes of Europe. Henry II's loyalty, upon which depended the allegiance of England, Normandy and Anjou, and perhaps also Aquitaine, was crucial to the maintenance of his position. The king, then, was in a very strong position to press for concessions; and he was not above threatening secession to the anti-pope, if he did not get his way.

If Pope Alexander was vulnerable, so was Thomas, for Roger of York and Clarembald of St Augustine's had launched appeals against him, with the king's approval and support, and Gilbert Foliot, the new bishop of London, had refused to renew his profession to Canterbury. Political isolation was becoming ecclesiastical isolation. The pope had to manage the situation as best he could. The York case was deferred; the legation excluded Canterbury and its archbishop (and so was worthless); London was not required to repeat his formal profession to Canterbury, since the one given as bishop of Hereford was still binding; Clarembald was ordered to make profession.[32] In the major and potentially much more damaging case, however, Alexander resisted the king's blandishments, but sought to achieve some kind of accommodation – not compromise, but a formula for reconciling the English Church with its king. To this end, he sent letters and personal emissaries to the archbishop, strongly urging that he should do all in his power to make peace.

> We have received with special attention the letter which your fraternity has sent to us, and listened attentively to what your messenger [Master Henry of Houghton] transmitted to us by word of mouth, and we are giving deep consideration to the serious anxieties and sorrows which afflict your spirit. Our spirit was deeply moved and disturbed when we heard and learned these things, for just as we delighted in your prosperity so do we suffer with you in your adversities, as with a dearly beloved brother. As a steadfast and experienced man, you should remember the scriptural saying, 'The apostles went forth from the sight of the council rejoicing, because they were found worthy to suffer insults for the name of Jesus,' and patiently bear trials of this kind, and do not let your spirit

be troubled more than is necessary, so that you may
receive fitting consolation and we and you may be
consoled in him who has chosen you to defend Catholic
and Christian truth at this moment of crisis, and whose
pleasure it is now to remove the stain of those things
which you have less than lawfully committed, and to
punish them by various afflictions, so that they should not
be reserved for punishment at the Last Judgment. As for
the other matters, do not be troubled or alarmed for any
reason – as we have heard from the letter which you sent
to your clerk – because you have been appealed to
the Apostolic See [Roger of York and Clarembald of
St Augustine's], since it is our pleasure and desire that if
those who have appealed against you come to the Curia
you should, if you think it appropriate, prosecute the
appeal in your own person without any hesitation
or delay. And no one should be able to strike your
steadfastness with fear or doubt by the authority of the
Roman Church, for with God's help we shall strive
steadfastly to preserve for you the rights and dignities
of the church entrusted to your charge as far as we can,
saving justice and reason, as for one whom we find to be
a steadfast and able defender of the Church. Finally we
direct and order your fraternity to return to the church
of Canterbury and travel as little as possible about the
country, and keep with you only the smallest number of
attendants whom you absolutely need. We are giving you
this particular advice so that you may not be compelled to
renounce the rights and dignities of your church by any
fear or misfortune which might befall to you. Given at
Sens on 26 October [1163]. (*CTB*, i, no. 19)

This papal advice needs to be weighed very carefully. In the general
literature, it is generally interpreted as evidence of Alexander's 'exasperation' with Becket. Professor Barlow thought that 'from the point
of view of the papal curia, Thomas was a liability, even a menace'.[33]
This judgment is too simple. The timing could hardly have been
worse, given the vulnerability of the papacy; yet Becket had more
friends among the cardinals than is generally recognized,[34] and objective observers could see that the issues were raised not by Becket but
by Henry II. Far from there being 'little merit in his cause',[35] the criminous clerks issue had implications for the whole Latin Church.

Professor Barlow saw the command 'to travel about the country as little as possible' as evidence of the pope's hostility to Becket's flamboyant behaviour; but that advice needs to be understood in the context in which it was written. Far from commanding capitulation to Henry's demands, the allusion to the Apostles' steadfast witness to Christ before the Jewish council in Jerusalem in the Acts of the Apostles (Acts 5: 26–42) contained coded approbation of the stand taken at Westminster. The Apostles' defiance of the council's mandate to stop preaching was founded on the priority of God's law to man's – as they said, 'We must obey God rather than men' (Acts 5: 29). For Becket and the bishops the inference was clear: they stood in the place of Peter and the Apostles; they, like them, were defending 'Catholic and Christian truth at this moment of crisis'. What lay behind the advice of the last sentence can only be guessed at, but it suggests fear for Becket's physical well-being. Henry's own envoys, as well as Becket's, no doubt painted a very bleak picture of the likely outcome of Henry II's famous rage. Even Gilbert Foliot later alleged fear of the king to explain his acquiescence in Becket's election; and a contemporary letter from Becket's old friend and colleague from Theobald's household, Bishop John of Poitiers, skirted the possibility of flight and exile for himself and Thomas: 'I hope that I may share your exile, or even anticipate it ... our Pisan [Cardinal Henry] is still struggling to have me provided with a safer place, and he said that he told the abbot of l'Aumône [Philip] to let you know the same thing.'[36]

By the time these letters were written, in late October 1163, at least two of Becket's supporters (John of Salisbury and Ralph of Sarre) had been exiled, and the wolves were gathering. The two Johns (of Salisbury and of Poitiers) thought the situation close to hopeless, seeing the precarious position of the papal Curia. Arnulf of Lisieux and Richard of Ilchester criss-crossed the channel three times between October and December 1163 in a vain attempt to persuade Pope Alexander to accept the king's Westminster proposals; Hilary of Chichester tried to persuade Thomas; and, finally, in December, Alexander sent three men, the bishop-elect of Hereford (Robert of Melun, whom Becket had heard at Paris), the Cistercian, Philip of l'Aumône, and Count John of Vendôme, to press Becket to find some formula to save the situation. Abbot Philip, particularly, was a man of high reputation, for he had been a companion of St Bernard of Clairvaux. It was he, speaking in the pope's name, who said that King Henry had assured Pope Alexander and the cardinals that in demanding the 'customs', he was not seeking anything prejudicial to the Church, only recognition of his honour in the presence of his nobles.

Under this pressure, Becket agreed, at Woodstock, around Christmas 1163, to give an oral acceptance to 'the customs of the realm', having been assured that no more would be required of him.[37]

For Henry, however, this was the breakthrough he desired, so he summoned a great council of nobles and bishops to attend him at Clarendon *c.* 25 January. There was played out the next stage of Henry's plan. Becket and the bishops were required to express their formal adhesion to the 'customs of the realm' in the presence of the baronial council. Thomas at first resisted; the bishops were shut up together for two whole days, while extreme pressure was applied. In an atmosphere of threat and intimidation, the bishops' unanimity began to weaken. Jocelin of Salisbury and William of Norwich were particularly afraid of the king's displeasure, and begged Becket to spare them; two earls, of Cornwall and Leicester, warned of terrible retribution if the bishops continued to resist; two templars, Richard of Hastings and Hostes of Saint-Omer, who had the king's ear (it was they who had handed the castles of the Vexin over to King Henry in 1160), painted an equally bleak picture of the dire consequences for the clergy if the king were further provoked;[38] and four bishops (Roger of York, Hilary of Chichester, Gilbert of London and Jocelin of Salisbury) were alleged to have said that if he held out, 'he would fall into the king's hands and be condemned as a disturber of the royal majesty and enemy of the crown, and killed'.[39] Becket acquiesced. He promised to accept the customs *in the word of truth*, and ordered the bishops to do the same. Although not an oath, this was a solemn undertaking – a promise, on their honour as bishops, to abide by the customs.

Worse was to follow. The king sent the 'older and wiser nobles' out of the room, accompanied by his clerks, to record the customs in writing. They produced a chirograph, a tripartite written memorandum that contained not only the 16 clauses of what became the Constitutions of Clarendon, but a preamble declaring that they had been acknowledged by 14 named members of the episcopate, who had promised, in the word of truth, to keep them 'in good faith and without any subterfuge', in the presence of 38 witnesses, headed by ten earls and the justiciar, Richard de Lucy.[40] Presented with this binding document, Becket accepted one of the three copies as proof of their content, but refused to append his seal.[41] For Gilbert Foliot, these actions were the breaking point in Becket's relations with the bishops. He broke their unity; he gave way; he ordered them to accept the obnoxious undertakings, then abstracted himself from their confirmation. If this wasn't an example of 'Yea' and 'Nay', then what was?[42] David Knowles thought that Becket's actions at Woodstock and Clarendon stemmed from weakness of character:

> He lacked still the inner strength to stand firm, and he displayed once more that lack of political or social judgment that was to do harm to his cause on more than one occasion: he changed direction suddenly without warning or seeking to persuade his colleagues.[43]

But some of the colleagues had been persuading him to accept the customs, and earls and royal familiars had warned of extreme action. Had they persisted in their defiance, Henry's immediate recourse could have been to call them all traitors, seize their estates and drive them all into exile. During his son John's reign, indeed, all but two bishops went into exile rather than break the papal interdict that had been imposed in the wake of John's refusal to accept Stephen Langton as archbishop of Canterbury. There was nothing to prevent Henry using his ultimate weapon – sequestration of the lands held by homage and fealty – as he was to do with the Canterbury estates at the end of 1164. It might have been better, as Knowles thought, to have led the episcopate in a desperate defiance rather than to have employed a stratagem that backfired; but that argument presumes that the bishops were willing to follow him in such a course, which, *pace* Foliot's assertions,[44] is highly uncertain. Thomas seems to have been of the same mind, however, for he was bitterly remorseful. He could not have anticipated that a written schedule would be presented or that he and the bishops would have been required to set their seals to such a document. His tactical recognition of the unwritten customs had come very close to being an irrevocable confirmation of a formally promulgated programme.

Becket's refusal to seal the Constitutions created a new crisis; and when Rotrou, bishop of Évreux (soon to be archbishop of Rouen), who had come to report on cross-Channel affairs, attempted to mediate between archbishop and king, Henry said that the only way to resolve the situation was for Rotrou and Becket to petition the pope for confirmation of the Constitutions.[45] This was done; but Alexander refused his approval and, on 23 February 1164, commanded Becket and the bishops 'to revoke [whatever promise they had made] and to strive to make [their] peace with God and the Church in respect of that unlawful promise'.[46] Thomas duly suspended himself from celebrating mass, until he was absolved by the pope on 1 April.[47]

The Constitutions of Clarendon

Not all the Constitutions were disadvantageous to the Church; indeed six of the sixteen clauses were tolerated by Alexander III (clauses 2, 6, 11, 13, 14 and 16), and it is clear that the Church's attitude was far from intractable. In accepting clause 2, the pope recognized the legitimacy of royal proprietary rights over royal churches; and he also acknowledged the obligation of prelates who held land by knight service from the crown to participate in all judgments of the royal court that did not involve the spilling of blood (clause 11), and the rights of landowners over their serfs (clause 16). Even more significantly, he accepted three clauses that required cooperation between secular and ecclesiastical jurisdictions (clauses 6, 13 and 14). The important clause 6 declared that laymen should be accused in episcopal courts only by reliable (*certos*) and lawful (*legales*) accusers, and that if an accused were of such power that no accusers dared appear against him, then the bishop could require the sheriff to summon 12 lawful men from the neighbourhood to declare the truth of the matter on oath from their own knowledge. In this way, ecclesiastical courts were enabled to use the sworn jury, which was becoming one of the linchpins of the more integrated system of criminal and civil justice (the common law) that was being constructed. Equally, where a lord attempted to obstruct the exercise of episcopal or royal jurisdiction in his lands, each authority was to support the other in the maintenance of its rights (clause 13), and in clause 14, royal officers were allowed to breach the sanctuary of churches and cemeteries to secure for the king the property of felons that might be hidden there.

But if these six were deemed 'tolerable', the remainder seriously impinged on ecclesiastical rights. Freedom of episcopal and abbatial election was undermined in clause 12, which declared that all such elections should take place in the king's chapel, and with his consent; and clause 4 required archbishops, bishops and beneficed clergy to seek a royal licence before travelling overseas. Equally seriously, eight of the clauses were concerned to define, directly or indirectly, the competence, authority and procedure of the courts Christian on the basis of what Henry claimed were the customary rights exercised by his grandfather, Henry I (1100–35). In respect of competence, three areas of jurisdiction were excluded from ecclesiastical courts: disputes about rights of patronage over churches (clause 1); the determination of whether ecclesiastical property was held in lay fee or in free alms (clause 9); and debt (clause 15); and a fourth, the trial and punishment of clerks accused of criminal offences, was subjected to radical change (clause 3). In respect of authority: the rights of prelates (bishops and archdeacons) to impose spiritual penalties of excommunication and interdict were restricted (clauses 5, 7 and 10); in respect of process, ecclesiastical appeals were to follow a predetermined path (clause 8).

These Constitutions have been dissected by generations of scholars in an attempt to establish whether they were indeed 'ancient' custom, as Henry claimed, and whether, even if they were, they were compatible with the Church's claims to independent rights and status within the kingdom. No easy answer can be given to either question, since English and canon law were being rapidly transformed.

Quite independently of Anglo-Norman custom, the Latin Church was developing its own corpus of law and procedure on a Europe-wide level. The teaching and practice of ecclesiastical law had acquired something approaching professional status in the second third of the twelfth century, following the establishment of schools of law in some of the leading centres of advanced education in Europe – principally Bologna in Italy, Arles, Nîmes and Montpellier in Provence, and Paris, Tours and Reims in France. The ecclesiastical reform movement associated with Pope Gregory VII had accentuated the search for authoritative law; reformers like Ivo of Chartres had compiled highly influential collections of canon law – which were used and cited across Europe. With the reintroduction of Roman civil law in Provence and Bologna in the early years of the twelfth century, the teaching and study, and therefore the practice, of canon law took on a much more professional form. The *Decreta* (Decrees), commonly known as the *Decretum* (*Gratiani*), compiled by Master Gratian, a teacher at Bologna, became the fundamental source of ecclesiastical law. The first recension, compiled at Bologna between 1120 and 1139, was supplemented in the next five or six years, particularly with procedural texts from Roman law. There is no doubt that it became the basis of the teaching and indeed practice of canon law throughout Europe. The papal Curia itself was employing *legistae*, and John of Salisbury cited Gratian in legal letters written for Archbishop Theobald of Canterbury in the 1150s. That same archbishop had invited the Roman lawyer Vacarius to England in the mid-1140s, and he had encouraged Becket's legal studies in the early 1150s. Gilbert Foliot, bishop of London, had learned Roman law somewhere in continental Europe. In 1153 he had a copy of the *Digest* corrected and glossed for his uncle Robert de Chesney, bishop of Lincoln;[48] and he cited elements of the *Corpus iuris civilis* (*Codex*,[49] *Digest* and *Institutes*) more frequently than the *Decretum*.[50] King Henry's campaign to assert and confirm the 'customs of his ancestors', then, coincided with – and may have been inspired by – the revival of what historians have come to call the learned law. His proposals were not all hostile to ecclesiastical rights, as we have seen, but there were major objections to their promulgation. There had been no discussion with the bishops; their recognition, in the manner described, implied full compliance; and the 'customs' included two clauses (3, relating to the trial and punishment of 'criminous clerks'; 8, on appeals within the ecclesiastical system), which were particularly problematical from the Church's point of view.

Constitutions of Clarendon, Clause 3

> Clerks cited and accused of any matter shall, when summoned by the king's justice, come before the king's court to answer there concerning matters which shall seem to the king's court to be answerable there, and before the ecclesiastical court for what seems to be answerable there, but in such a way that the king's justice shall send to the court of holy Church to see how the case is there tried. And if the clerk shall be convicted or shall confess, the Church ought no longer to protect him.

It was on this clause that debate centred in 1164; and there has been much debate since, both about its 'customary' character and its conformity with contemporary canon law. How far the proposal represented the established 'custom' of Henry I's time is moot. Precedents for many of the processes used by Henry II are found in the first Henry's reign: the sworn juries of recognition and presentation, itinerant justices, royal intrusion into baronial jurisdiction by writ; but the sources are largely silent about the treatment of criminous clerks. There is, however, some evidence that clergy were not generally subjected to secular punishment. Two clauses from King Ethelred's code of 1014 set penitential exile at the pope's discretion as the penalty for homicide or other serious crime; another imposed degradation and exclusion from the fellowship of the clergy for bearing false witness or perjury; and a clause in Cnut's laws (1020–23) declared that 'If a man in holy orders commits a capital crime, he is to be seized and kept for the bishop's judgment according to the nature of the deed.'[51] During that late Anglo-Saxon period, bishops had sat with shire reeves at the county court, but they dealt with clerical malefactors separately. William I ended that practice in the 1070s, when he mandated that ecclesiastical cases be heard by the bishops in their own courts.[52] There is little secure evidence of common practice in Henry I's day, but recognition of the separate estate of the clergy was given high profile in King Stephen's Second Charter (1136), in which the king declared, 'I maintain and command that the jurisdiction and authority over ecclesiastical persons and over all clerks and their property ... is in the hands of the bishops.'[53] John of Salisbury, in his 1159 *Policraticus*, maintained that a cleric was immune from secular punishment 'unless he again raised a bloody hand' against the Church;[54] and while he was still bishop of Hereford (1148–63), Gilbert Foliot asserted the principle uncompromisingly to Elias de Say, who had tried a priest in his court:

> I am much more astounded to hear that you subject
> to the judgment of your court a priest of ours and a
> dean and that you claim against the Church this power
> which kings and emperors, in spite of much sweat
> and labour, have not been able to obtain against
> her until this day.[55]

Of course, this letter, like the three cases already cited, in which high-profile cases were secured by the Church after dispute with the king, are evidence that the principle of clerical immunity was not firmly established in England. There were countervailing pressures, and the king and nobility were pressing for its abandonment. But that does not mean that it had not existed after William the Conqueror had separated episcopal and county courts, or that the Church's claims were false. Henry's policies here and elsewhere were more aggressive than his claim to be reviving the customs of his grandfather implied. Graeme White has recently argued, in this context, that 'the king was now manifestly seeking business for his own courts'; and the claim to ancient precedent in the Clarendon code was 'doubtless based on suitable cases recalled by his investigators'.[56] More broadly, Paul Brand has presented a strong case for the novelty of Henry II's legal reforms.[57]

Becket and the bishops, however, argued, not on the basis of local English customs, but on the basis of canon law, which they deemed was contrary to Henry's formulation. About this contention there has been much debate since the great F.W. Maitland argued, more than a century ago,[58] that the king's compromise was not only consonant with canon law, but rested on a better understanding of the legal texts than that presented by Becket. That view held the day until the 1960s, when it was challenged by Charles Duggan; and Duggan's arguments were then challenged in 1978 by Richard Fraher, who argued that contemporary canonical opinion favoured Henry more than Becket, and that it was only in the wake of his murder that Bolognese opinion hardened against the process.[59] Here we enter very tricky territory, for a great deal hinges on the dating and interpretation of scholastic commentaries, but some investigation of the legal problem is necessary if Becket's case is to be understood.

If, in 1163–64, a lawyer turned to Gratian's *Decretum*, he would have found 50 chapters of citations relating to the *privilegium fori* (court privilege) of clergy in its Causa 11, quaestio 1. Broadly, they were assembled to demonstrate that clergy and laity belonged to separate jurisdictions, based on the concept that each has his own court (*forum*). Where there is a (civil) dispute between a lay person and a cleric, or *vice versa*, the dispute should be determined in the court of the defendant, according to the Roman legal principle that the plaintiff should seek redress in the defendant's court (*actor forum rei sequatur*).[60] This meant that clergy should not be summoned before lay courts either by other clergy or by laymen;[61] but where a clerk wished to pursue a layman, he had to sue in the layman's court. In secular criminal proceedings, however, clergy should be tried and punished by their own courts – that is, by their bishops.[62] There is no doubt that the whole tendency of the 50-chapter treatment in Gratian was to define and defend the principle of clerical judicial privilege.

But the matter was complicated by four apparent exceptions, which challenged the general principle. The first, *Si quis sacerdotum*, attributed to 'Pope Pius' (Causa 11, questio 1, c. 18), reads,

> If any priest or any other cleric is disobedient to his bishop,
> or plots against him, or inflicts insult, false accusation, or
> abuse upon him, and can be convicted of it, as soon as he
> is deposed, he is to be handed over to the *curia* (*mox
> depositus curiae tradatur*), and receive retribution for his
> wrongful act (*et recipiat quod inique gessit*).

This short text raises many difficult questions. Far from being an authentic decree of Pope Pius I (*c.* 140–*c.* 154), the text was 'confected' in northern France in the ninth century and transmitted in a compilation known for convenience as Pseudo-Isidore (because it was falsely attributed to Isidore of Seville, *c.* 560–636). The second exception (Causa 11, questio 1, c. 31), which is equally dubious, reads,

> We decree that if any cleric is rebellious or plots against
> his bishop, having been removed from the clergy

(*submotus a clero*) in the presence of the court (*iudicium*),
let him be handed over to the curia (*curiae tradatur*),
which he is to serve all the days of his life, and remain
defamed without hope of restitution (*et infamis absque
ulla spe restitutionis permaneat*).

Although attributed to Pope Fabian (236–50), it was another forgery from the same Frankish workshop.

At a quick reading, these two chapters seem to authorize a condemned cleric's transmission to a secular court, at the bishop's
behest, there to suffer a secular penalty. But the word *curia* had various meanings. In addition to court of law, it could mean 'household',
'house', 'courtyard' or 'prison'. Some English readers will be familiar
with Great Court in Trinity College Cambridge. In the second example,
indeed, *curia* seems to mean something different from a judicial forum.
Having been 'removed from the clergy in the presence of the court
(*iudicium*)', the condemned cleric is to be handed over to the *curia*,
there 'to serve all the days of his life'. This clause implies submission,
not to judgment, but to a form of servitude, in or of the bishop's house
or household. Since both texts were devised in the same context
in the mid-ninth century in order to strengthen episcopal authority
over clergy, it is likely that *curia* meant the same in both – that is, the
bishop's household or prison. In both cases, the convicted cleric is
degraded and reduced to penitential servitude. There is no involvement
of secular authority.

By the time these texts found their way into Gratian's compilation, however, the particular interpretation attached to *curia* by the
Carolingian forgers had been superseded by its more general juristic
meaning of 'court', and particularly 'secular court'. Gratian's own
summary in his comment following c. 30 (*dictum post* c. 30), which
cites 'Pope Fabian', shows that he understood *traditio curiae* to
mean handing over to a secular court:

> … in a criminal case no cleric is to be produced before a
> civil judge, except with the consent of his bishop, as, for
> example, when they [*sic*] are found incorrigible, and then,
> having been deprived of office, they are handed over to
> the *curia*.

Bolognese commentators in the 1150s and 1160s (Paucapalea,
Rolandus, Rufinus, Stephen of Tournai) followed his interpretation
of the phrase. Setting aside the question of the original meaning and

intention of the clauses, however, it is clear that the cases were regarded as exceptional, and that the initiative for transferring a degraded cleric to the *curia* lay with his bishop. The justification in both is incorrigibility. If a disruptive or rebellious cleric remains defiant, the bishop may deprive him of his clerical status and 'hand him over to the *curia*'.

The third case, in Causa 11, questio 1, c. 20, was taken from a genuine letter of the sixth-century Pope Pelagius I (556–61) to the Byzantine general Narses, who was in control of northern Italy in the aftermath of the Gothic wars, although it was wrongly attributed to Gregory I (590–604). The key passage read, 'We request that you send the pseudo-bishop Paul of Aquileia and the bishop of Milan to the most merciful prince under appropriate guard, so that … [each] may be subject to the punishment of the canons (*ut … canonum uindictae subiaceat*)'. It, too, related to a form of 'handing over', but not in the judicial sense. Pope Pelagius asked the recipient (General Narses) to have the patriarch Paul of Aquileia and the (arch)bishop of Milan transferred to Constantinople, where the emperor (Justinian) could impose the appropriate canonical penalty on them.[63] Gratian's rubric summed up his understanding of the example: 'Those whom the Church cannot correct may be corrected by princes.'

The fourth example (Causa 11, questio 1, c. 45) was much more inimical to clerical immunity. It derives from a sixth-century *novella* (new law) of the Emperor Justinian (*Nov.* 83.1), contained in the summary of Latin constitutions made in 554 by Julian, a teacher of law in Constantinople, and known as the Julian epitome.[64] As transmitted by Gratian, its key clause read,

> If a case concerning a criminal matter arises, competent [judges] may, when required, impose a judgment consonant with the laws, but in such a way that the discussion of the case should not exceed two months from its formal presentation (*litis contestatio*).

Even so, 'A cleric may not be punished unless having been found guilty he is deprived of the priesthood or the clerical honour by his bishop.' This decree of Justinian subjected clerics accused of secular crime to secular process, but the cleric cannot be punished – that is, subjected to the penalties of the public law – unless he is deprived of his clerical status after his guilt has been proved. In the sixth century bishops and clergy belonged to the category of *honestiores personae*, for whom most forms of degrading punishment were deemed inappropriate, so that they, like the lay élite, were punished for the most part by fines, exile and the like: hence the separation between the judgment and the penalty. Only if the bishop judged that the cleric deserved a dishonourable punishment would he be degraded. As long as he remained a cleric, he was protected from what the Roman world considered degrading penalties.

These exceptions modified but did not destroy clerical privilege; in the first two cases, the cleric is subject to his own bishop, and those who wish to bring a case against a cleric must do so in his own (that is, the bishop's) court, but where the cleric is himself contemptuous of that jurisdiction, or takes part in sedition against the bishop, the bishop may put him outside the protection of the Church, as a last resort, when all else has failed. Indeed, this was the explicit intention behind the inclusion of the Pelagian text, which was supplied with an unambiguous rubric, 'Those whom the Church cannot correct may be corrected by princes.' In the third case, a pope was invoking imperial Byzantine authority against suspected Arians. In the fourth, Gratian's chapter heading extracted only the emphasis on episcopal jurisdiction: 'Anyone with a legal dispute with a cleric should approach [the cleric's] bishop.'[65] He may not have realized that the 'competent judges' were secular. Gratian was trying to derive a consistent doctrine from apparently 'discordant canons',[66] but he left some questions only partly resolved. In this case, the extract from the *Authenticum*, combined with his misunderstanding of the 'Pius' and 'Fabian' canons, gave ammunition to the opponents of the immunity he was striving to confirm.

It was largely on the basis of these *canones* that Maitland made his famous conclusion that Henry II had a better case in canon law than Thomas Becket (and the bishops). But the great legal historian ignored the weight of the evidence accumulated by Gratian and the interpretation that he, a teacher at Bologna, had put upon it. Gratian's book strongly supported clerical immunity, but it allowed derogations from it, at episcopal initiative, in exceptional circumstances. The king's advisers produced a formula that applied to all cases and suppressed the essential feature of episcopal initiative. As proposed at Westminster and Clarendon, clerics would first be arraigned before a secular court, then tried in episcopal courts in the presence of royal officers, who would secure their persons and then, after degradation, carry them to the secular court for punishment, normally corporal punishment, in accordance with secular practice. The king was seeking to turn exceptions into an invariable procedure. Moreover, there was considerable ambiguity in the wording of Clause 3. It defined neither the cases that would be subject to the overview of royal officers nor the kinds of penalty that might be imposed. Not only was the phrase 'accused of any matter' dangerously vague, and perhaps deliberately so, the words, 'come before the king's court to answer there concerning matters which shall seem to the king's court to be answerable there', left the interpretation to the king's justices.

Fraher's assertion that the early decretist commentators produced an interpretation that supported Henry II's proposals at Westminster and Clarendon misinterprets their conclusions.[67] His first two commentators, Paucapalea and Rolandus, remained very close to Gratian's summary: in criminal cases, a cleric could be taken before a secular court only after he had been degraded by his bishop; but neither implies that the bishop was obliged to degrade the cleric concerned, and Paucapalea confined the 'presentation' to cases of incorrigibility.[68] Rufinus, writing *c.* 1157–59, provided a much fuller analysis of the four main categories of litigation, which distinguished between private (or civil) and criminal cases, and between ecclesiastical and secular jurisdictions. After arraying the authorities in Gratian's Causa 11, which supported the various definitions, Rufinus summarized the civilian text (*Novella*) in c. 45. But after contrasting the *Authenticum* with the *canones*, with the comment that the canons were more lenient, he concluded, as Gratian had, that a clerk convicted in an episcopal court could be deprived of office by his bishop and sent to the secular judge for punishment according to the 'public laws', *if his crime was sufficiently terrible* (*adeo horrendum*).[69] Unfortunately, Rufinus did not define *horrendus* – but he may have been thinking of the cases of clerical plotting and rebellion against bishops that formed the focus of the 'Pius' and 'Fabian' texts discussed above.

Such was the state of play on clerical immunity on the eve of the English crisis. Stephen of Tournai, writing in the 1160s, followed Rufinus closely. He also contrasted the severity of the *Authenticum* with the mildness of the *canones*, and attempted to bridge the chasm between them with the conclusion that 'in all crimes the cleric must be charged before an ecclesiastical judge and, after condemnation by him, handed over to the curia – that is, abandoned (*relinquendus*) – so that the curia may punish him according to the *leges*.' This seems to support Henry II's proposals almost to the letter; but Stephen went on to say, 'Some argued that he could neither be accused nor punished by a secular judge, since this amounted to double process, which the *lex* (Roman law) forbade; others that he could'; and, he concluded, the degraded cleric was not to be punished 'unless he was again charged and lawfully judged before a secular judge, and thus condemnation or acquittal should follow according to the *leges*.'[70]

There is ambiguity in the verbal formulation, but Stephen opposes transfer from the ecclesiastical to the secular court for punishment, on the grounds of double process, and concludes that a degraded cleric becomes liable to secular judgment and punishment only if he commits another crime. This had been the conclusion of John of Salisbury in his *Policraticus*, which he dedicated to Chancellor Thomas Becket in 1159. Anyone who lectured on Gratian's *Decretum* in the law schools had to deal with the apparent contradictions the juxtaposition of such varied material presented; and some opposing views were voiced, like the anonymous opinion recorded in one Anglo-Norman manuscript: 'When he (the plaintiff) accuses him (a cleric) of a civil crime (*civili criminali*), he should bring him before the bishop, who should deprive him, and thus hand him over to the judgment of the secular judge.'[71] How widely held was this view is difficult to determine, and its authority as a statement of the Church's position is doubtful. It should be compared with the mandate issued by Pope Alexander III to King Henry, cited below.

In opposing Clause 3, the bishops were not claiming that all cases involving clerics belonged to the ecclesiastical forum. The world was a complicated place; and even the strictest interpretation of the law accepted that some cases involving laymen should be tried in the appropriate lay court; and many cases were so mixed that arguments could be advanced for the one or the other. At the same time, some clerics sought advantage wherever they could find it. In the Symphorian vs Osbert case, Symphorian may have judged that he stood a better chance of securing a conviction according to the procedures of the king's court than in the ecclesiastical court, where different levels of proof were required. Not only was he prepared to sue a fellow cleric before the king, but he offered not evidence and witnesses but proof by ordeal. He failed to make his case in the ecclesiastical court, 'because of the subtlety of the laws and canons' – a phrase that probably means the 'sophistication of the Roman and canon law'.

Becket and the bishops were in line with current thinking about clerical immunity, including the proviso that exceptional cases required exceptional action; and they raised no objection to royal jurisdiction over secular land tenure. Their principal concern seems to have been with criminal prosecutions. When it came to a public defence of the ecclesiastical position, however, Becket opposed the king's proposals with the declaration *non iudicabit Deus bis in idipsum* – 'God will not judge twice in the same matter' or *non vindicat Deus bis in idipsum* – 'God does not punish twice in the same matter'.[72] However

Clause 3 was read, it appeared to propose a dual process with double judgment and double punishment for the same offence. Barlow thought the argument weak; but John of Salisbury had stated the principle very clearly in *Policraticus*,[73] and, as Beryl Smalley demonstrated, a similar issue had been debated by theologians in Paris.[74] Moreover, there was opposition to double jeopardy in Roman law (cited by Stephen of Tournai);[75] it has been a principle of English and American law in modern times, and the proposal to abandon it in England has raised fierce debate and strong opposition from some legal quarters. It may be that Becket was advised to base his opposition not on the intricacies and ambiguities of the written canon law, but on an appeal to scriptural law. To be tried and/or punished twice for the same offence would seem to go against the claims of natural justice. In the Philip of Broi case, cited above, there was no second trial of the murder case, which was declared to be *res iudicata* – a matter already judicially determined, and the unrelated matter of insult to a royal official was tried for diplomatic and not legal reasons, to satisfy the king's honour.

In defence of the king's position, Maitland argued that there were not two trials in the process described in Clause 3 of Clarendon, since the trial and conviction or confession were in the ecclesiastical court and the punishment in the secular court, so that the second court was merely completing what the first had begun. Furthermore, he argued that there was no secular trial or punishment of a cleric, since the man punished in the secular court had been degraded, and no longer enjoyed clerical status. That argument has some theoretical force, but since the now-degraded cleric was being punished as a layman for crimes committed when he was a cleric, this process would have negated the principle of immunity. He also laid great stress on Innocent III's decretal, *Novimus expedire* of 1209, which directed that where a degraded cleric was transferred to the secular forum for punishment, the Church should ensure that the penalty did not endanger life. For Maitland, this represented an *ex post facto* justification of Henry II's procedure and, supported by the Pius and Fabian canons, proved Henry to be the better canonist. But he ignored the weight of contrary opinion, the emphasis on episcopal initiative and Innocent's conclusion, which ordered the forger of papal documents to be degraded and detained in the bishop's prison. Innocent's *Novimus* did not reverse or supersede the existing principle of immunity, which remained a formal part of canon law until 1917.

Clause 3 was indeed skilfully designed to avoid the prescriptions of the canon law. This means, of course, that its drafters were aware of that law and sought to circumvent it; but the proposal subverted the intention of the ecclesiastical law, which was to protect clerics from the brutal physical penalties which were the hallmark of the secular law: mutilation (amputation of hands or feet), castration, blinding and death by hanging. The ecclesiastical penalties were degradation, deprivation of benefice, loss of clerical status, imprisonment in a bishop's prison or consignment to a strict monastery, or severe penances, including pilgrimage and crusade. Moreover, a degraded cleric who committed another crime was not protected from the penalties of the secular law. It was not Becket's aim to protect the violent and recalcitrant for ever; but there were issues, both about the nature of secular penalties, to which the Church was opposed, and the application of those physically deforming penalties to men who had been ordained and consecrated to God. The position the Church was adopting struck a balance between complete immunity and modified immunity. John of Salisbury and Stephen of Tournai were arguing that a degraded clerk could not be subjected to secular punishment for crimes committed when he was a cleric, but once he was degraded, he would be subject to all the penalties of the secular law. Degradation, however, was not an automatic penalty. A papal letter to Henry II himself, almost certainly issued before the crisis broke in England, mandated the king to order his bailiffs and administrators, 'for the honour of God's Holy Church', not to lay hands on the sub-deacon I., who was accused of murder, or to bring him before a secular judge. Those who wish to proceed against him must do so before the 'ordinary' ecclesiastical judge (meaning, the bishop).[76] The principles were later spelled out very clearly in a decretal of Pope Celestine III (1191–98) – the former Cardinal Hyacinth, whom Becket regarded as a friend – to Archbishop Eirik of Trondheim:

> You have asked us whether a king or any other secular person is allowed to judge clerks of any rank who have been arrested for robbery, homicide, perjury or any other kinds of crime. We reply thus to your consultation, that if a cleric of any rank is lawfully seized or convicted of robbery, homicide, perjury, or any other crime, he is to be deposed by the ecclesiastical judge. If the deposed is incorrigible, he should be excommunicated; then, if his contumacy increases, he should be struck with the sword of anathema; and if then, falling into the depths of wickedness, he remains contumacious, since the Church has nothing more that it can do, he should be restrained

by the secular power, lest he become the ruin of many, so
that, he is either sentenced to exile, or some other lawful
punishment is inflicted on him.[77]

As Charles Duggan concluded long ago, the problem with Henry II's
proposals was their open-endedness. 'Had Henry II claimed that
degraded clerks could be delivered to secular judgment in certain
cases, his claims would not have conflicted with established canonical theories';[78] but the formulation of Clause 3 was so general as to
embrace any kind of action or offence in which the king's officers
chose to claim an interest; and the principle of episcopal approval
was entirely swept aside.

Constitutions of Clarendon, Clause 8

Although the records of the Becket controversy concentrate on the
issue of criminous clerks, almost to the exclusion of everything
else,[79] one further clause was of the gravest importance to the jurisdictional structure of the Church. This read:

> With regard to appeals, should they arise, they should
> proceed from the archdeacon to the bishop, and from the
> bishop to the archbishop. And if the archbishop should
> fail to do justice, the case must finally be brought to the
> lord king, so that by his command the dispute may be
> determined in the archbishop's court, in such wise that it
> proceed no further without the assent of the king.

Here there can be little debate about the meaning of the clause.
Appeals in ecclesiastical cases were to proceed according to a pre-
ordained path: from archdeacon's court to bishop's court to the archbishop's court, and no further without royal licence. Although there
is no mention of the papal court, the aim was severely to restrict, if
not prevent, the free flow of appeals to the papal court. Appeals to
'Rome' were no new invention. There is evidence of a clerk accused
of murder appealing to Rome before the Norman Conquest, but such
instances had been infrequent until the 1150s. Part of the fallout from
the professional development of law was the parallel development
of the concept of appeal from a lesser to a higher tribunal and, in the
Latin Church, the highest tribunal of all was the papal court.
Litigants of all kinds, men and women in marriage disputes, clerics in
dispute over churches, monasteries in dispute over rights and tithes,
began to appeal from the judgment of their local bishop or archbishop

directly to the pope. Gratian's *Decretum* had proclaimed the concept of the pope as 'universal ordinary', which implied that the pope had universal jurisdiction. 'Judge of all [but] judged by none' was the succinct summary of the papal position given by Gratian. Not everyone agreed with the development of this appellate jurisdiction; and clerical opponents criticized not only the judicialization of the papal office but the employment of paid advocates and the use of Roman civilian procedures. But there are two sides, at least, to every dispute; and there were enough willing appellants to swell the numbers of those clamouring for judgment in or from Rome, despite the time and expense involved. Motives were no doubt mixed: then, as now, litigants could appeal to avoid justice as much as to obtain it; and the same pressures that swelled recourse to Henry's new processes also fuelled the appeals to Rome. Henry's proposals would at the very least have subjected such appeals to his approval; at the most, they could have stopped them in their tracks, by diverting those the archbishop's court could not deal with to the king's, making it the final court in ecclesiastical cases.[80]

Both in Clause 3 and in Clause 8, the king's proposals marked a considerable advance on 'the customs of his grandfather' and they constituted a serious threat to the status of the English Church at the time. Even Professor Barlow concluded that, 'Thomas did right to hesitate before accepting the procedure laid down in clause 3. A custom which *may* in the past have been sporadic and operated usually only when to the advantage of the church, was being turned into a rule' (my italics). The customs 'were intentionally old-fashioned in outlook. They view the king as the real head and master of the English church. The ultimate decision always lies with him; the liberties of the church are what he concedes.'[81] Thomas Becket may be credited with seeing the danger and perceiving, perhaps, like his sixteenth-century successor, William Warham, that 'It were indeed as good to have no spirituality as to have it at the prince's pleasure.'[82]

If the cause was worth fighting for, how are we to judge Becket's conduct of the campaign? There is no doubt that he failed to maintain the solid backing of the bishops, and that his own behaviour appears uncertain and wavering. That he gave way, not once but twice, challenges the biographers' depiction of him as God's unbeaten champion; but it also challenges the historians' image of unbending arrogance. Here, in fact, was a man assailed by contradictory forces. His own assessment of the situation led him, first, to oppose the king on criminous clerks, and then to interpose the standard clerical saving clause in recognizing the unspecified 'customs of the realm'; but the weakness of the papacy, the fear of some bishops and the opportunism of others, and the desperate need, as it was presented to him from many quarters, to avoid alienating King Henry, drove him down the road of (temporary) concession. Gilbert Foliot later loaded all the responsibility on to his shoulders, but his *Multiplicem*, which Beryl Smalley rightly saw as 'a tissue of half-truths and inconsistencies',[83] was less than frank about the behaviour of Roger of York, Hilary of Chichester, Jocelin of Salisbury, William of Norwich and, indeed, of himself, during October 1163–October 1164.

3

The trial

Having failed to bend Becket to his will at Clarendon, Henry tried to circumvent his authority by having Roger of York appointed papal legate for England. The ruse failed, because Pope Alexander granted a legation that specifically excluded the person and diocese of the archbishop of Canterbury. The result was an uncomfortable impasse. Then, some time between the archbishop's presiding at the consecration of the new church at Reading Abbey (17 April 1164), where Henry I was buried, and early September, there occurred another commonplace dispute between Thomas and one of his tenants. In this case, however, the tenant was John FitzGilbert, marshal of the Exchequer, and an important member of the king's government. His status can be gauged not only from his position at the heart of Henry's fiscal administration, but from his marriage, no doubt through the king's favour, to Sybil, sister of Earl Patrick of Salisbury. The second son of that marriage, William Marshal (I), became the great earl of Pembroke.[1] Some time in the summer of 1163, John obtained a royal writ to bring a case in the archbishop's court, claiming the manor of Mundham, a dependency of Pagham in Sussex. He seems to have lost the case and then claimed on oath that the court had defaulted in doing him justice. He then secured another writ, which cited Thomas to appear before the king on 14 September. But Becket did not appear; instead he sent a deputation to rebut John's appeal. This incident enabled Henry to arraign Thomas on purely secular grounds, namely default of justice. Consequently, the archbishop was summoned to appear before a great council of the realm at Northampton.

Apart from the murder, the royal council at Northampton is the most fully recorded event in Becket's life, with resulting contradictions between the accounts. Of the five most extensive accounts, those by William FitzStephen and Herbert of Bosham, who were both present throughout the proceedings, provide the best coverage, in terms of precision and detail; Grim and William of Canterbury reported what they heard at Canterbury after Becket's death; and Anon. I, equally, relied on hearsay evidence.[2]

Preliminaries: Tuesday 6 October 1164

On his arrival, he found that some of the lodgings that had been arranged for some of his staff were occupied by members of the royal entourage, on the king's instructions, and Becket lodged in the Cluniac Priory of St Andrew in Northampton. Nothing further happened on that day, because the king was hawking along the banks of the river Nen, and did not reach the castle until the evening. This behaviour was not anything out of the ordinary. The king was devoted to hunting, and inviting his nobles to join him in one of his favourite sports was a way of binding them closer to him. But what was unusual, and an augury of the future, was that the archbishop of Canterbury had been summoned, not by individual writ addressed personally to him, but indirectly, through the sheriff of Kent. This was done to avoid having to send Becket even the formal greeting of a letter. At its simplest such a writ would have read, 'The king to Thomas, archbishop of Canterbury, greeting.' By that point, Henry could not even bring himself to keep up the basic formalities of epistolary intercourse. The king's action amounted to a public humiliation and it demonstrated that Becket was emphatically *persona non grata*.

Day 1: Wednesday 7 October

The message was driven home the next morning. Becket went to give Henry the kiss of peace outside the chapel, where the king had just heard mass, but he was denied; when he raised the question of the marshal's appeal, he was told that John was on royal business in London (at the Exchequer), and ordered to return to his lodging. Like the salutation at the head of a letter or writ, the exchange of the kiss of peace was part of the protocol of social intercourse between men of rank. It implied the existence of peace and concord between the parties. Its basis was Christian fellowship – it was, for example, denied to excommunicates – and a king's refusal of the kiss was open to the most serious interpretations. It could be read, for example, as a proclamation of the king's enmity – that the victim no longer enjoyed the king's peace (which meant protection) and grace (which meant favour). In Becket's case, it was another indication that the king's mind was firmly set against him; and the consequences of that enmity unfolded on the following five days.

Day 2: Thursday 8 October

In the presence of the full council of bishops and barons, Thomas was accused of contempt for failing to obey a royal writ in the case of John the Marshal. The archbishop's defence – that John had made a false plea supported by perjury, that jurisdiction in the case belonged to him, and that his court had delivered a just judgment – was not accepted, and the king demanded judgment. 'Everyone' believed that because of the respect due to the royal majesty, his own liege homage and the oath to maintain the king's earthly honour, there was no valid defence, since he had not alleged a pressing reason that could excuse his absence. He was condemned to forfeit all his movable goods at the king's mercy, and the amercement was assessed at £500. Historians on the whole have accepted this verdict as valid, and have censured Becket for failing to answer the writ. FitzStephen, however, recorded that, far from arrogantly ignoring the summons, Becket sent four knights to present his rebuttal of the marshal's case to the king, supported by a letter from the sheriff of Kent, which confirmed the findings of the archbishop's court: that John had initiated the appeal by perjury: instead of taking the oath (technically the *iuramentum calumpnie*, an oath that he was acting in good faith and not maliciously) on the sacred scriptures (Bible or Gospels), he had extracted a book of tropes (minor service book) from under his cloak and taken the oath on that. The king, however, had rejected the testimony and abused the envoys. There is no reason to disbelieve that circumstantial report. If that is so, then the case against Becket was very weak. His defence was brushed aside. Becket was the disgraced ex-chancellor and no one was prepared to support him. The king's assertion that his honour had been slighted was enough, for no one could challenge the statement of the king of England.

Despite 'everyone' having agreed that the king had been injured, when it came to delivering the sentence, there was uncertainty about who should do it. The barons tried to foist the responsibility on the bishops, saying that since they were laymen, the bishops, as ecclesiastics and fellow priests, should pronounce the sentence. One of the bishops said, 'But this is a secular case. You and we are equally barons here. It is useless for you to raise the question of our clerical status, for, if you consider it in us, you should also consider it in him.

In any case, we as bishops cannot judge an archbishop.' At this point the king intervened and commanded Henry of Winchester to pronounce the judgment of the court, which he did, with some reluctance. On the advice of the bishops, Becket accepted the judgment, 'because it is not lawful to challenge the sentence and record of the court of the king of England'.[3]

The fact of this unseemly wrangling in the king's own presence should alert us to the novelty of the process. Becket himself said at the time that it was unheard-of for an archbishop of Canterbury to be tried in such a way by such a court on such a charge, and the buck-passing, which was resolved by the king's intervention, gives some colour to his complaint. It is likely that, as at Clarendon, the court was led along a pre-arranged path. Thomas had been summoned on the marshal case, but he was charged with something completely different – contempt of a royal writ. As for the judgment itself, an amercement of £500 was far beyond what was customary. Where forfeiture of movables at the king's pleasure was imposed, the king took not the goods but a fine of between £2 and £5 according to the custom of the county. Unless Becket's enemies (Foliot and Chichester) were party to the plan, it is likely that the bishops went along with the judgment as a means of appeasing the king and bringing a quick solution to all their difficulties. It enabled them to express a general disapprobation of the archbishop's behaviour; it was a way of clipping Becket's wings without, as they thought, doing any serious damage to their own status. All the bishops, except the bishop of London, agreed to act as sureties for the payment.

The king then raised the question of John the Marshal's case, to which Becket replied that he had not defaulted in justice, but that John had failed to establish his case, being unable to prove his right, and having taken an invalid oath to undermine justice. When the king found that he could make no headway in that case, 'he turned to other matters'. The general explanation of this defeat for the king is that the barons were likely to have been on Becket's side in a case in which the judgment of a baronial court was challenged by one of its suitors and appealed to the king. That is certainly so; but the absence of the suitor, John, may well have weighed heavily; and they may also have felt that the matter was a subterfuge. The absence of one party, without legal substitution, would normally mean that the case would be lost. In fact, as we know, John did not lose the land: the king used his authority, without the judgment of his court, to award it to John anyway, and in 1202 it was held from the archbishop of Canterbury for the service of half a knight's fee and 100 shillings a year by John's son, the famous William Marshal, earl of Pembroke.[4]

Having failed to obtain a judgment in the Marshal case, the king raised the first of a series of pecuniary charges. In FitzStephen's words, 'the archbishop was sued for three hundred pounds received from the castellanies of Eye and Berkhampstead.' One of the important offices Thomas had had as chancellor was custody of these two royal castles. These were not only significant military strongholds, but the centres of estates producing significant income. The implication of the charge was that Thomas had embezzled the money. Not surprisingly, the archbishop was astonished at the turn of events, and his first reaction was to refuse to answer the charge, since he had not been summoned to Northampton on that matter; but he said, 'that he had spent that money, and much more besides, for the repair both of the palace (= Westminster Hall?) in London and of the said castles, as could be seen.' King Henry 'refused to confirm that this had been done on his authority', and demanded judgment. Without conceding the charge or entering into litigation, Thomas agreed to repay the money in order to mollify the king, and put forward three lay vassals as guarantors of £100 each: Earl William of Gloucester, William of Eynsford (whom he had earlier excommunicated over the patronage of Eynsford church), and a third, unnamed man. There does not seem to have been a judgment against Becket in this case. So ended the second full day.[5]

Thomas had been found guilty of contempt (expressed in the ominous phrase *lesae maiestatis*, treason), condemned to total forfeiture of his property (compounded to £500), for which the bishops were sureties, and forced to promise repayment of a further £300, which he had probably spent, as he said, on necessary repairs to the Palace of Westminster, and expenses in relation to the castles of Eye and Berkhampstead. Apart from the humiliation and disgrace, the amount was extortionate. The ordinary income that passed through Henry's own Exchequer in 1163–64 was about £20,000; the levels at which free men were obliged to supply themselves with weapons and armour for the king's service were set at annual income or assets (movables) worth 16 marks (£10 13s 4d) and 10 marks (£6 3s 4d) respectively in the Assize of Arms of 1184; a simple knight could live for a year on £20; the customary relief (entry tax) paid when a baron inherited his lordship was £100. By the end of the second day at Northampton, Thomas was theoretically destitute. But the king did not leave the matter there.

Day 3: Friday 9 October

As FitzStephen recorded in his lawyer's language:

> On the third day the archbishop was sued through
> intermediaries for the specific sum of five hundred marks
> (Herbert of Bosham says £500) on the ground of a loan
> made in the Toulouse campaign and for a further five
> hundred marks on the ground of the surety which the
> king had given to a certain Jew there on his account.
> He was also sued by an action for guardianship for all
> receipts from the vacant archbishopric and from the other
> bishoprics and abbacies which had been vacant during his
> chancellorship: and he was ordered to show an account
> for all these incomes to the king. (WF, 53–4)

A silver mark was two-thirds of a pound sterling, 13s 4d; 1000 marks
was £666 13s 4d; and the incomes from the seven years of the chancellorship were variously reckoned at £30,000, or 40,000 marks
(averaging £4285 per annum). Becket's response was to declare, quite
correctly, that he had not come to the council prepared for such
demands, nor had he been so cited. But if it was appropriate that he
should be sued, then he would answer his lord in the appropriate
place and at the appropriate time. According to Herbert of Bosham,
the king secured judgment against him for the £500 loan (which
Thomas claimed had been a gift), and five further men offered to
guarantee its repayment at £100 each. But this may be a mistake on
Herbert's part. In FitzStephen's account, there was no judgment on
the individual points, but the king demanded a warranted guarantee.
That is, he demanded that the archbishop find sureties to guarantee
payment of these enormous sums (on the assumption that he was
found liable). Becket said that he needed to take the advice of his suffragans. The king allowed it; and he withdrew, and, in FitzStephen's
words, 'from that moment no barons or knights came to visit his
lodging, having understood the king's mind.'[6]

Day 4: Saturday 10 October

The next day was spent in anxious discussions. No doubt at his summons, all the ecclesiastics present at the council went to Becket's
lodgings in St Andrew's priory. There he discussed the issues separately with the bishops and with the abbots. There is no record of the
abbots' advice, but the bishops' counsel is reasonably well recorded,

and a tolerably full account can be reconstructed from two sources that have the advantage of being independent of one another, William FitzStephen, who was present throughout, and Master Alan of Tewkesbury. This latter, the monk (from 1174) who became prior of Canterbury (1177–86) and abbot of the Benedictine monastery of Tewkesbury (1186–1202), was certainly nowhere near Northampton in 1164, but he had the advantage of association with a man who was. By an extraordinary coincidence, he acquired a canonry in the cathedral of Benevento *c.* 1171, where Becket's Bolognese legal eagle Master Lombard of Piacenza, then cardinal priest of S. Cyriaco, was appointed archbishop (1171–79).[7] Although not named in any of the reports of the council, Lombard was certainly there, since he was with the small band that accompanied Becket into exile, and he is the likeliest source for Alan's knowledge of the advice given to the archbishop on that fateful Saturday.

FitzStephen concentrated on Henry of Winchester, Hilary of Chichester and (regrettably unnamed) clerks. Henry of Winchester, Henry's cousin and brother of King Stephen, one of the wealthiest bishops in England, and renowned for his taste in precious objects and patronage of his cathedral and also the foundation of the hospice of St Cross, still in existence outside Winchester city, thought that an offer of 2000 marks might be enough to satisfy the king. He duly made the offer from his own resources (after all, Becket now had none), but he was summarily refused. Some of the clerks, who included at least two professional lawyers, Master Lombard of Piacenza and FitzStephen himself, laid out the problem. The duties of Becket's office as archbishop required him to protect the Church, to defend the rights and status of his office, and to honour the king in all things, 'saving the reverence due to God and the Church's honour'. Formulaic this assessment may seem, but it summed up the duality of a prelate's position in words that would echo not only through the remainder of Becket's life but down the centuries to a second Thomas (More), who proclaimed that he died, 'the king's good servant, but God's first'. The clerks added that Becket should not be afraid of the opposition, since he had been accused of no crime or infamy. Moreover, he had been relieved of all liability for his conduct as chancellor when he was elected to Canterbury, in the same way that when a monastery elected a monk from another monastery he was freed from all obligation to his own former abbot before assuming his new charge. In their professional opinion, Becket had no case to answer. Since he was innocent, he had no need to fear the outcome of the proceedings. Others, however, 'who were more in touch with the secret ear and mind of the king', counselled abject submission: 'Our Lord the king is grievously angry with him. From certain indications we interpret his mind to be this, that the lord bishop should in everything, and above all by resigning the archbishopric, throw himself on the king's mercy.' Party to this view was Hilary of Chichester, also a trained lawyer, whose reading of the legal situation was nothing like as rosy as the clerks':

> Who would stand surety for you for so great a reckoning
> or for so uncertain a sum? It is safer to leave everything
> to his mercy, lest (God forbid) he should arrest you or
> lay hands on you as his chancellor and (ecclesiastical)
> procurator,[8] sued for his money, guilty of extortion,[9] and
> lacking sureties, whereby the English Church would suffer
> distress and the realm shame. (WF, 55)

If the clerks thought that his status would protect him, and that no serious charges had been laid against him – that is, no criminal charges that would destroy his reputation – if nothing else, Hilary's use of the phrase 'guilty of extortion' implied that something more sinister was afoot. As defined in Roman law, the crime of extortion embraced a wide spectrum of official malpractice and applied to 'anyone holding a magistracy, a position of power or administration, a legateship, or any other office, duty, or public employment', or a member of their staff 'who accepts money in return for giving or not giving a judgment or passing a sentence'[10] 'or for doing more or less than his duty'.[11] It was punished 'for the most part by exile, or some even harsher penalty, depending on what they have committed.'[12]

This is not to suggest for a moment that the Julian Law on Extortion, issued by Julius Caesar in 59 BC, was current in Angevin England, but that, as in the formulation of Clarendon, Clause 3, legally trained members of Henry II's staff used a suitable Roman law text to formulate the charge against Thomas. Master John of Oxford, indeed, was named as compiler of the Constitutions in a marginal note in the earliest surviving copy of Alan of Tewkesbury's collection of Becket letters,[13] and his hand, though not his alone, may be sought in the construction of the charge sheet against Becket.

Roman law was not an unknown exotic. Gilbert Foliot of London, for example, was thoroughly familiar with the main components of Justinian's *Corpus iuris civilis*. Not only did he have a copy of the *Digest* corrected and glossed for his uncle Robert de Chesney, bishop of Lincoln in 1153,[14] but during the 1150s he is found citing the *Codex*, specifically by name, in judicial cases. In *c.* April–May 1150 a letter to a layman, Ralph of Worcester, included four citations from the *Codex* to explain why Gilbert (then bishop of Hereford) could not take cognizance of Ralph's case for breach of sanctuary against the earl of Hereford;[15] and five citations were used to elucidate the question of whether an appeal to the pope was possible in 1150–59.[16] During the same period, John of Salisbury quoted verbatim from the *Lex Iulia* (contained in the *Digest*) in the treatise on politics that he dedicated to Thomas himself (then royal chancellor) in 1159,[17] and it was cited by name in a letter John drafted for Archbishop Theobald in the late 1150s.[18] It is, therefore, not impossible that in seeking suitably secular charges to bring against Becket, Henry's legally literate clerks would have sought examples from the learned law. The author of the treatise on the laws and customs of England, which passed under the name of *Glanvill* and was compiled very probably by a member of Ranulf de Glanvill's staff, began his book with a paragraph that echoed the opening of Justinian's *Institutes*,[19] and the list of the grounds upon which an action for debt could be brought in the king's court was an abbreviation of the *actiones bonae fidei* in the *Institutes*.[20]

Hilary's allusion to the *crimen repetundarum*, however, may have been scare tactics, intended to intimidate Becket with the possibility that the serious criminal charge of corruption might be launched against him. FitzStephen identified the major case relating to the conduct of the Chancery as an *actio tutelae*, an action for guardianship. There was no such process in English law at the time, but it was one of the numerous forms of action available in Roman procedure. Its relevance to Becket's chancellorship seems extremely remote, since the action applied to guardianship of the property of children under 12 for girls and under 14 for boys. Twelfth-century lawyers, however, could argue from analogy. Becket's duty of care for the administration of vacant churches could be held to be analogous to the Roman *tutor*'s responsibility for his ward's estates. The classical process – in which the guardian was required to present his accounts to the court and could be obliged to indemnify the ward for any fraudulent or negligent administration so revealed[21] – provided a perfect model for the case initiated against the former chancellor.

Alan of Tewkesbury's account of the Saturday consultations provides more detail; it also reveals that the advice was not given haphazardly or informally. As he tells it, the bishops spoke in their hierarchical order, beginning with Gilbert of London, as dean of the Canterbury province, and ending with Roger of Worcester, not only the youngest in age but the most junior in rank, since he was the last to be raised to the episcopal order (23 August 1164). In the light of the 'ruin' his resistance might bring 'to the Catholic Church and to us', Foliot recommended submission to the king's mercy; Henry of Winchester, no doubt speaking second, as the most senior in episcopal rank (consecrated 17 November 1129), counselled resistance, since a very dangerous precedent would be set if a bishop were forced to resign his authority and pastoral care at the threat of the prince; Hilary of Chichester (consecrated 1147) rebutted. If the Catholic Church were not in difficulties, that conclusion would stand, but he thought 'that we should submit to the king's will, lest worse befalls'. Robert de Chesney of Lincoln, Gilbert Foliot's uncle (consecrated 1148), turned the pressure more directly on to Becket: 'It is clear that they are seeking the life and blood of this man, therefore he must lose either his life or the archbishopric.' Bartholomew of Exeter (consecrated 1161), came to a similar chilling conclusion:

> Since these are evil times, if we can survive this storm
> by dissimulation, then we should, especially since the
> persecution is personal, not general. It were better for
> one head to roll than that the whole English Church
> should be exposed to inevitable harm.

That Robert of Lincoln should agree with his nephew of London is not surprising, especially since both belonged to the nobility and considered Becket an upstart, and Hilary of Chichester may still have resented his humiliation in the Battle Abbey case; but the support for their position given by Bartholomew of Exeter, who may have owed his bishopric in part to Becket's intervention with the king, must have been particularly galling. But it is also telling. 'Dissimulation' meant, quite simply, ignoring the unlawfulness of the process and giving Becket up as a sacrificial victim to assuage the king's rage and avert reprisals against themselves. It was the advice of a very frightened man. Bartholomew had no axe to grind against the archbishop, but he was not prepared to take any risks to defend him. If the king wanted a blood sacrifice, let him have it; then relations between the crown and the episcopate could return to normal. This was not a judgment on the merits of the case that had been brought against Becket, but capitulation to circumstances.

Last to speak was Roger of Worcester, the king's cousin, whom Becket had consecrated just short of six weeks before, and he sat on the fence:

> I do not give advice on this matter, for if I say that the
> cure of souls received from God should be given up at the

threat and will of the king, then my mouth would be speaking against my conscience to my condemnation. But if I say that the king should be resisted, there are those here listening who will report it to the king, and I shall immediately be thrown out of the synagogue: therefore I do not say the one nor do I counsel the other.[22]

It is significant that the only two to show any courage in the face of Henry II's *vis et voluntas* were men who shared his royal blood: Henry of Blois (Winchester), a grandson of the Conqueror, and Roger of Gloucester (Worcester), a grandson of Henry I, and even Roger was afraid to commit himself to a formal expression of opinion that might be carried back to the king. They also saw beyond the crisis of the moment to the possible consequences of the establishment of such a precedent. No English bishop, still less an archbishop, had been forced to resign in such circumstances. Even in the three notorious cases (Odo of Bayeux, 1082, William of Durham, 1088, and Anselm of Canterbury, 1095) in which bishops were tried for 'treason', there had been no depositions; and they had occurred more than 60 years earlier in a very different political and ecclesiastical environment.

After this, Alan says, Becket sent for two earls and told them that he did not have with him the men who had knowledge of the financial matters, and he asked for respite until the next day (meaning the following Monday, the next day on which the council met). Presumably in response to their advice, Becket sent the bishops of London and Rochester – being respectively the dean of the Canterbury province and the archbishop's vicar – to carry his request to the king, but Foliot, according to Alan of Tewkesbury, deliberately misled the king by saying that Becket was preparing a document-based defence. No one has taken this charge seriously, but in the light of Foliot's assertion that Becket should have constructed a specific defence against the king's charges, it is possible that Foliot did indeed add his support to the building of the legal trap that had been set.

Sunday 11 October

Sunday was a *dies non*: a day on which no official business was conducted. For Thomas, however, it was a day of ceaseless discussions with his entourage, the bishops and other ecclesiastics – but there is no secure information about what was said, or by whom. One can imagine that the desperation of the situation became increasingly plain to the archbishop. Apart from Henry of Winchester, who had the courage to spell out the danger of the precedent which would be set by the enforced resignation of an archbishop of Canterbury, and the young Roger of Worcester, who had given a coded response, the bishops were not prepared to take the risk of offending Henry. Gilbert Foliot was already hostile, and his own position could only improve from the fall of the king's former favourite; Norwich, Chichester and Exeter were terrified. One reads in their attempts to justify the unjustifiable the ratiocinations of frightened men. The 'evil of the days', 'the danger to the Church (both at large and in England)', the 'danger' to Canterbury itself were all put forward as justifications for pressing Thomas to abandon a hopeless contest and sacrifice himself for the common good. Whether they would have been prepared to support a different archbishop is an open question. In a sense, though they would not have been comfortable admitting it, they had been driven up the same cul-de-sac; but separating themselves from Becket might, they thought, have bought valuable time. By the end of that terrible Sunday, Becket was himself terrified and was struck with a recurrent ailment, which has been described as renal colic. Whatever it was, he was too ill on the Monday to attend the council.

Monday 12 October

On his non-appearance, members of the king's staff were sent to require his attendance; their report only inflamed the king's anger even more, and he sent the earls of Leicester and Cornwall, and a deputation of barons, both to check that he was really sick and to demand whether, now that he had taken counsel, he was willing to give a sworn guarantee (*fideiussoriam prestare cautionem*) that he would render an account of the revenues from the vacant churches received during his chancellorship and submit to the judgment of the king's court on the matter. Becket's reply, which was conveyed by the bishops, is very interesting. It does not say anything about sureties – none of them was prepared to risk the financial ruin that would follow such an unwise action – but he did say that, his health permitting, he would come to the council on the next day, there to do 'what he ought (*quod deberet*)'. No doubt this reply was very carefully pondered. 'What he ought' did not include standing trial on a trumped-up charge; nor did it include submitting to the judgment either of the bishops or of the barons. According to Grim and

William of Canterbury, he was warned that some of the king's supporters had conspired either to kill or imprison him, with the king's approval, if he came to the council.[23]

Tuesday 13 October

Whether physically revived or not, Thomas prepared for the dénouement with particular care. Hostile witnesses describe his actions as additional provocation of the king, further defiance;[24] but they can be read very differently – as the actions of a man with no other recourse than to take steps to protect his person by whatever means available. He seems to have spent the night of 12 October behind an altar in the church of St Andrew's. That an archbishop of Canterbury, and one, moreover, who was not lacking in physical courage, should have been reduced to seeking the sanctuary of a sacred place in such a way, should alert historians to the fear that Henry II inspired. Early in the morning, he had a final consultation with the bishops. Again, he heard the counsel of very frightened men. They told him that the only way out was submission to the king on all counts, including the archbishopric, otherwise he risked condemnation for perjury and treason, for failing to preserve his lord's earthly honour and for defying the customs he had sworn to maintain. Realizing, as he said, that they were prepared to participate in his condemnation in a secular court, he forbade them to act as his judges, appealed to the pope and ordered them to use their ecclesiastical powers against anyone who laid violent hands on him. Gilbert of London immediately counter-appealed; and all the bishops, except Winchester and Salisbury, withdrew immediately.[25] It was at this point that, following the advice of a religious man (one record names his chaplain, Robert of Merton), he said the mass of St Stephen, the first martyr, with its *Introit*, 'Princes also did sit and speak against me; but thy servant is occupied with they statutes', and its Gospel, which referred to the slaying of Zachery.[26] This was reported to the king as directed against him and his evil advisers, perhaps by Foliot, who later reported to the pope that Becket had celebrated the mass as a kind of sorcery, and in contempt of the king.[27] No doubt Becket was both invoking the aid of the first martyr and highlighting his own predicament. The scriptural text was particularly apt. We might see it as an act not of bravado but of desperation. The same may be said of his taking a consecrated Host with him, and his insistence, when he reached the castle, on carrying his own metropolitan cross and holding it throughout the ensuing process. Much was made of this 'provocation', at the time and subsequently. One of Becket's clerks, Hugh of Nonant, asked Gilbert of London if he was going to let the archbishop carry his own cross, to which he replied with the famous, 'My good man, he was always a fool and always will be.'[28] But was it any more than a legitimate assertion of his episcopal rank and the spiritual authority that flowed from it?[29] It was a reminder to all that Thomas of London was not merely a royal vassal, but a consecrated archbishop. The cross thus functioned both as a symbol of sacerdotal authority and as a protection to its bearer. The incident may be a measure not of Becket's 'arrogance', but of his fear of reprisals.

Becket went into the inner room on the ground floor and sat 'in his usual place', with the bishops arranged around him in their hierarchical order, with Foliot by his side. As they sat down, Foliot asked him to hand over the cross to one of his clerks, since it looked as if he were ready to disturb the whole kingdom. 'You are holding the cross in your hands, what if the king should gird on his sword? There will be a king bravely adorned and an archbishop likewise.' Becket refused to budge: 'Say what you will. If you were in my place, you would do the same. But if my lord the king were, as you say, to take up the sword, that would hardly be a sign of peace.' According to Grim, Roger of York (who had just arrived, having his own cross borne provocatively before him)[30] took up the refrain: 'You are entering, armed, against the king; but be certain that the royal sword strikes heavily, if you do not act with more circumspection, and it has already been unsheathed against you.' To which Thomas replied, 'The cross brings peace, not a sword, pacifying alike the things of heaven and of earth.'[31] The archbishop's clerks, meanwhile, gave contradictory counsel. Herbert of Bosham advised him to issue excommunications against any who should lay hands on him; FitzStephen counselled him to suffer whatever might come with resignation, for, if he were to 'suffer for justice and the freedom of the church' his 'soul would be at rest and his memory blessed'. When they heard these words, John Planeta (an archiepiscopal clerk) and Ralph of Diss (Diceto), archdeacon of Middlesex, burst into tears. At this point, the bishops were summoned upstairs to the king's presence.[32]

In the upper room, then, the bishops strove to distance themselves from their archbishop. They told the king that Becket had reprimanded them for being more hostile to him than the barons and for having judged him more severely than was right in condemning him to the loss of all his movable property for a single absence, which was not contumacious. This was contrary to custom, he had said, because a monetary settlement was established in various places for such amercements. In London it was set at one hundred shillings (£5), while in Kent, which was more lightly treated because of its forward position in defending the country from invasion, the sum was 40 shillings (£2). Since his residence and see were in Kent, he should have been judged according to the law of Kent. They also reported that he had said that within ten days of their sentence he would appeal them to the pope, and that he had forbidden them by papal authority to take part in any other secular case relating to the time before he was made archbishop.[33] Nothing could demonstrate more clearly the bishops' collective pusillanimity in the face of king and baronial council.

The king, angry, sent the earls and a deputation of barons to ask whether what the bishops alleged was true, especially since Becket was his liege vassal and had given his word at Clarendon to observe the customs, among which was the stipulation that bishops should participate in judgments of the king's court, apart from judgments of blood. They also asked if he were willing, having given sureties, to render account for his chancellorship and accept the judgment of the court therein. Remaining seated, holding the cross firmly in his hands, he replied. FitzStephen gives the text of the speech.

> Gentlemen, brothers, earls and barons of the lord king,
> I am indeed bound to our liege lord the king by homage,
> fealty, and oath: but the oath of a priest has justice and
> equity as its special companions. In honour and fealty to
> the lord king am I bound in due and devoted submission
> to offer him for God's sake service in all things, saving
> obedience to God and ecclesiastical dignity, and the
> archiepiscopal honour of my person. I decline this suit
> since I was summoned neither to render accounts nor for
> any other case except the case of John [the Marshal], nor
> am I here bound to answer or listen to judgment in the
> case of another [meaning, the king]. I acknowledge and
> I recall that I received many commissions and dignities
> from the lord king, in which I served him faithfully both
> here and beyond the sea, and also, having spent all my
> own revenues in his service, for which I am glad, I bound
> myself as a debtor to creditors for a considerable debt.
> But when by divine permission and the lord king's grace
> I was elected archbishop and was due to be consecrated,

I was released by the lord king before my consecration and given to the church of Canterbury free, quit, and absolved from every secular suit of the king, although now in his anger he denies it; but this many of you and all ecclesiastical persons of this realm, know well. And I pray, beseech, and abjure you who know the truth of this matter, to put these matters to the lord king, against whom it is not safe, even if it is lawful, to name witnesses, nor indeed is there need at this time, since I am not litigating. After my consecration, I set myself with all my strength to watch over the honour and burden I had received and to advance the church of God over which I am seen to preside. If it is not given to me to go forward in this, if I am unable to make progress against the blasts of adversity, I impute it not to the lord king or to any other man, but principally to my own sins. The Lord is able to (give an) increase (of) grace to whom and when he wills.

I am not able to give sureties for rendering an account. I have already bound all the bishops and my helpful friends, nor should I be compelled to do it, since it has not been judged against me. Nor am I engaged in a case about accounts, because I was not summoned for that cause, nor have I a citation for any case except for the case with John the Marshal. As to the prohibition and appeal which the bishops have this day alleged against me, I recall that I did say to my fellow bishops that they had condemned me for a single absence and not for contumacy more severely than was right, and contrary to custom and the example of long ages past. For this I have appealed against them and I have forbidden them, while this appeal is pending, to judge me again in any secular plaint relating to the time before I assumed the archiepiscopal office; and I appeal now, and I place both my person and the church of Canterbury under the protection of God and the lord Pope. (FS, 63–4)

How should we judge this declaration – an arrogant refusal to submit to the judgment of the king's court on charges of embezzlement, or the justified repudiation of a prejudiced process? If the former, then Becket's reputation must be seriously damaged; if the latter, then he emerges from this trial as a man of principle and courage. But what of the view that he should have sacrificed himself for the sake of the Church? His reply would have been that he was no longer merely Thomas Becket, whose personal fall would have meant little to anyone but himself. Just as Henry was more than the son of Geoffrey of Anjou and the Empress Matilda, Thomas was more than the son of Gilbert and Matilda Becket of Cheapside. He was the archbishop of Canterbury and primate of England, successor of Augustine. If the king had two bodies, so had the archbishop, and injury to one entailed injury to the other. His destruction by such means would set a very dangerous precedent for the future, and his successors would have reason to rue it.

While Becket's formal rejection of the case against him was being reported back to the king, some of the barons came down, casting sideways glances at the archbishop, and talking in such a way that he could hear:

> King William, who conquered England, knew how to rule
> his clergy: he seized his brother, the rebel bishop Odo of
> Bayeux and thrust Stigand archbishop of Canterbury into
> a black dungeon; and Count Geoffrey (of Anjou), the lord
> king's father, had Arnulf elect of Séez and many of his
> clergy castrated and forced to carry their members before
> him in a basin, because he had accepted the election and
> they had made it without the count's assent.[34]

Although the barons (or FitzStephen) were mistaken as to the name of the bishop – who was called Gerard (1144–57) – this was no exaggeration of the barbarity that was perpetrated in 1144 and which Gerald of Wales cited on three separate occasions.[35] Warren skirts around it, however, alluding only vaguely to the count's 'persecution' of the bishop, of which he 'repented' 13 years after the event (1157), to the extent that he allowed the men who had acted on his instructions to be indicted in the ecclesiastical courts and was reconciled with Gerard through the good offices of Pope Eugenius III.[36] The meaning was clear. If Becket did not submit, the king would deal with him as his ancestors had dealt with recalcitrant bishops and archbishops, and he would do it with the barons' support.[37]

In the upper room, the king insisted that the bishops, by reason of their homage and fealty, should join the barons in their judgment. They said they could not, since the archbishop had forbidden it; the king rejoined that such a prohibition could not supersede their undertakings at Clarendon. They said that the archbishop could make it very difficult for them and that they should be excused, in the interests of the king and kingdom. The king was persuaded, and they returned to the archbishop. Robert of Lincoln was in tears, and so were many of the others. Chichester, however, led the attack, saying that they been greatly injured by him, that his prohibition had put them between the hammer and the anvil: if they did not observe it they would be guilty of disobedience; if they obeyed it, they would infringe the Constitution (of Clarendon), which they, led by Becket himself, had promised to observe, and trespass against the king. Becket was now asking them to act contrary to that undertaking by forbidding them to take part in the judgment, so they appealed against Becket to the pope, thereby forestalling obedience to his pro-hibition.[38] Becket's rebuttal is reported in full by FitzStephen.

> I hear what you say and, with God's grace, I shall go
> to prosecute the appeal. At Clarendon nothing was
> conceded by me or by you on my account except 'saving
> ecclesiastical honour'. For, as you have yourselves said
> to me, we kept three limitations, 'in good faith, without
> fraud, and lawfully (*in bona fide, sine dolo malo,
> et legitime*)', by which were saved the dignities of our
> churches which we have by episcopal right. For what
> is contrary to the faith (*fidem*) due to the Church and
> against God's laws cannot be observed 'in good faith and
> lawfully'; further, there is no dignity for a Christian king
> where ecclesiastical freedom, which he has sworn to
> uphold, perishes. In addition, the lord king sent a written
> copy of what you call the royal dignities to the lord Pope
> for confirmation, and they were brought back from him
> rejected rather than approved. He has given us an
> example for our instruction, that we should do the same,
> being prepared with the Roman Church to receive what it
> receives, to reject what it rejects. Moreover, if we fell at
> Clarendon, for the flesh is weak, we ought to take fresh
> courage (*spiritum resumere*) and strive in the strength of
> the Holy Spirit against the ancient enemy who arranges
> that 'he who stands shall fall and he who falls shall not
> rise up again'. If under the stipulation 'in the word of
> truth' we there conceded or swore unjust things, you well
> know that those who swear unlawful oaths are not bound
> by any law. (FS, 66–7)

As in the address to the earls, FitzStephen was probably relying either on the accurate memory of a lawyer who had helped to shape the arguments or on copies of the drafts themselves. Although described as Becket's responses, the clarity of their exposition suggests careful planning. Becket was surrounded by an excellent household, which contained both lawyers and theologians. This address was skilful. It attacked the validity of the promises made at Clarendon on the basis that an oath to do something unlawful cannot be considered lawful and binding. Moreover, the king had spectacularly failed to get papal approval for the customs; and if Becket and the bishops had lapsed at Clarendon (as he acknowledged that he had), then it was up to them to repair the damage. Other biographers supply further details.

The bishops then went back upstairs to the council. There, according to Grim, Anonymous I and Bosham, in return for their undertaking to appeal against Becket to the pope, the king excused them from participating in the judgment, and they sat apart from the barons. Some of the senior sheriffs and barons of middling rank were summoned to make up the numbers and be present at the judgment. What transpired is not recorded, since none of Becket's people was present – and it is evidence of FitzStephen's veracity that he does not speculate.

After some time, the nobles returned to the archbishop. Earl Robert of Leicester (who was co-justiciar with Richard de Lucy, and a man of high repute) tried to persuade some of the others to pronounce the sentence, but they refused. As he began to recapitulate the Constitutions of Clarendon article by article, Hilary of Chichester cut through the presentation with the comment that the archbishop 'was clearly guilty of treason through his breach of the promise made there *in the word of truth*', and signified to Becket that he must listen to the sentence.[39] But Becket refused to allow the earl to proceed.

> What is this that you would do? Are you come to
> judge me? You have no right to do so. Judgment is
> a sentence given after trial. Today I have said nothing
> as in a judicial case (*ut in causa*). For no suit have
> I been summoned here, save only the case of John the
> Marshal, who was not here to go to law with me. You
> cannot pass sentence in respect of this. Such as I am, I am
> your father, and you are magnates of the household, lay
> powers, secular persons. I will not hear your judgment.
> (FS, 67–8)

What explains Robert of Leicester's reluctance to pronounce the sentence? Was it realization that he was participating in a procedure that mocked all the forms of law with which he was acquainted? He was, after all, co-justiciar. Becket's statement as to his summons was a simple statement of the fact of the case. He had been summoned at the suit of the marshal, based on a fraudulent oath, and John had made no appearance. Moreover, the barons had evidently demurred from finding Becket guilty of false judgment. As to Clarendon, Becket had accepted the customs *in verbo veritatis*, but he had refused to seal them, and not only suspended himself from saying mass but sought absolution from the pope. Moreover, Alexander III had refused Henry's request for confirmation and had absolved Becket for his lapse, advising him to make confession to a good priest and accept penance.[40] (One wonders if that was the point at which he began to wear the hair shirt that was revealed after the murder in the cathedral.)

At the same time, Thomas had not been present at any of the proceedings in the king's presence in the upper room, nor did he have any legal representation at any time. The bishops moved backwards and forwards between the upper room and the inner downstairs' chamber where Becket and his household were seated; groups of the baronage did likewise. In the light of Hilary of Chichester's intervention, one could conclude that Becket could have been declared guilty of treason on the grounds of Clarendon alone, and that he would have been condemned for failing to submit the accounts of the chancellorship that the king had demanded; but what penalty would have been attached to these offences is unknown. In the light of Hilary's earlier fear that the intention was to condemn the former chancellor on charges of peculation on the basis of the Roman *Lex Iulia repetundarum*, however, the possibility of very serious penalty becomes greater. Henry's court could not depose the archbishop, but it could, if he were not protected by his clerical status, banish or outlaw him; the king could seize the lands belonging to the archbishopric; and he might have proceeded to physical punishment. Even without proceeding to extremes, however, condemnation and sequestration would have made it impossible for Thomas to carry out his duties as archbishop; and the pope might have been faced with a fait accompli, in which his only option would have been to depose Becket or to arrange his translation to a see outside the English king's extensive dominions.

This case raises many issues about the king's treatment of his archbishop. To cast Becket in the guise of aggressor, it is necessary to justify the king's procedures in October 1164. No modern historian has attempted to do that. Even Warren found the process unlawful – 'Henry had acted throughout with scant regard for decency, legality, or justice' – and Barlow considered the charges 'trumped-up'.[41] Northampton was an example of the way in which the traditional procedures of the king's court could be subverted by the king for his own purposes. No one dared speak against the king; no witnesses or evidence could be brought against him; no defence was admitted on behalf of the archbishop. Henry demanded not trial but judgment – that is, condemnation.

Why did the bishops go along with it? They were, of course, barons as well as bishops, obliged by their fealty (as well as by Clause 11 of Clarendon), to participate in judgments of the king's court; but they might have raised objections to the process. As it was, they seem to have gone along with the series of 'trials' until the last, when they persuaded the king to excuse them from participating in the final judgment. Why had they not done so earlier? Had they not been party to the judgments on defiance of a royal writ, the incomes from Eye and Berkhampstead and the loans for Toulouse? Why stop at the chancellorship accounts? We may speculate that they found themselves in a fix. They may not have thought that matters would come to such a pass. Their strategy had been to avoid confrontation with the king – to sacrifice the one in the interests of the many. But it was one thing to participate in relatively minor cases; to collude in a criminal[42] conviction against the primate of England would have established a precedent that would put them all in jeopardy. And it is possible that, even at that late stage in the process, they recognized that what was being done was contrary to justice, although none of them had the courage to say so.

Silenced by the archbishop's refusal to listen to the formal sentence, those charged with its pronouncement withdrew. Becket then rose and, still carrying his cross, walked to the door of the chamber, pursued by angry nobles, who called him perjurer and traitor. Among those named were Hamelin, the king's illegitimate half-brother, and Ranulf de Broc. His responses are variously recorded. Grim says that he kept a calm silence; William of Canterbury that he insulted them; and Anon. I said that he shouted to those who were calling him traitor that, if his priestly order had not prevented it, he would defend himself in arms against their charges of perjury and treason.[43] As he passed through the outer *aula*, which seems to have been thronging with servants, he stumbled over some firewood, but did not fall, and made it out to the courtyard. There he and his household quickly mounted their horses – so quickly in fact that Herbert of Bosham could not find his own mount and had to share Becket's – and they rode without incident to the priory of

St Andrew, where, after supper, the knights of the Canterbury estates renounced their homage to him and, with his permission, went away. This is another defining moment. The lay tenants did not risk continuing their association with a man marked with the king's anger. Then Becket sent the two bishops whom he had consecrated, Robert of Hereford and Roger of Worcester, and his episcopal chaplain, Bishop Walter of Rochester, to seek safe conduct and permission to leave the country, but the king deferred his reply to the following day. Becket saw the writing on the wall. He was not going to be allowed to withdraw with dignity to pursue the appeals in the papal court, and so he fled before daybreak.[44]

The Becket business had thus ended unsatisfactorily for the king, for the archbishop's resolution had prevented the pronouncement of the formal judgment of the king's court. Yet there was no pursuit; quite the contrary. Following a request from Robert of Melun, bishop of Hereford, or someone else, the king sent out a crier to forbid any insult or injury to the archbishop or his staff; and the council returned to dealing with other pressing matters, mainly the king's preparations for an expedition against Owain Gwynedd of Wales, planned for the following May. Henry's strategy, however, perhaps guided by the bishops, was to transmit his own version of events to interested parties. His primary objectives were to denounce Becket's perjury and treason to King Louis and the count of Flanders, and possibly close the French kingdom to him; and also to present the king's and the bishops' complaints before the papal Curia in Sens, in the hope of securing papal condemnation, which would mean the end of Becket as archbishop. In pursuance of these objectives, he issued a letter for Louis VII, witnessed by Robert of Leicester at Northampton. Its contents were stark and uncompromising.

> You should know that Thomas, who was archbishop of
> Canterbury, has been publicly judged in my court by the
> full council of the barons of my realm as a lawless and
> perjured traitor of mine, and he has unlawfully (*inique*)
> withdrawn with the reputation of a convicted traitor,
> as my envoys will tell you more fully. Therefore I
> earnestly pray you not to allow a man disgraced for
> such wickedness and treasons or his men to be in your
> kingdom; nor should so great an enemy of mine receive
> any counsel or aid from you or yours, since neither I nor
> my land shall ever afford such to your enemies in my
> kingdom, nor shall I allow counsel and aid to be offered.

Rather, if you please, help me effectively to take vengeance
for my dishonour on so great an enemy of mine and to
seek my honour, as you would wish me to do for you,
should the need arise.

> Witnessed by R[obert] earl of Leicester at Northampton.
> (*MTB*, v, no. 71: October 1164)

That this was the letter which Henry's messengers presented to
Louis VII at Compiègne is confirmed by its survival, not in the
Becket collections, but in a manuscript with unimpeachable connex-
ions with Louis' own chancery (and similar letters probably went to
the counts of Flanders and Boulogne). The terms of the missive,
drawn up in the terse style of Henry's chancery, need little comment,
but it is remarkable that Becket is not only denounced as a traitor
and an enemy of the king, but *former* archbishop of Canterbury.
There was to be no way back.

4

Flight and exile

If Becket's performance at Northampton is sometimes presented as arrogant refusal to submit to the king's justice, his flight has been seen as a cowardly abandonment of his episcopal colleagues and his cultivation of King Louis of France as treasonable.[1] Serious charges indeed, but what alternative did he have, apart from abject submission? Thomas of Canterbury fled from Northampton just before dawn on Wednesday 15 October, without waiting for the king's formal refusal. Although Bishop Arnulf of Lisieux later told Becket that the king had allowed his departure –

> If he had wished to prevent your departure, no calm
> breeze, no favourable winds, no peaceful sea, no diligent
> sailors would have carried you away, for everywhere the
> hand of royal power would meet you, which diligence
> could not deceive nor power control. (*CTB*, i, 189)

– it is possible that the king had not expected him to flee so quickly. Moreover, the path taken by the archbishop was wholly unexpected. Instead of riding south along the main Roman roads from Northampton to London (via Bedford and St Albans) and thence to one of the Kentish ports, he and his small group of clerks, accompanied by their guides, slipped out of the north gate of the city (which was unguarded) and made, first for Lincoln, more than 80 miles to the north-east, and then by boat down the River Witham, deep into the fenland around Boston. There they seem to have lain low for at least a week, moving between granges (agricultural outposts) of the Gilbertine Order. From there, they made for the Gilbertine monastery of Chicksands in Bedfordshire, where they were taken in charge by one of the canons, named Gilbert, and Becket put on the habit of a Gilbertine lay brother and adopted the false name of Christian or Dereman. Becket wasn't easy to disguise. His height alone and distinguished bearing made him readily recognizable as something other than he pretended to be. Much of the travelling was by night and along the less frequented ways. In this way, they made their tortuous way down to Eastry, an archiepiscopal manor close to the coast, and thence to Sandwich, where, in the early hours of Monday 2 November, they were able to take ship for the Flemish coast. They landed at Oye, between Marck and Gravelines, and then had to negotiate the tricky currents of French and Flemish politics.[2]

This unexpected route and the assistance afforded by the Gilbertine canons regular may have taken the king by surprise. There seems to have been no pursuit, perhaps because Henry expected that he would easily be spotted on the highway. Henry's kingdom was well regulated. Every town shut its gates at dusk; strangers were suspect; and traders and pilgrims had to have modes of identification. Leaving the kingdom without similar written warrants was difficult and risky for the sailors who conveyed unknown or suspect persons in or out of the country. After all, Becket had tried twice before to slip out of the country and had failed, partly because no sailor dared risk the king's wrath. The difference in October 1164, however, was that Thomas was not just attempting to go abroad without the king's leave, he was fleeing for his freedom, or perhaps for his life. He did not travel along the known or expected ways, and he travelled as a fugitive, with few attendants and no state, and mostly by night. By the time he reached Sandwich, at exactly the same time as the king's imposing company of bishops, nobles and their attendants reached Dover,[3] it is possible that the watch on the ports was relaxed.

Foliot's comment on Becket's flight is severe.

> having begun your flight by night, in disguise, as if he were devising plots against your life or your family, after lying hidden for a short while, you secretly crossed from the realm, with no one in pursuit, with no one expelling you, and chose to make your abode for the time being outside his dominions, in another kingdom. From there, you are arranging to pilot the boat which you had abandoned without an oarsman amidst the waves and tempest ... For what was accomplished by bowing the knee at Clarendon, beginning a flight at Northampton, changing your dress to skulk for a while, and secretly slinking out of the confines of the kingdom? What did you achieve by these actions, except that you very carefully avoided the death which no one thought fit to inflict? (*Multiplicem*: CTB, i, 525–7)

Apart from the bitter sarcasm, the bishop of London's comments are disingenuous. Gilbert may be giving away something of the king's disappointment at Becket's successful flight and its consequences, but he surely underestimates the threat to Becket's person. Writing a furious denunciation of the archbishop's behaviour, he has chosen to forget the advice given at Northampton, in which he had shared: submit or risk imprisonment, mutilation or death. There is a general consensus among historians that Henry would not have proceeded to extreme measures, but he was capable of taking savage reprisals against the Welsh who resisted the invasion, planned at Northampton. Following his defeat in the Berwyn mountains in August 1165, he had 22 sons of Welsh princes, whom he had earlier taken as hostages, castrated and blinded. The mutilated included one of Owain Gwynnedd's sons, as well as two sons of Rhys ap Gruffydd, prince of south Wales.[4] Becket's clerical status might have protected him, but it had not protected the clergy of Séez against Henry's father in 1144 (to which the barons had threateningly alluded), and the Constitutions of Clarendon had laid down a process for the secular punishment of condemned clerics that would have deprived him of any remaining protection. Guernes de Pont-Sainte-Maxence, in fact, says that at Northampton, two barons had threatened him with imprisonment, blinding and death; and Edward Grim recorded his fear of imprisonment.[5] From his point of view, the successful flight did enable him to summon support outside Henry's lands and to keep up something of a fight. He was probably right in his judgment that there was no hope for him in England. The bishops were firmly attached to the king's policy, willy-nilly, and the few who recognized the danger of the situation were in no position to protect him.

Part of Becket's problem, of course, was that he was forever identified with the sword-wielding chancellor. He had not even been ordained priest until the day before his consecration as archbishop of Canterbury, so it was easy to describe the flight as pusillanimous. If he wanted to be a martyr, why did he not meet his martyrdom then? For Thomas, however, there was still a fight capable of being fought. He already had the pope's absolution and some form of condemnation of Clarendon, but it was necessary to counter the denunciations of his actions being carried to the courts of Flanders and France, and the papacy. He knew well enough that condemnation in the Curia would be the end of the line; and how could he defend himself on the other side of the channel if he and his clerks were shut up in England? There is no doubt that he was a fugitive, but was he running from a justice and retribution he richly deserved or from a fate that might have been worse than death?

Becket's delay in getting to a port from which he could safely cross is explained by his need to evade detection, but the slowness of the king's embassy is puzzling; unless, of course, they were waiting to be sure that Becket had not been caught, or they were held up by storms in the Channel. The king's party then split into at least two different missions – to Philip of Flanders and Louis VII[6] – so that the main group only reached the papal court at Sens around 24 November. But the emissaries sent to King Louis were shadowed by Herbert of Bosham and another archiepiscopal clerk, and these two had an extremely satisfactory audience with Louis VII on the day after Henry's envoys left. The French king showed them Henry's letter of denunciation[7] and, after discussing the matter with his own courtiers, announced that he would give his 'peace and security' to Becket.[8] This was a considerable coup; it meant that unless Louis changed his mind for any reason, Thomas could find refuge in the lands subject to the lordship of the king of France. There he already had friends and access through them to a nexus of like-minded ecclesiastics who could exercise their influence in the councils of the great. Weak as Louis VII was sometimes perceived to be in comparison with Henry II, Louis was Alexander III's principal supporter, and it was in his lands, not Henry's, that the pope had sought refuge in 1162. The French king's influence could therefore balance Henry's at the papal court.

Louis, of course, had many grievances against Henry: his marriage to Louis' former wife Eleanor of Aquitaine and acquisition with her of the largest duchy in France; the precipitate marriage of the younger Henry to Louis' daughter Margaret and occupation of the Norman Vexin; and the attempt to seize Toulouse. Louis had good reason to be wary of Henry II's stratagems. Moreover, Louis knew Becket quite well: he had seen his magnificence as chancellor in 1158; he had experienced his military prowess in 1159 and 1161; and he had probably met him when he attended the council of Tours in May 1163, by which time he was archbishop of Canterbury. From the very beginning of the public dispute between Church and king in October 1163, Louis VII had been kept abreast of the unfolding crisis and had offered support. Master Henry of Houghton reported to Thomas *c.* 9 November 1163,

> At Soissons the king of France received me and that which I brought with great joy, and he immediately sent the prior of Saint-Médard of Soissons [Ralph, prior of the Benedictine abbey of St-Médard, Soissons], a man of great discretion and authority, to the Pope with his letters,

adding oral instructions relating to your affairs, which I
cannot safely entrust to the scribe. When I was taking my
leave of him, he took my hand in his and promised on the
word of a king, that if you should come to these lands he
would receive you not as a bishop or an archbishop, but
as the co-ruler of his realm. The count of Soissons,[9] also,
in the same way declared on oath that he would turn the
whole county of Soissons and its revenues over to your
use, and he said that he would put that promise in writing
to you if I should pass his way on my return journey.
(*CTB*, i, 50–3)

Louis' pressure was effective. On 6 November Alexander III
responded with approval to the French king's request for support of
an unnamed person, which Ralph prior of St-Médard had brought
to him, and asked Louis to give his own protection and aid to that
same person, should the need arise.[10] There were more clandestine
communications between them the following summer. An unnamed
emissary, who may be Ralph of Sarre, reported in July 1164 that King
Louis had given him a letter whose contents were too sensitive to
entrust to the courier who carried his own: 'The king sent you a letter,
full of his great love and consolation, which I have not risked entrust-
ing even to the present bearer because of some things contained in it,
but I have kept it with me.'[11] Becket's reply, which can be assigned to
July 1164, is preserved:

When we received and read your highness's letter, we
were fully aware of the palpable signs of your generosity
and kindness towards us, although, to acknowledge the
truth, no merits of ours have gone before to obtain what
you are freely offering. ... May he who is the rewarder
of all good men reward you; and we indeed are ready to
respond to your kindness, according to our capacity,
with whatever service we can offer in respect of God and
men. Even so, although we have long experience of your
generosity toward us, we now realize it more fully and
more thankfully, since you have deigned to visit us in our
desolation with your letter and offered us the refuge of
your consolation, if it should be necessary. By that offer
you have acquired what was left of our heart – if there
was any left – and bound it entirely to yourself, and you
have buoyed up our hope. For, apart from my lord the
king of England, there is no mortal man in whom I have

greater hope for good and honour and assistance, if
we should need it, although we have never deserved it.
Nevertheless, discussions about peace are being conducted
between my lord the king and us, and we hope that God
will sway his mind to turn his anger away from us. But
if you happen to speak to him, please reprove him for
having ever believed anything bad about a man who has
served him so well and so faithfully, and who has always
loved him with sincere affection, and on whom he has
conferred so much honour. If, however, there is anything
that we can do for your honour or pleasure, please
command us, dearest lord, for there is no man in the
world who would more willingly do it than us. Farewell.
(*CTB*, i, no. 35)

The proffered 'consolation' no doubt meant safe lodging and
material support. In the eyes of some writers, such communications
were not only clandestine but treasonable; and Henry II would no
doubt have viewed them in the same light. Becket, however, was
very careful of the legalities, as the above letter shows. He would have
been imprudent not to have sought to make some provision for himself, if the worst came to the worst.[12] So it was that Herbert of Bosham
and his companion approached the French king in mid-November and
duly obtained his support. Exile had been a possibility since the débâcle
at Clarendon; two of Becket's clerks, John of Salisbury and Ralph of
Sarre, had already experienced it themselves, John for the second time
in five years; and John of Canterbury, bishop of Poitiers, was actively
considering exile to Pontigny for himself if the pressures became too
great for him in Poitou. There was, moreover, an honourable tradition
of archbishops of Canterbury fleeing from various kinds of persecution in England, from the times of Dunstan, through Anselm, to
Becket's own patron, Theobald.

The king's great embassy reached the papal Curia at Sens on 24
November. If they had hoped to steal a march on Becket, they were
soon undeceived. Although the accounts we have are all hostile, it is
clear that the embassy failed. Despite the eminence of its members
and the liberal promises they made on the king's behalf, they got neither Becket's condemnation nor a commitment to judicial review. It
seems that Foliot and Chichester,[13] as the most legally experienced,
took the lead. The core of Foliot's argument, transmitted by Alan of
Tewkesbury, seems to have been that the dissension between the king
and the priesthood related to 'a minor and unimportant matter',

'which could easily have been settled if discretion and moderation had been shown'; and that it was 'my lord of Canterbury, following his own individual opinion and not acting on our advice', who 'pushed the matter to extremes, not taking into account the evil of the times or the harm which might arise from such hostility, and in so doing has laid a trap both for himself and for his brethren.' This version of events, which suppressed the bishops' own opposition and the seriousness of the Constitutions, and made Becket the scapegoat for the breakdown in relations between crown and Church, became the main plank of anti-Becket propaganda from then on. Ignoring the proceedings at Northampton, where the bishops' behaviour was at best dubious, Gilbert described Becket's flight as unnecessary and calculated to embarrass his episcopal colleagues:

> In order to cast infamy on us, his brethren, he has taken
> to flight, although no violence has been used, nor even
> a threat uttered against him – as it is written, 'The wicked
> flee when no man pursueth.'

At this point, says Alan, the pope intervened with, 'Refrain, brother', to which Gilbert replied, 'My lord, I will spare him'; and the pope, 'I am not saying that you should spare him, but that you should restrain yourself.' This rebuke, which implied that the learned bishop had misconstrued the pope's Latin, silenced Foliot.[14] Hilary of Chichester took up the refrain of Becket's indiscretion, but committed a grammatical error in using the impersonal verb *oportere* as if it had been a personal one, and he fell silent amid the amused laughter of the consistory. Roger of York was more circumspect, but he emphasized Becket's obstinacy. It was left to Bartholomew of Exeter to cut to the key purpose of the mission. Rightly saying that the case could not be decided in the archbishop's absence – and they were clearly not prepared to confront him in the Curia – Bartholomew asked for the appointment of legates to determine the case between the king and the archbishop. This request was reinforced by the earl of Arundel, who, speaking in Norman French, reminded the pope of the king's loyalty. According to FitzStephen, the earl promised privately that the king would extend Peter's Pence to every household in England, which would provide £1000 a year for the papal treasury; and the bishop of London also asked privately that the legates should be sent to judge without the possibility of appeal, which the pope would not allow. It was this unsatisfactory papal response that the envoys brought back to the king at Marlborough on Christmas Eve (1164).[15]

After securing King Louis' promise, Herbert of Bosham and his companions reached the Curia on 25 November, the very day after the departure of King Henry's envoys. They were immediately given an audience, and poured out to Alexander the full story of the archbishop's treatment at Northampton, where he 'fought with beasts', and of the numerous perils through which he had come: 'perils on his flight, perils on the way, perils in the sea, and even in the port, of his labour, poverty, and distress, and his change of dress and name in order to avoid the snares of his enemies'. In Herbert's colourful language, Becket has become another Joseph (who was betrayed by his brothers and sold into slavery): 'Joseph was still alive, but ruled no longer over the land of Egypt; on the contrary he was oppressed by the Egyptians and well-nigh destroyed.'[16]

This Herbert was no shrinking violet. He was a secular cleric who liked to dress in the latest fashion and he feared no one. An encounter he had with the king himself at Angers on 1 May 1166, described by FitzStephen, gives a flavour of his daring outspokenness. After John of Salisbury had been dismissed from the king's presence, Herbert entered wearing a splendid suit of green cloth of Auxerre, with a short cloak hanging from his shoulders in the German fashion. As they discussed the customs, to which Herbert, like John of Salisbury, refused to swear, Herbert said that there were many bad customs against the Church in the land of the king of Germany, at which point the king said, 'Why do you slight him by not calling him emperor?', to which Herbert replied, 'He is king of the Germans, but when he writes he writes "Emperor of the Romans forever triumphant".' At this, the king said with great displeasure, 'For shame! Does this son of a priest trouble my kingdom and disturb my peace?' Herbert replied, 'Not I indeed; nor am I the son of a priest, since I was not conceived in the priesthood, for my father became a priest afterwards; nor is he the son of a king unless his father was king when he was born.' This pointed reference to the fact that Henry was the son only of a count (of Anjou) and not the son of a king (or even queen, for his mother Matilda, from whom he derived the claim to England, had never been crowned queen) took some courage. One of the nobles standing by (Jordan Tarsun) is reported to have said, 'I don't care whose son he is, but I would give half my land to make him mine!'[17]

Herbert was more than just a flashy cleric, however. He had been a pupil of Peter Lombard at Paris, he studied with Parisian rabbis, and wrote a treatise on the Hebrew Psalter, which demonstrated some knowledge of Hebrew. His forte was the Old Testament, peopled with high priests, prophets and kings, and much of his writing

was heavily laced with citations and allusions to it. Christopher de
Hamel believes that he was also a consummate scribe and manuscript artist, for the finely executed transcriptions of Peter Lombard's
great gloss on the Pauline epistles, which he began at Pontigny and
intended for Becket, are thought to be in his own hand. It had been
Herbert who had urged Becket to excommunicate the lot of them at
Northampton! This was the man who bore the responsibility of presenting Becket's case in the two courts where it counted most: that of
the French king and the pope. The image of Joseph and his brothers
was both apt and, as it turned out, prophetic; and its meaning would
not have been lost on the learned Curia to which it was addressed. As
told by Herbert, an eyewitness and fellow sufferer, the betrayal of the
bishops, with two honourable exceptions, would have loomed large in
the account.

Meanwhile, the main Becket party made its way to Soissons, where
it was royally received by Louis VII, who confirmed his earlier promise.[18] It then rode directly to Sens, arriving on 29 November to find
a Curia already buzzing with conflicting accounts of the English crisis.
It is not entirely clear how long the Becket party remained at Sens:
Herbert of Bosham, who was there, but who wrote 15 years after the
event, describes a number of presentations over a number of days;
Alan of Tewkesbury, whose source was probably Lombard of
Piacenza – although there is a possibility that drafts of the speeches
had survived among Becket's records – describes two sessions.[19] In the
first, Thomas told the Consistory that he could have made peace with
the king, if he had been willing to endorse the Constitutions, which,
according to Anon. I, were solemnly read out, clause by clause, while
Becket himself presented the canonical arguments against them,
despite the obstruction of Cardinal William of Pavia. 'Rightly have
you come, dear brother,' said Alexander, inviting Thomas to sit beside
him; and he formally condemned the Constitutions.[20] It may have
been at this point that Becket presented his rebuttal of the charges laid
by Gilbert Foliot and defence of his appeal and flight:

> Then ... they hurled accusations and malicious charges
> as pretexts for my prosecution; and I preferred to be
> expelled rather than to allow it. Added to these wrongs
> was the fact that I was summoned before the king to
> make satisfaction as a layman, and I was deprived of
> what I had hoped would be my defence. For I knew that
> those lords, our fellow-bishops, were prepared to censure
> me according to the will of the courtiers. ... Before [your]

audience I stand, ready to demonstrate that I should not
have been judged there, or by them. ...

I am not surprised that laymen have constructed such a
conspiracy against the clergy, but I am surprised that our
lords and brothers were not only aware of this faction,
but even its advocates. ...

They will say again, that the prince should not have been
provoked at this time. How subtly do they who give
wings and support to his excesses and adduce evidence for
their own slavery ... .

Nothing of this should be imputed to the lord king, for he
is the servant of this conspiracy rather than its author.
(*CTB*, i, no. 37)

The focus of this presentation was the actions of the bishops at
Northampton, and their charges against him. His adversaries at Sens
were primarily the bishops, though supported by the king, whose
own interest was made manifest by the presence of Earl William of
Arundel. And it had been the bishops, led by London and Chichester,
who had been in the forefront of the attack, and blamed the whole
crisis on Becket's 'rashness', 'indiscretion' and 'obstinacy'. So he
turned the attack on their pusillanimity and willingness to connive
with the nobility in his destruction; and, in a piece of verbal economy,
exonerated the king from any blame. This last was part of the political game. Ministers are blamed for the actions of their masters. Here
one can see Becket keeping his oath of fealty to preserve the king's
'earthly honour', at least formally.

At this point, it seems that Becket went into secret session with
the cardinals and the pope. There Alan of Tewkesbury put into
his mouth the following confession, which is corroborated by
FitzStephen's summary:[21]

Fathers and lords ... I willingly confess with sighs and
groans that these distresses have befallen the English
Church through my wretched fault. For I climbed up into
the sheepfold of Christ, not through Him who is the door,
as one summoned by canonical election, but I was
forcibly intruded by the secular power. Although I
accepted this burden unwillingly, nevertheless it was the
will of man and not the will of God which induced me to
do so. What wonder, then, if it has brought me to this

misfortune! Yet, had I, at the threat of the king,
renounced the jurisdiction of episcopal authority
conferred upon me, as my brother bishops urged me to
do, it would have constituted an evil precedent, dangerous
to the interests of princes and the will of the Catholic
Church. I therefore delayed to do so until I should appear
before you. But, recognizing that my appointment was far
from canonical and dreading lest the issue should become
even worse for me, realizing also that my strength is
unequal to the burden and fearing lest I should involve in
my own ruin the flock to which, such as I am, I was given
as shepherd, I now resign into your hands, father, the
archbishopric of Canterbury. (AT, 342–3)

Sometimes regarded as an admission of guilt, this confession
enhances rather than destroys Becket's reputation as a man of courage
and honour. It was a frank acknowledgement of what everyone
knew. He had been thrust into Canterbury by royal power in a
process that mocked the spirit of canon law. The resignation, however, was a spontaneous act, related to the form of his election; it was
not a recognition of guilt for his actions in England. Moreover, if he
were to be reinstated, it would be by papal authority in the presence of
the full consistory, and any lingering doubts about the validity of his
election would be scotched.

Alan of Tewkesbury and Herbert of Bosham reported that there
was a party among the cardinals who favoured acceptance of the
resignation as the easiest way of resolving the problem – especially
since that was what the king wanted; but Alexander and an influential group favoured restoring his power, because 'he is fighting for all
of us'.[22] We can guess at how the cardinals split. A careful analysis
of their correspondence with Becket and their known actions suggests that at least one cardinal bishop (Bernard of Lucca),[23] three
cardinal priests (John of Naples,[24] William of Pavia[25] and John of
Sutri)[26] and perhaps one cardinal deacon (Peter de Mizo)[27] overtly
supported the king, while Becket seems to have been able to count on
two cardinal bishops (Hubald of Ostia[28] and Walter of Albano),[29]
who were later joined by a third (Conrad von Wittelsbach),[30] two or
three cardinal priests (Albert de Morra,[31] Henry of Pisa[32] and perhaps Hildebrand)[33] and four cardinal deacons (Boso,[34] Hyacinth,[35]
Manfred of Lavagna[36] and Otto of Brescia).[37] Most of these men
knew Becket. The older cardinals had first met him at the council of
Reims in 1148; others had seen him sitting at the pope's right hand

at Tours in 1163; and he regarded at least five of them as friends: Hubert, Albert, Henry, Boso and Hyacinth. Henry of Pisa, indeed, had already emerged as a protector, negotiating with the monks of Pontigny for a safe haven for him and John of Poitiers, and about the time of the appearance at Sens, Cardinal Hyacinth wrote to King Louis in defence of Becket's flight. Calling him 'our dearest friend', he justified the archbishop's appeal to Louis' protection. 'As God is our witness,' he wrote, 'we believe that it is because the king of England is so seriously and irrevocably exasperated against our same friend that, in his difficulties, he has ventured to seek your aid and protection.'[38]

It would have been possible to provide an honourable escape for the archbishop. His resignation could have been accepted and he could have been honourably accommodated, so to speak, with a bishopric in France, given King Louis' favour. But that would have given King Henry a free hand to appoint an archbishop more to his liking and the Constitutions of Clarendon would have remained set in stone. The proceedings at Northampton, however, did much to confirm Becket's claims that the Constitutions were not harmless restatements of custom, or little local variants that the Church could live with. The consequences of depriving clerks of the protection of their clerical status went far beyond the hanging of a few criminal clergy, and the restriction, if not prohibition, of appeals to the Curia could be subversive of the general order of the Church. Thomas was, therefore, restored to his archiepiscopal office and, together with his closest *familia*, he went to the Cistercian monastery of Pontigny, where he was to remain until Henry II's threats against the Order in England made his continued residence there a danger, not to Pontigny, but to the numerous houses in England.[39]

We know little of his daily life at Pontigny, but it was very different from that which he had experienced as chancellor or archbishop. Although he wore a monastic habit that had been blessed for him by the pope himself, he did not make a monastic profession. He would have followed the monastic horarium of hours and mass, but no doubt enjoyed more freedom than an ordinary monk. A core household remained with him: Herbert of Bosham, with whom he studied the scriptures, Master Lombard of Piacenza (until 1166/67), who deepened his knowledge of the canon law, Alexander Llewelyn, his cross-bearer, Master John Planeta, and his chaplain, Robert of Merton. Others had already found refuge elsewhere. Master John of Salisbury was staying with his old friend Peter of Celle, then abbot of Saint-Rémi at Reims; Ralph of Sarre, also, was in Reims, but attached to the cathedral; and Gerard Pucelle was in Cologne. With his small entourage, Thomas was probably accommodated in the guest house as a long-term guest. Pontigny was no Cluny. Still one of the most renowned Cistercian houses in France, it did not offer the lavish entertainment on which the older Benedictine houses prided themselves. Life was primitive. The biographers who saw his exile as a preparation for the martyrdom, if not a form of martyrdom in itself, were probably not far off the mark.

But he did not intend to be an exile for ever: for although he retained the office of archbishop, he was deprived of the means of discharging most of its duties. So, the first imperative was to negotiate a return to England. That meant reconciliation with the king. In fact, it was to take just short of six years for a peace of sorts to be patched up at Fréteval on 22 July 1170. Whose fault was it that it took so long? Henry's intransigence, or Becket's, or both, or the difficulties intrinsic to the situation? As in much else in the Becket story, answers depend on how the situation is read. If it is concluded that it had been Becket's unreasonable, even treasonable behaviour, that had got him into exile in the first place, then his continued resistance in exile was further demonstration of his unsuitability for the office. But if it is considered that the flight was defensible, that the opposition to the implementation of Clarendon had some justification, then much might be said in Becket's favour. That opinion might be further supported by the king's own actions.

Henry was informed at Marlborough on 24 December of the failure of his démarche at the papal Curia. His immediate response was to sequestrate the archbishop's estates, which were placed in the charge of Randulf de Broc, to deprive Becket's clerks of their incomes, and to forfeit and expel all the relatives of Becket and his household from England. The writs are uncompromising. The first, addressed to every English bishop, read:

> You know how wickedly Thomas archbishop of
> Canterbury has acted against me and my kingdom, and
> how wickedly he has gone away. And therefore I
> command (*mando*) that the clergy who were with him
> after his flight, and the other clergy who detracted from
> my honour and from the honour of my kingdom, shall
> not receive anything from the incomes which they have in
> your bishopric, except with my permission. Nor are they
> to have any aid or counsel from you.
> Witnessed by Richard de Lucy at Marlborough. (*MTB*, v, no. 77)

The second, to the sheriffs, read:

> I order you to arrest any clerk or layman in your
> bailiwick who appeals to the Roman Curia, and to keep
> him in strict custody until you receive my will; and you
> are to seize into my hand all the revenues and possessions
> of the archbishop's clerks, as Ranulf de Broc and my
> other ministers shall instruct you. And you are to put the
> fathers and mothers, brothers and sisters, nephews and
> nieces of all the clerks who are with the archbishop, and
> their chattels, under secure pledges, until you receive my
> will in the matter; and you are to bring this writ with you
> when you are summoned. (*MTB*, v, no. 78)

Henry's 'will', which seems to have been expressed soon afterwards, was for their chattels to be sequestrated and their persons to be expelled from the country. This action was not merely vindictive – Becket and his household were out of reach, but their relatives were easy targets for the king's rage – it was intended to put enormous psychological and financial strain on Becket. Not only were some 400 persons sent across the Channel in mid-winter with only the clothes they stood up in, but they were ordered to present themselves to Becket before seeking refuge.[40] Not surprisingly, this action featured prominently in the perception of Becket as 'victim' and Henry as 'tyrant'.

No one should underestimate the extent of the arbitrary power over the property and persons of his subjects that Henry II possessed, or his willingness to use it. These people, most of them lay men and women, had committed no wrong; nor had they been convicted in any court. In an action reminiscent of the worst days of the communist regimes in eastern Europe, the families of 'enemies of the state' were made to suffer for the 'crimes' of their relatives. Nor should it be overlooked that the agents of this particular expression of Henry's *vis et voluntas* were not his household knights or the mercenaries he frequently employed, but what one may call the normal law enforcement structures of the kingdom. The writs were witnessed by the justiciar, Richard de Lucy, and executed by the county sheriffs, who had to bring proof of their actions when summoned – presumably to the next session of the Exchequer, which met after Easter (1165). Meanwhile, the estates of the archbishopric were placed in the hands of Randulf de Broc, who took up residence in Saltwood Castle.

We have no records of the exploitation of those estates during the six years they were in this man's charge, but we can speculate on the basis of the accounts of the treatment of the monastic estates under

King John. In order to estimate the amount of the indemnity to be paid by King John after his reconciliation with the Church, an enquiry was made into the management of ecclesiastical estates in the king's hand. From the numerous records compiled, only one, relating to the lands of the monks of Christ Church Canterbury, records the activities of Fulk de Cantelu and Robert of Thornham, who succeeded one another as 'keepers of the see', and it makes chilling reading. Independently of receiving the ordinary agricultural revenues, the pair systematically denuded the estates of livestock (including breeding animals) and timber, and they sold so much grain that no seed was kept for planting and land was left fallow. In Orpington, for example, Fulk sold 13 beef cattle, 10 stots, 7 cows, 60 ewes, 82 sheep, 6 sows, 24 lambs and 17 piglets; Robert found only 2 beef cattle, 1 cow and 1 draught animal, which he sold. In Monkton, Fulk sold 3 draught animals, 12 cows, 18 beef cattle, 250 sheep and 110 pigs; there was no stock left in 1211. In Cliffe, Fulk sold 1980 ewes and 38 lambs; Robert found no sheep when he succeeded! The story was the same on the other 19 manors of the monks' estates. The title *custos* – 'guardian' or 'keeper' – borne by these men was grimly ironical. Their guardianship amounted to systematic asset-stripping, most of which was carried out in the first six months.[41] The catastrophic effects of such destruction of the rural economy on the majority of the ordinary people of Kent – men, women and children who depended on it for their livelihood – is not hard to imagine. There is no reason to believe that the de Brocs behaved very differently on the archbishop's lands in the six years they had them in their charge (1165–70 inclusive),[42] so that the execration they received from Becket's biographers was not merely clerical bias.

One can also understand why the community at Christ Church did all it could to keep a low profile. It was not necessarily disapproval of Becket's general stand – they would have been as anxious to preserve clerical immunity, the right of appeal to the papacy and some form of canonical election as any member of the clerical order – but they did not want to be expelled from their monastery or to see their estates suffer the same fate as the archbishop's. And the same, it must be said, went for the bishops. The king's power to seize the material assets of their sees and hand them over to the tender mercies of such 'custodians', constituted the chief hold the king had over them. In consequence of the homage they swore before consecration, they held the territorial endowment of their dioceses *per baroniam*; and, as Archbishop Lanfranc told William of St Calais, bishop of Durham, in 1088, he was not being judged as a bishop but *de feudo suo* (as William I had judged his half-brother Odo, bishop of Bayeux, in 1082); his episcopal status was not at issue, but he was forfeited because he refused to plead in the king's court and because he appealed to the pope.[43]

The king's strategy was to force Becket to capitulate in one way or another. The forfeitures and expulsions, the sequestration of Becket's estates, the prohibitions of counsel and support by the English episcopate, were all intended to isolate Becket's household and family and to render his continued survival in exile insupportable. In what was a double-edged letter of advice written soon after knowledge of Becket's total destitution was known in Normandy, Arnulf of Lisieux summed up his problems:

> ... strangers ... bring instant assistance with kind and
> profuse generosity at first, but afterwards, their affection
> grows cool with the tedium of the passing days, and
> slackens in proportion to the generosity of the outlay.
> In fact a modest burden is certain to grow heavier as it
> grows longer, and the burden of one's own cares often
> outweighs that of someone else ... (*CTB*, i, 194–7)

Becket's household and family, and all their relatives, could not live on charity for ever; the support network was bound to fail sooner or later. Arnulf, who often spoke with forked tongue, was not alone in his belief that the battle could not be won. John of Salisbury expatiated on the uselessness of relying on the law and bemoaned the weakness of Louis VII; even Alexander III recommended that Becket should accept suitable 'sustenance' (a bishopric?) from Louis VII, while simultaneously commissioning the bishops of London and Hereford to intercede with Henry II; and John of Poitiers advised the same thing.[44] Even worse, just before leaving France, the pope sent a very dispiriting letter, which opened with the same quotation from Ephesians the bishops had used to Becket at the height of the crisis in Northampton: Alexander urged accommodation, as long as 'the Church's freedom and the honour of [his] office' were preserved, and he forbade the archbishop to issue any ecclesiastical censures (excommunications or interdicts) for the coming eight months or so.[45]

It was clear that there would not be a quick resolution. The intervention of Rotrou of Rouen and the Empress Matilda had elicited only a demand for Becket's submission. The king's opinion was passed on by Rotrou:

> It is plainly known that he has acted unjustly against
> me and my realm, and how pompous, rebellious, and

seditious he has always shown himself against me, and
how wickedly he attempted to defame my name and good
reputation, and tried as far as he was able to diminish the
dignities of my realm.

Rotrou's comment did not offer any encouragement: 'See if you have
any appropriate explanation to give to these charges and consider in
what humility and affection you can present yourself to him.'[46] This
was the same advice that had come from some quarters in late 1163
and mid-1164. It amounted to throwing himself on the king's mercy.
That he did not do so, and clung on in Pontigny, in the midst of such
discouraging advice, can be read as the steadfastness of a man of
principle or the obstinacy of a self-obsessed megalomaniac; or it may
be that he was aware of a wider band of support than has been
recorded. Prior Nicholas of Mont-Saint-Jacques, an Augustinian
hospice outside Rouen, who approached the Empress on Becket's
behalf around Christmas 1164, promised him the prayers of his own
community and assured him that his cause had the support of the
population at large: 'the devotion of the whole people is offering you
support in God, and a good opinion about what you are doing is
blazing through the discourse of the entire population.'[47] And, with
reference to the pope's letter, whose opening phrase, 'evil times', he
echoed in his own later allusion to the 'difficulties of the times',[48]
John of Poitiers committed himself to a criticism of the papal caution that implied support for what Becket had done:

> ... what the Lord Pope has written to you by way of advice
> reflects his own concerns rather than yours. For although
> his cause may be the cause of all of us, he will handle it in
> the first instance in such a way that he may retain the king's
> professed fidelity and pretended obedience in the meanwhile,
> at the cost of some loss of liberty for the rights of the
> church for which you are suffering exile. Nevertheless it
> seems certain to me that it would have been much better
> for him and for the whole Church which looks to him, if,
> after appropriate canonical warnings, he had set his course
> against the king from the very beginning and followed the
> strict path of justice. (*CTB*, i, 255–7)

This was an opinion that Becket himself held firmly. Rightly or
wrongly, he believed in strong action, by which he meant interdict of
the kingdom and suspension or excommunication of the bishops who
had either actively plotted against him or had connived in the trial at
Northampton.

5

Defiance? The Vézelay excommunications

It was clear by the end of 1165 that the king's strategy of sequestration and expulsion had failed to break his adversary. The material support given by the French king and some of his nobles, and by bishops and religious houses, had softened the blow considerably; and Thomas was safe in the great monastery of Pontigny. The situation for Becket was far from rosy, however. Without a negotiated settlement with Henry II there was no way that he could be repatriated; no way that the 400 or so exiles could be restored to their properties; no way that his faithful clerks – mostly men of excellent education and prospects – could be restored to their offices and careers; and Henry's price was unlikely to be low. As far as the king and his supporters were concerned, Becket remained the ungrateful, perjured traitor he had been declared in October 1164; the English bishops and church were still bound by their promise to observe the Constitutions of Clarendon; and Henry's quest for the public vindication of his honour remained firm. Becket's absence from his province did not seriously affect the running of the church, since all episcopal functions could be carried out by the remaining bishops, while Foliot could be a kind of 'acting primate', and Walter of Rochester could discharge all episcopal functions in Becket's diocese of Canterbury in his capacity as archiepiscopal vicar. The longer the dispute went on, the greater the risk of the tedium to which Arnulf of Lisieux had alluded: Louis of France and the monks at Pontigny might tire of their guest; the papal Curia might lose interest in the case or be forced by the threat of Henry's secession to the anti-pope to sacrifice the exiles. Even worse, an imperial victory in Italy would end Pope Alexander's reign, and an imperial pope and Curia would have few qualms about abandoning an archbishop who had challenged a king. King Henry would have been well aware that Frederick I had no difficulty in substituting his own man, Christian von Buch (1165–83), for the archbishop-elect, Conrad of Wittelsbach in the great archbishopric of Mainz, when he refused to acknowledge or receive consecration from the new anti-pope, Paschal III, in May 1165; and the pro-Alexandrine Oberto (1146–66) had been replaced as archbishop of Milan. An imperial win could spell disaster.

At the same time, as these imperial examples show, Thomas of Canterbury was not the only high-profile prelate enduring the rigours and risks of exile for opposition to the ecclesiastical policy of the ruler. There were parallels between his position and theirs, for the emperor was as committed to the recuperation of what he claimed to be imperial rights over the Church in Burgundy and Italy as Henry was in England, and both regarded such rights as part of the inalienable honour of the crown, imperial or royal. Henry's 'traitor' was therefore in good company; and many ecclesiastics saw his dispute with Henry II as part of the wider tension between the institutional church and secular rulers of every kind. Even so, Becket could not just sit in monastic isolation in Burgundy and hope for the best. Unlike the archbishops of Mainz and Milan, his place had not been taken by another nominee. He might be in exile, but he remained archbishop of Canterbury. Henry had the honour of his crown, Becket had the dignity of his office. Inactivity on his part would have played into the hands of his adversaries.

In fact, strenuous efforts were made through 1165 and into early 1166 to effect some kind of reconciliation. The initial attempts of the Empress Matilda, Rotrou of Rouen, Gilbert Foliot and Robert of Hereford failed to move the king. Thomas consulted widely among his friends and familiars. One of the most experienced, his old friend Bishop John of Poitiers, wrote a carefully worded letter of advice, which laid out the dangers of trying to negotiate with the king in person, especially if he were to return to England,

> You know that there everyone says only what they think
> will please the king. Indeed I fear that you would have
> to go into a second exile under some legal pretext, and
> the new situation would be worse than the first, with
> everyone bearing witness against you by writing and
> speech, both in the Lord Pope's Curia and in the French
> king's court. *Let no one persuade you to this, therefore;
> do not be tempted to return except on secure and
> absolutely certain conditions, unless you want to leave*

> *everything relating to yourself entirely to the pleasure of*
> *the king, a thing I would not venture to persuade you to*
> *do.* (*CTB*, i, no. 66)

The extreme caution expressed by John of Poitiers should be borne in mind in relation to the whole business between Becket and the king, as well as his comments on the attitude of 'people in England', including the bishops. His comment on the papal court was also accurate. Although in fact Becket had more friends there than even his other friends knew, the Curia had to keep its powder dry. However, there was also more than a hint in John's letter that he was in favour of more stringent action. His statement that the pope ought to have followed 'the strict path of justice' – that is, placed or threatened an interdict on England, could also be read by Becket as a hint that he should use his own authority. The shoring-up of that authority became the principal focus of his diplomacy. Masters Gunther of Winchester and Hervey of London travelled back to Rome with the pope in November 1165.[1] This meant that they could keep a watchful eye, not only on Henry II's envoys, but also rebut their arguments, and keep Becket's cardinals on the *qui vive*.

Their principal campaign in early 1166 was to secure the confirmation of Becket's status as primate and augment it by conferring on him the office of papal legate, and forbid the archbishop of York to have his cross borne before him in Becket's province. The first two objectives were achieved. Far from Alexander abandoning the English embarrassment, he confirmed Canterbury's primacy, as it had existed in the days of Lanfranc and Anselm in April, and appointed Becket legate for England on 24 April.[2] The key sentence of the notification addressed to Thomas himself read,

> ... considering the steadfastness of your wisdom and
> reputation, we have, with the common counsel of our
> brethren, appointed you legate of the Apostolic See for
> the whole of England, except the bishopric of York,
> and we commission your discretion to act there as our
> representative: that is, in our name, you are there to
> amend what should be amended and establish what
> should be established for the good of souls, with the
> Lord's help.[3]

The exclusion of York from Becket's legatine authority was something of a blow, but the document confirmed that he was still emphatically archbishop of Canterbury; and that papal recognition

was published in Henry's continental lands by letters addressed to
the archbishops and bishops of the provinces of Rouen and Bordeaux
(and possibly also Bourges and Tours), which urged the prelates of
Henry's continental dominions to work for the repatriation of 'our
venerable brother, Thomas, archbishop of Canterbury, who is loyal
and devoted to [the king]'.[4] According to John of Salisbury, these
prelates were also told to obey whatever sentences Becket might
issue, although such a mandate is not contained in the surviving collections of materials. There may, of course, have been further letters,
which have not survived. These papal actions, which were paralleled
by the conferment of extra dignities on Conrad of Wittelsbach
(December 1165: archbishop of Mainz and cardinal priest of
S. Marcello; April 1166: cardinal bishop of Sabina), reflected a temporary strengthening of Pope Alexander's position. There was a lull in
imperial military action in northern Italy, and the first manifestations of what became the Lombard League of cities opposed to
Frederick's Italian policies were being seen.

Perhaps sensing that a more favourable breeze was blowing in
papal circles – he was hopeful that Conrad of Mainz would be able
to use his influence to secure the grant of his petitions – Thomas
began to take the initiative himself. He wrote directly to Gilbert
Foliot, sent a sequence of three letters to the king, and, most dramatic of all, travelled to Vézelay, where St Bernard had preached the
second crusade, and there, on Whit Sunday (12 June), he promulgated a series of ecclesiastical censures against those who were occu-
pying Canterbury lands, those who composed and implemented the
Constitutions of Clarendon, the two royal clerks (Richard of
Ilchester and John of Oxford), who had attended the imperial council in 1165 and, according to the emperor's own encyclical, had
taken an oath in Henry II's name to accept the authority of the new
anti-pope, 'Paschal III'. In addition, he suspended the two bishops
whom he regarded as key players: Gilbert Foliot of London and
Jocelin de Bohun of Salisbury.

The letter to Foliot is sharp and acerbic, and full of bitter irony:

> ... how conscientiously you bore what happened, with
> what anguish of mind you concealed the wrong done to
> God in us – the wrong done to us because of God, the
> wrong, indeed, done to you through us – when in us the
> Lord Jesus Christ was again dragged before the prince's
> judgment seat, again in us ordered to be crucified. Was it
> to protect yourself and your relations from the burden of

> confiscation and the inconvenience of exile? … Not thus
> did the Apostles, who were not afraid to preach the faith
> and name of Christ before the princes and potentates of
> the world. (*CTB*, i, no. 65)

Professor Warren thought such language almost blasphemous; but bishops and priests represented Christ, and their dignity in Christian society derived from that association. A quick glance at the legislation of the Christian Roman emperors would have demonstrated that similar ideas existed long before their particular association with what Warren called the 'high clericalism' of the Gregorian period,[5] and they were being systematically developed in the schools of theology in northern France through the twelfth century. Those who lectured on scripture took for granted the primacy of spiritual over temporal matters and therefore the superiority of priestly authority, and the pages of the Bible and the Gospels provided a rich source of political and ecclesiastical allegory. One particularly influential exponent of this opinion was Hugh of St-Victor, whom Becket may have heard in Paris, and whose very popular treatise on the sacraments had been completed in the 1130s. In it he laid out the theory of the two powers, earthly and spiritual, headed respectively by king and pope. Each had its own sphere; each owed respect to the other; but the powers of the earthly order could not infringe the rights of the spiritual, and secular judges could not lay hands on clerical offenders.[6] The comparison between Christ's arraignment before Pilate and Becket's before Henry II came naturally to writers saturated with such learning. Present problems could always be seen as reflections of sacred history.[7] Becket's letters to Gilbert Foliot, the bishops and the king should be set in this context.

Of the three letters to the king, the first two were carried by Urban I, abbot of the Cistercian monastery of Cercamp-sur-Canche (dép. Pas-de-Calais), which was a daughter house of Pontigny. The choice of messenger was made carefully. He was already an old man (he died on 31 August, about a month after discharging his second mission), and as a Cistercian abbot commanded respect and immunity from vindictive action. It was unlikely that any messenger connected with Becket would have gained access to the king's presence; the last was carried by Gerard, a barefoot monk. All three have been judged either as outrageous (how could a subject address his king in that manner?)[8] or as fatuous (what hope did such letters have of persuading a king like Henry II?). Do they not prove that Becket's judgment was faulty? Do they not smack of the arrogance of which he is accused? Who was Becket, of all people, to write to the lord of the Angevin Empire in such terms?

> To speak about God (*Loqui de Deo*) requires a serene and quiet mind. Therefore I would speak to my lord (Gen. 18: 27) and I wish he were peaceable to all. I entreat you, my lord, to bear with a serene mind this small hint of admonition, bestowed by God's grace, which is never in vain, for the salvation of your soul and my delivery. Difficulties surround me on all sides. Distress and danger have sought me out: set between two very grievous and fearful things and fearful between two very heavy imperatives, between silence and admonition. But if I am silent, it will be my spiritual death, nor shall I escape the hands of the Lord who says, 'If you do not tell the wicked man his transgression and he dies in his sin, I shall require his blood from your hands.' (Ezek. 3: 18) If I speak a warning, I fear that I shall not escape my lord's wrath, which God forbid, and that it might happen to me, as the wise man says, 'When he who does not please comes or is sent to mediate, we must fear lest the spirit of the angry man be provoked to worse things. (Gregory I, *Registrum*, i. 24) What therefore shall I do, speak or hold my peace? Either way certainly lies danger. ... Often indeed are good things bestowed on the unwilling, especially when their advantage rather than their pleasure is considered.

> In your land, the daughter of Syon, bride of the Great King is being held captive ... . Free her, and allow her to reign with her Spouse, so that God may bless you ... . The Lord indeed is a patient requiter, and waits for a long time, but he is a most severe avenger. Listen to me and do good. If you do not, we must fear, which God forbid, that the Most Powerful will gird his sword upon his thigh and come with strong arms and a great army to free his Spouse from the oppression and servitude of the oppressor ... (*CTB*, i, no. 68)

It comes as a shock to read a letter like this from the son of a middling Londoner to an anointed and powerful king. Critics would have looked for humble apologies and submissive appeals, if not for pardon, then for the king's grace. Would Becket not have been better advised to have taken the path of 'humility'? Eighteen months of 'humble approaches' had produced nothing but demands for his unreserved acceptance of the Constitutions; and *Loqui de Deo* was a sermon, not a petition. Moreover, it was drafted to have maximum effect when read aloud before the court, and contained not the words of Thomas of London but the solemn admonition of the successor of Augustine. Yet the opening was flattering. The first paragraph likened Henry to the Almighty, whereas Becket used the words with which Abraham opened his plea that the Lord spare Sodom and Gomorrah for the sake of even one just man; and the imagery of biblical kingship was used to encourage the king to free the Church from the abuse of her enemies. The threat of divine retribution is unexceptional. It was part of the repertoire of preachers everywhere. No specific charges were made; no condemnations were issued.

The real message, however, was 'in the mouth of the bearer', an old man of unimpeachable reputation, a 'holy man', a mediator, unconnected with the dispute between king and archbishop. His pleas, spoken in the French vernacular, were likely to have been on the level of personal appeal to the king's justice and mercy, and presented with befitting monastic humility. That part of the message has not been recorded, but whatever was said fell on deaf ears, and Thomas wrote a second, more strongly phrased letter, which was presented to the king at his great castle of Chinon by the same Abbot Urban. This time, we have the real message, not the formal statement, for one manuscript transmits the heading, 'These are the words of the lord of Canterbury to the English king.' The appeal begins with a compelling biblical echo of Christ's words at the Last Supper, 'With longing have I desired to eat this Pasch with you before I suffer' (Luke 22: 15), and a moving allusion to Becket's present plight:

> With longing have I desired (*Desiderio desideraui*: Luke 22: 15) to see your face and speak to you, much indeed on my account, but more particularly on yours. On my account, that when you have seen my face you would call to mind the services I rendered to you, when I was in your service, with devotion and loyalty according to the judgment of my conscience – so help me God in the final judgment, when all of us shall stand before his tribunal to receive according to what we have done in the body, whether good or ill; and so that you might be moved with pity for me, who now must live by begging among strangers. (*CTB*, i, 293)

Followed by a statement of his threefold relationship with the king:

> Because you are my lord, I owe and I offer you my
> counsel and service, whatever a bishop owes his lord,
> according to the honour of God and holy Church. Because
> you are my king, I am bound to reverence and warn you.
> Because you are my son, I am bound to reprove and
> restrain you by reason of my office. … (*CTB*, i, 293–5)

The phrase, 'according to the honour of God and holy Church',
which was to echo through the controversy to the end, was a coded
assertion of the limits of clerical obedience to the king. Henry was
reminded of the dignity of Christian kingship and the obligations
attached to it. If kings were claiming to rule by God's grace, they
were responsible to Him, and the Old Testament was full of examples of 'good' and 'bad' kings. There was nothing offensive or exceptional in this line of argument, which could be traced back in
ecclesiastical discourse to the eighth century, and beyond.

> Kings are anointed in three places, on the head, on the
> breast, and on the arms, which signifies glory, wisdom,
> and strength. Those kings who did not observe God's
> laws and violated his commands in ancient times, had
> their glory, wisdom and strength taken away from them
> and from their heirs, like Pharaoh, Saul, Nabuchodonosor,
> Solomon, and many others. But those who after their
> fault humbled themselves before God in contrition of
> heart, recovered God's favour, together with all the above
> graces, more abundantly and perfectly – like David,
> Hezekiah, and many others. (*CTB*, i, 295)

Kings indeed had a sacred – a consecrated – ministry, but their
authority extended only to secular affairs, and it was paralleled by
another:

> God's Church consists of two orders, the clergy and the
> people. Among the clergy are apostles, popes, bishops, and
> the other teachers of the Church, to whom is entrusted the
> care and rule of the Church itself, who have the ability to
> conduct ecclesiastical affairs so that they may direct the
> whole to the salvation of souls. This is why it was said
> to Peter, and in Peter to the other governors of God's
> Church, and not to kings or princes, 'Thou art Peter, and

upon this rock I shall build my Church; and the gates of
the underworld shall not prevail against it.' ... if you allow
me to say so, you do not have the power to command
bishops to absolve or excommunicate anyone, to draw
clergy to secular judgments, to pass judgment concerning
churches and tithes, to forbid bishops to hear cases
concerning breach of faith or oaths, and many other things
of this kind, which are written down among your customs,
which you call 'ancestral'. For the Lord says, 'Keep my
laws'; and again, he declares through the Prophet, 'Woe to
them who make unjust laws and set down injustices in
writing to oppress the poor in judgment and deprive God's
humble people of their right'. ...

Therefore, my lord, if you desire your soul's salvation, do
not for any reason take away what belongs to the Church
or oppose it in anything beyond what is just; rather, allow
it to have in your realm the freedom which it is known
to have in other realms. Remember also the profession
concerning the preservation of the liberty of God's
Church which you made when you were consecrated
and anointed by our predecessor, and placed in writing
upon the altar at Westminster. Restore the church of
Canterbury, from which you received promotion and
consecration, to the condition and dignity in which it was
in the times of your predecessors and ours, and restore
in full the possessions belonging to that church and to
us – the villages, castles, and estates which you have
distributed at will, and all the goods sequestrated from us
and the clergy and laity connected with us. And further,
allow us, if it please you, to return freely to our see in
peace and with full security, and to exercise our office
freely as we should and as reason requires. And we are
ready to serve you as our dearest lord and king, loyally
and devotedly with all our strength in whatever way we
can, saving the honour of God and of the Roman Church,
and saving our order. If you do not, you may know for
certain that you will suffer the divine severity and
vengeance. (*CTB*, i, 295–9)

Described as 'the threatening letter in which you left out the salutation' in the bishops' appeal composed by Gilbert Foliot *c.* 24 June
1166,[9] this letter so enraged the king that he protested to the

English-born abbot of Cîteaux against Cistercian monks acting as agents for Thomas, naming the abbot of Cercamp as the bearer of an impudent 'scriptum' from 'a certain Thomas, who was our chancellor', and 'which he read with his own lips, in which he denounced us and appeared to accuse us of broken faith and schism'; and its predecessor, 'contained words of anger and pride ... which demeaned our honour and person'. And he threatened the head of the Cistercian order that he would have to 'seek a remedy himself' if the abbot failed to take steps to correct the 'excesses' of his monks.[10]

How justified was the king's rage? The sentiments could hardly have been more traditional and the 'threat' referred to God's judgment, not Becket's or the pope's. The address, however, was delivered at Chinon, probably in the presence of the bishops and nobles of Touraine, and Henry may have been particularly stung by the reference to his trafficking with the schismatics – Frederick I and his anti-pope – at the very moment when he was organizing a tax for a proposed crusade. His contemptuous reference to 'a certain Thomas, who was our chancellor' demonstrated that he did not recognize Becket's episcopal rank, so that what would have been accepted as the normal admonition of a high cleric became arrogant insult on the lips of his disgraced servant. He was also aware that the archbishop was now free to use his powers of ecclesiastical censure (which had been suspended by the pope until Easter – 24 April), and he did not want Cistercian monks to be the transmitters of such offensive material. He may also have taken offence at the style. Both letters were couched in the first person – an informal, intimate mode of address. That construction was appropriate between equals, or between friends – Henry may have felt that neither designation applied in the circumstances.

The second letter had scarcely been presented when Thomas delivered his most controversial blow. Unknown to the royal administration, he went to the great Benedictine monastery of Vézelay, where he issued a series of sentences against persons most closely involved in the king's policies. They were almost certainly promulgated in the abbey church, and a stream of letters reported the sentences to the pope (whose confirmation was sought) and leading cardinals, Rotrou of Rouen, Robert of Hereford, Hilary of Chichester,[11] and no doubt others, and a general letter was sent to the bishops of the province of Canterbury. It begins with a rebuke:

> Dearest brothers, why do you not rise up with me against the wicked? Why do you not stand 'with me against the

workers of iniquity'? ... We have borne with the lord king of England enough and more than enough, and no advantage has come to God's Church from our forbearance. ... And, because he has scarcely listened to us, and never yet paid any heed to us, after invoking the grace of the Holy Spirit, we have publicly condemned and quashed the document which contains those perversities, rather than customs, by which the English Church is for the moment being thrown into disorder and confusion, together with the authority of the document.

Furthermore, we have excommunicated all who observe, enforce, counsel, support, or defend them. And, by God's authority and our own, we absolve all you bishops from the promise which binds you to observe them, contrary to ecclesiastical ordinance. ... In like manner ... we have nullified and quashed the authority of the text itself and the document in which it is written, together with the perversities it contains, especially these:

That there can be no appeal to the Apostolic See in any case, except with the king's licence [cf. Clarendon, cl. 8];

That an archbishop or bishop may not leave the realm to come at the summons of the Lord Pope, without the king's licence [cf. Clarendon, cl. 4];

That a bishop may not excommunicate anyone who holds of the king in chief, without the king's licence, or place his land or the lands of his officials under interdict [cf. Clarendon, cl. 7];

That a bishop may not punish anyone for perjury or broken faith [cf. Clarendon, cl. 8];

That clerks may be drawn to secular judgments [cf. Clarendon, cl. 3];

That laymen, whether the king or others, may try cases involving churches and tithes; and other clauses of the same kind [cf. Clarendon, cll. 1 and 9]. (*CTB*, no. 78: Vézelay, 12 June 1166)

It is probable that this list of particularly obnoxious clauses was composed from memory, since there is no attempt to reproduce either the language or the order of the chirograph. The high profile given to clauses that affected the relationship between clerics and the papacy has been interpreted as intended to ensure the continued support of the papal Curia, but Henry had made the issue a matter of current and not merely theoretical importance when, in December 1164, he had ordered the arrest of any cleric or layman who appealed to the Roman Curia. Depending on how it was implemented, this could have been used to isolate the English Church from the developing system of general ecclesiastical law.

Whatever one thinks of the Constitutions, it was necessary from his point of view to make clear where the archbishop stood. In a sense, this declaration was only part of the business unfinished after Clarendon. Henry believed that he had a binding contract between church and kingdom; that belief had to be challenged and the bishops relieved of their promise to uphold the customs. More irritating from the king's point of view was the series of disciplinary sentences. John of Oxford was excommunicated for having communicated 'with that notorious schismatic Rainald of Cologne' and accepting the deanery of Salisbury in defiance of papal and archiepiscopal mandates; Richard of Ilchester was similarly excommunicated for communicating with Cologne, but also for 'devising and scheming all manner of evil things with those schismatics and Germans to the detriment of God's Church, and especially of the Roman Church, from the agreements made between the lord king and them.' These sentences related to the embassy these two royal clerks had conducted in Germany, when they attended the imperial council of Würzburg in May 1165. The emperor's own encyclicals proclaimed that they had sworn allegiance to 'Paschal III' in the name of their lord, the king of England, and Rainald of Dassel cited the imminent defection of Henry II and his 'more than fifty bishops' as justification for his own action.[12] Either the emperor was deceiving or he was deceived!

There is no doubt at all that the two were important delegates at the council; but there is some doubt about what they did there. Certainly they were engaged in discussing marriage alliances. Henry II's second daughter, Eleanor, was destined to marry Frederick's son, Frederick, and his eldest daughter, Matilda, was to marry Henry the Lion of Saxony. These would have been splendid matches for the young princesses; and they would greatly have strengthened Henry's position vis-à-vis Louis VII of France. In fact, one can detect in Henry II's marriage policies a policy of encirclement. Before the envoys returned, however, Rotrou of Rouen wrote a letter denying that any such oath had been taken;[13] and some historians argue that Henry could not have gone forward on such a policy without the agreement of the local episcopates of England, Normandy, Anjou and Aquitaine. But it is perfectly possible that Henry did flirt with the idea, and that either he found that the local episcopates were hostile or that he simply thought better of the idea. In any case, the mere fact of the rumour – and it was more than a rumour – would have been enough to send a clear message to Alexander III. Even without the acknowledgement of the anti-pope, however, there is no doubt that the two envoys 'communicated with schismatics' and therefore incurred automatic excommunication. They were, however, primary agents of Henry's ecclesiastical policy, and their excommunication was intended to paralyse their capacity to continue to operate in the king's service, since they could be excluded from all forms of Christian communion. Richard de Lucy and Jocelin de Balliol[14] were excommunicated for their part in drawing up the Constitutions.

Becket then turned his attention to the agents and beneficiaries of the king's seizure of Canterbury property: Randulf de Broc, 'who seized and holds the goods of the church of Canterbury ... and who seized our men, both clerks and laymen, and holds them captive in prison';[15] Hugh of St Clare[16] and Thomas FitzBernard,[17] 'who seized and still hold the goods and possessions of the church of Canterbury without our consent'. To these specific miscreants, he added a general sentence against 'all those who shall in the future lay violent hands on the possessions and goods of the church of Canterbury, against our will and without our consent', and those who conspire with them. Not only did he order the bishops to promulgate the excommunications in the usual manner – by 'setting them in a prominent place at the entrances of churches', but he added a direct command to Gilbert of London, as dean of the bishops, to ensure that copies of the sentences were circulated throughout the province of Canterbury: 'Moreover, by the power of obedience we enjoin you, brother bishop of London, to publish this letter and lay it before our other venerable brothers and fellow bishops in our province.'[18] The last two clauses, addressed to the bishops and to Foliot, put the bishops in a quandary: whether they liked it or not, Becket was still their archbishop and they were bound by the canonical obedience they had sworn to Canterbury, when they were themselves consecrated (and of which they left a written copy in the Canterbury archives),[19] to obey his lawful mandates. In addition, however, he suspended the bishop of Salisbury for his alleged connivance in the appointment of John of Oxford to the Salisbury deanery, and summoned him and Geoffrey Ridel to his presence within 40 days, or face sentence for contumacy.[20]

These Vézelay sentences have been severely judged as evidence of Becket's tendency to take precipitate action and to inflame a situation that was already tense. This action, like his letters to the king, was merely stoking up the flames of royal indignation. Moreover, it was striking at the servants rather than the master. All of them, after all, were merely discharging their due service to the king. Yet it is hard to see how the issue of censures 18 months after the expulsion of Becket's household and their families, and the failure of all the diplomatic efforts made on his behalf, can fairly be called precipitate. That the Vézelay sentences specifically excluded the king should be read, in fact, as reluctance to press the issue too far at that point: 'we have so far deferred imposing a sentence on the person of the lord king, since we are waiting to see if perchance he comes to his senses under the inspiration of divine grace', although he added the ominous rider 'nevertheless, we shall soon impose it, if he does not very quickly see reason.'[21]

The response to this courageous or foolhardy action was mixed. Nicholas of Saint-Jacques, who had the Empress's ear at Rouen, supported it warmly:

> We were overwhelmingly delighted when we learned from your letter that you have publicly condemned with anathema the bad customs to whose observance your prince wished to bind the English bishops. ... In this, indeed, you have begun more nobly and more earnestly than if you had issued a sentence against the king's person. For, in condemning the fore-mentioned perversities, you have closed off any possibility of your return which is short of the freedom of God's Church. (*CTB*, i, no. 95)

Nor were these merely empty words. Nicholas goes on to say that he had read Becket's letter to the archbishop of Rouen, and that he was keeping the one addressed to Chichester until he had an opportunity to present it in person. He further reported that 'when the Lady Empress heard the names of those you had sentenced, she treated it as a joke and replied that they were already excommunicated. Afterwards, when she was greeted by Richard of Ilchester, she did not reply.' The Empress, of course, had disapproved of the writing down of the Constitutions and their imposition by oath, even though she approved of some of them. How many others shared this view is difficult to assess. One suspects that there was a split between 'regular' and 'secular' prelates – that is, between members of religious orders and bishops, since the latter were far more vulnerable as individuals to the king's power.

The reaction in Normandy and England was swift. Nicholas reported that Rotrou of Rouen, Arnulf of Lisieux and Froger of Séez were preparing to undermine the sentences, and Gilbert of London, with the king's permission, drafted an appeal, not against the sentences, which are denounced as canonically invalid, because the condemned had not been given an opportunity to defend themselves in advance, but as a protection against the issue of an interdict in England or an excommunication of the king. The text of the appeal to Rome begins with a highly sanitized résumé of the dispute about criminous clerks, stressing the king's good intentions and his zeal for justice, then asserts that all was going well in the quest for Canterbury's peace and repatriation until the archbishop upset everything with 'the harsh and terrible letters', which threatened the king with interdict and excommunication (probably *Desiderio desideraui*, whose presentation at Chinon so enraged King Henry, although it is not as explicit as Foliot implies) and the (Vézelay) sentences against the leading members of the royal administration. 'Therefore', the appeal continued,

> lest the Church be so miserably overthrown in the time of
> your papacy, lest our lord the king and the populations
> who serve him be turned away from your obedience –
> which God forbid, lest all that is being plotted against us
> by the advice of men of no official status be made possible
> through the anger of the lord of Canterbury, we have
> appealed *viva voce* and in writing to your highness
> against him and his mandates containing injury against
> the king or kingdom, against us or the churches entrusted
> to our charge, and we set the term of the appeal at
> Ascension Day (Thursday, 18 May 1167), choosing rather
> to humble ourselves before you in whatever pleases your
> holiness than to be wearisomely grieved from day to day
> according to the movements of his proud spirit, when we
> have not deserved it. (*MTB*, v, no. 204)

It is not clear whether all the English bishops in fact associated themselves with the appeal, even though it was couched in the name of all the bishops and dignitaries of the Canterbury province. We know that Foliot had to write to ask Bartholomew of Exeter to seal the document, and William of Canterbury recorded that he had done so very reluctantly, declaring that it was only because 'he did not wish to be viewed with distrust by the lord king'; and he attached a series of highly significant saving clauses: 'saving the honour due to God and the lord king, saving obedience due to the Roman Church, and saving reverence for the archbishop of Canterbury.'[22] John of Salisbury reported that only three bishops, Gilbert himself, Henry of Winchester, and Robert of Hereford sealed the notification that was sent to Becket.[23] That letter blamed Becket's ingratitude for the crisis, held up the spectre of royal secession from Pope Alexander, and urged 'patience and humility'.

Meanwhile, Thomas sent a third and much more threatening letter to Henry.[24] After quoting Gelasius I on the relationship between priestly and royal authority –

> There are indeed two things whereby the world is
> principally ruled, the sacred authority of the priests and
> the royal power; of these the authority of the priests is the
> greater to the extent that they will render an account for
> the kings themselves in the divine judgment

– he cited precedents for the excommunication of Christian emperors: Innocent I's sentence against Arcadius (395–408) for deposing St John Chrysostom, patriarch of Constantinople[25] and Ambrose of Milan's condemnation of Theodosius (379–93),[26] reinforced by King David's acceptance of rebuke by the prophet Nathan, and urged his 'dearest son, most serene king, most respected lord' to do likewise, otherwise

> Unless you come to your senses, unless you cease
> attacking churches and the clergy, unless you keep your
> hands from causing disorder among men, the Son of
> the Most High will indeed come in the staff of his fury
> (Isa. 10: 5), in response to the sighs of captives and the
> voices crying out to him; because it is already time to pass
> judgment against you in the equity and sternness of his
> spirit. Truly he knows how to take away the spirit of
> princes, and is terrible before the kings of the earth
> (cf. Deut. 10: 17). (*CTB*, i, no. 82)

Of the three letters sent to King Henry, this was certainly the fiercest in its Old-Testament rhetoric, but, like them, it needs to be put into its contemporary rhetorical framework. The art of effective composition was one of the most useful skills taught in the schools. Popes, emperors, kings and archbishops employed its practitioners to express their arguments, and hyperbole was one of its characteristics.[27]

But it was only rhetoric. There were no direct threats of interdict of the kingdom or excommunication of the king. Becket knew well enough that a direct assault might have driven the king into schism.

The shock of the Vézelay sentences and the furious responses of king and whatever bishops in fact joined the appeal had scarcely passed when the arrival of the papal letters that conferred the legation and the primacy, and ordered the restoration of revenues assigned to other clergy by the king, gave further ammunition to a man whose armoury was thought to have been neutralized by the appeal of 24 June. In an extraordinary coincidence, the bulls and mandates were received at Pontigny between 12 and 24 June, when the appeal was being organized in England; and Thomas lost no time in issuing further mandates. To Gilbert Foliot and the English bishops, he sent copies of the papal letter that, on 3 May 1166, had ordered the restitution of all property expropriated 'by the king's command';[28] to Robert of Hereford and Roger of Worcester, the two bishops whom he had consecrated, and who therefore were considered especially bound to him, he sent copies of the legation letters, with instructions to show them first to the bishop of London, who should communicate them to the other bishops and also to the bishop of Durham, as well as to the bishops of Winchester, Bath, Salisbury, Chester, Exeter and St David's,[29] and, with a separate letter to Gilbert Foliot (90), he sent the original of the legation bull, ordering him to promulgate it to the bishop of Durham and the bishops of the Canterbury province. Becket was taking no chances. If Foliot suppressed the mandate, there was a chance that either Hereford or Worcester would have the courage to circulate it to their fellow bishops.[30] The two letters to the bishop of London (87 and 90), with the papal mandate for restoration of properties and revenues and the bull appointing Becket as legate, were in fact delivered to Gilbert in dramatic fashion on 30 June, as Gilbert ruefully explained in a letter to the king.

> When, on the feast of St Paul, we were standing before the altar [of St Paul's] in London, we received from a person wholly unknown to us letters from the lord Pope, in which the legation of all England, except the bishopric of York, is granted to the lord of Canterbury and confirmed by apostolic authority. All the bishops of this realm are commanded by the same authority to give him humble obedience as legate of the apostolic see, to go to his presence when summoned, to answer in full for what pertains to our offices, and to receive whatever he

commands for firm observance. In addition, we are to
compel all clerics, who have at your command received
benefices of his clerks in their absence, to make full
restitution of them within two months, under sentence
of anathema, without right of appeal. We have been
ordered to collect St Peter's Pence from our fellow brother
bishops and hand it over in full to envoys who will be
sent. (*GFL*, no. 168 = *MTB*, v, no. 208)

That Becket had somehow managed to have a battery of papal and
archiepiscopal mandates smuggled into England and delivered into
the hands of the dean of the Canterbury province at mass in his own
cathedral, and on the patronal feast, less than a week after the appeal
was drafted, was no doubt shocking to the bishop. He had based
his own strategy, and his advice to the king, on his ability to nullify
Becket's metropolitical authority in England. The bishops, almost
certainly led by Foliot, had managed to extract themselves from the
most damaging of the Northampton judgments only by assuring the
king that if they were allowed to appeal they would be able to protect king and kingdom from Becket's authority, and continue to
observe the Constitutions undisturbed by troublesome interdicts,
suspensions or excommunications. The right of appeal to the pope
could be used to tie Becket's hands. Now, Foliot was placed in a serious quandary. Whatever he thought of Becket as a man, he could not,
if he remained a faithful Catholic bishop, ignore the papal mandates
he had received. Thomas was now legate for the greater part of
England, including the bishopric of Durham, only the *diocese* of York
being excluded, because its archbishop was legate for Scotland.[31]
The recent appeal notwithstanding, Foliot was driven to beg abjectly
for royal support. His letter explains a great deal about his relationship with the king.

Prostrate in spirit at the feet of your highness we beg you
not to turn your eyes away from us on account of the
great royal business which you are conducting, but with
royal piety to make provision lest we be reduced to
nothing, to our immense disgrace. This indeed will you
achieve admirably, if you allow us with your grace to
obey the apostolic mandates for the present, and when
Peter's Pence has been paid and the clerks who are in your
mercy have been restored, you command all the bishops
that they may immediately appeal with confidence to the
lord Pope or to legates sent to us, if they perceive any

infringement of the custom of the realm in the archbishop's letters. In this way will you bring to perfection the labour of mercy and preserve us from disobedience, and through the general appeal of everyone you will provide that our position (*causa nostra*) does not suffer damage in anything. ... (*GFL*, no. 168 = *MTB*, v, no. 208)

This letter leaves no doubt at all about Foliot's very close association with King Henry and his connivance with the king in devising strategies that would nullify Becket's authority, provide a smoke-screen of apparent obedience to papal commands, and protect Foliot's own position by the subterfuge of a general appeal. The readiness with which Foliot embraced the whole gamut of the Constitutions of Clarendon calls into question the honesty of his statements about the king's willingness to negotiate, and the danger of Becket's opposition. This letter should be set beside the arguments put to the pope in the appeal that Foliot drafted, his condemnation and vilification of Thomas in the notification, and his wholesale destruction of Becket's character in *Multiplicem*; it should also be compared with his assertion that all the bishops had been adamantly opposed to the Constitutions until Becket broke ranks and sold the pass at Clarendon.

Foliot's motivation is a puzzle. He was a man of education, a Cluniac monk of long standing, an experienced abbot (of Gloucester) and bishop (successively of Hereford and London). He seems on the whole to have been a good bishop, though heavily tarred with nepotism. Is it the contempt of a monk and an aristocrat for the curialist? Since he was willing to do almost anything to appease the king during the Becket controversy, he aligned himself with the curialist circle. Was it, perhaps, frustrated ambition, whose denial appears too shrill? Or was it, as Becket hinted, simple fear for his position and status, and for the security of his extended family? The latter is understandable; but it might challenge the sincerity of his carefully crafted arguments if one concludes that he was merely a paid pen: paid, not in money but in the protection and security the king afforded. The Becket party seems to have believed the latter. Both his authorship and the intention of the appeal were recognized by John of Salisbury, whose identification of Foliot with Achitophel and Doeg left little to the imagination of those who knew their Old Testament. Achitophel was the ambitious miscreant who had conspired with King David's son Absalom against the king, advising armed rebellion and patricide; Doeg was the chief of King Saul's herdsmen who, at the king's command, slew 85 priests and destroyed Nob, their city.[32] Needless to say, John was warm in his approbation of the form and tone of Becket's response to the appeal; and, from that point on, he threw himself unreservedly into the mobilization of the defence of Becket's position.

Becket's situation in July–August 1166 was complicated. On the one hand, he had issued sentences that the pope confirmed in August,[33] and his own position had been immeasurably strengthened by the grant of the legation of England; on the other hand, with the king's full support, Gilbert of London had organized another appeal and was geared up to use every legal device available to paralyse Becket's authority. John of Salisbury's support had become more vocal, however, and Becket's supporters began to sense that all was far from lost. There was much consultation of the interested parties. Nicholas of Mont-Saint-Jacques advised him to emphasize to Rotrou of Rouen, Arnulf of Lisieux and Froger of Séez that he had always been prepared and was still prepared to return to Canterbury

> and there submit to whatever judgment an archbishop of
> Canterbury should submit, according to the authority of
> the canons, as long as they are able to obtain a safe return
> for you from the king, guaranteed by the lord of Rouen
> and the Lady Empress

and 'if the Church is fully restored both to the freedom it had when the dispute first arose between [him] and the king – that is, when the bishops were not obliged to the observance of perversities ... .'[34] That became a blueprint for all later negotiations. John of Salisbury advised circumvention of the appeal by summoning some of the bishops on any suitable pretext, especially those who sealed the letter (London, Winchester, Hereford),[35] and to write to all of them, taking precaution to avoid any 'appearance of arrogance or excess'; and he suggested that some of Hereford's academic and monastic friends should be asked to urge him to live up to his reputation for learning and piety.

John, however, was not very hopeful, either of the bishops or of the Roman Church, which he thought would consult its own interests and succumb to bribes when it came to judging the appeal.[36] When he saw Nicholas's advice, he warmly endorsed it – that is, he, too, pressed Becket to seek reconciliation under the protection of the empress and the archbishop of Rouen. But whereas Nicholas had stressed the aspect of Becket's personal security, John said that he should not be too meticulous about the wording of the agreement, and he hinted that Becket should be prepared to take the risk of martyrdom: 'Whoever suffers for justice, is a martyr, that is, bears witness to justice, proclaims the cause of Christ.' He advised Becket, nevertheless, to keep up his battle of words, 'in season and out of season', since the bishops 'will all use the appeal as a cloak to cover themselves', although he believed

> that there are some among the bishops who stand firm in their wishes and their prayers, with you, indeed with God and his Church, even though in deed and word in many ways they communicate with the Church's enemies and persecutors.

The only firm advice was to avoid laying an interdict on the kingdom or excommunication on the king.[37] The advice in this letter is subtle and shifting. John wants a swift resolution, and he seems to be willing to sacrifice Becket on the altar of martyrdom. As he reported it, the advice of Peter of Celle, abbot of Saint-Rémi, Master Fulk and Master Ralph of Sarre – all then in Reims – gave the same advice as Nicholas, though they had not seen his letter, but they put a different spin on the process:

> If there is any possibility of confronting the peril or aiding the churches, you ought not to set such value on your life and soul, that for its salvation and the liberation of your ship-wrecked church, you fail to enter into discussion with the persecutors, and to put to the test what the fatherly kindness of Jesus may be ready to perform through your humbleness – since after the glory of his ascension he announced, as is found in authentic writings, that he is still prepared to die for the humble and carry the shame of the Cross.

If this is an allusion to the *Quo vadis* story,[38] in which St Peter deliberately returned to Rome and martyrdom by crucifixion following a vision in which Christ said that he was going to be crucified again, then it is a clear invitation for Becket to risk his life as St Peter risked (and lost) his. And John concluded,

> The counsel of your best friends, from which Master Philip and I do not dissent, is that if you have been summoned by the Empress, you may safely visit her, escorted by the archbishop of Rouen. If you hear good news there, give thanks to God; walk in all things so that

your moderation may be known to all. If it turns out otherwise (Heaven forbid!), let the archbishop of Rouen escort you back to the land of your pilgrimage safely and honourably. (*CTB*, i, no. 102)

A friend, possibly Master Walter de Insula, whose dismissal it records, reported that the king was hoping that either Becket or the pope would die; and this well-wisher, who knew the mind of the king and the attitude of his inner circle intimately, gave very different advice:

> Therefore, while you still have time, stretch forth your hand in retribution, and you should know that it is written that 'The Lord copiously repays those who act with pride.' Let your sharp judgment punish those who set themselves against God. Quickly cut off the head of the treacherous serpent with the staff of the upright, so that Satan may be swiftly trodden under your feet. Truly, God's Church will not have peace except through a strong hand and raised arm, nor can this lion, wholly asleep in his treacherous infidelity, be roused except by the roar of the father. Go then, draw back your bow, let loose your arrows, until they become enfeebled, because it is failing in respect for God to be gentle in a place where duty to God is destroyed and Faith imperilled. (*CTB*, i, no. 112)

And he was not alone. At about the same time, Nicholas of Mont-Rouen reported that the king would allow no one to mention Becket's name in his presence, and that Rouen and the Norman bishops were taking no overt action to admonish the king (no. 113): they, too, were broken reeds. Henry, meanwhile, demonstrated that peaceful negotiation was not what he had in mind. He sent a letter to the General chapter of the Cistercian order, which met annually on 14 September, proclaiming that Becket was his enemy and declaring that he would remove all their houses from his land, unless the Cistercians expelled him from Pontigny (reported in no. 115). Becket bowed to the inevitable in early November, and accepted the charity of the Benedictine monastery of Sainte-Colombe in Sens, where he was under the direct protection of the king of France, supplemented from 1168 by that of the new archbishop of Sens, William of the White Hands, Louis' brother-in-law.

All of the anxiously debated advice of Becket's friends was summarily nullified by matters outside their control. Not only was the king's implacable enmity even more manifest, but he seems to have flirted again with renouncing his allegiance to Pope Alexander and throwing in his lot with the schismatics. At some uncertain date he wrote to Frederick I's chancellor, Rainald of Cologne, requesting safe conduct through imperial territories for an extremely powerful embassy, consisting of Roger of York, Gilbert of London, Richard of Ilchester, John of Oxford and Richard de Lucy, who were to go to Rome to threaten withdrawal of obedience from 'Pope Alexander and his perfidious cardinals', if they did not abandon 'the traitor Thomas, former archbishop of Canterbury', revoke his sentences and confirm the 'royal customs of Henry, my grandfather'.[39] Nothing came of that explosion of rage, but it should not be set aside as merely empty posturing. The German emperor had crossed the Brenner Pass in October 1166 with a great army,[40] and the outlook for Pope Alexander's papacy looked bleaker than ever. If Frederick were to achieve the total conquest of the Italian peninsula, including the Norman kingdom in the south (which was his principal aim), then the establishment of 'his' pope (Paschal III) would have been a serious possibility. In the event, however, Henry set about achieving his aims by making another démarche on the Curia. Perhaps bearing a safe-conduct from Chancellor Rainald, a powerful embassy, consisting of John of Oxford (representing himself and the bishops), John Cumin and Master Ralph of Tamworth (representing the king), was dispatched to the Curia. Its aim was to obtain confirmation of John's deanery and the appointment of papal legates to settle the Becket question once and for all. His preferred judge was William of Pavia, cardinal priest of S. Pietro in Vincoli, a man of considerable weight in the Curia, and generally recognized to be favourable to the king. When he got wind of this delegation, Becket counter-appealed, begging that the royal envoys be sent back with what he thought they deserved – after all, one of them (John of Oxford) was excommunicate.[41] Thus 1166 ended, with the king confidently expecting triumph and the exiles fearing that the worst would befall them, despite all their endeavours.

6

God's honour and the Church's liberty

If Becket's actions in 1166, especially the Vézelay excommunications and the letters to the king, were criticized at the time and since as ill-considered, arrogant and inflammatory, his manoeuvrings during the three papally organized negotiations through the years 1167–69 are said to smack of vacillation and subterfuge. He was unwilling, so it is argued, to submit to any judgment but his own, and he constantly undermined perfectly good agreements by last-minute changes. If only he had adopted the mode of simplicity and humility, if only he had been more ready to trust the goodwill of the king, if only he had been ready to pass over slights to his honour or to soft-pedal the questions of restitution and compensation, all would have been well and a perfectly honourable peace (to quote Foliot's words in *Multiplicem*) could have been secured. This is the general interpretation, and upon it one important segment of Becket's reputation for awkwardness and arrogance depends. How well founded is it? As in much of the judgment so far, a great deal depends on how one evaluates the situation; how one assesses the sincerity of the other side in the controversy. Were the king or his negotiators honest brokers? Did Becket have reason to be distrustful and to seek in careful phraseology the protection of his position?

The discussions themselves were fraught with difficulties. Most of the time, the negotiations were carried out by third parties: the papal legates spoke to the king and his supporters, and to Becket and the exiles separately, and proposals were carried backwards and forwards across the Norman border. At no time did all the interested parties meet together. Not only was the papacy involved through its representatives (who had their own individual interests and outlooks), but the king of France was represented through his own envoys, either officially or unofficially, and Norman and English bishops, as well as Henry II's own skilled clerks and advisers, also played their parts. Involved were not only a multiplicity of persons with a multiplicity of agendas, but also a multiplicity of legal questions. The consequence was that the attempts to reconcile the two parties took on the appearance of a peace process between international agencies; and each side was aware that it was operating in an international arena. The involvement of papal legates, commissioners or envoys not only transformed the nature of the debate but gradually tilted the balance of advantage towards the exiles. Where Gilbert Foliot had been able to exploit loopholes in the law to his and the king's advantage from 1164 to 1166, from 1167 to 1169, it was Becket who established an advantage.

But it was not only the legal process that helped him. Although the first papal commissioners were appointed in December 1166, and their identity confirmed in February 1167, they made such snail-like progress (perhaps deliberately), that they did not reach Normandy until Autumn 1167. By the time they were ready to begin real negotiations, however, the pope's situation had taken a decisive turn for the better; and with the improvement in his own prospects came a slightly firmer hand in dealing with the English question. The great event, which was trumpeted with delight by Becket's friends, was the disaster that overtook Frederick I's army outside Rome in August 1167. The emperor was forced to flee north through Italy in disguise. At the same time, the continuing tensions between Louis VII and Henry II – fuelled by Henry's chicanery, which made Louis highly distrustful of any peace or truce agreement they negotiated – helped to maintain Louis' protective stance towards the Becket exiles.

The first mission: Cardinals William and Otto, autumn 1167

The shift in papal fortunes is clear in hindsight, but it would have taken considerable powers of clairvoyance to see even as far as Easter 1167, let alone to November 1169. The visible auguries were not encouraging. In early February, the royal envoys, John Cumin and Master Ralph of Tamworth, accompanied by John of Oxford (who had conducted his own business while furthering the bishops' and the king's), returned triumphantly from the Curia with virtually all of the king's petitions granted. To Becket's chagrin, John of Oxford was confirmed in the deanery of Salisbury (and sported a golden ring to prove it), and boasted that the pope had placed him under papal protection so that he was subject only to papal discipline, not to Becket's. Even worse, they brought with them a further restriction of Becket's disciplinary powers. Becket remained archbishop, primate and legate, but he was a lame duck. The papal letter makes painful reading:

> After receiving the letter [*lost*] and messengers [Oxford, Cumin, and Tamworth] from our dearest son in Christ, Henry, illustrious king of the English, we have proposed once more to admonish him by letter and envoy and to assuage his wrath by careful exhortations, so that he might reconcile you to himself and restore you to his grace and affection. Indeed we hope and trust in the Lord that he will fall in with our admonitions and exhortations and restore your church to you freely and peacefully. For this reason, we ask, advise, and counsel you as a prudent man, to bear with him patiently until we can see the end and outcome of this affair, *and you may not in the meanwhile decree anything against him, or anyone in his kingdom, which appears harsh or offensive to him.* But if he is unwilling to accede to us through our envoys, whom we shall perhaps send, by the Lord's will, we shall not for any reason abandon you, but we shall take care to preserve the right, honour, and dignity of you and your church, as far as divine grace shall allow. Finally, if he cannot be persuaded by any other means, you shall not lack the authority of exercising your office without restriction. *We desire nevertheless that you keep this detail secret.* (CTB, i, no. 119)

Even more painful for Becket was the letter addressed to the king from the Lateran on 20 December, which announced that the pope was sending legates,

> in accordance with your wishes ... with full power to hear ... judge ... and conclude (*terminare*) the ecclesiastical cases (*causas*) which have arisen between you and our venerable brother Thomas, archbishop of Canterbury and that between the same archbishop and the bishops of your realm in respect of the appeal made to us.

Becket would be forbidden to issue any further sentences, and the legates would absolve the excommunicated members of the king's household and council (the Vézelay list), although if they were in danger of death, any bishop might raise the sentence[1] – a message reinforced by the letter, secured by John of Oxford on 1 December 1166, which relieved the English bishops of the need to prosecute their appeal at the Curia.[2] All the gains of 1166 had been negated in these two letters. Not only that, but the man whom Becket most feared, William of Pavia, cardinal priest of what the exiles thought was the aptly named church of St Peter in Chains (S. Pietro in Vincoli), was appointed as one of the two legates.

There is no doubt that he was the king's choice. His name was being touted at court when the king's envoys set out for the Curia, and Thomas made frantic efforts to have his powers curtailed. In a letter written in November 1166, he pleaded with the pope to

> ensure that our innocence is not overthrown by the
> mission of Lord William of Pavia, through whom our
> persecutors are openly boasting that they will bring about
> our deposition. We do not yet know whether or not he is
> coming with such power, but we are certain that unless
> we are compelled by your majesty we shall not entrust
> ourselves to the judgment of anyone except your holiness.

To his friend, Conrad of Mainz, he said that Prester, William of Pavia's clerk, had promised Henry II that his master would determine the case between him and Becket according to the king's pleasure.[3] William was certainly *persona grata* at the English court. He had helped to win Henry II over to Pope Alexander in 1160; he had approved the formal marriage of the infant Prince Henry and Princess Margaret of France in 1160; he had been papal legate in Aquitaine 1161–62; and in mid-1164 he was named as one of three royalist cardinals.[4]

Historians can see these actions as another example of the pope's serial vacillation, and it was certainly read by the exiles and by the French court as a partial betrayal, but at the time of writing, Alexander's position was threatened by yet another German invasion of Italy, whose aim was even more ambitious than those that had preceded it. The succession of a minor (William II) to the Sicilian throne on 7 May 1166, following the death of William I, created what seemed to be a golden opportunity for Frederick I to conquer the *mezzogiorno* and incorporate the Norman kingdom into his imperial dominions. Having assembled one of his largest armies, stiffened with a contingent of the feared mercenaries from Brabant, the emperor had reached Lodi by November 1166; by February 1167 he was on the Via Emilia, between Parma and Bologna; and he would be on Monte Mario, about to launch his assault on the city of Rome on 22 July.[5] The concessions to the English king were made in mid-December and the temporary restriction of Becket's powers was issued on about the twentieth of the same month.

The emergence of this new crisis for Alexander's papacy explains the change of tack in the English storms and it probably added to the euphoria that was evident in court circles as the royal envoys returned with the news of the legation and the gagging of Becket. When Gilbert Foliot heard the news, at Winchester, where he was making preparations to obey Becket's earlier summons, he is reported to have cried out with delight, 'Thomas will no longer be my archbishop.'[6] That euphoria was equalled by the consternation among Becket's supporters. John of Poitiers was the first to get wind of the awful fulfilment of their worst apprehensions. He had met a tight-lipped Cumin and Tamworth at Tours on 2 February 1167, but wormed useful information out of Bartholomew of Vendôme, dean of the cathedral, with whom they lodged in Tours, and from a cleric from Saintes who had travelled with them. The news was all bad. Not only were the papal envoys to be legates, they were to have overriding judicial power: 'For the full power of the legate will, so they say, bring a preliminary judgment against every exception and every decree.' This implied that any legal objections which the Becket party might make would simply be overruled. As for John of Oxford, he had been wholly exonerated, largely because he had assured Pope Alexander that peace could be restored between Becket and the king 'if there were someone to conduct it honestly – and he promised that he would do all that he could in the matter', although Cumin and Tamworth were calling John a traitor to the king, 'because he promised to do that which the king considers impossible in order to make better progress in his own affairs'. More alarmingly, the king's envoys had obtained copies of letters sent to the Curia in support of Becket by bishops and members of the king's own court, as well as some of Becket's own letters! John also passed on the rumour that John of Oxford had gone to England 'to procure, prepare, and persuade witnesses and informers against you, with the advice of those who are thirsting for your blood.' With at least one favourable judge already in his pocket, so to speak, Henry was planning a re-run of the Northampton trial, this time supported by witnesses and presided over by papally appointed judges. 'Against their shameless and ominous plots', wrote John of Poitiers, 'I counsel you to take action by whatever means you can, while you have time. For many great men are about to rise up against you and accuse your innocence of serious crimes.'[7] John of Oxford had indeed gone to England, where he prevented Robert of Hereford from crossing the

Channel in response to the archbishop's mandate; and in a meeting at Oxford, where he acted 'almost like a cardinal', he forbade the other bishops to obey Becket's summons.[8] The only glimmer of light in that exceedingly bleak prospect was the news that Otto of Brescia, cardinal deacon of S. Nicola in Carcere Tulliano, had been appointed as William's associate. Otto was also well known to Henry II, since he had acted with William in the early 1160s, but he was not as closely identified with the English king. John of Poitiers, indeed, expressed the hope 'that the more propitious and benevolent star may nevertheless temper and lessen the malice of the star joined to it, even if it does not extinguish it.'

Nothing can express Thomas Becket's sense of betrayal more than the letter he immediately wrote to Master John Planeta, his agent in the Curia.

> The manner in which we were again made a figure of
> shame to our neighbours, a mockery and delusion to those
> not only in our circle but indeed to almost all people in
> both kingdoms, French and English, and even in the
> Empire, and what kind of rumour, not to say infamy and
> scandal against the Lord Pope, is flying around the ears
> and mouths of everyone ... and the serious verbal attacks,
> insults, and shameful reproaches being cast against the
> whole Curia, you can gather to some extent from what is
> written below, and tell it very privately to the Lord Pope
> and his friends, if he has any. (*CTB*, i, no. 123)

To the cardinals he wrote in similar vein:

> You have in fact set us up, wholly undeserved, as a target
> for the arrows, so that we are unable to avoid the spears
> of the spear-throwers attacking us on every side, nor can
> we escape the arrows of the bowmen, except through the
> powerful hand of God. You have made us shameful to
> every passer-by, a mockery to our neighbours, a joke to
> those who are around us; I hope that you have not also
> made yourselves an object of mockery! (*CTB*, i, no. 125)

Such directness of speech is considered more evidence of Becket's intemperate language, but its context has to be fully understood. He was, in fact, outraged, and felt that he had been sold down the river; and not only he. Lombard of Piacenza, his legal adviser, now a sub-deacon of the Roman Curia, reported the dismay of the French king at the triumphant return of John of Oxford, not only with extraordinary status, 'only slightly less than a cardinal', but having obtained the appointment of legates who would determine everything against the archbishop of Canterbury to the king's pleasure. Not only that, but he had obtained a papal dispensation for the marriage of Henry's son Geoffrey to Constance of Brittany, related in the third degree, enabling another region to be added to his 'empire' and thus encircling the French king's domains even more comprehensively. King Louis declared that he would not allow the legates to enter his lands, and expatiated at length on the damage to his honour that the betrayal of Becket implied.[9] The French king's own letter reinforced the message, reminding the pope that he had commended Becket to the pope on his departure from France. 'Many are scandalized', he wrote, using that word in its full meaning of being alienated by outrageous behaviour, 'and they do not hesitate to blame and stigmatize you'.[10] All Becket's letters to the Curia rehearsed the same sense of betrayal and outrage; and all declared unequivocally that he would not under any circumstances enter King Henry's lands to litigate; nor would he submit to the judgment of an enemy, especially William of Pavia.[11] Was this arrogant contempt for justice or prudent avoidance of another kangaroo court?

All these letters – Becket's, the French king's, Master Lombard's and probably many others that have not survived – were sent off posthaste to the Curia in early February, but it is unlikely that they reached Rome before the legates' mandates were drawn up. Becket's earlier (November) letter, however, may have produced some modification of the wide powers that had been promised to the king in December 1166. For when Alexander's chancery drafted the announcement of the appointment of William of Pavia and Otto of Brescia, probably some time in March, there was an apparent diminution of the legates' power. As announced to Thomas, they had been appointed 'to discharge the office of legate in [the king's] lands on this side of the Channel, and particularly to restore peace and concord between you and the same king and make an amicable settlement, with the Lord's help.' This was not the language of a judicial mandate; it was the language of mediation; and it said nothing about the bishops' appeal. It did, however, in terms reminiscent of the pope's advice before Clarendon, urge the archbishop to do his best to find a path to peace:

> bend your mind and will to the establishment of peace
> and concord between yourself and the said king, as far
> as it is possible, *saving the honour of yourself and the*

> *Church*, and if everything does not go forward according
> to your good pleasure, you should for the present conceal
> it, so that you can gradually by the Lord's will restore to
> their former state the things which need correction.

That notification was written probably in March, by which time
Frederick I's army had moved to Imola. It is a mark of Alexander's
desperate plight that he added a surprising rider to the letter, in
which he asked Thomas to use his personal influence with Philip of
Alsace, count of Flanders, to secure a monetary subvention for the
support of the papacy:

> we request and instruct you, brother, to approach the
> noble count of Flanders in your own name and encourage
> him very forcefully to endeavour to assist us generously in
> any way he can, when he has seen our needs and those of
> the Church.[12]

There were, nevertheless, some shreds of consolation in the letter.
Whatever the legates did would not be *appellatione remota*, without
right of appeal; the double repetition of *saving the honour of his
person and of the Church* could be interpreted (and may have been
intended) as a kind of lifeline. His and the Church's honour were to
be weighed against that of the king. There was much more leeway in
this summary of the legates' mandates than the exiles could have
hoped for in the midst of the rumours that had been floating around
between November and March. The game was not yet up.

The legates' journey to France was slow even by twelfth-century
norms, for Otto had to elude the imperial armies as he travelled
north through Italy, and William was sent to encourage the Sicilians
to stand firm against the German invasion, before setting forth for
France. Otto did not reach Saint-Gilles-en-Provence until August,
and from there he was going to Montpellier to wait for his colleague.
For the exiles, it was a long and nerve-racking wait, filled with anxiety
about how the legates would react. Otto's first letter was friendly –
indeed it called Thomas 'dearest friend' – although it gave nothing
away; but he sent a very confidential message in the mouth of his clerk,
who was to be trusted as much as Otto himself.[13] Cardinal William, on
the other hand, attempted to mend some bridges by acknowledging
his earlier ambivalence – which he explained by the need to preserve
Henry II's loyalty to the Apostolic See in those perilous times. That part
of the message was satisfactory enough: it demonstrated recognition

of the need to work with Becket, not against him, but the next sentence contained what was for Becket the alarming assertion that William and Otto had been sent 'to determine the questions which have arisen between you and [the king], in the manner we deem most beneficial to God's Church.'[14] That was precisely what the pope's notification had not said, and Thomas drafted a sharp response, along the lines of his earlier declaration that he would not accept such a man as his judge.

> We have just received your highness's letter, offering
> the semblance of honey in the beginning, poison in the
> middle, and oil at the end. It says that you have now
> come down to these regions to determine the questions at
> issue between the king of England and us, as you shall
> consider expedient. We do not believe that you have come
> to do this, and we certainly do not accept you for this
> purpose, for many reasons, which we shall reveal at the
> appropriate time and place. Nevertheless, we thank God
> and you for any good or peace that may perchance come
> to us through your hand. May your highness flourish, so
> that we may thus have better fortune. (*CTB*, i, no. 133)

This letter, and a second, were submitted to the diplomatic judgment of John of Salisbury, who rightly condemned them for discourtesy, and they were never sent.[15] One wonders, in fact, why they were drafted at all. Were they simply expostulations, expressions of the combination of desperation and anger which William's appointment had occasioned? It was certainly believed fairly widely back in February that Henry's envoys had obtained a tainted judge who would preside over Becket's ignominious deposition – and even that Henry's bribe had included the archbishopric of Canterbury, after he had done the deed. And the news from the court in Rouen was particularly dispiriting. Nicholas of Mont-Saint-Jacques was afraid to visit Becket in case the king should learn of it, 'for the very mention of your name is hard and hateful to his ears, nor does anyone come forward who speaks well of you or dares even to make an allusion to you in his presence.'[16] Sometimes it helped to call a spade a spade. To Cardinal Otto, in contrast, Becket sent a more considered letter. After applauding him as a saviour – 'the whole company of Christ's exiles and ourselves were overjoyed, and rejoiced as if an angel had been sent from heaven to comfort the Church and free the clergy' – the letter pointed out that the Constitutions of Clarendon had been condemned in his presence at Sens, but concluded with an upbeat:

> if it seems right, pursue God's honour and the Church's
> peace, and tell us what we should do that God's Church
> may enjoy its due liberty. For there is nothing we would
> not most willingly do, saving our conscience and our
> reputation, to recover the lord king's affection.[17]

Probably unknown to Becket at this time, however, was the fact that despite the grave danger that threatened him, Pope Alexander had responded to the avalanche of protests that John of Oxford's boastings had unleashed. On 7 May he sent an extraordinary missive to the legates in which he castigated the rumour-mongering of John of Oxford: that he (Alexander III) had withdrawn the bishops and other secular and ecclesiastical persons from Becket's jurisdiction, that he was intending to depose the archbishop in accordance with the king's will and had sent them for the purpose, all of which greatly tarnished his own reputation. He commanded them immediately to write reassuringly to Becket and then to strive to reconcile him with the king, in such a way that they 'preserve for him and his church their ancient rights and liberties'; nor were they to carry out any important action in the king's land, nor were they to enter the kingdom, on any pretext, should the king wish it, unless he was 'fully' reconciled with the archbishop:

> We desire, moreover, that you should handle yourselves
> in all things with circumspection, maturely and
> providently, so that no material can arise for detraction
> against us, and the fidelity of both realms for us and the
> church may be augmented by your mode of conduct, that
> you may thus earn eternal praise and renown.

This was supplemented, three months later, by another mandate that ordered the legates to strive to reconcile the two kings and to be even-handed in their negotiations with each; and it strictly forbade either legate to go to England, or to deal with matters touching that kingdom, especially relating to the consecration of new bishops, unless Archbishop Thomas was first 'fully' reconciled with the king.[18]

By the time that personal contact was made with the cardinals, then, their instructions had been clarified. After meeting them at Châteauroux in September–October, Archdeacon Humbert of Bourges was able to report to Thomas that 'absolutely nothing has been permitted them against you, but rather for you.'[19] This man was a far more important person than his archidiaconal title suggests. As Master Umberto Crivelli of Milan he had taught canon law at Bologna to a galaxy of influential clerks, including Peter of Blois, Baldwin of Exeter, archdeacon of Totnes (successively abbot of Forde, bishop of Worcester and archbishop of Canterbury), and no less a person than Conrad of Wittelsbach, cardinal bishop of Sabina. It is not known exactly when he established his connexion with Thomas Becket, but Alan of Tewkesbury called him a 'former clerk of Archbishop Thomas'; and Herbert of Bosham regarded him as an honorary member of Becket's *familia*, listing him as one of the archbishop's learned men (*eruditi*).[20] Like Becket and Conrad of Wittelsbach, he was an exile from home and office, his pro-Alexandrine sympathies having forced him to flee from Bologna when Frederick I tightened his grip on Italy in the early 1160s.

At Bourges, however, he was in an excellent position to observe and indeed to influence the French court. Although the city was the primatial see of Aquitania Prima, a key province in Henry II's continental dominions, it was itself situated in French lands and its Archbishop, Peter de la Châtre, had established close relations with the French king.[21] Even more importantly, he was one of Becket's secret supporters: his sympathies were unmasked when one of his letters to the pope was betrayed to Henry II's agents in early 1167.[22] As a close collaborator of this powerful francophile archbishop, Humbert was able to speak to the legates with considerable authority, not only on his own account as a leading canon lawyer and a casualty of the papal crisis, but as a man who had the ear of the French king. He was able to reinforce the tenor of Alexander's latest communication, which he may have seen. Louis VII had given the pope and his Curia refuge before (1162–65), and there was a strong possibility that his protection would be needed again.

Suddenly, however, the Italian situation was transformed by the intervention of Providence. Having progressed through northern Italy, though not without difficulty, and having had his wife Beatrix of Burgundy crowned as empress by the anti-pope Paschal III (Guy of Crema) in St Peter's on the feast of St Peter in Chains (1 August), the army encamped outside the city fell victim to the perils of the summer heat in that region. A particularly lethal combination of bacillary dysentery and various forms of malaria sped through the camps, literally decimating the army and enfeebling the survivors. So terrible was the pestilence that Frederick's right-hand man, Rainald of Dassel, archbishop of Cologne, was carried off by it. With him also died some of the luminaries of Frederick's empire, headed by six bishops (Conrad of Augsbug, Alexander of Liège, Daniel of Prague, Eberhard of Regensburg, Gottfried of Speyer and Hermann of Verden), three dukes (Frederick of Swabia, Welf VII and Theobald of Bohemia), and numerous counts and lesser nobles.[23] It is impossible to exaggerate the delight and relief at the emperor's discomfiture that was felt by the Becket exiles as soon as rumours of the debacle filtered north to Sens, probably some time during September–October. Scarcely able to contain his delight, Becket compared the decimation of Frederick I's army to God's destruction of the camp of Sennacherib, king of the Assyrians, during the war with Hezekiah (Ezechia), king of Juda (4 Kings [2 Kings] 19: 35):

> No more manifest demonstration of God's power has
> been heard of since the beginning of time ... no justice
> more just, than that by which he dashed to pieces those
> who brought this wickedness about ... for he consumed
> them with an infamous death. (*CTB*, i, no. 139)

That letter, and its companions, addressed to Cardinals Conrad (of Wittelsbach) and Hyacinth,[24] then turned the full weight of its rhetoric against the judicial pretensions of William of Pavia: 'Certainly he is not the man to whose authority we should be subject in this case, especially since it was the king's insistence which constrained you to send him ....'[25] At the same time, perhaps in response to John of Salisbury's urging, Thomas established better relations with William. Not only did he himself intercede with Louis VII to obtain permission for the two cardinals to enter his lands, but he frankly requested his favour – 'we pray that your dear self will be more kindly disposed to us, out of love and respect for him [Louis VII] who is, as you say, very much concerned about us and our affairs.'[26]

All the omens were now better than anyone could have imagined at the beginning of the year, and it was with high expectations that the exiles went to meet the cardinals in the marches of Normandy (since Becket, of course, would not enter Henry's territory), at a place called Planches, between Gisors and Trie, on 18 November. The cardinals had had an audience with King Henry at Caen at the end of October, where they also discussed matters with English and Norman bishops summoned by him. There is no record of those discussions, but we can deduce something of what was said from the line taken by the legates when they met the exiles 'between Gisors and Trie'. Henry's position, from which he never retreated, was that no peace could be made without confirmation of the Constitutions of Clarendon. The Planches conference, however, was recorded at the time by an eyewitness, probably John of Salisbury, who described the interview with the legates as a 'formal process (*actio*)', conducted in public. The legates, who came as mediators, not as judges, explored his responses to a series of points put forward by his adversaries – rather as members of ACAS present proposals to the opposing sides in an industrial dispute; and the procedures were governed by the protocol of formal mediation.

After a long disquisition on the pope's affection for Becket, the difficulties of their own journey, the power of King Henry, the situation of the Roman Church and the great favours which the king had conferred on the archbishop, 'They went on to recount the complaints and injuries which the king claimed he had suffered from the archbishop, charging him among other things that he had stirred up the king of the French to war against him' – which would, of course, have been treason.

> To every point they had put forward, one by one and in the same order, he gave answer; on genuine grounds which could be established he annulled the king's complaints and expounded plainly the Church's injuries and insupportable losses. Since they demanded humility and due show of honour from him, he replied that he would show all humility, and as much honour and reverence to his lord the king as was *consistent with God's honour and the Church's liberty, with his own and his office's good name and the possessions of the churches. …*

The legates then asked whether he would permit the observance of the 'customs of Clarendon' in his own province,

> To this the archbishop replied *that none of his predecessors had been compelled to make such a profession by any of the kings*; that with God's help he would never promise to obey customs patently opposed to God's law, repugnant to the privilege of the Holy See, destructive of the Church's liberty; customs which the Lord Pope condemned at Sens in the presence of many witnesses, themselves included. 'I have followed the Pope's authority', he said, 'and condemned certain of the customs along with those who practise them'.

They then enquired if Thomas would promise, if not to confirm, at least to dissemble and tolerate the customs of *Cleridamnum*; or at all events to return to his see, to accept peace, with no specific mention made of the customs, to which he replied, 'It is a proverb of our people that "silence implies consent."'[27]

Finally, the cardinals asked if he were willing to accept their judgment on the issues between himself and the king – presumably the financial charges that had been raised at Northampton. Since they had not been commissioned as judges delegate, they could not compel the archbishop to submit to their judgment, but they could so act, if Becket were willing to accept their jurisdiction. Thomas did not reject their offer as much as side-step it: his answer was based on the principle that no one could be required to litigate until the goods and properties of which he had been despoiled had been restored to him. This was a masterly defence, known in canon law as the *exceptio spolii*, the defence of despoliation. A defendant was not required to answer pleas relating to right or damages until he had been restored to the properties of which he had been despoiled.[28] Becket used it, however, to avoid raising the defence of *recusatio iudicis* against William of Pavia. This was a Roman defence taken over by the canonists in the course of the twelfth century, which enabled a defendant to challenge the competence of a judge on the grounds of bias or prejudice.[29] Becket had in fact said more than once that he would not accept William as judge, because he was an enemy and known to favour the king,[30] but he chose not to say it to his face at Planches, perhaps because he knew that the cardinal's wings had been severely clipped. Without any comment, the legates then raised the question of the bishops' appeal. Was he willing to respond to their appeal, since they were present? He replied that on this issue he had 'received no papal mandate, and that when it came he would give a considered answer and do what was right.'

What had transpired at Planches was a stage in a consultation process. It was not a trial, and since Becket did not have to submit to judgment, unless he wished to have them as his judges, it would have been foolhardy to enter the judicial lists unless he had to. On the following day, accompanied by Becket, they had an audience with Louis VII, where the French king declared on oath that Thomas had never instigated war between him and the English king. At that point, Becket asked the legates to point out to him any errors he had committed, 'but', says the report, they 'did not say that anything in his course and purpose should be changed'; and, at the end of the meeting, Cardinal Otto sent a secret message, 'informing the Lord Pope that he will be neither the agent nor the abettor of your deposition, although the king seems to want nothing else but your head on a platter.'[31]

As the cardinals returned to Normandy to relay Becket's responses to the king, Becket sent a report of the Planches Conference to the pope, which voiced his fear that William of Pavia might still be out-manoeuvred by King Henry:

> We fear that by a carefully devised plan such petitions
> may be presented to you which will be grievous to hear,
> impossible to carry out, displeasing to God, and hateful to
> the world. ... Be certain of this, serene lord, there would
> be no need for the intervention of any cardinal or any
> man at all if we had been willing to accept the bad
> customs from the beginning...

He emphasized that 'it is not safe or possible for us to submit to judgment, except in the presence of your holiness, and under your own examination.'[32] Further letters to Cardinals Albert and Theodwin, John of Sutri and Boso reinforced the message,[33] supported by letters from King Louis and Queen Adela of France, and testimonials from French bishops, ecclesiastics and nobles.

Meanwhile, William and Otto had the unenviable task of reporting back to King Henry, whose demeanour is described in an anonymous report that was sent to Becket immediately afterwards.

> The cardinals came to the monastery of Bec on the
> Thursday immediately after the octave of St Martin [23
> November]; on the next day they were at Lisieux; on the
> third at Saint-Pierre-sur-Dive, and on the fourth, that is
> the Sunday before the beginning of Advent, they came
> to Argentan [26 November]. On that day the king went
> out two leagues to meet them, showing them a smiling
> countenance, and he accompanied each cardinal to his
> lodging. Summoned fairly early, after Mass on the next
> day, that is the Monday [27 November], they came to
> the king and entered his chamber for deliberation,
> accompanied by the archbishops, bishops, and abbots
> who were allowed to enter. After they had spent
> something like two hours in the chamber, the cardinals
> came out, and the king accompanied them outside to the
> door of the chapel, and there, as he was leaving, the lord
> king said openly, in the hearing even of the cardinals
> themselves, 'I hope that I may never set eyes on a cardinal
> again.' He dismissed them in such haste, moreover, that
> they did not wait for their own horses to come, although
> their lodging was nearby, but were given the horses which

chanced to be standing close by in front of the chapel for
their departure. And the cardinals left with at most four
men in their company. The archbishops, bishops, and
abbots, however, remained with the king, and they
entered his chamber to deliberate. After they had
remained there almost until the hour of Vespers, they
came to the cardinals' lodging, and all their faces seemed
very worried. When they had spent some time with the
cardinals, they returned to their lodgings. On the next day
[28 November], after staying with the king until the sixth
hour, they came to the cardinals, then returned to the king,
and afterwards back to the cardinals, transmitting secret
replies backwards and forwards. On the following day,
that is, on the vigil of St Andrew [29 November], the king
rose at the crack of dawn and went out to hunt with dogs
and birds of prey, deliberately absenting himself, according
to the general belief and assessment. (*CTB*, i, no. 149)

This report does not provide any information about the nature of
the discussions between the cardinals, the bishops and the king, but
it provides ample evidence of the difficulty of reaching any kind of
agreement. Having failed to bend the legates to his will, the king
effectively walked (or rather, rode) out of the discussions, leaving
the bishops to bring the proceedings to a conclusion. Unlike the earlier secret meetings, the last formal action took place in public, so that
all should hear the grievances of the king and the English bishops.

On that same day [29 November], they all gathered at
the king's chapel fairly early in the morning and went
immediately into the king's chamber; and having had a
discussion there in the king's absence, they went out to
the church, near which the cardinals had their lodgings.
There, when the cardinals had taken their seats, and
the archbishops of Rouen and York, the bishops of
Worcester, Salisbury, Bayeux, London, Chichester, and
Angoulême, numerous abbots, and a great crowd of
clergy and laity, summoned to hear what they proposed,
had seated themselves around the church, London stood
up, and his tasteless and not very graceful address gave
evidence of the agitation of his mind. He began thus. 'You
have heard that the Lord Pope's letter has been brought to
us, and we have it in our hands, in which the Lord Pope
informed us that when we were summoned by you,

we were to come to meet you, and that the case which had
arisen between the lord king and the lord of Canterbury
and between us, the bishops of England and the same
Canterbury was commissioned to you with full power.
So, after hearing of your arrival in these parts, we hurried
to meet you, entirely prepared and willing to accept
your sentence, and to initiate or answer a legal action.
Furthermore, the lord king is offering the same thing, that
he will ratify whatever sentence you pronounce between
himself and the lord of Canterbury. Since therefore neither
the lord king nor you nor we have taken any action to
impede the fulfilment of the Lord Pope's mandate, let the
blame be placed where it should.' (*CTB*, i, no. 149)

Foliot, of course, was shifting the blame for the failure of the
negotiations on to Becket and the legates; but his grounds were
weak. The papal mandate, 'which he held in his hands', and which
announced the imminent appointment of 'dignitaries from our presence with full power' to decide the questions at issue between them
and the archbishop, had been issued on 1 December 1166,[34] and had
been superseded by events. William and Otto had not come as judges
and could not compel the archbishop of Canterbury to litigate. Denied
the hoped-for trial, Gilbert Foliot launched a second appeal. Its purpose, as before, was to paralyse the archbishop's disciplinary powers, but the bishop presented particular grievances of his own, which
would have been presented in the trial that never was. One was the
preposterous charge that Becket had taken 'about sixty churches'
from his jurisdiction. This allegation referred to the deanery of
Arches, an ancient Canterbury 'peculiar' in the London diocese, over
which the archbishop and not the bishop had jurisdiction. In most
cases, the subordination of the churches within the deanery to
Canterbury dated from pre-Conquest times, and to allege that
Becket had 'taken about sixty churches from his jurisdiction' was
dishonest.[35] Even more significantly, however, was Foliot's declaration that the king had intended to include the Chancery incomes in
his case against Becket: 'the king is demanding from you 44,000
marks of silver on account of the incomes which were entrusted to
you when you were Chancellor.'[36] Henry and Foliot had hoped for
compliant judges, who would find Thomas guilty on as many counts
as possible and depose him by papal authority. The court party was
understandably furious that the cardinals' power had been curtailed
and that the archbishop had eluded the trap they thought they had
prepared.

The legates seem to have remained at Henry's court for five more days, but to no avail, although as they were leaving (on 5 December), he made an emotional appeal to them

> to intercede on his behalf with the Lord Pope to free him
> from [Becket] entirely; and he wept uncontrollably in the
> presence of the cardinals and the others; and lord William
> the cardinal was seen also to weep. Lord Otto could
> hardly keep himself from laughing.

William of Pavia's distress and Otto of Brescia's mirth reflect their divergent attitudes to the case. William had set out from Rome in May with high hopes of being able to negotiate a settlement. He may even have made some kind of promise to the king, and his total failure would have been a matter of genuine grief. Otto had, if anything, favoured the archbishop, and he probably concluded that Henry's tears were false. The bishops of London and Salisbury, and Geoffrey Ridel, archdeacon of Canterbury, renewed their own appeals; King Henry sent a large and imposing embassy to the Curia, including Master Henry Pium of Northampton, Reginald FitzJocelin, Clarembald of St Augustine's and Simon of La Châtre; Cardinal William sent a secret message to the pope by the hands of an unnamed relative of Master Lombard of Piacenza; and the cardinals, no doubt at the request of the king and bishops, expressed Henry II's furious rage and formally instructed Becket to defer to the appeal and to desist from any disciplinary action in the meantime.[37]

Becket's dismay at this outcome, which opened up the prospect of endless delays and endless exile for him and the 400 exiled with him, was poured out in another letter to the pope, carried by Master Alexander Walensis, who had been his cross-bearer at Northampton, and Master John Planeta. They, no doubt, carried much more in their memories, and their eyewitness reports of how the cardinals had proceeded would have added considerably to the weight of the written message. Its focus, however, was on William of Pavia. Although the cardinals had withdrawn from the court, they had not left the region; and Becket was still fearful that Pavia might yet make some kind of accommodation in accordance with the king's wishes.[38] What particularly alarmed him was that Cardinal William had hinted to King Henry that the pope might be willing to translate him to another see, and he sent a special courier to overtake Alexander and John with an adamant rejection of the idea:

> Let the Lord Pope and our other friends know – and
> continually and firmly remind them – that we would

rather allow ourselves to be killed ... than allow ourselves
to be thrown down from our mother the church of
Canterbury while yet we live .... (*CTB*, i, no. 161)

It was in this context that he dispatched a fierce denunciation to
Cardinal William himself, which opened with the words: 'I did not
believe that you would set me up for sale in the market place so that
you could make a profit on my blood and make a name and reputation for yourself from the price of iniquity.'[39] Not the way to make
friends or influence people, it would seem, yet Cardinal William did
shift his position towards Becket in the aftermath of his encounters
with King Henry.

Who was to blame for the impasse? All sides, perhaps. Henry had
hoped for compliant judges who would duly find Becket guilty and
perhaps depose him, or at least arrange his transfer to a see outside
his domains. Either way, he would be free of the troublesome archbishop and the path would be open to appoint a more compliant
prelate – Foliot, perhaps, or one of his loyal clerks – and the
Constitutions would remain firmly in place. Anything less was
unacceptable. The episcopal opposition, also, wanted Becket out. As
for the archbishop, he was committed to defending both his position
and his cause. He could have capitulated and accepted a safe see, but
what would become of the cause for which he was contending? The
two were bound up together. If he were deposed or translated, the
cause would be lost. Unless compelled by direct papal mandate,
then, he would have been foolish indeed to submit himself either to
the judgment of a man whom he did not trust or to the mercy of a
king who 'wanted his head on a platter'. And the legates themselves
found that their hands were effectively tied. As for Alexander III, the
year 1167 saw him propelled along by the tides of imperial advance
and retreat in Italy, the conflicting pressures of two kings and the
contradictory arguments of an exiled archbishop and an adamantly
hostile episcopal clique. As long as an imperial anti-pope remained,
there was the risk of an even greater schism, but if he pleased King
Henry, he would alienate King Louis. In any case, he was politic
enough to know that once a favour has been given it loses its value.
No man remembers past favours when he is pressing for new ones.

So the carousel began another turn. Just as at the end of 1166, so
now, at the end of 1167, Thomas of Canterbury found his hands
tied by yet another appeal, not against something that he had done,
but something that he might do; and the cardinal legates had turned
out to be broken reeds.

7

God's honour and my order

If legates *a latere* were afraid to displease the English king, then it was unlikely that Alexander, nearly a thousand miles away in Benevento, would be emboldened to take strong action. His initial response to the first set of reports from Normandy was to repeat his earlier virtually impossible advice. On 30 January 1168 he sent a short advisory note to Becket, the core message of which was, much as before,

> you may not work to restore peace with the English king
> in any way which leads to the abasement and reduction
> of ecclesiastical honour. Nevertheless, you should strive
> by all means to recover his grace and love, and humble
> yourself before him, as far as can be done, *saving the
> honour of your office and the Church's liberty*; nor should
> you fear him more than is right, or require greater
> securities from him than necessary, because, as we believe,
> from the moment he makes peace with you, he will not
> harm you in any way, or allow you to be harmed by
> anyone. (*CTB*, i, no. 162: Benevento, 30 January 1168)

Although not stated overtly in any surviving letter to the pope, fear of physical injury was not far from Becket's mind. He had refused to enter Henry's territories, despite promises of protection from the archbishop of Rouen and the Empress Matilda, because he did not trust the king. The empress had died at Rouen on 10 September 1167, however, and her death may have accentuated his unwillingness to trust himself to the tender mercies of King Henry. It is therefore likely that the messenger sent from the first meeting with the cardinals had been more explicit.

Any assessment of his attitude must take into account Henry II's reputation. It is clear from the words and actions of Cardinals William and Otto, the former of whom was counted as a friend of the king, that they were afraid to do or say anything that might inspire his fearsome *ira*. At the very least, he could withdraw his protection. He needed only to let it be known that the cardinals had offended his honour and they would not have been safe on the roads of Normandy. It is unlikely that they would have been murdered, but robbery, mistreatment, imprisonment or being held to ransom were all within the arsenal of possibilities. Becket, as a proclaimed traitor, was even more vulnerable. The treatment meted out to the Welsh hostages in 1165 was unlikely to inspire confidence.[1] Only his own calculation of the effect on his reputation could restrain the king. Alternatively, critics say, Becket should have been willing to sacrifice himself to bring the dispute to an end. But from his perspective, his death, or imprisonment, or translation to another see, would have handed Henry the Constitutions of Clarendon on a plate and left the English Church even more at his mercy than it already was.

Alexander, meanwhile, continued the policy of maintaining a delicate balance between the contesting sides. During late April and early May 1168 he issued a series of letters relating to the English crisis, in an intricate balancing act, which, although it conceded little of substance to either side, nevertheless marked a subtle shift in Becket's favour. In late April, he rebuked the English bishops for their disobedience to the archbishop of Canterbury, but, 'at the wish of our dearest son Henry, illustrious king of the English and swayed by the insistent pleas of his envoys', he released them from prosecuting the second appeal, which they had launched on 29 November 1167;[2] and on 16 and 19 May respectively, he ordered Christ Church to accept a prior chosen by the archbishop, condemned the *prava consuetudo* of lay investiture of clergy, quashed all grants made in that way, ordered all who had received ecclesiastical offices through lay intervention to resign them and assign their incomes to the diocesan bishops, and ordered the bishops to excommunicate within 40 days any cleric who refused to obey the mandate.[3] Probably at the same time he ordered John Cumin to give up the archdeaconry of Bath, which he had secured through lay action,[4] and mandated Bishop Roger of Worcester to return to his church only if he were able to discharge his episcopal functions freely, without observing 'those evil customs', but he was not to risk imprisonment.[5] In the light of Becket's fears of detention or worse, this advice to the king's own cousin is very telling.

Simultaneously, the pope responded to the imposing embassy that the king had sent after the failure of the legates' mission. If there was any doubt about the king's disposition towards Becket, the message his envoys gave orally to the pope should dispel all doubts. They said, as Alexander repeated in his letter, that the king 'was so greatly agitated that [he] could not in any way receive the archbishop of Canterbury into his grace nor was there any way that his opinion could be softened.' In order to give divine grace time to mitigate the king's temper, however, he declared that Becket's powers would be restricted until peace was made. And he frankly explained the difference between what he had said in his earlier letters to King Henry and the performance of Cardinals William and Otto by a change of mind on his part, in the expectation of a negotiated peace.[6] To Thomas, meanwhile, he sent yet another letter of restriction, to last until Easter (1169). Its terms, however, reveal that Henry's envoys had threatened the withdrawal of obedience (and perhaps something worse) if the king's petitions were refused.

> Your discretion has already heard that Henry, illustrious
> king of the English, sent his messengers to us, and what
> hard and harsh things he sought from us through them ...
> putting forward terrible threats, if we did not give way to
> his will ... (*CTB*, ii, no. 166: Benevento, 19 May 1167)

The delay between the reception of Henry's envoys (late February?) and the issue of this batch of replies suggests that the papal Curia anguished over the best way to respond to the contradictory pressures being applied by the kings of England and France, to say nothing of the numerous defences of Becket that had been launched by Louis VII and members of the French Church and nobility. It is possible that the Sicilian court was also engaged on Becket's behalf. At the end of 1167 he had sent two letters to Sicily. The first, addressed to Stephen of Perche, the Norman nobleman who had just become archbishop-elect of Palermo and chancellor of the kingdom, begged him to use his influence; the second, to the English-born Richard Palmer, bishop-elect of Syracuse, criticized William of Pavia.[7] These two men were at that time major players in the Norman kingdom, where they were the leading advisers of the queen mother, Margaret, who was governing the kingdom during the minority of her son, William II. Since the papacy was even more dependent on the Sicilians than he was on the kings of England and France – it was being supported by Sicilian gold – and the city of Benevento was an enclave within Sicilian territory, support from that quarter was very valuable indeed. John of Salisbury reported to Baldwin of Exeter that Henry II's envoys had tried to persuade the Sicilians to their side, but were defeated by envoys from France.[8] Becket, in fact, commended his nephew Gilbert to both of them; and other Canterbury exiles found refuge in the south.[9] Louis VII's envoys, at any rate, made it clear that their lord would not tolerate a shameful abandonment of his protégé. The Curia had therefore to keep finding ways of squaring the circle. Henry II had to be mollified; Thomas of Canterbury had to be given just enough support to keep him safe; formal confirmation of Clarendon had to be avoided; and the king of France (and perhaps the Sicilian court and even the count of Flanders) had to be assured of the papacy's integrity in respect of the English matter. Moreover, the eyes of the whole Western Church were now on the dispute.

The second mission: Simon, prior of Mont-Dieu, Bernard de Corilon, prior of Le Bois de Vincennes, and Engelbert, prior of Val-Saint-Pierre, 1168–1169

In this almost impossible predicament, the Curia came up with another scheme. Formal adjudication had been abandoned before William and Otto had set out for Normandy in the previous May, so the way of religious persuasion was adopted. Two parallel commissions of monastic leaders were appointed: Basileus, prior of La Grande Chartreuse, and Anthelme de Chignin, the Carthusian bishop of Belley, formed one; the Carthusian Simon, prior of Mont-Dieu, the Grandmontine Bernard de Corilon, prior of Le Bois de Vincennes (perhaps representing Louis VII), and another Carthusian, Engelbert, prior of Val-Saint-Pierre, formed the other. Both orders were high in Henry II's esteem and, unlike the Cistercians, neither was contaminated with support of Becket. In order to avoid the problems of distance from the Curia, they were provided with alternative letters of admonition and commination addressed to Henry II, which they were to use sequentially.[10] In the milder of the two, after reminding the king how far he had given way to him in the matter of his venerable brother (he hoped not contrary to justice) and prevented him from uttering sentences against the king or his kingdom, Alexander hoped that God would so far soften the king's heart that he would be prepared to honour God in the archbishop, in accordance with the advice of the religious and God-fearing men whom he was sending.[11] The stronger letter is much fiercer. It informs the king that the pope had borne with his obduracy long enough and that he will not silence the archbishop of Canterbury any longer. If the king does not listen to the advice of the 'religious men', then he 'will dread what will come.'[12] The mandate to the commissioners set the following Easter (1169) as the deadline for lifting the restrictions on the archbishop's powers.

The pope may have thought that the monastic leaders would have more success than their eminent predecessors. They were all French; they did not come from the Curia; and they were able to approach the king more directly on the spiritual plane. Unfortunately, however, whatever hope there may have been was undermined by the swift return of the king's envoys (Master Henry Pium of Northampton, Reginald FitzJocelin of Salisbury, Clarembald of St Augustine's and Simon of La Châtre). With their one gain, they had travelled back from Benevento much more quickly than they had gone out, and from them rumours of the extension of his suspension reached Becket by the end of June; and again, as in mid-1167, he wrote in pained protest. This time, however, he was able to use Master Lombard of Piacenza as his mouthpiece. That man had become a rising star in the Curial firmament, a skilled lawyer and no doubt a keen observer of the Norman-French scene. He had been with Becket at Northampton, had fled with him from England; and was in a perfect position to explain in the Curia what really was at stake.

Meanwhile King Henry delightedly published the announcement of Becket's suspension[13] at an assembly at La Ferté Bernard at the beginning of July, and broadcast the welcome news that Becket's authority was again restrained. As before there was widespread consternation in what one may call the 'Becket camp', and an avalanche of protests, from Becket himself,[14] from Louis VII,[15] William aux Blanchesmains (bishop-elect of Chartres and soon to be archbishop of Sens), Stephen, bishop of Meaux, Queen Adela[16] and Matthew, precentor of Sens. This cleric had just returned from Benevento, where he had secured papal approval for the elevation of the bishop-elect of Chartres to the archbishopric of Sens. His extremely interesting letter of protest reminds Alexander of the secret message he had transmitted on the pope's behalf to the French king, urging him to remain firm in his hope for Canterbury's relief, even if the English king's envoys should secure something damaging to the archbishop. When Louis learned that *Excellentie tue nuntios* had been read out before an assembly of bishops, he accused Matthew of lying and declared that the Roman Church could not be trusted![17]

So strong was Becket's feeling that he broke with his usual formal practice and wrote to the pope in the first person singular to emphasize the anguish of his spirit: 'My soul, father, is overwhelmed in bitterness, for together with my unfortunate fellow-exiles I have been made a thing of shame to men and rejected by the people by the letters in which you were pleased to suspend us.' And he pointed out, again, that he could have had a splendid career 'if I had been willing to leave God's Church unprotected and acquiesce in his will. Indeed, I could have flourished and luxuriated in the riches and delights of the realm, feared, courted, and honoured by all.'[18]

David Knowles spoke of 'the ennui of the reader' with 'the frequent repetition in different letters of similar narratives and similar arguments', many of which 'consist of a stream of words carrying a minimum of factual information.'[19] Modern readers certainly find the constant repetition of Becket's anguish not only tedious but also embarrassing. Such letters, however, were only the formal dressing for the real message – for the detailed report that the messenger could speak with his own lips from his own observation. The letter's function was to accredit the envoy and express in the high-flown rhetorical style being taught in the best schools (Orléans and Paris, for example) the broad lines of their author's position. Every mission to the Curia had to carry such letters, and since the circumstances repeated themselves again and again in the Becket dispute, the letters of protest revolved around the same fears and grievances. A short matter-of-fact note saying, 'this is Master John Planeta, my clerk: you can trust what he says in my name', would not have cut much ice in the papal Curia; and the stronger the emotion, the more powerful the rhetorical language had to be.

Alexander's reply, issued on 9 October, said that if Henry II 'had caused the letter to be carefully read from the beginning to its end, and understood it in its entirety, he would not truly have found in it any justification for insulting either us or you'; and he confirmed that Becket's powers would be restored as promised, but that he was waiting for a report from the religious men he had commissioned.[20] The pope also responded to King Louis' protests, in the same vein, explaining that he was treating Henry II like a wise physician, but that he had not changed his opinion about the archbishop and would restore his powers, without right of appeal, on the specified day.[21] To Henry II, however, also on 9 October, he wrote a circumlocutional letter, referring obliquely to the Becket affair, which he said he would be happy to discuss with him if they were able to meet. The pope was in Benevento, and that hope could have been realized only if Henry went on crusade and travelled by way of Sicily (as his son Richard was later to do). The letter also took up the particular complaints that Becket had made in late November 1167 about the king's failure to allow the filling of five vacant sees (Lincoln, Bath, Hereford, Bangor and St Asaph), which he lists.[22] In what was an oblique assault on Clause 12 of the Constitutions, Alexander advises Henry not to confuse the rights of Caesar with those of God, and to permit free and canonical elections to take place: 'Nor should you desire to nominate a person to those who are to make the election.' And he went as far as to end the letter with a threat: 'Otherwise ... we shall not be able hold back the hands of St Peter and ourselves from doing you an injury.'[23]

That Alexander should have taken such particular care to ensure the execution of the mission and to choose monastic leaders of such eminence (Anthelme was later canonized) suggests that this was not a delaying tactic. Every effort seems to have been made to find mediators who were beyond reproach from either side. Neither party could suspect that any of them were in the other's pocket. Moreover, even the king of England would not think it beneath his dignity to treat with such unworldly men, who came from the most austere religious orders of the period, Chartreuse and Grandmont. The latter was a particular favourite of Henry II, for its headquarters was in the Limousin, and he had such regard for its saintly founder that when he was taken seriously ill in 1170 he asked to be buried at the feet of St Stephen Muret.[24] In the event, and probably by agreement, it was Simon the Carthusian and Bernard the Grandmontine, supported by another Carthusian, Engelbert, prior of Val-Saint-Pierre in Picardy, who executed the papal mandate. Even more importantly, however, the pope had skilfully shifted the ground. There was no question of trial or judgment. All reference, both to the king's case against Becket (relating to the chancellorship) and to the bishops' second appeal, was dropped. This cleared away the possibility of condemnation or deposition. The whole focus was on the necessary conditions upon which reconciliation and repatriation could take place.

Conference at Montmirail, 6–7 January 1169

The commissioners were certainly punctilious in carrying out their instructions and they achieved more than had been thought possible a few months before. Not only did they arrange a formal meeting between the king and the archbishop – the first since the council of Northampton in October 1164 – but they were able to engage in the process virtually everyone who was interested in the matter, for the encounter took place at a peace conference between Kings Louis and Henry, which was held at Montmirail, a border town in the county of Chartres on 6–7 January 1169. Apart from a meeting in the presence of the pope himself, the context could not have been more high profile. The Montmirail conference was the equivalent of a summit meeting between the kings of England and France, where the two monarchs entered into a series of accords intended to secure the future of Henry's continental territories, the inheritances of his sons and mutual harmony between the two realms. It was to be sealed by the marriage of Henry's third son, Richard, to Louis' daughter, Alais. Henry's eldest son, the younger Henry, was recognized as seneschal of France. The two Henrys paid homage to Louis for Normandy; the younger Henry paid homage for Brittany, Maine and Anjou; Richard paid homage for Poitou and Guienne; and Geoffrey was to hold Brittany from the younger Henry. Both royal courts were present, attended by a large gathering of nobles and ecclesiastics from the two realms. It was at this great gathering that Simon, Bernard and Engelbert, acting on the mandate of the milder papal letter,[25] presented Thomas before the king on the feast of the Epiphany (6 January). The formal report of Simon and Engelbert, which was supported by an oral statement to Master Lombard of Piacenza by the Grandmontine Bernard de Corilo, the rules of whose order forbade him to write to the pope on any matter, is the most authoritative account of the proceedings.

> Constrained by the counsel of the king [of France] and of the archbishops, bishops and barons, the archbishop assented and in the presence of all he came to the king of England and, kneeling, placed himself [in the mercy] of God and the king, to the honour of God and the king, using this form of words that he might thus be able to earn his peace and grace. But the king refused to receive him because of the phrase, *ad honorem Dei* (for the honour of God), saying aloud that it should not appear that the archbishop wished to preserve God's honour, and the king not; but after saying much more (would that he had kept silence) he said that the was seeking nothing from the archbishop except that as priest and bishop he

would promise him in the word of truth and without subterfuge (*in verbo veritatis et sine [malo] ingenio*) in the presence of everyone that he would keep the customs which holy archbishops of Canterbury had kept for their kings, and which the archbishop had himself promised him on another occasion. But the archbishop replied that he had done fealty to the king, in which he was bound by oath to preserve his life, limbs, and earthly honour, *salvo ordine suo* (saving his [own] order), and that he was ready to fulfil that oath very faithfully, nor had anything more been required by any of his predecessors nor was it exacted from anyone. And when the king had insisted strongly on this point, the lord of Canterbury added that, although none of his predecessors had done or promised this, nor was he in any way bound by law to do it, he said that for the Church's peace and for his grace he would promise to keep those customs which his holy predecessors had kept to their kings, *salvo ordine suo*, as far as he could according to God; and that, to recover his affection, he would do whatever he could *salvo ordine suo*, claiming that he had never served him more willingly than he would now, if it pleased him. The king refused to accept this, unless he promised observance of the customs to him precisely and absolutely under oath, because he was demanding nothing more from him. Because the archbishop refused to do this, although many urged it, the king withdrew, with the peace unconcluded. (*MTB*, vi, no. 451: Montmirail, *c.* 7 January 1169)

Although this formal résumé accurately conveys the *acta* of the interview – rather as the minutes of a meeting record the conclusions reached – it does not capture the highly charged atmosphere or the pressure put on Becket to suppress his caveats. For that we have to turn to the long report that John of Salisbury sent to Bishop Bartholomew of Exeter and to Herbert of Bosham's account in his later Life of Becket. The king let it be known to members of Becket's entourage, but not formally, that all he wanted was an honourable reconciliation, so that he could then go off on crusade. Henry, it seems, made the most of the public forum to appear alternately severe and mild and reasonable; and his demand for absolute acceptance of the customs 'which saintly archbishops of Canterbury had observed to his predecessors' seemed eminently reasonable, even to

Louis of France, who is said to have asked Becket, 'My lord, do you wish to be more than a saint?' In Bosham's words, 'They one and all entreated, urged, and advised the archbishop to suppress the tiny little phrase, *saving God's honour*, so that he and his might soon obtain peace, to their honour and glory in the sight of the kings and princes.' Herbert says that he himself, as one of the learned entourage, particularly urged the archbishop to stick to his guns, since he had bitterly regretted dropping the phrase *saving his order* at Clarendon.[26] If some at least of Becket's advisers were pressing for the retention of some kind of saving phrase, the king's clerks – *his* learned men – were, according to John of Salisbury, another eyewitness, equally pressing the king to insist on its removal.[27] No names are given, but one can imagine who they are likely to have been: John of Oxford, Geoffrey Ridel and perhaps Richard of Ilchester.

Certainly, the Montmirail interview was the best hope so far, and peace – some kind of peace – was within Becket's grasp. But historians must ponder whether he was justified in holding out. Was it just another manifestation of his pride and arrogance – as the king claimed and as many historians think – or was he, as Herbert and John thought, justified in his caution? On the one hand, it is surely clear that whatever form of words Henry used in public, his principal aim remained formal and unqualified confirmation of the Constitutions of Clarendon, and his opposition to *saving God's honour* or *saving my order* derived from that overriding motive. As long as the king insisted on the Constitutions and Thomas tried to find a formula that would reserve the Church's position in respect of them, no peace could be made. Should he have thrown himself unreservedly on the king's mercy? The answer will depend partly on how King Henry II is judged and partly on the importance given to the Constitutions themselves.

After the painful meeting at Montmirail, Thomas wrote a very short personal appeal to the king, re-stating his willingness to agree to the king's demands, *saving his order*.

> Your royal nobility may remember that I offered you in the presence of the lord king of the French, and of many others who were there, that for God's honour and yours I was ready to place myself entirely in God's mercy and yours, so that I might thus earn your peace and favour. But, my lord, that form of words did not please you, unless I promised to observe the customs which our predecessors had observed to yours. I conceded, therefore,

my lord, that I would observe them, as far as I could,
saving my order, and that if I should know of anything
else that I should promise more fully and more clearly, I
was prepared to do it, and I am still prepared to do it, to
recover your favour, and that I have never more willingly
served you than I am still prepared to do. Since it did not
please you to accept those assurances, I beg your majesty
to remember my service and the favours which you
conferred on me, for I remember that I am bound by oath
to preserve your life, limbs, and all earthly honour, and
I am prepared to do whatever I can do for you, according
to God, as for my dearest lord. God knows that I have
never served you more willingly than I shall in the future,
if it should please you. May my lord prosper for ever.
(*CTB*, ii, no. 186: after 7 January 1169)

This letter spelled out very clearly Becket's readiness to fulfil the
obligations of his homage and fealty, subject to the customary reservations allowed to prelates. Flimsy as they were, these reservations
were the only protection that stood between ecclesiastical personnel
and a potentially vindictive king. At the same time, however, he
urged the papal commissioners to present their more severe letters,
as instructed by the pope.[28]

Secretly, however, the king had already sent messengers to the
Curia (Archdeacon Reginald FitzJocelin of Salisbury, followed at a
short interval by Archdeacon Ralph of Llandaff), whose mission was
to convince the pope of the king's readiness, at last, to allow Becket's
repatriation, on the understanding that he would perform his full
duty as archbishop of Canterbury, as his predecessors had done, and
obtain a papal mandate to the archbishop to accept the proffered
peace. If a great assembly of nobles and bishops had been unable to
induce Thomas to concede, then the pope might be persuaded to use
his authority to end the affair.[29] It was unlikely, therefore, that the
king would make any concessions while that embassy was pending.

Conference at Saint-Léger-en-Ivelines, 7 February 1169

Nevertheless, a month after the Montmirail meeting, on 7 February
at Saint-Léger-en-Ivelines, he did accept the second, comminatory
letter, and in what was virtually a re-run of the exchanges at

Montmirail, Henry rehearsed his attitude to Becket and his requirements for peace. The commissioners' report records their exasperation at the king's wordplay. It was impossible to tie him down to any specific undertaking in respect of Thomas. It is probable that he was only going through the motions, and that, short of a capitulation by the archbishop, there was little chance of agreement between them. After emphasizing that he had not expelled the lord of Canterbury from his realm, he declared that, nevertheless,

> out of respect for the lord Pope [the archbishop] could return to England and there have peace, if he is willing to do what he should for me, and *to keep for me what his predecessors observed for mine, and those things which he promised* ... And because he frequently changed his answers, we asked if the archbishop was permitted to return to his see and enjoy his peace. *To this he replied that the archbishop would never enter his kingdom before he did for him what he should and promise that he would observe what the others observed and which he had promised*. Then we asked if he would write and seal his response in letters patent, because we needed to be able to send a reliable response to you, which we did not yet have, because he was changing his replies so often, But he would not agree to this ... (*MTB*, vi, no. 464)

This report from Simon and Engelbert, who had no particular axe to grind in respect of Henry and Becket, deserves to be considered very carefully. Not only does it demonstrate King Henry's slipperiness, it confirms that whatever form of words he used, the sworn maintenance of the Constitutions of Clarendon was his overriding aim. Becket's own letter to the pope said much the same, and emphasized the dangers inherent in making an open commitment. More importantly, however, it reveals that Becket's insistence on the standard reservations had been mandated by the pope himself. The archbishop had been tricked into a dangerous open-ended commitment at Clarendon. He was not to make the same mistake again.[30]

The intervention of John of Poitiers

Similarly fruitless, because of Becket's opposition, was the attempt by Bishop John of Poitiers to find a way round the impasse. John was an old friend and a skilful diplomat. He had weathered his own storm with King Henry in Poitou and had a good chance of devising a compromise. With respect to the phrases that caused the rupture of the peace, he tried to persuade both king and archbishop to submit the peace formula to the judgment of bishops from Henry's continental dominions, naming himself, the archbishop of Rouen and the bishops of Le Mans and Séez as possibilities. Becket rejected that proposal, requesting instead an interview with the king. Henry's response was characteristically evasive. John reported that Henry 'would observe God's honour in the first place and then his own and his realm's, and that he would provide for you in such a way that he would not injure your person, *as far as he reasonably could*', and he proposed a meeting in the environs of Tours on 22 February. Thomas, however, would have none of it, reproachfully telling his friend that his proposals would amount to selling the pass completely, for the king would proclaim 'that we have completely and absolutely submitted ourselves to his counsel, suppressing every condition, and without reference either to God's honour or our order ... since it is his primary aim and definite purpose that they should be passed over in silence.'[31] Although Becket did not comment on it in his response to John, the clause, 'he would provide for you in such a way that he would not injure your person, *as far as he reasonably could*', must have raised Becket's suspicions to fever pitch.

Meanwhile, as Easter 1169 was approaching, and with it the restoration of his powers, his two chief episcopal adversaries, Gilbert Foliot and Jocelin of Salisbury, made another pre-emptive strike, by appealing yet again against the risk that he would impose a sentence of excommunication or interdict on the king, the realm, the bishops or their churches, setting the octave of the Purification (9 February 1170) as the term. As before, they were principally concerned with their own vulnerability; as before, they sought to include the whole English Church and the king under its umbrella, although there is no evidence that they even went through the pretence of consulting anyone outside their own circle before taking action[32] – although they did try, unsuccessfully, to widen the constituency two months later. This time, however, with his authority restored at Easter, Becket did not defer to the appeal, considering it specious. In a spectacular replication of the Vézelay sentences, he went to Clairvaux, one of the leading Cistercian houses, and there, on Palm Sunday (13 April 1169), he issued a set of excommunications, which included the two bishops, seven occupiers of Canterbury property, including Randulf de Broc (the 'custodian' of the see), his brother Robert, Nigel de Sackville and also Earl Hugh of Norfolk. Foliot was denounced for his 'disloyalty clothed in the cloak of religion' and 'treachery'. The excommunication of Hugh of Norfolk was of course a breach of Clause 7 of Clarendon, which forbade excommunication or interdict of tenants in chief of the crown without prior royal consent; but it was also an attempt to bring to an end the long-running dispute between the canons of Pentney in Norfolk and William de Wall, a tenant of the earl of Norfolk, who had expelled them from their property on the grounds that his father had not given it to them. The controversy had already involved appeals to the pope and a papal excommunication of the earl and his tenant in July 1166, which had not been effective.[33] In addition, a further six, headed by Geoffrey Ridel, Richard of Ilchester and Richard de Lucy, were threatened with excommunication on 29 May (Ascension Day) if they did not in the meantime make satisfaction to the archbishop. He also threatened with the same sentence whole categories of unnamed individuals: occupiers of Canterbury property, those who advised the king on his anti-ecclesiastical policies and those who prevented the execution of papal and archiepiscopal mandates. Altogether, it was a very comprehensive list and included many of the king's leading advisers and administrators.

Was this another precipitate and foolhardy action? It certainly enraged the king; but he was already wholly opposed to Becket's return except on the most humiliating terms. It did produce three positive consequences. It showed that Henry's watch and ward was porous; that Becket's disciplinary power could be used effectively; and, most surprisingly and significantly, that the attitude of the other English bishops was changing dramatically in his favour. This last was demonstrated most graphically in mid-May, when an attempt was made at an assembly at Northampton to persuade the rest of the episcopate to join London and Salisbury in renewing their appeal on the octave of Whitsun (15 May). The attempt failed. Not only did it transpire that Henry of Winchester had already published the Clairvaux sentences and was refusing to have any contact with the excommunicated, but that Bartholomew of Exeter was also obeying the decrees. Neither wanted anything to do with the proposed appeal. The bishop of Winchester did not even attend the council, using the excuse of age to avoid involvement. Bartholomew was more circumspect, but equally reluctant. If all the bishops agreed that it would be to the advantage of God's church, and the king allowed him to go abroad to prosecute it, then he would be willing to appeal 'against not actual but feared oppression'; but he thought that 'a special protection could be obtained against all appeal', and, 'if he were to learn that this were so, then he would obediently accept the sentence laid upon him by his pastor.' In this roundabout way Bartholomew was indicating both that he considered the Clairvaux sentences valid and that he was willing to accept Becket's disciplinary mandates. Foliot 'ridiculed his scruples' but made no headway, and 'Exeter was thenceforward outside the synagogue.' Even Hugh of Durham would not be drawn into the action. He said that he had not been consulted nor had he heard anything about the first appeal, but that 'he would discuss the matter with his own metropolitan, and would then prudently do whatever was lawful, *saving God's order and his own*' – a carefully phrased statement that echoed Becket's much repeated *saving my order*.

What induced this change of heart? The whole concept of appeal *ad cautelam* was novel. Moreover, if used more generally, it could have the effect of paralysing all ecclesiastical discipline. Becket's spiritual authority depended on the same foundations as that of his episcopal colleagues. They were bishops, too; and if their clerical subjects – priests, deacons, archdeacons, abbots and priors – could launch such appeals against their ordinary jurisdiction, then their disciplinary powers would evaporate. It is also possible that they were not very happy with Foliot's close association with Henry II. They knew as well as the Becket party that Foliot had been the architect of the first appeal in 1166, which only a few of them had sealed, and that the appeal had been launched to tie the archbishop's hands. We do not know how widely Becket's letters were circulated, or how extensively John of Salisbury's arguments were transmitted through the clerical order, but the king's treatment of Becket's clerks' families, his implacable hostility to Thomas and his insistence on the full operation of the Constitutions of Clarendon were not likely to be popular. They could also see that the king had failed to have Becket condemned, deposed or translated, despite his strongest efforts. Thomas was still archbishop and legate, and the tide was turning in Alexander's favour. It may also be that the bishops felt bold enough to stand out against the pressure because King Henry was not only overseas, but in the far south, in Gascony, and he had been out of the kingdom since late March/April 1166. News of the Clairvaux sentences had percolated into England by the time of the Northampton meeting, and some bishops, at least, were executing the sentences; this means that they were publishing the excommunications and observing them themselves.

Some two weeks after the Northampton assembly, the letters containing Gilbert Foliot's excommunication and its notification

addressed to the dean, archdeacon and clergy of London were
dramatically delivered to the celebrant in St Paul's Cathedral on
Ascension Day (29 May 1169), the very day on which Becket's second wave of excommunications became effective. An eyewitness
who wrote under a pseudonym to avoid detection sent a lively
dispatch to Becket in Sens:

> I have deemed it appropriate to bring to your notice how
> Berengar handed over your letters in the church of St Paul
> on Ascension Thursday [29 May]. After the Gospel had
> been read, as I stood by and watched, the messenger came
> to the altar and thrust your letters into the hand of the
> priest, named Vitalis[34] – who thought that he was about
> to receive an offering from him – and tightly held his
> hand and the letters, commanding him in the Lord's name
> and yours to give one letter to the bishop and the other
> to the dean,[35] and not to proceed with the celebration of
> Mass until the letters had been read. He called William of
> Northolt,[36] who had read the Gospel on Ascension Day,
> to witness what he said, enjoining him similarly in your
> name not to participate in the Mass until the letters were
> read, and he said the same to the sub-deacon, William
> Hog.[37] After this, Berengar turned to the congregation
> and said in a loud voice: 'Know that Bishop Gilbert of
> London has been excommunicated by Thomas, archbishop
> of Canterbury and legate of the Apostolic See.' ... The
> priest refused to celebrate the Mass against your
> prohibition, and William of Northolt refused to serve it.
> William notified these things to Archdeacon Nicholas,[38]
> who responded, 'Would the priest stop eating if a man
> told him in the archbishop's name not to eat?' And the
> Mass was said, with the letters being read only privately,
> as I heard. (*CTB*, ii, no. 207: after 1 June 1169)[39]

The news of this unwelcome event was transmitted to Bishop
Gilbert in his Stepney manor, about a mile to the east of the City.
The bishop was clearly stunned. For a second time an archiepiscopal
sentence had been served on him in his own cathedral church; and,
having failed to build the bulwark of a general appeal, he could not
simply ignore a personal excommunication issued by a man who
was now legate of the apostolic see. Instead, he set about organizing
the strongest defence he could. First, he summoned a convocation of
London clergy on 31 May 1169, where Vitalis handed the letters to

the bishop and the dean of St Paul's. 'Enraged by the bitterness of his spite, the bishop knitted his eyebrows and read the letter, the words scarcely escaping from his lips', and sought to defend himself from the published sentence by claiming (rather weakly) that London had good claims to metropolitan status independent of Canterbury in its own right; that Becket could not exercise legatine authority since he had not entered the land to which it applied; and that the sentence was invalid because he had not been judicially condemned. He then renewed his appeal, supported by dean and chapter of St Paul's and the archdeacon and priests of London; significantly, the canons of St Bartholomew's, St Martin's and Holy Trinity refused to join the appeal.[40] He then called a wider meeting of ecclesiastics on 7 June, the details of which are unknown, and he sent Master Henry Pium of Northampton to seek Henry II's support for his action and permission to go abroad to await the return of his envoys. As before,[41] the bishop sought the king's gracious support in his difficulties – 'recalling your and our injury, may your royal clemency bring us aid in our great need' – and implored the king to write to the pope in support of his appeal. Henry, then at St Machaire in Gascony, duly complied with Gilbert's requests, authorizing his exit from England and even offering to pay all his travelling expenses:

> I have heard the injury which that traitor Thomas my
> enemy has imposed on you and other people in my realm,
> which I bear no less ill than if he had spewed out his
> poison against my own person. Know for certain
> therefore that I shall do all I can, through the lord Pope
> and the king of the French and all my friends to see that
> he is not able to harm us or our kingdom in the future.
> Therefore I wish and advise that you should not be
> disturbed in spirit in any way ... if you come to me and
> if you wish to go to Rome, I shall supply you with all
> necessaries for the journey, honourably and sufficiently.
> (*MTB*, vi, no. 505)

He duly sent a letter of vehement denunciation to the pope, requesting annulment of the sentences against the bishops of London and Salisbury, and those threatened against members of his household, issued without judicial process.[42] Meanwhile, Foliot assembled a dossier of testimonials for his clerk, Master David of London, to take with him to the Curia – from the dean of St Paul's (Hugh de Mareni), seven abbots (Westminster, Ramsey, Chertsey, Llanthony Secunda, Reading, St Osyth's and Stratford Langthorne) and one prior (Holy Trinity Aldgate), to which were added letters by Rotrou of Rouen and Arnulf of Lisieux.[43] Deprived of the support of his episcopal colleagues, Gilbert was driven to rely on his monastic confrères. They did not join in the appeal, however; they merely wrote letters testifying to the good character of the bishop and declaring their belief that he had not done anything to harm the archbishop.

Meanwhile, of course, the king's envoys had presented the king's proposals to the pope in Benevento. His response, as before, was to deflect the king's petitions by appointing another papal mission, this time to comprise not cardinals but two rising Curial officials, the subdeacon Gratian and Master Vivian of Orvieto. They were nominated in a letter to the king on 28 February,[44] although, as before, it would be many months before they reached Normandy; indeed, he did not even issue the letters informing Becket of their appointment until 10 May, when he urged him to suspend any sentences that he might have issued in the meantime, and on 11 May he again asked Thomas to spare Jocelin of Salisbury until the nuncios' arrival, and confirmed John of Oxford in the deanery of Salisbury.[45] Although in his letter of 28 February the pope had praised Henry's commitment 'to allow our venerable brother Thomas archbishop of Canterbury … to return to his own and hold his church in peace, as long as he is willing to do for you what he ought', nothing was said about restraining the archbishop's powers. Reginald and Ralph returned from their fruitless journey to find that the Clairvaux sentences had been promulgated, and Ralph was sent back immediately to try to secure annulment of the sentences.[46]

Not only were Becket's letters getting into England, but information was being passed to him regularly, even if the writers hid their identities under pseudonyms. He was thus informed of Foliot's failure to bring the bishops into line and of his response to the publication of his excommunication. Such news can only have buoyed up Becket's spirits, and he went forward to drive home the attack. Foliot's raising of the spectre of metropolitical status for London enabled him to appeal to the monks of Christ Church Canterbury to support his defence of Canterbury's dignity, as he confirmed the excommunication of Archdeacon Geoffrey Ridel and his vicar Robert,[47] and released the clergy and people of Kent from their jurisdiction. At the same time, he invoked the assistance of the venerable Bishop Henry of Winchester and Roger of Worcester, congratulating the former for his resistance to the general appeal and informing the latter, then in France, that the bishops had denied communion to Gilbert Foliot and had published his excommunication throughout their dioceses; he asked both to write to the pope in defence of Canterbury's rights.[48]

Thomas may have been unexpectedly successful in imposing his sentences this time around, but their notification caused some disquiet in Benevento. By the time that news of the Clairvaux excommunications reached the pope in mid-June, he had already sent his holding letter to King Henry and committed himself to the appointment of new papal envoys. Alexander therefore expressed surprise that the archbishop had not waited for the return of his own envoys before issuing his sentences, and ordered him to suspend the sentences until the papal envoys (Gratian and Vivian) reported whether or not the king would grant his peace to the exiles. If, however, peace were not forthcoming, the sentences were to be re-imposed *ipso facto*.[49]

8

God's honour, king's honour, Becket's honour

The third mission: Masters Vivian and Gratian

The conditions of the third mission were very different from the earlier two. There was no general episcopal appeal; the archbishop's powers were not suspended, although his Clairvaux sentences were put in abeyance pending the outcome of the mission; there were significant signs of a split among the English bishops, with London and Salisbury (and probably also York) distinctly isolated, and London recognized as a royal collaborator. Moreover, the purpose of the mission was spelled out more emphatically:

> To impress upon him [Henry II], as forcefully as we can,
> that he must restore you to his peace and grace, recall you
> to your church with dignity, and preserve both to you and
> your church all your former rights and liberties, dignities
> and honours, whole and unimpaired, and allow you and
> yours to live in all peace and tranquility. (*CTB*, ii, 204:
> Benevento, 10 May 1169)

Even more importantly, the two envoys were highly trained lawyers, more likely than the monastic agents to be aware of the nuances of language and alert to Henry II's verbal gymnastics. They were also closer to the pope. Alexander described the first, Master Gratian of Pisa, as 'our subdeacon and notary, a man of honour and education, whom we hold very dear, both because of the memory of our father and predecessor of holy memory, Pope Eugenius, and from recognition of his own true faith and service'. This Gratian was Eugenius III's

nephew, a graduate of the law schools of Bologna, where he had
heard the lectures of the great Bulgarus (one of the famous 'four doc-
tors' of Roman law in the twelfth century),[1] and had from March
1168 been head of the papal chancery (*datarius*), though without the
title of chancellor, an office he held until 1178, when he became
cardinal deacon of SS. Cosma e Damiano (1178–1206).[2] There
can be no doubt that he was fully in the pope's confidence. He was
also attached to the Becket circle, however, through John of
Salisbury, whom he had met at Ferentino in 1150–51, when another
'Englishman', Baldwin of Exeter, was appointed as his tutor.[3]
Moreover, his respect for Becket was manifested at the beginning of
the mission, when he announced his arrival in France with a letter
accompanied by a gift. Thomas replied with a request for admission
to his friendship circle: 'We nevertheless ask you most particularly,
if it is agreeable to you, to have us – and indeed the church of
Canterbury – as your friend.'[4] Gratian's older associate, Master
Vivian of Orvieto, was also a trusted agent of the pope, whom he
loved 'with the sincere affection of our heart for his long-standing
friendship, prudence, and education'. In 1169 he was a jurisconsult
in the Curia, and later rose to be cardinal deacon of S. Nicola
in Carcere Tulliano (May–September 1175) and cardinal priest of
S. Stefano in Monte Celio (1175–84).[5] From the outset, they were
regarded much more hopefully by the Becket circle, although there
were fears that Vivian might be bribed or cajoled by the king to concede more than he should. John of Salisbury's first report, after
meeting them at Vézelay on 22 July, was hopeful;[6] and he was not to
be disappointed. Thomas, meanwhile, kept up his diplomatic pressure on the Curia (with letters to Cardinals Hubald and Hyacinth,
William of Pavia, John of Sutri and Hugh of Bologna) and to the
Sicilian court.[7]

The papal envoys' first series of encounters occupied almost three
weeks, from 15 August to 2 September, and took place at four different locations – Argentan (15–16 August), Domfront (23–24
August), Bayeux (31 August) and Bur-le-Roi (1–2 September) – as
they followed King Henry's court from point to point in Normandy.
In many ways the progress and the outcome were very similar to the
process at Montmirail and Saint-Léger at the beginning of the year.
The papal nuncios were working to a specific mandate; the king
wanted to preserve his public honour – which meant that he would
recall Thomas to his see on his terms, without conceding the
Constitutions of Clarendon and without appearing to give way to
pressure of any kind; and Thomas, for his part, wanted to restore the

status quo ante – the situation in all respects before he fled the realm, with all the rights and privileges and properties of the archbishopric intact, and, most importantly of all, without obligation to the written Constitutions. This meant that he expected to be free to exercise the legal rights of the metropolitan see, with power to issue ecclesiastical censures against disobedient subordinates. But he was also concerned to protect his physical safety. The aim, simply, was to work out an agreement that would enable Becket and all the exiles to be restored to all their offices and possessions in peace and security and with no loss to those possessions. This question of restoration proved very difficult, since the king's agents and appointees had exploited the lands and churches to the best of their own advantage for almost six years, and there was also the problem of prising the properties out of the clutches of those who had them. Would the king be prepared to deprive his loyal supporters of the lucrative tenures they had been enjoying?

This time, however, the venues were all in Normandy, which was one of the most tightly governed regions of Henry's domains and where the customs of the Norman kings in relation to the relative powers of duchy and Church were virtually undiluted from the time of the Conqueror's Constitutions of Lillebonne (1082), which had defined some of the duke's rights over the institutional Church. Even more than the English Church, the Norman Church was in the king's pocket, so to speak, and its leading ecclesiastics – bishops and abbots – were generally accustomed to working within that system. This time, also, there was no high-level political business to which the Becket question could be attached, so that Henry was more elusive than ever. It is clear from the very full accounts of the conduct of the papal mission that the king was disinclined to give much time to the debate. He wanted a quick fix that would leave him free to interpret the repatriation terms as he saw fit, after Becket was safely back under his own lordship. The absence of the king of France and the array of Franco-Norman-Angevin nobles that had thronged the castle and halls of Montmirail deprived the meetings of the formal structure that had existed in January. Henry was constantly on the move, with what can only be called snatches of discussion squeezed in between hunting trips, the normal business of the court, and its ceaseless movement from place to place.

This time Becket took no direct part in the business. He did not enter Henry's lands – that could happen only when a satisfactory peace had been secured – and it was left to the nuncios and their clerks, and Henry's Norman bishops (principally Rotrou of Rouen) to draw up the blueprint, which had to be agreed by both parties. So messages and proposals had to be ferried back and forth as the envoys tried to hammer out a short form of words that would be acceptable to both sides. The exiles, therefore, were on tenterhooks throughout the negotiations, watching anxiously to see what the nuncios would allow and fearful that their position would be undermined by the addition or subtraction of a word or phrase from the *forma pacis*, the written peace formula, which would prove their only protection once they returned to England. This time, also, we can see the king's tactics at very close quarters, and perhaps understand why he acquired a reputation for government by fear and threat, including the outbursts of anger that terrified his vassals.

There are two excellent accounts of the mission: the formal report from Master Vivian to the pope and an anonymous account compiled for Becket by an eyewitness who calls himself simply 'a friend', in order to hide his identity, in case the letter was betrayed. These can be supplemented by Henry II's own version of events.[8] The 'friend' had some access to the court, but not to the private meetings in the king's chapel, but he is unlikely to have been one of Becket's clerks. A possible author is Master Walter de Insula, the royal clerk whose sympathies for Becket caused him to be deprived of the office of deputy keeper of the seal in 1166; another possibility is Nicholas of Mont-Rouen, but the style is direct and matter-of-fact, totally lacking the biblical metaphors that Nicholas loved.

Vivian explains that he and Gratian were delayed, since the king was in Gascony when they arrived in France; so they went first to see the king of France at Soissons, then to Sens (where of course Becket was staying), there to await the arrival of the king of England in more accessible parts. They were, Vivian wrote, received 'honourably enough' (at Argentan on the feast of the Assumption, 15 August), and presented the pope's letter. This was the missive that had been drafted when the envoys were about to leave on their mission, and functioned as a letter of credence – accrediting the two papal clerks as papal nuncios with power to represent the mind of the pope. They were not cardinals, however; nor were they given legatine powers. They occupied an intermediate position between legates – who, as it were, carried the full force of the papal office in their own persons, with power to summon and coerce by ecclesiastical sentences, and messengers, who merely carried a message (written and oral), but without the power to make their own judgments on the matter in hand. Gratian and Vivian were accredited negotiators, acting in the pope's name. Alexander's letter, which much displeased

the king when it was read, opened with an unusually long *arenga*,
which reminded the king of the many graces bestowed on him by
God and his responsibility to repay the Almighty in due measure –
an argument similar to Becket's in 1166. This was stiffened by a
quotation from a homily of Pope Gregory I:

> The truth of the Gospel warns us to ponder carefully lest
> we, who are seen to have received more than others
> (*ceteris*) in this world, should consequently be judged
> more severely. For when the gifts are increased, the
> reckonings for those gifts increase also.

> Therefore by apostolic letters we ask, advise, and exhort
> in the Lord, but also, for the remission of your sins we
> enjoin on you in the name of Almighty God, of St Peter
> Prince of the Apostles, and of ourselves, mercifully to
> receive the said archbishop into your grace and love,
> all indignation and rancour set aside, for God and his
> Church, for your honour and also for that of your whole
> realm, and allow God to triumph and your will to be
> defeated in this regard ...

One can see why the king was displeased with this approach. It was
the strongest letter yet to be received from the Curia and it neatly
subordinated the king's earthly honour to that of God, 'by whom
kings reign'. It is clear that Alexander had been paying careful heed
to the questions raised at Montmirail, and the king's insistence on
the preservation of his own honour. A king's honour was great, but
for a Christian king, God's was greater. More than that, of course,
it stressed that Thomas was a man of God; and in despising him the
king was despising the author of all. So, God's honour, king's honour and Becket's honour – as God's man – were all laid out in a neat
logical triangle, with God's at the apex, and Henry's royal and
Becket's episcopal honour balancing one another at the two angles
of the base. According precedence to God's honour was no disparagement for a Christian king; and part of God's honour was to show
due respect for his ministers. But the pope went further still. Acting
in the names of God and St Peter, and with the full authority of his
priestly office, he commanded the king for the remission of his sins
to grant his peace to the archbishop. Vivian and Gratian were designated to intimate 'our will more fully by word of mouth', and the
king was urged 'for the reverence of God's Church, for St Peter's
honour and ours' to receive them kindly and treat them honourably,

and to accept their oral communication in respect of this matter 'and the others which you have signified through Reginald, archdeacon of Salisbury', and carry out their instructions 'for the honour of God and the Church, but also for the eternal praise and glory of your name and equally for the advancement of your heirs.'[9]

Henry's first response was to raise the question of the absolution of the excommunicates and then to attack Becket as he had to Cardinals William and Otto, but he agreed to 'take counsel' on the mandate to receive Becket into his peace 'for the remission of his sins'. Dean John of Salisbury and Archdeacon Reginald were sent to meet the nuncios on the following day. Then, in Vivian's words, they were dragged about from place to place (he does not say where), with 'much bending of words and many twisted paths'. They reached Domfront on 23 August, where the king and his son were hunting. The Anonymous account describes events as they happened:

> when it was already evening, the king came in from the wood and turned aside to the nuncios' lodging before going to his own, and received and greeted them with much respect and humility. And, while he was still standing in conversation with them, lord Henry, the king's son, came to the door of the lodging, and many young men with him, all blowing hunting horns in the usual manner to announce the taking of a stag, which he gave whole to them; this was done so that the sojourner would hear – and as a show for the people's benefit.
> (*CTB*, ii, no. 227: *c.* 3 September 1169)

One of the king's venison was a princely gift indeed, and intended to flatter the papal envoys and put them in a good mood for their discussions, which were conducted in private. But before getting down to the question of Becket's peace, Henry demanded that those of his clerks that had been excommunicated in April and May 1169 should not only be absolved, but absolved without the usual oath to accept the archbishop's judgment on their offences. Their excommunication had indeed been an embarrassment, not because they or he observed it, but because an increasing number of English bishops did. He had been obliged to employ other clerks to conduct his business with the pope, and Geoffrey Ridel and Nigel de Sackville had withdrawn from Domfront because they could not risk the embarrassment of being publicly humiliated by being denied the formal kiss of peace by the papal clerks. There would have been no difficulty about absolving the clerks in the traditional manner – subject to their submission to Becket's authority – since that had been laid down by the pope as a concession that should be made in the interests of peace, but Henry's requirement that they should be exempted from the requirements of canonical discipline was a calculated blow against the archbishop's jurisdiction. The matter generated some heat, but Henry gradually wore the envoys down, although he could not persuade them to take the bait of going to England to absolve those who were still in the island.

The king had clearly expected to be able to reach an accommodation, for he summoned all the Norman bishops, led by Rotrou of Rouen, together with Bishop Roger of Worcester, Bishop John of Poitiers and Bertrand I de Montant, archbishop of Bordeaux; William de Passavant, bishop of Le Mans happened to be present on business of his own. Also present, however, were the Cistercian, Brother Geoffrey of Auxerre and eight abbots from neighbouring Norman monasteries (two Cistercian – Beaubec, Mortemer – six Benedictine – Bec, Caen, Cérisy, Fécamp, St-Wandrille, Troarn), in addition to the abbots of Rievaulx (Yorkshire) and Tiron (diocese of Chartres). No attempt was made to involve the English episcopate, except Worcester, who had withdrawn from England in the wake of Becket's summons to him, probably because the king was aware of their changed attitude and their refusal to participate in the latest appeal. His episcopal allies, London and Salisbury, could not be present, since they were excommunicate. Essentially, then, this was a council of Norman prelates, which could be relied upon to support the king's arguments and present a solid front to the *missi*. Even so, the meetings were spread over three days (31 August–2 September) and in two different places, Bayeux and Bur-le-Roi, and the king played a cat-and-mouse game with the envoys, returning again and again to the question of absolution for his clerks.

> On the next day [1 September], all the bishops assembled with the nuncios at a place called Le Bur [Bur-le-Roi], and immediately after the nuncios arrived, the lord king went into the park, and all the bishops went with him, but only those who had been summoned by name. Then the lord king immediately took counsel with the nuncios alone, asking them to absolve his clerks without oath. When the nuncios steadfastly refused to do this, the lord king ran to his horse and mounted and, in the hearing of everyone, swore that he would never for the rest of his life listen to anyone concerning your peace and restoration, neither

the Lord Pope nor anyone else. When they heard this, all the archbishops and bishops who were present came to the nuncios and implored them to absolve the clerks for the love of God. The nuncios conceded, but with the greatest reluctance.

When this was done, the lord king dismounted and again took counsel with them. And immediately afterwards, having summoned all who were present in the park, the lord king began his address and said that he desired them to know that you had not been exiled from England by him, and that he had many times recalled you to come and make satisfaction to him concerning the matters which he held against you, and that you had refused; but now the situation was this, that, at the prayer and precept of the Lord Pope, he was restoring the archbishopric to you in full and granting his peace to you and to all who left the country on your behalf. The lord king made this grant of peace at about the ninth hour, and after this he remained exceedingly cheerful, and he had various other matters discussed in his presence. When this other business had been transacted, he came again to the nuncios, and asked them to go into England to absolve the excommunicates who were there. When they steadfastly refused to agree to this, the king became angry, and again asked that one of them at least should go while the other remained, or that they should send one of their clerks, and that he would give that clerk an income before he returned. When Gratian, whom we hope is a son of grace, again refused, the lord king left them in a great rage, and declared in their hearing, 'Do what you like; I don't rate you and your excommunications and doubt if they are worth an egg.'

After making this outburst, he mounted his horse to leave. But all the archbishops and bishops who were present followed him and said that he had spoken badly. Then he dismounted and spoke to them. The sum of their advice was that they would all write to the Lord Pope, saying that he had offered you peace in their hearing, and that he had been ready to carry out every command of the Lord Pope, and that it was the nuncios' fault that none of this had happened. Then, after they had lost a great deal of

time in writing the letters, seeing that the king had often
left them extremely angry, the archbishops and bishops
came to him, saying that the nuncios had in their
possession and had already revealed a mandate from the
Lord Pope, that everyone was to do whatever the nuncios
commanded. The king replied, 'I know; I know; they
will interdict my land. But cannot I, who can capture a
well-fortified castle every day, capture a single clerk, if he
interdicts my land?' But after they had promised that they
would do some things in accordance with his will, the
tempest of rage ceased entirely, and he came to his senses
and said: 'If you do not make peace tonight, you will
never come again to this point.' Afterwards, when
they had been troubled by that statement for some
considerable time, he called them all together and said:
'It is proper that I should do much in response to the
Lord Pope's prayer, for he is my lord and my father, and
therefore I restore his archbishopric to him, and my peace
to him and to all who are outside the country on his
account.' Then the nuncios and all the rest expressed their
thanks. And the king then added, 'If I have now done less
than I should, tomorrow I shall make it up at your advice.'

On the next day, that is the 1st [correctly, the 2nd]
September, they all assembled at the same place at around
midday, and after there had been a long discussion about
the absolution of the excommunicates, namely that they
should not take an oath, he finally agreed that Geoffrey
Ridel, Nigel de Sackville, and Thomas FitzBernard
should, with their hands stretched out towards the
Gospels placed before them, give their word that they
would carry out the nuncios' command. Then the nuncios
were asked that however many of your churches the lord
king granted in the intervening time should all remain in
the hands of those to whom the king had granted them.
But, as we have heard, he finally agreed that they should
freely return to your gift. Later it was determined that the
bishops should draw up the formal contract of the peace
which the king had granted, and the lord king tried very
hard to persuade one of the nuncios to cross over to
England to absolve the excommunicates. And when they
had broken up – it was already towards the end of the third

hour of the night – the king said that the words '*saving the dignity of his realm*' should be inserted into the peace contract; but Gratian, so we have heard, vehemently denied that he would allow it for any reason. And they are still standing by this decision, intending to return to Caen on the Nativity of the Blessed Mary [Monday 8 September] to confirm it more fully. Lisieux bent his energies to flatter the king; Rouen to please God and the Lord Pope. Farewell. (*CTB*, ii, no. 227: *c.* 3 September 1169)

Responsibility for this sudden reversal on the king's part was attributed by Becket to Geoffrey Ridel in a letter to Hubald of Ostia at the end of September:

Archdeacon Geoffrey ... obstructed the peace when it was all but made, convincing the king not to make any agreement except after extorting a pledge to observe the customs, which he called by the more acceptable term of 'dignities', so that they might be obtained more easily.

It was probably at this point that the letters required by the king were drafted, one from Rotrou of Rouen and the other from the Norman episcopate, which duly reported to the pope that in response to his petition and out of love from him, with the advice of the archbishops, bishops, abbots and religious dignitaries and nobles of his realm, he had granted that the archbishop 'could return to his archbishopric and receive it as fully as he held it when he left, and thenceforward possess it in peace, for the honour of God, saving, of course, the pristine dignity of his realm.' They said, and Henry's own letter, written at the same time for transmission to the Curia by Reginald of Salisbury, Ralph of Llandaff and Richard Barre, also alleged, that the nuncios at first happily accepted that phraseology and then, at dawn, rejected it;[10] but their version is contradicted by the anonymous account just quoted and by Vivian's own report. One suspects that there was some sleight of hand on the king's part.

In a move reminiscent of the manner in which the Constitutions of Clarendon were reduced to writing after an oral approval had been given to unwritten customs, the nuncios agreed to the peace proposals presented to them, only to find that 'it was determined that the bishops should draw up the formal contract of the peace which the king had granted.' That *forma* has not survived, but its content can be recovered from the king's letter, witnessed (and perhaps drafted) by Geoffrey Ridel, archdeacon of Canterbury, which was sent from

Bur-le-Roi to the abbot of Cîteaux and the Cistercian order in time to reach the annual General Chapter, which met at Cîteaux on 14 September. Its aim was to demonstrate to the Cistercians that, despite his own reluctance, the king had obeyed the papal mandate and had offered his peace to the archbishop:

> Nevertheless at the petition and out of respect and love for the lord Pope, although it is very burdensome to me and quite repugnant to my will, and seems very troublesome to me, I grant that he may return to England and have his archbishopric as fully as he had it when he gave it up; and his followers in the same way may have theirs. And he and his may have peace for God's honour and mine, saving the dignities of my realm. (*MTB*, vii, no. 568)

That letter was carried by Brother Geoffrey of Auxerre, whose opposition to Becket's residence at Pontigny had resulted in his enforced abdication as abbot of Clairvaux in 1165,[11] and the abbots of Rievaulx (Yorkshire), Mortemer and Beaubec (Normandy). On the face of it, the concession seems to give Becket everything he wanted, except for the final clause. Since 'dignities' and 'customs' were interchangeable, saving the realm's 'dignities' meant saving the customs – as the envoys well knew.

As far as the king was concerned, this really was the end of the matter, for he immediately sent new envoys to Alexander III with his letters and those of the Norman bishops, saying that the nuncios had played him false by accepting and then rejecting the *forma pacis* with its dignities clause. Becket, also, having been informed by the anonymous letter, and probably by messengers from the papal nuncios, sent off letters to the pope and to his envoys, Alexander and John, defending the actions of the pope's men and begging the pope to oppose Henry's requests for the coronation of his son, the younger Henry, and the consecration of new bishops by hands other than Becket's.[12]

These latest royal petitions represented a new and dangerous development in royal policy. They suggest that Henry was manoeuvring to obtain papal privileges that would enable him to act without Becket. With his son crowned by a prelate of his choice – perhaps York – and five or six new bishops 'elected' according to his choice, and consecrated by an archbishop other than Becket – either York or Rouen – the stage would be set for an English Church functioning normally without an archbishop of Canterbury. Thomas Becket would have become completely redundant. With a more compliant bench of bishops, who knows what might not have been possible?

The men who had dared to hold off from the third appeal in 1169 would effectively be sidelined. Once the king had secured these concessions, the formation of an English Church on the Norman model could have proceeded apace.

Despite these moves and counter-moves, Rotrou of Rouen did not despair of securing a settlement. He conducted the nuncios to Caen, which they reached on 8 September, and when the King set out to meet the count of Flanders at Rouen, he commissioned the archbishops of Rouen and Bourges, and five bishops (Lisieux, Worcester, Séez, Bayeux, Rennes), together with Geoffrey Ridel and Reginald FitzJocelin and some nobles, to reconsider the peace. According to Master Vivian (vii, 80), the *missi* insisted that if the king kept the clause *saving the dignity of his realm* it should be matched with *saving the liberty of the Church*. But the king would not accept the addition of such a phrase. It was at this point that Rotrou, with the agreement of the bishops, suggested a way of cutting the Gordian knot. He suggested that a slight rewording of the formula, which should omit the saving clause and so avoid any terms that could give rise to debate, would solve the problem, if the king would accept it.[13] This was accepted by Vivian and Gratian; but when they travelled, at the king's summons, to Rouen, they were not even admitted to Henry's presence. Instead, Henry informed them by messenger that he would not retreat from *saving the dignity of his realm*.[14] The envoys therefore told the prelates that, if there was no peace by the time they withdrew, those who had been absolved would be returned to their excommunicated state in conformity with the papal mandate. Becket therefore re-imposed the sentences at Michaelmas (29 September) and reiterated the other censures;[15] and then, taking advantage of an embassy from Archbishop Øystein of Trondheim, he sent another batch of letters to the Curia: to Bishop Stephen of Meaux, who had been many months in Benevento, and who may have been instrumental in obtaining the appointment of Vivian and Gratian;[16] to the pope; and to four cardinals (Hubald, Albert, Hyacinth and Theodwin).[17] He emphasized Gratian's steadfastness and the deliberate ambiguity of the king's language. His letter to Hubald opened with a sharp comment on the Curia's gullibility in believing the promises and stories told by representatives of the English king.[18]

Meanwhile, in what should be seen as a complement to the isolation policy his envoys to the Curia were hoping to advance, King Henry set about insulating his realm from the worst that Becket and the pope could do. At Michaelmas (29 September), in an act that showed he was prepared to go almost as far as schism, he sent Richard of Ilchester and Guy of Waltham to England to impose a series of mandates, whose aim was to prevent a repetition of the successful transmission to England of the Clairvaux sentences. Everyone above the age of 12 was to be compelled to swear to observe decrees and, like the order to exile the kindred of Becket and his household in late 1164, the mandates were to be imposed and enforced through the ordinary legal and administrative system. The sheriffs would impose the oaths and carry out the mandates; the judges would in due course execute the sentences. The decrees themselves were fierce.

> Anyone bearing interdict letters from the Pope or 'Canterbury' was to be seized and kept in captivity until the king or his justices declared the king's will,
>
> No cleric, canon, or monk was to be permitted to cross the sea in either direction without letters of crossing from the justices or the king: anyone who did was to be seized and held
>
> No one might carry mandates from the Pope or 'Canterbury': anyone who did was to be seized and held.
>
> No one might appeal to Pope or archbishop or hear pleas on their mandate or receive any of their mandates in England: anyone who did was to be seized and held.
>
> Any bishops, abbots, clergy, or laity who observed a sentence of interdict were without delay to be cast out of the kingdom, with all their kin, taking nothing with them, and their chattels [movables] and properties were to be taken into the king's hand. All clergy with incomes in England were to be summoned to return to them within two months: if they did not, their incomes would be taken into the king's hand. Peter's Pence was to be seized and kept until the king's will was known.[19]

The view that these decrees were simply a response to the threat of interdict narrows the focus far too much. If the king were merely concerned with interdict, he could have framed the mandates accordingly. But they were much more wide-ranging than that. The 1169 decrees should be set in the context of the king's dismay at the failure of the existing controls on the passage of individuals through the ports and the consequent ability of 'his enemy' to insinuate his sentences into England. More than that, he was incensed that bishops and other ecclesiastics had obeyed them and had, moreover, refused to take the path of defensive appeal. He was also incensed at the failure of his papal policy. No longer able to coerce, or at least control, Becket by means of pressure on Alexander III, he determined to shut both out of his realm. Comparison with Henry VIII's use of *praemunire*, and his prohibition of appeals and annates is very instructive. They are chillingly similar both in form and motive. For both kings the object was essentially the same: to protect themselves from papal censures against policies they were determined to pursue.

The reaction in England was consternation. Geoffrey Ridel, Richard of Ilchester and other officials summoned the bishops to London to give security that they would observe the king's edict. According to a letter sent by Becket after 18 November to his clerks Alexander and John, who were still in the Curia, all the bishops and abbots, apart from a messenger from Clarembald of St Augustine's Canterbury, refused to attend the assembly. Henry of Winchester declared that

> in all things he would loyally obey the apostolic
> mandates, and those of the church of Canterbury, to
> which he owed loyalty, obedience, and devotion by
> reason of his profession, as long as he lived, and he
> commanded his clergy to do the same.

He was followed by Bartholomew of Exeter, who took refuge in a religious house; and William of Norwich provocatively excommunicated Earl Hugh and the others listed in the Clairvaux and subsequent sentences in the very presence of royal officials and,

> coming down from the pulpit, he placed his crozier (that
> is, his pastoral staff) upon the altar, saying that he would
> like to see who would stretch out a hand to touch the
> lands and property of the Church, and, having entered
> the cloister, he is living with the brethren.

Richard Peche of Chester, also, declared his willingness to obey papal mandates, and 'withdrew into the area of his bishopric where the Welsh live, in order to be safe from the officials.'[20]

This was a very significant episcopal revolt. The only bishops known to have been in England not mentioned by name are York, Durham, Salisbury and Rochester, and it is not clear that the province of York was included in the mandates. If that is so, only Salisbury and Rochester are unaccounted for: London and Worcester were abroad; Bath, Chichester, Ely, Hereford and Lincoln were vacant. If indeed no abbots turned up either, apart from Clarembald's messenger, then the defiance of English Church leaders was almost total. But this resistance to Henry II's directives was not entirely new. It was foreshadowed in the willingness of many of them to execute the Clairvaux excommunications. The reason for their defiance in late 1169 and early 1170 was similar to their defiance in May–June 1169, but probably much more serious. The *ad cautelam* appeal was seriously subversive of all ecclesiastical authority; the 1169 decrees challenged the bishops' sense of their own integrity. Here was the king demanding public oaths against papal and archiepiscopal mandates, and imposing them on the whole population under threat of sequestration and exile. What many had connived at or dissembled in respect of Becket himself was now being visited on them, and they could see the awful consequences of further dissimulation.

Bishops and abbots could, if they dared, resist and go into hiding. It was not so easy for laity or the lesser ecclesiastical fry. Becket had to issue absolutions for those who had taken the oaths under duress.[21] From one point of view, Henry's 1169 decrees justified Becket's initial opposition to the Constitutions of Clarendon. From another, it could be argued that Becket drove him into taking more and more authoritarian and tyrannical action.

At the very moment that his agents were imposing oaths that cut at the heart of ecclesiastical authority in England, the king made another effort to organize a peace to his liking. Almost certainly in the knowledge that the more uncompromising of the two envoys had already set off on his return journey to Benevento, Henry attempted to entice Vivian into another series of interviews, possibly in the hope that he would be more amenable to persuasion (or even bribery) than his colleague. The result was a meeting at Saint-Denis outside Paris at Martinmas (11 November), whose purpose was to finalize the details of repatriation, including compensation to the Becket party for the confiscations. As earlier, at Montmirail, the splendid location and the presence of King Louis of France seemed to offer better chance of agreement than the locations in Normandy, where Henry controlled the show:

> The lord king of the French and Master Vivian and other
> wise men compelled us to attend that meeting, so that
> when we were established in Paris, and he at Saint-Denis,
> our peace could be very conveniently discussed from close
> quarters.

Henry proved to be as wily as ever:

> When Master Vivian pressed him very insistently and
> assiduously to carry out the promise he had made, he
> demurred in his usual fashion, and revealed himself to
> Vivian in such a way that when Vivian returned to us, he
> openly said, with many people present, that he could not
> recall ever having seen or heard a man so mendacious.[22]

Nevertheless, a second attempt was made to reach some kind of
agreement. The two kings were together at Montmartre on 18
November, where Rotrou of Rouen presented a written petition in
Becket's name. This is how Thomas described what followed:

> we went to meet the English king when he passed near
> Montmartre on his way back from Saint-Denis, and,
> through the venerable lord of Rouen, the bishop of Séez,
> and others who had put themselves forward to carry the
> message, we asked him, *for the love of God and the Lord
> Pope, to restore his grace, peace, security, and all
> possessions and sequestrations to us and our followers,
> while we offered ourselves, ready to show him whatever
> duty an archbishop owes to a prince.*[23]

The king's response was that he would 'freely remit whatever offences
and quarrels he had had against us from the bottom of his heart', but
that he would prefer to submit the specific issues of restitution to the
judgment of the French king, the French Church, or the scholars of
Paris. This can only have been a tactic to avoid getting down to brass
tacks. While his ministers in England were extorting oaths to subvert
Becket's and the pope's authority, Becket's restoration was not at all
what Henry had in mind. When Becket's petition was presented to him,

> he replied in his mother tongue, so twisting the meaning
> of words in his usual fashion that he seemed to the more
> simple-minded to be granting everything, while to the
> more cautious he seemed to include perverse and
> intolerable conditions.

More significantly, he refused to offer the kiss of peace. At this,

> The most Christian prince [Louis VII] immediately
> concluded that not for all his weight in gold could he
> advise us to enter his territory, without first receiving the
> kiss of peace in public. And Count Theobald [V, of Blois]
> added that it would be a very foolish presumption, while

many of those standing around recalled and reminded one
another of what had happened to Robert de Sillé [Sillé-le-
Guillaume, near Le Mans], for whom even the kiss had
not seemed a sufficient guarantee of the maintenance of
peace and safety. (*CTB*, ii, no. 243)[24]

Earlier, it had been words and phrases that had impeded 'peace';
now it was a symbol. Was Thomas being unreasonably scrupulous?
The issue was essentially one of trust. The kiss of peace was far more
than a polite gesture between friends: according to the conventions
of the day, it was a necessary ritual of reconciliation.[25] In the absence
of this universally recognized sign of concord, what reliance could
be placed on Henry's assurances?

So, at the end of another year, the wheel of fortune turned yet again. As
King Henry sent yet more envoys (Archdeacon Giles of Rouen, John of
Oxford and John of Séez), Thomas wrote more letters, to William of
Sens, travelling to the Curia with Gratian, to Gratian himself, to
Cardinals William of Pavia, John of Sutri, Bernard of Porto and John
of Naples, and to Bishop Stephen of Meaux (who was at the Curia),[26]
warning them against the royal envoys and denouncing Gilbert Foliot,
who had set out for the Curia to prosecute his appeal in person. To
his clerks, Alexander and John, however, he gave details of the 1169
decrees and the resistance of the bishops and abbots, and instructed
them to secure papal mandates ordering the king to give the kiss of
peace and restore the sequestrated properties.[27] In the full knowledge of
the bishops' refusal to withdraw from his authority, Thomas not only
reiterated the excommunications but went forward with the promulgation of an interdict to be imposed in England if there was no peace, to
begin on the feast of the Purification, 2 February 1170.[28]

There had been a considerable shift in papal attitudes during this
year. Whether from the arguments relentlessly presented by Becket
or from the reports of his various envoys, the pope seems to have
come round to adopting a more aggressive stance. There is some evidence, also, that William of Pavia had shifted his ground. He was
now much better disposed to Becket than he had been in 1167;
Simon, Engelbert and Bernard had expressed their exasperation in
1168; Lombard of Piacenza had witnessed Henry's shiftiness in
1169; and Vivian and Gratian had seen it too. Even more serious for
Henry's reputation, Lombard had been insulted and abused. This
mistreatment of a member of a papal embassy may have done quite
a lot to change the pope's mind.

9

A hollow peace: Fréteval and after

The year 1170 opened with Thomas of Canterbury poised to impose the interdict that he would have liked to impose at the very beginning of the controversy with the king. Almost certainly, if the international situation had been different – if the pope had not been in exile and a powerful German emperor were not supporting an anti-pope – there would have been little question about the issue of the standard censures. Whether they would have been successful or not is another matter – Becket thought that they would. As it was, however, Becket's resolve to use the most powerful weapons in his armoury was at last supported by the pope. For the first time, pope and archbishop were agreed on severe action. At the same time, however, Alexander had, as always, to manage the situation in such a way that King Henry was not so alienated that he withdrew his obedience altogether. He was approached by emissaries from three parties simultaneously: Henry II, Gilbert of London and Thomas of Canterbury; and he was aware that the joint mission of Vivian and Gratian had failed. His formula for peace had been rejected. He had little option but to appoint a fourth commission, this time of two local prelates, Rotrou of Rouen and Bernard, bishop of Nevers, to try to persuade Henry, even then, to receive Becket into his favour and allow his honourable restoration to office and property in England.

The tone of his letters was very different from those written earlier, however. The statements of the king's agents (John of Oxford, Giles of Rouen and John of Séez) were countered by those of Master Vivian, just returned to Benevento, who could give his own account of the most recent proceedings. The pope did appoint new commissioners, no doubt at the petition of the royal envoys, but he insisted on the implementation of the peace promised by the king at

Montmartre, which was to be sealed with the public conferment of the kiss of peace (which Henry had refused). In addition, Thomas was to 'humble himself before the king as far as he could, *saving the honour of the Church and danger to himself and his followers.*' Rouen and Nevers were to execute the mandate within a month of its reception and, if Henry refused to comply, they were to impose an interdict on his continental lands, without right of appeal. Further, if peace were made, after a suitable interval they were to enjoin the king 'to cancel entirely those bad customs, and especially those which he has recently added [1169 decrees] and which are contrary to his salvation and to the liberty of the Church, and free the bishops and other prelates of the realm from their observance.'[1] The response to the king said much the same thing, though without reference to interdict, and it emphatically rejected the petitions his envoys had presented (presumably for the coronation of Henry's son and consecration of bishops).[2] Gilbert Foliot had better luck with his petition, for Alexander authorized his absolution by the same Rouen and Nevers.[3] The threat of interdict was then considerably firmed up with the issue of a series of mandates to English and continental prelates to obey the interdict to be imposed by the legates (Rouen and Nevers) on Henry's continental lands or by Becket himself in England, following failure of the peace.[4] A further mandate was issued to Rouen and Nevers about the absolution of excommunicates, with the requirement that they surrender any uncanonically acquired properties, with special reference to Geoffrey Ridel's wrongful acquisition of the church of Otford.[5] More support for Becket's position was given in a general mandate prohibiting Roger of York and the other English bishops from infringing the rights of Canterbury, and in the bull that forbade Thomas and the English bishops to participate in the coronation, unless the new king took the customary oath to protect the Church and Canterbury, and absolved the men of England from the oaths and customs (1169 decrees) recently imposed upon them.[6]

Before these letters could be delivered, however, another false hope of reconciliation appeared briefly on the horizon. An embassy from the Latin kingdom, which included Archbishop Frederick of Tyre and King Amaury I (1162–72) of Jerusalem, produced an equally fleeting plan for an Anglo-French crusade, and Henry declared his intention of making peace with Becket. Alexander of Cologne, abbot of Cîteaux, Geoffrey Foulquia, master of the Temple, and Brother Geoffrey of Auxerre summoned Becket to Chaumont to receive the king's peace, but when Becket had travelled as far as Pontoise, the proposal was scuttled by the return (*c.* 20 February) of Richard Barre and

Archdeacon Ralph of Llandaff, who alleged that they had obtained a further restriction of the archbishop's power.[7] Becket therefore wrote to his suffragans, congratulating them on their new-found obedience and unity, and warned them against Ralph and Richard, the recently returned bearers of false prophecy.[8] Meanwhile, to Becket's chagrin, Gilbert Foliot was absolved by Archbishop Rotrou at Rouen, and returned triumphantly to England,[9] at which the archbishop sent a strongly worded letter to the pope, denouncing Foliot's absolution, which allowed him to go to England, there to participate in the coronation of the king's son, 'so that the Church of Canterbury should never be free .... The bishop of Séez ... is boasting that he will do it on the basis of your personal mandate, if the others are absent.'[10]

The nomination of Rotrou and Bernard offered some small hope of forcing a reconciliation before the coronation could take place. Probably with this in mind, Thomas sent a long and carefully considered letter to the bishop of Nevers in late March, deeming him to be the more reliable of the two. After a very forthright description of Henry's customary behaviour, he laid down his own requirements for peace: a written statement, to include specific references to the restoration of property; the kiss of peace; a list of the sequestrated properties; and the 1000 marks promised through Vivian to be given to Becket (but which could be remitted as a bargaining point). Once peace was made, the bishop was to approach the king for full restitution and abolition of the evil customs, but he must exercise caution in absolving the excommunicates – this was to be done only if peace was really expected and after they had taken public oaths to obey the archbishop. What is particularly interesting about this letter is that Becket did not trust Henry II to keep his word, unless his promises were supported by a written guarantee.[11]

Prevention of the coronation then became the focus of attention. Since most of the bishops had held out against the 1169 decrees, there was hope that they would also refuse to participate in a coronation that infringed the rights of the church of Canterbury, so he wrote in that vein to all the bishops of the province, and also to Roger of York, forbidding them in the strongest possible terms to take part in the illicit ceremony,[12] and he commanded Roger of Worcester (who was still in France) to show the papal prohibitions to York and the other bishops, and to prohibit them, and particularly London and Salisbury, from participation. He stressed that this action was not directed against the young Henry, whom he would willingly crown with his own hands.[13] At the same time, Becket commissioned a woman, a nun with the pseudonym 'Idonea' ('the appropriate one') to present a copy of the original papal mandate to Roger of York, if possible in the presence of other bishops.[14] It is highly possible that this lady was Mary of Blois, daughter of King Stephen and abbess of Romsey, who had been compelled by Henry II to abandon the religious life in 1161 and marry Matthew, younger brother of Count Philip of Flanders, so that he could acquire the county of Boulogne to which she had become sole heiress. After giving birth to two daughters, Ida and Maud, she retired to the monastery of Sainte-Austreberth de Montreuil in 1169/70. As the daughter of a king, she would certainly have had the status to confront Roger of York; and she had good grounds for hostility to Henry II![15]

All these precautions were to no avail, however. As an observer at the court reported from Caen, the coronation of Prince Henry would take place on the following Sunday (14 June), his wife, Princess Margaret of France, having been left with Queen Eleanor at Caen. The papal letters forbidding the coronation had indeed been smuggled into England, but they had been suppressed by the person (Roger of York?) to whom they had been given and could achieve nothing. Even worse, Richard of Ilchester, who had conducted the young prince from Caen to escort him across the Channel, had confirmed to the writer that the king was adamantly opposed to reconciliation with the archbishop, and would hold out until he died, even against God. One correspondent summed up Henry's policy towards Becket as 'trickery and wickedness', and he drew a fearful picture of the consequences for Becket of this coronation of an enemy king by an enemy archbishop and the alienation of the king of France through his daughter's disparagement. In such a perilous situation, he urges Thomas to use all his powers, for the king will never forgive him.[16]

The young Henry was duly crowned and anointed in Westminster Abbey by Roger of York, assisted by the bishops of London and Salisbury. This was an entirely new situation and a very difficult one. What was the best way forward? One correspondent counselled great caution and advised that no sentences be issued, except perhaps against the archbishop of York.[17] None was issued. It was difficult to condemn the archbishop of York and his collaborators without impugning the validity of the coronation. Instead, Thomas decided to take action not on his own authority but through that of the pope, sending a messenger to obtain papal censures against the delinquent prelates,[18] but Archbishop William of Sens supported immediate imposition of the interdict on Henry's continental lands. His position as papal legate for 'France' gave him jurisdiction over much of Henry II's continental territories, and he urged Becket to send copies of the papal mandates to the archbishops of Rouen and Tours, and copies of William's to the archbishops of Auch and Bordeaux.[19] And so it was done.

The coronation of the young Henry, called 'Henry III' in contemporary chronicles, turned out to be a political disaster for the old king, for it created exaggerated expectations on the part of the younger Henry, which drove him into the arms of Louis VII and set him on a collision course with his father, which poisoned relations until his premature death in 1183. In the short term, the circumstances in which it was carried out – in the teeth of papal prohibition, by an archbishop of York acting within the Canterbury province, with Margaret of France, the boy's wife, and Eleanor of Aquitaine, the boy's mother, deliberately excluded, and general interdicts poised to strike throughout his realms – were hardly auspicious. Its impact on the Becket question was immediate. Archbishop William of Sens, who, as papal legate for 'France', had issued interdict letters for the two southernmost provinces of Aquitaine (Auch and Bordeaux), seems to have taken the lead in applying pressure on Henry II and urging the peace commissioners, Rouen and Nevers, to play a more energetic role. Bernard of Nevers, in fact, had been described as either deliberately slow, travelling 'through the bishoprics and monasteries and royal houses as far as Mont-Saint-Michel with an ant-like pace' in the days before the coronation, or deceived by royal agents – 'taken in by lies' – with an emphasis on the former.[20] One of the deceptions may have been the transmission to Rotrou of Rouen of a royal letter, dated at Westminster in late May and witnessed by Richard de Lucy, which declared the king's readiness to grant his peace to Becket in the form drawn up by Rotrou and approved by the pope. This had been brought to Normandy by Thomas 'Agnellus', archdeacon of Wells, in what seems to have been an elaborate device to prevent Rouen and Nevers getting to London in time to impede the coronation on 14 June. Becket's informant implies that the two prelates may have been willing dupes.[21]

After the coronation, however, the king had either to keep his promise or face interdict, and he chose the former. Rouen and Nevers met Thomas on 16 July and arranged that he and his household would come to Fréteval to receive the king's peace on 22 July, at the end of a three-day conference between the French and English kings. 'After taking the advice of many learned men, and especially the counsel of the lord of Sens', Becket agreed. The consequence was the peace of Fréteval.

This was an extraordinary event. After King Louis had withdrawn, the archbishop, accompanied by William of Sens, went to meet the king in the open air. Both men were on horseback and, for the first time since 1164, spoke privately to one another. It is clear that both parties, the king and the archbishop, carefully avoided referring to the matters that had caused the rupture of discussions again and again: no customs or dignities of the realm; no honour of God; no saving my order. The best account, in fact the only firsthand account, comes from Becket's report to Alexander III. It stresses the king's courtesy and amiability:

> when he saw us approaching in the distance, leaving
> the crowd milling about him, he advanced closer, and,
> with his head uncovered he anticipated our salutation,
> exultantly pouring forth words of greeting, and, after
> saying a few words in the presence of ourselves and the
> lord of Sens, he turned aside and, to the amazement of
> everyone, led us apart and spoke for a long time with
> such familiarity that it seemed there had never been
> any discord between us. (*CTB*, ii, no. 300)

But there was no discussion of the substantive issues. Instead, they spoke about the most recent event and Becket's grievance at the injury to Canterbury's rights in the coronation. Becket's account of the conversation, to which he gave considerable space, offers considerable insight into the king's intellectual skill and ingenuity. He defended his actions first on the grounds of precedent, that Thomas of York had crowned William I, to which Becket replied that exceptional circumstances explained that and the other exception: the schismatic Stigand had been archbishop of Canterbury in 1066, for example, and Henry I's coronation by Gerard of Hereford (a mistake for Maurice of London) had occurred during Anselm's exile, and was rectified after Anselm's return. Moreover, William II, Stephen and Henry II himself had been crowned by Canterbury in the presence of archbishops of York who raised no challenge. Then Henry claimed that he had a papal mandate that allowed him to have his son crowned by any bishop of his choice, which Becket countered by pointing out that it had been obtained during the vacancy after Theobald's death (in fact in 1161),[22] and that the later letters had nullified it. The king promised to remedy the situation:

> I do not doubt that the church of Canterbury is the
> noblest church in the Western world, nor do I wish

her to be deprived of her right, but rather, following
your advice, I shall take action to see that she is relieved
in respect of this matter, and that she recovers her early
dignity in all things.[23]

The amount of space devoted to this conversation in the letter to
the pope has led many commentators to conclude that Thomas was
more concerned with the rights of Canterbury than with the Constitutions of Clarendon. This is to misunderstand the situation. It is
almost certain that the question of the customs was deliberately passed
over in silence by both men. 'He did not presume even to mutter the
customs which he used to claim with such pertinacity. He required
no oath from us or from any of our supporters,' wrote Becket to the
pope: but that dissimulation was no doubt part of the package. The
forma pacis had already been agreed between the king, the papal
commissioners (Rouen, Nevers and Sens) and Becket. York's illicit
coronation was a new event, and could not be passed over without
risk to Canterbury's future rights. Without challenge, future archbishops of York might substantiate a claim to crown and anoint the
future kings of England. What else was discussed is not revealed.
The first stage of the encounter ended with mutual courtesies:

> As I was kneeling at his feet after dismounting from my
> horse, he took hold of my stirrup and compelled me to
> remount, and said with tears in his eyes: 'What more need
> I say? My lord archbishop, let us restore the old affection
> between us, and each show what favour he can to the
> other; and let us forthwith forget the enmity that has gone
> before; but I ask you to show me respect in the presence
> of those who are watching from afar.' (*CTB*, ii, no. 300)

The two men then separated to prepare for the final formal act.
It is clear from Becket's account that, even then, in moves that had
been repeated at least twice before, great pressure was put on him to
submit himself to the king's judgment and mercy. The king's iron fist
was only just covered by the velvet glove of his negotiators. But
Becket held out, as before:

> And so we came to the king and his associates, and asked
> him in all humility, through the mouth of the lord of Sens,
> who was the bearer of our words, to restore his grace to
> us; to grant his peace and security to us and ours, and
> to return the church of Canterbury together with its
> possessions, which he had seen set out in the document;

and, in his mercy, to correct what had been presumed
against us and our church in his son's coronation: and we
promised him affection and honour, and whatever service
an archbishop might show to his king and prince in the
Lord. (*CTB*, ii, no. 300)

And so it was done: 'When he heard the petition, he nodded his
approval and received us and those of ours who were present into
his favour'; and Henry and Thomas talked again until it was almost
vespers.

On the face of it, all was sweetness and light; but there had been
no kiss of peace. Becket reported to the pope that the king had been
willing to give him the kiss of peace,

If we wished him to be pressed so far, considering not
merely that he would appear defeated on all points but
also because he might be called a perjurer by those who
had heard him swear that he would not receive us with
the kiss on that day.

This had clearly been dissimulation. For all its stage-managed amiability, there was a hollowness at the heart of the reconciliation.
Henry's oath, presumably one of his famous exclamations, 'by God's
eyes', had been made to the bishops in the preliminary discussions, in
which he had approved the terms of the peace. After agreeing minimum terms, one can imagine him shouting, 'By God's eyes, I shall
not give him the kiss of peace today.' That had been a sticking point
at Montmartre, and it had featured in the papal instructions to
Rouen and Nevers.[24] The king's excuse was more than paper thin –
and he had used it before – but by that point, no doubt with many
suppressed misgivings, Becket did not, or could not, insist.

The absence of the kiss of peace was ominous,[25] but there were
also many irksome questions still to be resolved. Not least among
these was the punishment of those who had collaborated in the coronation in blatant defiance of papal and archiepiscopal commands,
compensation for six years' lost incomes, and the restoration to
archiepiscopal power of churches that had become vacant during the
exile, and to which the king had presented clerks (e.g. Geoffrey Ridel
to Otford). There was also the problem of the transfer of the sequestrated estates back to Becket's own officials. It was one thing to
exchange fine gestures in public; it was another altogether to turn
the parchment grant into deeds. Even as the Becket party was leaving the king's presence, Arnulf of Lisieux, prompted by Geoffrey

Ridel, declared publicly that since the king had received his followers into his grace, the archbishop should receive all who had stood with the king into his. Becket demurred, but said that he would deal with the matter as moderately as he could, *for the honour of God's church, for the king's honour, and his own.*[26]

The interval between the peace of Fréteval and the murder in the cathedral was short of six months. What went wrong? Becket's critics blame him for destroying the peace by his insistence on the eve of his return to England on issuing the papal letters suspending York and Durham, and excommunicating London and Salisbury for their role in the coronation.[27] But they had already teamed up with Randulf de Broc, Reginald of Warenne and Gervase of Cornhill, sheriff of Kent, to intercept him as he landed; and they were preparing to collaborate in filling the vacant bishoprics without any recourse to the archbishop.[28] York, London and Salisbury then went to Henry in Normandy, complaining that Becket was bringing not peace but fire and sword into the realm. His furious outburst caused the four barons to embark on their fateful mission, which, fuelled further by Becket's excommunication of the de Brocs and others on Christmas Day 1170, led to his murder. That chain of events is continuous, but it should not be seen in isolation from what had preceded it.

Although Becket's letter to the pope had put a very positive spin on the Fréteval reconciliation, his letter to Cardinal Bishop Hubald of Ostia hinted that the 'whole substance' of the peace 'so far subsists in hope'; and his envoy, Master Gunther of Winchester, carried an oral report for the pope and cardinals, together with requests for mandates to the peace commissioners to reinstate the excommunications and the interdicts if the Canterbury properties were not restored.[29] Gunther did not reach the papal Curia, which was travelling northwards towards Segni, until late September, and he could not have been back in Sens with the papal mandates much before the middle of November at the earliest. During all that time, from 22 July to about the same date in November – four months – Becket imposed no new censures, and the existing ones were lifted by order of Rouen and Nevers immediately after Fréteval. During that time, therefore, responsibility for the implementation of the peace depended entirely on the king, and he moved with leaden steps. Although he had issued writs announcing that he had bestowed his peace on all those who had left England on Becket's account from Cloyes-sur-le-Loir soon after the reconciliation at Fréteval, which instructed the bishops to restore them to their properties, subject to their paying homage to him,[30] no mandates were issued in respect of the archbishopric itself until the end of September. This was bad enough from Becket's point of view, since it meant that he could not return to his own until the king's administrators had been removed; it also meant that he continued to be deprived of income, so that it was extremely difficult for him to wind up his affairs in France – pay debts, for example, or make suitable arrangements for his return to Canterbury. Not only did Henry keep him hanging on, but he embarrassed and humiliated him at every turn.

Some time in early August, Thomas sent two of his most distinguished clerks, John of Salisbury and Herbert of Bosham, to ask about three lordships in particular: the barony of William de Ros, Saltwood Castle (which had been confiscated with the estates of Henry of Essex, although it belonged to the lordship of Canterbury), and custody of Rochester Castle,[31] which the king had promised that he would restore 'when he came back to Normandy'. They found him very ill with tertian fever (malaria) at La Motte near Domfront,[32] but when he recovered,

> In his usual fashion, he deferred, delayed, and deferred again, and finally ... said to Master John, who was asking in the archbishop's name, 'Oh John, I shall never give a castle to you unless I first see that you behave differently towards me than you have hitherto done.'[33]

Probably in mid-September[34] Thomas attempted a personal approach. Taking advantage of a projected meeting between the king and Count Theobald of Blois at Amboise (or Tours), he and his entourage approached the court. Although the king went out to meet the archbishop's party, Becket and his clerks were treated with something approaching contempt. There was no formal greeting – no kiss of peace – and the king turned a stern countenance to him. That evening, no one from the court visited his lodging. The message to onlookers could not have been clearer. There was no concord between the two men. Next morning, the message was sealed in the most brutal fashion. To avoid having to exchange even the liturgical kiss of peace with the archbishop, Henry, on the advice of Nigel de Sackville, one of the Clairvaux excommunicates, who was still holding the church of Harrow by the king's grant, ordered the mass for the dead to be celebrated. Later that same day, when Becket, supported by Count Theobald and other nobles, asked that the Canterbury estates be restored to him, the king told him that he must return to his church before the estates were restored, so that the king could see in advance how the archbishop behaved towards royal authority.[35]

Their last meeting, at Chaumont a few days later, which was more private, was more amiable but equally unsatisfactory. 'Oh', the king is supposed to have said, 'Why do you not do my will? I would indeed put everything into your hands.' After promising to meet him in Rouen, where he would settle his debts and either give either him the kiss of peace or depute the archbishop of Rouen who would take him to receive it from the young king, the interview ended on an ominous note: 'Go in peace. I shall follow and meet you as soon as I can, either at Rouen or in England.' To which the archbishop replied, 'My lord, my heart tells me that I thus leave you as one whom you will never see again in this life.' 'Do you take me for a traitor?' said the king; to which Becket responded, 'Far be it from you, my lord.'[36] It was only after that last meeting that the king, from Chinon, issued the appropriate mandate to his son, who was technically in charge of administration in England.

> Know that Thomas archbishop of Canterbury has made peace with me according to my will. Therefore I command that he and his are to have peace; and you are to cause the archbishop himself and all who left England on his account to have all their property honestly, honourably, and in peace, as they had them three months before the archbishop withdrew from England; and you are to cause some of the more law-worthy and older knights of the honour of Saltwood to appear before you and by their oath have recognized what is held there from the fee of the archbishopric of Canterbury; and you are to cause the archbishop to have whatever is acknowledged to belong to his fee. Witnessed by Rotrou, archbishop of Rouen, at Chinon. (*MTB*, vii, no. 690)

Even in this writ there were irritants. Why was the term set at three months before Becket's flight and not at the beginning of his archiepiscopate? Why was there so long a delay between the making of the peace on 22 July and the issue of this writ at the end of September? On the first point, the reference date for restitution, around 16 July 1164, may have been chosen to exclude the various lordships and churches that had been contested during Becket's time at Canterbury; on the second, it is likely that he and his agents wanted to wring every particle of profit from the estates – especially the fruits of the harvest. The argument that Henry was waiting for the end of the financial year (Michaelmas, 29 September) so that the accounting would be easier does not seem very plausible, since the Exchequer was perfectly able to calculate portions of years.

Nevertheless, this was the only effective warrant that Becket received. Armed with this mandate, and perhaps a copy of the writ of peace issued after Fréteval,[37] Thomas sent some clerks, headed by Herbert of Bosham,[38] to England to make all the necessary arrangements for his return, which he expected would be in early November.[39] Their report makes grim reading.

> As far as we could we have fulfilled your mandate.
> We delivered your letters to William of Eynsford and
> William FitzNigel, and with some hardship we brought
> them along with us to London, together with Thurstan
> and Osbert [lay officials of the see]. And when we were
> ready to show the lord king's letter [mandate to the
> young king], which we had with us, to the younger king
> of England, none of them dared to appear in the king's
> presence. In fact, they had received advice from some
> people, who dissuaded them utterly from supporting us in
> this matter. But after consulting William FitzAdeline and
> Ralph FitzStephen [royal officials][40] we who were charged
> with the business boldly and diligently approached the
> king in his chamber at Westminster on the Monday
> immediately following the feast of St Michael [Monday,
> 5 October], in the presence of Earl Reginald [of Cornwall],
> the archdeacons of Canterbury and Poitiers [Geoffrey
> Ridel and Richard of Ilchester], William of St John,[41] and
> many others, taking with us only Robert, the sacrist of
> Canterbury. When Earl Reginald heard of the peace, he
> and many others gave thanks to God devotedly in the
> king's presence, but not all.

> After the letters were read, with us removed from the
> room, the king declared that he would take counsel on the
> matter. Then, having summoned Walter de Insula and
> taken counsel with him, we were recalled, and in our
> presence your archdeacon of Canterbury [Geoffrey Ridel]
> replied in these words: 'The lord king has received the
> mandate and command of his lord and father and has
> taken counsel on it. He therefore replies thus: 'Randulf de
> Broc and his officials, in the same way as other officials,
> have held the lands and possessions of the archbishopric

and the goods, churches, and incomes of the archbishop's
clerks in various places by command of the king his
father. And since he will not be able to have reliable
knowledge about the state of the archbishop's manors
in the absence of these same officials, or make enquiries
about them, the lord king appoints and assigns you
the Thursday following the feast of Pope St Calixtus
[Thursday 15 October 1170] as the day for the full
execution of this mandate.' Nevertheless, some, hearing
the delay and despairing utterly of firm peace, insistently
asserted that it was a bad omen for peace; but others
argued that they wished to have the incomes of this
period, which is more likely. For that reason all your
supporters whom we found in England were so despairing
of peace that they did not wish to believe, nor could they
believe either the lord king's letter, which we showed
them with the seal hanging from it, nor ourselves, who
were present at the making of the peace and affirmed it
with an oath viva voce. (*CTB*, ii, no. 311)

And this was almost three months after Fréteval! The letter continues:

... many of your friends are advising you privately through
us, to stay with the lord king for some time, if you can
possibly do so in any way, until you deserve to acquire
his favour and good will more fully. You would scarcely
believe how much almost all those we have spoken to love
your person and how ardently they desire your return and
your presence; but fear forces them to dissimulate and
pretend that they do not love you. (*CTB*, ii, no. 311)

But worse was to come. Not only did Becket not have his estates,
but the king was proceeding with episcopal elections without consulting him.

We have received reliable intelligence, my lord, confirmed
by one of your former friends, which we know to be true,
that through Walter de Insula and by writs carried to
England by him, the lord king of England has summoned
Roger, so-called archbishop of York, Bishops Gilbert of
London and Jocelin of Salisbury, and four or six clerks
from each vacant church in England, to elect bishops
in accordance with his will and the advice of the
aforementioned bishops, and to send the bishops elected

by his will and their advice to the Lord Pope for consecration, to the damage of the church of Canterbury and your confusion, which God prevent. This is why he desires your return to England so much and continues to discredit you so repeatedly and outrageously. Moreover, we see very clear evidence of this devilish plot, believed by all the inhabitants of the region. ...

... we are alone, leaderless, without aid, and destitute of counsel: for none of those whom you suggested to us has dared to obey your mandate or command except Robert the Sacrist, who gave his support to the task as far as he was able and had knowledge. If it should happen that they make restitution of your goods on the day specified, we shall immediately advise you, as we hear and learn it. May our lord fare well. (*CTB*, ii, no. 311)

There is absolutely no reason to doubt the veracity of this account. Popular feeling was with the archbishop, but fear of the king and disbelief that his peace was genuine made the envoys' task impossible. After writing the letter, they added an even more chilling postscript:

This bearer will tell you by word of mouth, in private, certain things which are believed to be true; they are disgraceful, and yet they are true. ... Again and again, my lord, we impress on your memory, that you should not hurry into England unless you are able to secure the unadulterated grace of the lord king. For there is no man in England, even among those you trust, who does not despair entirely of the peace; and those who should give us advice, whom we relied on especially, all avoid our conversation and flee our company. Farewell. (*CTB*, ii, no. 311)

After receiving this thoroughly disturbing report, Thomas sent urgent letters both to the pope and to the king. To the pope, enclosing a copy of the report, he commented on the king's failure:

he departed from his agreement in certain details, withholding from us until now certain possessions of the Church which our predecessor held all the days of his life without challenge ... when we approach him on the subject of their restitution, he promises that if we wait

and show him our earlier devotion, he will compensate
us in such a manner that no just cause of complaint will
remain. On the other hand, the well-known habits of the
man and the evidence of his actions undermine faith in his
promises, for we have been able to secure nothing from
him so far except words. ... in the mean time, we are
guarding against breaking the peace agreement just made,
as far as we can. (*CTB*, ii, no. 318)

At the same time, however, on King Louis' advice, he requested milder
letters of censure against the bishops than the ones he had just
received,[42] which should concentrate exclusively on the breach of
ecclesiastical order involved in the coronation, and leave the correc-
tion of all the bishops, except the archbishop of York, to his own
judgment. These were to be supported by a letter to King Henry
defending ecclesiastical discipline, mandates to the bishop of Meaux
and the abbot of Saint-Crépin-le-Grand to approach King Henry
about the implementation of the peace, and the restoration of his
own 'full' primacy. He also wrote to the king, complaining of the
delay in handing over his estates and also about Randulf de Broc:

> ... the aforesaid Randulf [de Broc] is in the mean time
> rampaging through the Church's property and even now
> openly gathers our provisions into Saltwood castle, and, as
> we have heard from those who are prepared to prove it, if
> it pleases you, he has boasted in the hearing of many people
> that we shall not long rejoice in your peace, because we
> shall not finish a whole loaf in England before he, as he
> threatens, takes away our life. ... (*CTB*, ii, no. 320)

The blame for this lawlessness is laid at the king's door, for 'what
could that Randulf do if he were not armed and supported by the
authority of your will?' And the letter ended on an eerily prophetic note:

> I had intended to return to your presence, my lord, but
> fate is drawing me, unhappy wretch that I am, to that
> afflicted Church; by your licence and grace I shall return
> to her, perhaps to die to prevent her destruction, unless
> your piety deigns swiftly to offer us some other comfort.
> But, whether we live or die, we are and will always be
> yours in the Lord; and whatever happens to us and ours,
> may God bless you and your children. May your highness
> always prosper, most serene lord. (*CTB*, ii, no. 320)

How should we interpret this last known letter to the king – and the events that gave rise to it? It is easy to say that from that point on the archbishop was courting martyrdom. But in fact, he was not so much courting as accepting the possibility that he would suffer some unspeakable fate when he reached England. What security could he have if the de Brocs were still in charge of Saltwood Castle and the military might that went with it? If they were prepared to murder sailors to get their hands on Becket's wine, if they had indeed uttered the kind of threats passed on to the king, what might they not do? And if they were to attack him, could Becket have believed that the deed would be done in his own cathedral, in front of witnesses, where the murder would automatically become sacrilege? Was it not much more likely that they would lie in wait for him on the coast, seize him as he disembarked, and carry him off, not to Canterbury but to Saltwood, where he could be imprisoned or quietly disappear? No martyrdom there; at least, no certain martyrdom there. When Eliot wrote his powerful play, he made the idea of martyrdom one of Becket's last temptations. But Thomas could not have known what would happen after such an event as his murder. It might have been a grubby and inglorious end in some filthy dungeon.

When John of Salisbury arrived in England a month later, on 16 November, where he represented the archbishop at a council in Canterbury on 18 November, which lifted the excommunications from all who had been forced to have dealings with excommunicated officials on the Canterbury estates, he found matters, if anything, worse. Despite the king's writ, as John reported later to Peter of Celle, abbot of Saint-Rémi in Reims,

> The third day before I landed [14 November] all the possessions of the archbishop of Canterbury and his followers were put under surveillance and his own proctors removed from their administration; and in the ports a public edict was issued prohibiting any of our colleagues who might wish to leave England from crossing the Channel under pain of exile and outlawry. The king's devout and filial officials took all careful measures ... to ensure that the archbishop and his followers on their return from exile should find nothing or almost nothing save empty houses largely in ruins, barns destroyed, threshing floors bare ... all the revenues which could have accrued up to Christmas have been seized in the [young] king's name. By authority of the

public power, curiales still hold many possessions which
ought to have been restored to the Church of Canterbury
according to the agreement. ... I found everything thus
in confusion quite contrary to our hope and the good
reputation and fine promises of the king; and so everyone
had given up hope of our peace and the archbishop's
return. (JS, *Letters*, ii, 714–20).

When Thomas took what was to be his last leave of the king (at
Chaumont), he was told that Henry would meet him at Rouen. But
when the time came, some time in November(?), he was met, not by
the king or by Rotrou of Rouen to conduct him to England and provide the necessary safe conduct, but by John of Oxford, whose deanery at Salisbury had been received in the face of his prohibitions,
bearing this writ:

> ... I was not able to come to Rouen at the time agreed
> between us. But I am sending Dean John of Salisbury,
> a clerk of my household, to travel with you to England,
> by whom I am informing my son, Henry, king of the
> English, that you are to have all your property honestly,
> honourably, and in peace; and furthermore, if any of the
> properties belonging to you were less well managed than
> they should have been, he is to have the matter put right.
> And because many rumours are being carried back to me
> and my son about the delay which you are making, which
> perhaps are not true, it would be expedient I believe for
> you not to defer your return to England any longer.
>   Witnessed by the king himself at Loches.
>   (*CTB*, ii, no. 322)

The non-appearance of the king on a rather superficial pretext and
the nomination of the particularly obnoxious John continued the
disdainful treatment. None of the king's promises had been kept. As
Becket said to the archbishop of Rouen, who had come out of courtesy to bid him farewell on his journey, there had been no kiss of
peace and no money to pay the creditors whom he had brought to
Rouen for payment. From his own funds, Rotrou gave him £300 to
help with his expenses. And the last sentence of the writ, which
spoke of the 'many rumours [that] are being carried back to me
and my son about the delay which you are making' must have been particularly galling, in the light of the total obstruction Becket's envoys
had encountered as they tried to make the necessary arrangements

for his repatriation. So, who had broken the peace of Fréteval? Was it Thomas or the king? The evidence speaks for itself.

From Rouen there was no turning back. John of Oxford was there with a royal writ that was just short of an order to return to England as quickly as he could, although the situation there was highly volatile. Becket knew that the de Brocs were still installed at Saltwood and still in charge of his estates; he knew that no revenues would be forthcoming; he knew that a process of election was already afoot that would fill five sees without his approval and probably with enemies; and he also knew that the archbishop of York and the bishops of London and Salisbury were adamantly opposed to his resumption of power. John of Salisbury claimed that they had earlier sent messengers to Henry, advising him not to allow Becket to return to the island until he had renounced the office of legate, given up all the papal letters he had received and promised to observe the laws of the realm. As he waited for a ship at Wissant, indeed, Milo, dean of Boulogne, transmitted the warning from Count Matthew that his enemies were waiting on the opposite shore, ready to arrest him as he disembarked. 'Make provision for yourself,' said the count.[43] This was the situation in which he sent a special courier on ahead with the very severe letters suspending York and Durham and excommunicating London and Salisbury, which were duly presented, individually, to York, London and Salisbury as they waited at Dover.

Although he had just sent off far milder letters, which would have enabled him to manage the situation that he found with some discretion, the emergence of another episcopal conspiracy whose purpose was to undermine both his legatine and episcopal authority compelled him to take some action to try to avert another round of time-consuming appeals and counter-appeals. He also carried with him the latest batch of papal bulls just brought back from the Curia by Master Gunther, whose intention was to strengthen Becket's authority as archbishop and legate. One series (of five letters) issued from Anagni and Segni between 28 September and 13 October, declared that York's coronation of the young king should not injure Canterbury's rights; authorized penalties of deprivation and excommunication against anyone clerical or lay who contravened interdicts imposed by the pope or their bishops; ordered the excommunication of any absolved by Rouen and Nevers who had not restored the properties taken from the church of Canterbury; reissued Becket's legation; and, finally, permitted Thomas to exercise his disciplinary powers over all persons subject to his legatine authority, except for the king, his wife and children.[44] These were supported by two further letters, which urged Henry II and the clergy and people of England to carry the peace into full effect.[45] A second series, obtained at the same time, was designed to enforce the peace. Letters to continental prelates provided for the imposition of an interdict if Henry II reneged on his undertakings: Archbishops William of Sens and Rotrou of Rouen were ordered to impose an interdict on Henry's continental lands within 30 days, if the sequestrated properties were not restored to their rightful owners and the 'execrable customs' utterly rescinded;[46] Rotrou of Rouen and Bishop Bernard of Nevers were commanded to reinstate the excommunication of any clergy who failed to give up Canterbury properties;[47] and all prelates in Henry II's continental territories were instructed to obey the interdict which the archbishops of Sens and Rouen would impose if the Fréteval peace were not implemented.[48] These mandates were distributed to their recipients before Becket left France.

Was this an act of impotent defiance or of prudence? One's conclusion will depend on one's judgment of the circumstances. His own clerks had encountered only contemptuous hostility from the king's ministers, there had been no kiss of peace, no restitution, no 'honourable escort' – only double-dealing. Although in the event, as Becket acknowledged, John of Oxford's presence did obtain safe passage when he landed in England, the nomination of John probably appeared deliberately insulting. The 'welcoming committee' he found at Sandwich on 1 December 1170 probably confirmed his suspicions. His last letter to the pope, written at Canterbury on 5 December, and carried by Gunther of Winchester, described what happened:

> When those enemies of ours had got certain news of
> this, fearing we know not what, they took counsel with
> the king's officials and with that most criminal son of
> perdition, Randulf de Broc, who, misusing the force of the
> public power, has for seven years raged without restraint
> in God's church. They decided therefore to have the sea
> ports to which they suspected we would come guarded
> and carefully watched by armed forces of their soldiers
> and henchmen, so that we should not be able to enter the
> country without their making a thorough examination of
> all our baggage and sequestrating all the letters which we
> have obtained from your majesty. But by God's will it
> happened that their machinations became known to us
> through our friends, and their overweening insolence and
> impertinence was not allowed to remain hidden. For the

henchmen ... were moving in arms around the shore,
directing their course as the aforementioned York and the
bishops of London and Salisbury instructed. They had
indeed chosen for the accomplishment of this spitefulness
those whom they knew to be especially hostile to us,
namely Randulf de Broc, Reginald of Warenne [brother of
William of Warenne, earl of Surrey], and Gervase, sheriff
of Kent, who openly threatened that they would cut off
our head if we presumed to land. ...

When their intentions had been very carefully discovered,
your letters were sent ahead, one day before we took ship,
and those in which York was suspended, and London and
Salisbury were again placed under sentence of anathema
were handed to them.[49] We boarded ship on the following
day and reached England after a fair crossing, taking with
us at the lord king's command, Dean John of Salisbury;
who, not without sorrow and shame, saw the armed men
we have spoken of hurrying to our ship to use force
against those who were arriving. Fearing that any wrong
done to us and ours would redound to the lord king's
dishonour, the said dean went out to meet the armed
men, commanding them in the lord king's name not to
harm us or ours, because such action would brand the
king with whom we had made peace with the mark of
treachery, and he persuaded them to approach us without
weapons. ... (*CTB*, ii, no. 326)

Despite these bad omens, however, Becket's return to his own cathedral city was a triumphant *adventus*. All along the 12-mile route the
ordinary people crowded out to meet and greet him, parish priests
led their congregations in procession; and, when he reached
Canterbury, the city and the cathedral were decorated as for a festi-
val, and Becket was received with a procession of monks and clergy.
'The cathedral resounded with hymns and organ-music, the hall
with fanfares of trumpets and the City with loud rejoicing on every
side.' Inside the monastery, he greeted each monk with the kiss of
peace and in the chapterhouse, he preached a sermon on the text,
'Here we have no abiding city.'[50] There is no reason seriously to
doubt the general accuracy of these descriptions. After six years of
exploitation and tyranny by the de Brocs and their cronies, backed
by the awful power of the king, which had witnessed the systematic
denuding of the archbishop's estates, his return would have been

seen as a delivery. However oppressive the regime of Becket's bailiffs, they were infinitely better than the exploiters whose only purpose was to extract as much profit as possible in as short a time as possible. There was even welcome evidence of the acceptance of his authority by those who were not tied up in the king's conspiracy. Arnulf of Lisieux, for example, recommended the reinstatement of a clerk who had been deprived of the Church at Saltwood[51] on Becket's account; the clerks of Earl Hugh of Norfolk, who had defied the interdict placed on the earl's land in the Pentney affair submitted to his discipline; and Earl Hugh himself had been reconciled to the Church by the bishop of Norwich, in accordance with his mandate.[52] A similar acknowledgement of his authority would have been enough to re-establish tolerable relations with the censured bishops; but they were more defiant than the earl.

> When we arrived at [Canterbury], the king's officials immediately approached us and commanded us in his name to absolve the suspended and excommunicated bishops, since the lord of York and the bishops of London and Salisbury had informed them that the action taken against themselves redounded to the king's injury and the overthrow of the customs of the realm, and promised that after absolution the bishops of our province would come willingly to us to obey the law, *saving the honour of the realm*. But we replied that it is not for a lesser judge to relax the sentence of a superior, and that no man is allowed to undermine what the Apostolic See has decreed. Nevertheless, because they were pressing insistently and threatening that the lord king would take amazing and extraordinary action unless we agreed to them, we said that if the bishops of London and Salisbury would swear in our presence according to the Church's form that they would obey your mandate, we, for the peace of the church and out of respect for the lord king, with his advice and that of the lord of Winchester and our other brethren, would … do whatever we could in that matter, saving the respect due to you, and love them as our dearest brothers in Christ, and treat them with all gentleness and humanity.

> When this was reported back to the bishops by the interlocutors, York, seeking partners in his rebellion and agitators for the schism, responded that an oath of this

kind should not be taken except by the king's will, especially by bishops, *because it was contrary to the prince's dignities and the customs of the realm.* He was told on our behalf that those bishops had been excommunicated by us before, and that they did not deserve to be absolved except after taking the oath ... And if our sentences ought not to be relaxed without an oath by the bishops, much less should yours .... The bishops were so moved by that reply, as those who were present told us, that they decided to go to you and receive absolution according to the Church's custom, not considering it safe to oppose the Church and attack Apostolic decrees in order to preserve the customs of the realm. But York ... dissuaded them, advising that they should rather go to the lord king, who always supported them, and that they should send messengers to the new king, to convince him that we wished to depose him, when we, as God can witness, would prefer him to have not one kingdom only, but the greatest and most numerous kingdoms on earth, if it would profit God's church. (*CTB*, ii, no. 326: Canterbury, 5 December 1170)

Roger of York's attitude is easy to explain. In the context of his long-term strategy to achieve an equal status for the province of York, his successful coronation of the new king would have been a very useful precedent for the future. If he could persuade Henry that the attack on him and the participating bishops was also an attack on the legality of the consecration of his son and heir, then there was a good chance that Becket's condemnations of his own actions would be countermanded in some way. The elevation of York to a position of leadership in the triumvirate is not just Canterbury prejudice, as Barlow argued,[53] but a recognition of the significance of his attachment to the London–Salisbury axis. He was an ecclesiastical heavyweight, with more to gain than the others; inveterately litigious[54] and, it was alleged, with a 'fighting fund' of £8000 to finance any necessary action. So it was that York, London and Salisbury hurried across the Channel, 'so that, which God prevent, they may deceive the lord king and rouse his anger against the Church.' These chillingly prophetic words, written on 5 December, were transmitted in Becket's last message to the pope.[55] The letter, and its bearer, Master Gunther, had reached only as far as Sens, when they were overtaken by news of Becket's murder.

10

Murder in the cathedral

Three images present themselves: that of a bitter and defeated man, lashing out in all directions, whose final acts of defiance against the four knights brought about his murder; or of a man who deliberately chose the way of martyrdom as the only way out of a desperate situation; or, following the theme begun by Foxe and given dramatic reality by Eliot, of an actor playing his finest role, and confounding his enemies by dying heroically and turning himself into a saint. As we have seen, there are hints – and more than hints – that some of his household were using the language of martyrdom,[1] and the story of a prophetic dream which he was said to have had at Pontigny was widely circulated. In it, Christ said, 'My Church will be glorified in your blood, and you will be glorified in Me.'[2] This latter may have been part of the posthumous image-making process, but two of Becket's letters from 1170 suggest that he was fully aware of the danger he was confronting. In late October 1170, after hearing from Herbert of Bosham how dire was the situation in England, he had concluded his last surviving letter to the king with the baleful statement:

> fate is drawing me, unhappy wretch that I am, to that
> afflicted Church; … I shall return to her, perhaps to die,
> to prevent her destruction, unless your piety deigns swiftly
> to offer us some other comfort. But, whether we live or
> die, we are and will always be yours in the Lord; and
> whatever happens to us and ours, may God bless you and
> your children. (*CTB*, ii, no. 320)

Six months earlier (in April 1170) he had written to Cardinal Albert:

> Let those who want to, attack; let the cardinals arm not
> only the king of England but the whole world to our
> destruction, if they can; by God's favour, I shall never
> withdraw from fidelity to the Church, neither in life nor

in death. For the future I commit the Church's cause to
God, for whom I am a proscribed exile; let him bring
healing as he knows it to be expedient. (*CTB*, ii, no. 278)

Should these statements be read as deliberate pursuit of martyrdom
or steadfast courage? Becket could not choose the time or the place
or the method of his killing, although the threat of physical violence
was never very far away. When Thomas sailed into Sandwich har-
bour at the start of December, he knew that many hands would be
raised against him. Indeed, he would have been seized by the armed
men in the service of Randulf de Broc, Reginald of Warenne and
Gervase of Cornhill, sheriff of Kent, if John of Oxford had not been
there to prevent it; and they seem to have been acting on the instructions of Richard of Ilchester and Geoffrey Ridel, probably representing Henry II, as well as York and the two bishops. By Christmas,
Becket knew that more serious measures were afoot: not only were
his estates still held by their occupiers, but he had been forbidden to
approach the young king's court and commanded, in pretty brutal
terms, to return to Canterbury and stay there. He also knew that
York, London and Salisbury had carried their grievances to the king
in Normandy, with consequences he could readily imagine. Not
surprisingly, his Christmas sermon alluded to Canterbury's martyr,
St Alphege, with the comment that it might soon have another.[3]
  A considered judgment on Becket's last days can be reached only
by considering his actions in their context. His first political action
was to seek reconciliation with the young king, who was in residence
at Woodstock. On about 9 December he sent Prior Richard of Dover
with a present of three fine horses to the young Henry, asking permission to come to pay his respects.[4] Richard, and his message, were
rebuffed. The prior was dismissed with the response that the king
would send his answer when he had consulted Geoffrey Ridel and
Richard of Ilchester, who were at Southampton, waiting to cross to
Normandy. Geoffrey's advice was obstructive. 'I know the will of
the father king; and I shall never be party to any counsel which concludes that [Becket] may enter the presence of the king's son, whom
he is striving to disinherit.' Earl Reginald of Cornwall and some others
dissented; but they were defeated by those who said that they knew
the older king's will.[5] Meanwhile, no doubt expecting a favourable
answer, for the young man had never been personally hostile, Thomas
set out for young Henry's court. Passing through Rochester, where
he was solemnly welcomed by the bishop and clergy, he proceeded
to London, en route for Woodstock or Windsor (Henry's court moved

to Windsor on 18 December). At Southwark Minster he was received, not only by the canons, but by streams of Londoners, clergy, men, women and students from the schools, about 3000-strong.[6]

These demonstrations of popular support for the archbishop, which mirrored those he had received along the road to Canterbury a week or so before, were not welcome to the royal officials. Claiming to be acting on royal authority, Randulf de Broc and Gervase of Cornhill (sheriff of Kent) summoned the leading churchmen and citizens of the City, and caused the names of all who had processed to meet the archbishop – the king's enemy, as they called him – to be written down, so that they would appear before the king's court to give sureties that they would submit to its judgment. But the priors and parish priests did not obey the summons, and

> the many citizens who did appear on the appointed day replied that they had not seen the royal letters which ordered them to be cited or to make provision for themselves, nor those of the justices. They were the king's citizens, and loyal to him, and not bound to answer to them: at the king's command they would do what they should. And so the matter rested.[7]

London was a chartered commune, with its own administrative and legal structure; and it had the defensive strength to withstand the threats of Randulf and Gervase.

Becket remained for a day and a night in the lodgings of the bishop of Winchester in Southwark, before continuing his journey; but he was intercepted by two of the young Henry's court (Thomas de Turnebu and Jocelin of Louvain), with orders to return to Canterbury and stay there, and he was forbidden to enter any royal cities, estates or towns.[8] It is possible that he had reached his manor of Harrow in Middlesex, when this disagreeable order was conveyed to him, for it was there, between *c.* 13 and 16 or 17 December that he was met by Abbot Simon of St Albans and Prior Richard of Dover, whom he sent back, accompanied by a London clerk (William FitzStephen?), to make another approach to young Henry, who was by then travelling to Winchester. He also sent his own doctor, William, to Earl Reginald of Cornwall at Braemore, near Fordingbridge. Confusing him with William of Canterbury, the monk who later compiled the miracles and a Life of the saint, Barlow calls the physician, somewhat disparagingly, a spy; but although William was instructed to discover what he could about what was afoot at the court, he was sent in response to the earl's request for medical advice on his cancer (*fistula*). Despite the earl's high status and royal blood, however, even he was afraid to disclose his opinions openly in the presence of his household. Presumably to put them off the scent, he declared publicly that the archbishop had 'greatly disturbed the country; and unless the Lord intervenes, he will drag it into perpetual disgrace; and soon we shall all be drawn into Hell by him.' Despite this subterfuge, one of the attendants recognized that the physician belonged to Becket's household, and Earl Reginald had to advise him, in private, to make his escape and warn John of Salisbury, John of Canterbury (John Planeta), Gunther and Alexander of Wales that if they were caught they would be put to the sword. He fled by night, and poured out the whole story to John of Salisbury, who declared himself ready for the swords of the young bloods (*garciones*).[9] Not to put too fine a point on it, the archbishop and his household were being treated as traitors on instructions from Henry II himself, conveyed through Geoffrey Ridel.

Abbot Simon, Prior Richard and the London clerk found the king at Fordingbridge, but were denied an audience. They presented a long list of complaints to the *tutores regis*, however: clerks were being imprisoned in secular jails and subjected to various physical penalties by secular judges; the Canterbury estates, including Saltwood, had not been restored as promised, and the manors were in a ruinous condition; Randulf de Broc had seized the wine shipment intended for the archbishop, and disabled and sunk the ships; churches were still wrongfully held by intruders; clerks were forbidden to cross the channel in either direction, making appeal to the jurisdiction of St Peter impossible. And the clerk added that if this did not stop, they as priests would have to do their duty.[10]

There was nothing exaggerated about these complaints. Becket's authority as archbishop of the see of Canterbury was almost wholly obstructed; his property was subject to open piracy and robbery; and the Constitutions of Clarendon were in full operation. The responses of the *tutores* were as disquieting as the secret message just given to John of Salisbury. Reginald of Warenne commented that 'Both sides are drawing wide their bows'; and Earl Reginald declared, 'Before the middle of Lent we shall have committed a terrible deed.' On the matter of their mission, however, the envoys were told that 'much appeared to need improvement', but that Becket's petitions would not be heard until he ceased his opposition to king and magnates; and one of the court told the London cleric that if it were not for the (young) king's presence, he would be severely punished.[11]

Declining the invitation of Abbot Simon to spend Christmas at St Albans, Thomas returned to Canterbury to celebrate the coming feast. There, on Saturday 19 December, the last of the three Ember days in December, he ordained new clergy, but deferred the ordination of monks who had been accepted into the monastery without his approval, with the exception of William of Canterbury, whom he made deacon; but during the following Christmas week, he received all of them in the chapter, to confirm their admission to the monastic life. Then, on Christmas Day, he solemnly excommunicated Randulf de Broc and his partisans, and published the papal sentences against the bishops.[12] Whether this was foolhardy or provocative is questionable. The wheels that would lead to his murder were already turning; the de Brocs were already geared up to resist. It is unlikely that they would have acted any differently had they not been excommunicated on Christmas Day.

On 27 December, the archbishop sent messengers to three different destinations. Herbert of Bosham and Alexander Llewellyn were sent to France (to Louis VII and William of Sens), Gilbert Glanville to the pope, and Richard his chaplain and John Planeta were sent to give conditional absolution to the clerics in the service of Earl Hugh of Norfolk, who had celebrated divine service while excommunicate. These embassies, in fact, may have been intended to safeguard the clerks in the light of the warning that Becket's physician had transmitted from no less a person than the earl of Cornwall, a son, though illegitimate, of Henry I. As he progressed through what were to be the last five days of his life, he followed the routine of public masses and Christmas festivities that the season demanded. What else could he have been expected to do? What else was he able to do? He could not have been other than fully aware that terrible storm clouds were gathering on all sides: he and his household had been made into virtual outlaws; the ports were closed to all traffic not licensed by the king; and Canterbury was almost under siege by Randulf de Broc and Gervase of Cornhill, who had stationed guards at the gates of the city. And both, it should be remembered, were royal officers.

Meanwhile, in Normandy, the other segment of the drama was being played out. Roger of York, Gilbert of London and Jocelin of Salisbury, supported by Richard of Ilchester (Geoffrey Ridel having been held up by rough seas), approached the king with their fury at having been sentenced again. As they told it, not only had Becket impugned the coronation by excommunicating York and suspending all the bishops who had participated in the ceremony, but he was also threatening the crown and the kingdom, and disturbing the peace by careering around the realm with a force of armed men. Whatever their opinion of Becket's ecclesiastical powers, which did not threaten either the king or the kingdom, their description of his travelling around England with an armed retinue, spreading disaffection, is a monstrous distortion of the truth. They had witnessed his arrival at Sandwich, where he was confronted by armed bands, not the reverse; and when they left him on the coast at Sandwich, which was in his own estates, he was on his way to Canterbury – a journey of 12 miles, where he stayed for eight days. Thereafter, his only journey was to Harrow in Middlesex (via Rochester and Southwark) on a projected visit to the young king at Woodstock, which he had duly notified, to acknowledge the young king's new status. Staying for a few days, perhaps from 14 to 16 or 17 December (he was back in Canterbury probably by 18 December, where he celebrated ordinations the next day) in one of his own manors, can hardly be called disturbing the peace of the realm!

The older Henry and his court were duly incensed at the lurid picture of Becket's behaviour that had been presented to them – and they may have been alarmed by the evidence of general support from the people, especially the London citizenry. In a scene reminiscent of the threats made at Northampton,[13] Enjuger (Engelram) de Bohun, Bishop Roger of Salisbury's uncle, advised punitive action – 'I don't know how you can punish such a man, except by hanging him on a cross-shaped gallows' – while William Malvoisin, nephew of Count Eudo of Brittany, recounted the story he had heard in Rome, on his way back from Jerusalem, of a pope who had been killed there for 'insolence and intolerable impudence'. Earl William de Mandeville, Saher de Quincy and Richard de Humet, constable of Normandy, were sent to seize the archbishop: Earl William and de Quincy set up a system of watch and ward on the Norman coast, while de Humet crossed to England, where he sent secret instructions to Hugh de Gundeville and William FitzJohn, the younger Henry's guardians. They were commanded to go immediately to Canterbury, without the young king's knowledge, while de Humet kept watch by the ports, to intercept the archbishop if he attempted to flee.[14] These complex arrangements demonstrate that the older Henry was resolved on a course of action that went somewhat beyond the sending of ordinary messengers: the intention was arrest, by force, if necessary, and imprisonment.

Henry's fury is manifest not only in the descriptions of his rage and his later acknowledgement that his intemperate words had encouraged the knights to leave his court, but also in the letter he issued in support of the appeal launched by London and Salisbury. The king's letter could not be more explicit in its bitter hostility:

> ... This most dangerous enemy of mine, very ready to use all his powers to destroy me and mine ... I received in peace in response to your mandates ... and I sent a member of my court to conduct him to his own. This peace was granted in full not only to him but to his men, who ... scurrying round the globe have filled the world with bad rumours about me ... . (*MTB*, vii, no. 729)

He begged the pope to relax the sentences, and he commended the bearer, Master David of London, who was a key member of Gilbert Foliot's staff. If, as seems likely, this letter was drafted by Foliot himself, it confirms Becket's opinion that Foliot was a dangerous enemy. This royal letter was supported by a dossier of defences written by Bishop Giles of Évreux, Archbishop Rotrou of Rouen and Bishop Arnulf of Lisieux. Giles stressed the 'peaceful and joyful' return of the archbishop and declared that nothing was said about the preservation of the customs in the oath taken by the new king, which Giles heard with his own ears; Rotrou also confirmed that there was no reference to the new customs. Writing at greater length, Arnulf proclaimed that the peace had been meticulously observed by the king, that the archbishop had been conducted by members of the royal household 'with the greatest honour', but 'in his hands he carried fire and sword', and promulgated censures against the bishops involved in the coronation. He denied that anything irregular had occurred in the coronation, although he was careful to say that this statement was based on the assertions of others, and he declared that the new king had sworn whatever was required about ecclesiastical liberty and dignity according to 'the laws and canons'; and that no mention was made of any kind of different customs, despite claims to the contrary. He also wrote testimonials for Gilbert Foliot and Jocelin of Salisbury. The first, for Foliot, largely recycled the testimonial he had written for him in 1169; the second, for Jocelin, claimed that the bishops believed that they had done nothing wrong in participating in the coronation, since they had the authority of papal letters.[15]

These versions of events should be compared with what is known of the king's actions: the tardy and in most cases non-compliance with the agreed restitutions, the status of the 'member of my court' sent to escort Becket to Canterbury, the reception at Sandwich and the systematic obstruction he encountered when he attempted to approach the young king's court, which was directed by the older king's agent, Geoffrey Ridel. As to whether Becket should be considered a troublemaker and a dangerous disturber of the realm's peace, his actions should be compared with those of Theobald in 1148. On his return from the council of Reims, which he had attended against King Stephen's command, he suspended all the bishops who had not attended the council for disobeying the papal mandate and reserved the absolution of Henry of Winchester to the pope.[16]

The king's manifest rage against Becket and some sort of taunt against the 'useless drones' who cluttered up his court, led four barons – Reginald FitzUrse, William de Tracy, Hugh de Morville and Richard Brito – to conspire together to repair the king's honour. Their aim, almost certainly, was to seize the king's enemy and bring him back to stand some sort of trial in Normandy, but it is almost certain that they did not have a written mandate from the king. They might have thought that Becket's capture would earn them the king's favour.[17] There has been much confusion about the precise identity and later careers of the four men, as historians were on the whole reluctant to accept the generalizations of Herbert of Bosham that they had all come to a sticky end within three years of the murder.[18] Fortunately, a very recent study has cleared up most of the problems. Reginald FitzUrse was the son of Richard FitzUrse of Bulwick, who had established himself in the service of Henry I and Stephen, and can be traced as witness to royal charters from 1158; Professor Vincent concludes from the marriage of his daughter to Robert de Courteney and other indicators that he was a man of some status at the court and, moreover, that he had sworn homage to Becket when he was chancellor. Hugh de Morville (not to be confused, as he usually is, with his cousin, Hugh de Morville of Burgh by Sands) was an important northern baron who had been educated at the court of the Scottish king. The second son of his father, also named Hugh, he was lord of Westmoreland and Appleby, and also frequented Henry II's court from at least 1157, when he was given custody of Knaresborough Castle, and he may have been an itinerant justice in Cumberland and Northumberland in 1169–Michaelmas 1170. Richard Brito has been identified as the son of Simon Brito of Sampford Brett in north Somerset, adjoining FitzUrse's estate of Williton. His attachment had not been to Henry II's court, however, but to the household of his brother, William, until his death in 1164; and he may have moved into the fringe of Henry's court in the train of William de Tracy. This latter, not to be confused with William de Tracy of Toddington in Gloucestershire, was lord of Bradninch in Devon and various fees in Normandy, especially Mortain, and can be traced in Henry II's court from 1163.

All four were linked by their estates in the West Country, and three of them – FitzUrse, Tracy and Morville – had all been associated with enemies of the Angevin cause and with Thomas as chancellor. 'Such men,' concludes Professor Vincent, 'were prepared to go to extraordinary lengths, even to the extent of murder, to prove their loyalty to the new regime.'[19]

The 'knights' left the court at Bur-le-Roi on the evening of 26 December and reached Saltwood on 28 December, where they spent the night, and then proceeded to Canterbury the following afternoon, with their numbers much enforced. Theirs was not a secret or clandestine approach. As they went, they called up the military support of the garrisons of three castles (Dover, Rochester and Bletchingley), in addition to their friends from Saltwood, proclaiming themselves 'king's men', and they stationed armed men around the small walled city of Canterbury to ensure that there would be no civil unrest and no attempt (or no successful attempt) to rescue the archbishop once they had arrested him. The best account is probably FitzStephen's. Clearly a large force of knights and armed men had been assembled, since a detachment of about 12 knights rode with the four ringleaders to the archbishop's palace, while their associates tried to rouse the citizens to join them. Finding that the people were not prepared to join in an attack on their archbishop, the knights ordered them to stay in their houses and pay no heed to whatever might happen. So the four, led by Reginald FitzUrse, entered the hall, where dinner had just finished (it was about 4 pm). As the servants were eating their meal in the lower part of the hall, Becket and his clerks and some senior monks had withdrawn into his private chamber. The four sat down with the clerks and monks, and FitzUrse declared that they had been sent by the king to demand the absolution of the bishops, and that he must then go to the younger king at Winchester to 'make satisfaction to him, whom you are trying to deprive of his crown', and there 'stand to the judgment of his court'. Becket pointed out that the sentences were not his but the pope's, and that they were deserved. Nevertheless, he continued,

> I have granted the petitions of the bishops of London
> and Salisbury for absolution and the removal of their
> suspension from the others, on condition that they
> humbly sue for pardon and agree to stand to judgment
> before the ecclesiastical court and to give security for the
> same. But they have rejected this offer, which, however,
> still remains open. As for the coronation of the new king,

it stands firm and unshaken. The lord Pope has punished
the agent of the coronation without detriment to the
dignity of the crown ... These penalties have been
imposed with the assent of the lord king and with his
express permission granted me at the time of the peace.[20]

This was a true statement, although it is not certain what kind
of disciplinary action the king had in mind when he gave his oral
approval at Fréteval. As they made threats, he reminded them that
some of them had been present at the peace (at Fréteval) and that he
had a letter of safe conduct from the king. John of Salisbury then tried
to persuade him to discuss the matter in private, but Becket refused:

Foot to foot shall you find me in the battle of the Lord.
Once I fled like a timid priest. Now I have returned to my
Church in the counsel and obedience of the lord Pope.
Nevermore will I desert her.

And he reminded Reginald, William and Hugh that they owed him
fealty. 'There is no bond between us against the king,' replied Hugh;
and Reginald added, more menacingly, 'We do well to threaten the
archbishop, and we will do more than threaten; come, let us withdraw.' As knights and clerks came into the chamber at the sound of
the commotion, Reginald ordered them in the king's name to leave
this man; when they did not, he told them to prevent his escape.
Becket said, 'It will be easy to guard me; I shall not run away.'[21]
John of Salisbury was dismayed at the turn of events and reproved
the archbishop for conducting the 'interview' himself in intemperate
terms, and for not seeking to conciliate the men who were no doubt
plotting evil against him. To this, Thomas replied, 'I am resolved. I
know what I must do', to which John responded, 'Please God, you
have chosen well.'[22]

What are we to make of this encounter? Generally Becket is found
guilty of failing to consult his entourage, of rudeness and of inflammatory language. In his defence, we might remind ourselves of the circumstances. Becket knew what was afoot: his ignominious arrest; and
he could guess at the likely outcome. His 'I know what I must do' was
his determination not to allow himself to be hauled off like a felon. He
had given way at Clarendon; he had fled from Northampton. At this
third crisis, he would neither flee nor willingly surrender. Was that the
point at which he decided to become a martyr? The answer is no.
What followed was largely the result of decisions made by other men –
monks and clerks – and the four barons themselves.

The four went outside into the courtyard, taking with them two of the archbishop's own knights – thus depriving him of any defence – and there not only donned armour and retrieved their weapons, but admitted a troop of soldiers into the courtyard to prevent Becket's escape from the precincts. Re-entry into the archbishop's palace was barred, because two servants had managed to shut and bolt the stout main door behind them, and they had to force an entry into the hall by means of an oriel window that was pointed out to them by Randulf de Broc (who had occupied the palace during the exile).[23]

These details are all well known, but their implications for the interpretation both of the barons' motivation and Becket's reaction are not generally explored. It is clear, surely, that the infamous four were not working alone. They had the support of Henry II's officials in Kent; they had assembled a large force of men-at-arms; and their assumption of weapons and armour manifested their readiness, if not their intention, to use ultimate force. The archbishop, on the other hand, was wholly unguarded. He had two immediate options. He could, when he heard the armed men breaking in, have gone to meet them and surrendered himself to their custody. One wonders if any of his post-Conquest predecessors would have done that? He seems, in fact, to have intended to wait for them in his chamber; but the monks who were with him urged him to seek the security of the cathedral, where vespers were being chanted, and some of them pulled him to his feet. So, preceded by his cross, carried by the French cleric Henry of Auxerre, he processed towards the monks' cloister and the door of the north transept, but he would not allow the monks to secure the cloister door. Why? Once inside the church, he began to ascend the steps leading to the upper altar where he used to say his private mass, but turned and came down to prevent the monks shutting the transept door. Again, why? Both actions were deliberate. As the four angry men, led by FitzUrse, rushed in, calling, 'Where is Thomas Beketh, traitor to king and kingdom?', and brandishing their weapons, all the clerks fled, except Robert the canon, William FitzStephen and Edward Grim;[24] so, too, did William of Canterbury (and most of the monks who had come down to the transept), being unworthy of martyrdom.[25] FitzStephen claims that had Becket so wished, he, too, could have fled, but that he chose to stand his ground and face what was to come.[26] Whatever might be thought about the 'provocation' of the de Brocs in the Christmas excommunications, none of the main protagonists had cause for personal grievance against the archbishop. He could not, in any case, meet force with force. The fact that he had ordered two sets of oak doors (cloister and transept) to be left unbarred supports the view that he did not intend to put up a fight. Instead, he replied, 'Here I am, no king's traitor, but a priest; why do you seek me?'

So, was this more evidence of eagerness for martyrdom or the courage of a brave man who chose to face what would come? Reginald FitzUrse first taunted him by flicking the cap off his head with his sword, saying, 'Fly, you are a dead man', and, his own action contradicting the advice, he grabbed Becket's cloak and tried to hoist the archbishop up on de Tracy's shoulders, while someone else shouted, 'You are our prisoner, come with us.' But Becket refused to allow himself to be bundled out of the transept. Reacting angrily to FitzUrse's sacrilegious assault, he wrenched his garment from his hand, called the baron a pimp and pushed him away with such force that he almost fell to the ground. 'I will not go hence. Here shall you work your will and obey your orders.' Realizing that the moment had come, Thomas bowed his head, joined his hands, and uttered his last prayer, 'I commend myself and the Church's cause to God and St Mary, to the holy patrons of this church, and to St Denis.'[27] While Hugh de Morville menaced any would-be rescuers, FitzUrse, shouting, 'Strike, strike', and de Tracy and Brito then rushed the archbishop. There is confusion over how many sword strokes it took to fell the archbishop and who struck the first blow, but it was a ferocious attack from three practised swordsmen, whose intention was to kill, not to wound or immobilize. There were no thrusts to the body or limbs: all three heavy swords, designed to cut through armour, slashed down on the victim's unprotected head.

In trying to protect the archbishop, Master Edward Grim thrust out an arm and so shared the first blow from FitzUrse (or de Tracy),[28] which glanced off the top of Becket's cranium, cut through his clothing to the shoulder bone, and nearly severed Grim's arm as the sword thrust down; another slashing blow or two to the head, perhaps from de Tracy, struck the archbishop to the ground, and, as he lay there, Brito sliced off the tonsured crown of his head with such force that his sword broke on the pavement: 'Take that for the love of lord William, the king's brother.' Then Hugh of Horsey, nicknamed Mauclerk, a clerk in the service of Hugh de Morville,[29] put his foot on the neck of the fallen man, and scraped his bloodied brains out on to the paved floor.[30]

Most commentators are at pains to excuse the murderers on the grounds of Becket's resistance. 'The situation got out of hand,' wrote Barlow.[31] The whole scene can be read very differently. Noting that, in his furious outburst, Henry II had emphasized Becket's humble origins, calling him a 'low-born clerk', and that the barons had called out for 'Thomas Beketh', thereby deliberately ignoring his episcopal status, Professor Aurell saw played out in the cathedral a demonstration of the aristocrat's contempt for the clever men of 'low' birth, whose learning had enabled them to rise high in royal and ecclesiastical service. Moreover, they concentrated their attack on his head, deliberately desecrating the tonsure that marked his clerical status.[32] Their very presence in the cathedral, wearing armour and carrying naked weapons, was a sacrilegious affront to the sanctity of the place; by so entering the cathedral, they were committed to the use of force and, armed as they were, that force soon became lethal.

However the story is told, it was a terrible and bloody murder. Nothing that Becket said or did could justify the slaughter. But was it martyrdom? From the declarations of Henry VIII onwards, one strand of historical commentary answers the question with an emphatic 'No'. Concentrating on the immediate circumstances, Becket's uncomplimentary remarks and his physical resistance to the knights' attempts at arrest are seen as the immediate cause; that in turn was provoked by his issue of the papal sentences on York, Salisbury and London, which in turn was provoked by the coronation of the young king in June 1170, and Becket's concern for the primatial claims of the church of Canterbury. No martyrdom there. For Henry VIII, John Foxe, Lord Lyttelton, Robertson, Warren and Türk, for example, the murder was as much his responsibility as that of the murderers, if not more so. If he had not resisted 'arrest', there would have been no violence against his person at that point, but he could be forgiven for having pondered what would have come afterwards. For the monks and clerics who described the terrible sacrilege, the sequence of events from the coronation to the murder was only the last series of links in a chain that reached back through the exile, to Northampton, Clarendon and Westminster. What linked them all was the archbishop's opposition to the establishment of the Constitutions of Clarendon. These constitutions/customs/dignities, whose recognition was made the *sine qua non* of reconciliation with the archbishop and his clerks, remained the point of contention throughout the six years of the exile. Their omission from the Fréteval peace was an exercise in dissimulation, and the focus on the coronation of 'Henry III' was almost certainly by pre-arrangement. As he faced his murderers in Canterbury Cathedral, Thomas would have seen in their violence the long-delayed consequences of his refusal to dance to the king's tune. Twice before, barons had threatened to execute the king's will; twice before, he had either given way (Clarendon) or fled (Northampton) – this was the end of the road.

> Here I am, no traitor, but God's priest; and I marvel that
> you have entered God's church in such a garb ... I submit
> to death in the name of the Lord, and I commend my soul
> and the Church's cause to God and St Mary and to the
> holy patrons of this church.[33]

The immediate reaction of the monks, clergy and lay people in the cathedral was shock and horror. Many historians remark that the monks did not immediately call Becket saint or martyr, and that it was only when his chaplain Robert of Merton revealed the hair shirt and the monastic habit, concealed beneath the black robe of a canon, that they took up the cause. The delay and hesitation, however, lasted short of 12 hours, and their hesitation, such as it was, was understandable. Becket's murder had been a terrible and terrifying act of violence carried out by a group of armed men in full sight of monks and clerks in the north transept of the cathedral. The assassins were not alone. They were accompanied not only by the de Brocs and their followers from Saltwood Castle, but by considerable military strength, to ensure that no one would attempt to defend the archbishop. Immediately after the murder, they ransacked the palace, carrying off whatever they could find, including horses from the stables. FitzStephen calculated the value of their booty at more than 2000 marks – a small fortune. While the marauders were still within the precinct of the cathedral – how long does it take to rob a palace? – the monks must have been petrified about what might happen next. This explains why, as FitzStephen describes it, the body lay 'for a long time (*diu*)' almost unattended, deserted by clerks, monks and all the rest; without even a light. This 'long time' cannot have been more than an hour or so, and it may have been less. As soon as it was known that the murderers and their escort had ridden off with their spoils,

> the monks and clerks and servants, and a crowd from
> the city came swarming round the dead archbishop. The
> silence was broken, and from every side groans and cries
> of lamentation were uttered, which before had been stifled
> for fear of the assassins.

The witnesses of the murder, the monks and the townsfolk were stunned and afraid. No doubt there was a collective state of shock as when an act of brutal violence or fatal accident occurs – the onlookers are first stunned and disorientated. What is the right thing to do when one has seen or heard an archbishop of Canterbury hacked to death before one's eyes and when the murderers, protected by their assertions of royal mandate, could still be heard looting the palace?

Once the knights had gone, the body was surrounded by a jumbled mass of people. They had not crowded in to see a saint, indeed, but to see the evidence of a frightful murder. Yet some were so affected by what they saw that they treated the body as a relic. Benedict of Peterborough, who was there, described how some smeared their eyes with the blood and others secretly gathered up small amounts in little containers that they happened to have with them, or cut off fragments of their own clothing and dipped them in the blood.[34]

FitzStephen does not try to hide the shock, the fear, the hesitation and the delay in preparing the body for burial. His word *diu* – for a long time – has been torn from its context and made to suggest callous disregard. What he describes is the natural reaction of frightened men (and probably some women, too). Thus passed 'most of the night'. Finally, 'it was resolved to cover and bind the martyr's broken skull with a clean linen cloth, and the body was then placed on a bier, carried through the choir, and deposited before the high altar. At this point Brother Robert of Merton revealed the hair shirt and the monastic habit. It was then that the monks acclaimed him as saint and martyr. Slightly later, a group of monks, including Arnold the Goldsmith, went to the place of the martyrdom, gathered up the blood and brains that had been scattered on the pavement, and put them in a clean basin; they then positioned movable benches over the place of his martyrdom, so that it should not be soiled by the feet of passers-by. Then the monks said the office for the dead.

Early the next morning, it was decided to hurry the burial because of the rumour that the de Brocs might drag the dead body out of the cathedral and either string it up like a felon's corpse or throw it into a drain. There were present the heads of two Kentish monasteries, Walter, abbot of the Cistercian house of Boxley, and Richard, prior of Dover, a dependency of Christ Church Canterbury, who had been summoned to advise on the appointment of a new prior for Canterbury. As the most senior ecclesiastics present, they supervised the burial. There was no funeral mass, because the cathedral had been violated; the outer, bloodstained garments, but not the hair shirt and monastic habit, were removed and distributed to bystanders;[35] the body was dressed in its archiepiscopal vestments without washing, the abbots deeming that it had been washed in its own blood. Thus clothed in the vestments he had worn on the day of his consecration in 1162, Thomas Becket was buried in the crypt, in a new marble sarcophagus, set in the floor between the altars of St John the Baptist and St Augustine of Canterbury.[36]

Murder, office and burial had all taken place within about 16 hours, at the most. There had been little time to assess the significance of what had happened, or to consult other ecclesiastical authorities, or to work out a strategy; and it cannot be assumed that the cathedral priory was enthusiastic about the prospect of a martyr's shrine in their midst.[37] Archbishops were not popular with Canterbury's monks, who resented their authority, whether or not they were monks by profession. Thomas was no different in that regard. Many of those who had witnessed his 'election' in 1162 would have been present in the cathedral to hear even if they did not see the dénouement. Opinions were likely to have been mixed. At least two monks said that Thomas had brought his troubles on himself.[38] On the other hand, the Becket who had returned to Canterbury after six years' exile was very different from the man who had fled with only a few silver vessels. The marks of his suffering were upon him; the murder was sacrilege; and the revelation of his secret mortifications did much to palliate the memory of his chancellorship. However divergent the views of the monks, however, lay people seem to have had fewer doubts. As news of the dreadful deed spread like wildfire through the city and county, stories of miraculous cures began to circulate.[39] One of the Canterbury laymen who had been present in the cathedral at the time of the murder, dipped his shirt in the blood to bring to his paralysed wife;[40] and on the third day (31 December), the wife of a Sussex knight was cured of blindness.[41] These two events are evidence of an immediate popular response to Becket's murder. The people who had scraped up some blood or acquired part of the dead archbishop's outer clothing found themselves in possession of valuable relics, which some sold on;[42] and stories of miraculous replication of blood began to be told.[43] A London priest was admitted to the crypt and given a tincture of water and blood, which restored his power of speech; a priest from Bourne acquired a blood relic and the cloak that Becket was wearing when he died, which itself became a source of healing.[44] What emerged in the first three months of 1171, was not a monk-led movement, however, for the cathedral was effectively closed until Easter (28 March), because it had been polluted by the spilling of blood; and it was only because of the clamour of the citizens, that the crypt, with the tomb, was thrown open to pilgrims on 2 April: the main church remained closed until 21 December.[45] Most of the 15 cures which were recorded during that period, in fact, occurred remotely.[46] Such evidence is significant, for it shows that popular veneration was growing, despite the efforts of 'the public power' to suppress all mention of the dead archbishop.[47] Becket's began as a spontaneous cult, inspired by belief that his death had been a martyrdom, and that, having made the supreme sacrifice that obliterated all the sins of his life, he was now with the great company of the saints and martyrs, and thus a conduit between heaven and earth.

Part of Becket's popularity in death flowed from his victim status. The people of Kent and Canterbury had been caught up in the oppressive exploitation of the de Brocs; some of them would have been related to the other victims – the 400 innocent exiles; and many of them had seen or heard about the build-up to the murder. Becket had faced it bravely. He had acted like a man, not like a pusillanimous monk or priest. Just as Henry could respect the tall knightly Becket, whose humble background he could overlook with royal disdain, contemporary men and women could recognize their kind of hero. There was something of the politically subversive about their recognition of Canterbury's martyr.[48] Royal barons had committed the crime; royal ministers were trying to suppress the cult. When, therefore, the monks granted general access to the tomb, there was a surge of pilgrims, many of whom claimed to have been cured through Becket's intercession, and the monk Benedict (later abbot of Peterborough), was deputed to check and record the miracles.[49] Three or four months later, the prior of Canterbury (Odo) sent a deputation of monks to the pope with a formal petition for the canonization of 'Thomas, of holy memory, once archbishop of Canterbury, who ... accepting the supreme penalty in defence of the Church's liberty, attained the crown of martyrdom, as the virtues of the miracles which God is working through him make manifest.' This request is known only from the pope's commission to Cardinals Albert and Theodwin, issued in late summer or early autumn 1171. It is highly likely that the monks presented a dossier of miracles that formed the basis of the legates' investigation. The mandate goes on to instruct the legates to cause the alleged miracles to be investigated by the local bishops and others, to send the pope a written report on them, so that he can decide whether or not to grant the monks' request and to authorize the expurgation of Canterbury Cathedral.[50] This is very important new evidence, which contradicts the assertion in William of Canterbury's *Miracula* that the monastery sent the clerk, William of Monkton, to petition the pope about the solemn celebration of the martyr, only to find that he was already inscribed in the list of martyrs.[51] Either William of Canterbury was mistaken or, more likely, the clerk was sent to the Curia in early 1173 to discover the fate of the earlier petition. This might collaborate the claim in Anon. II, that the first petition had been rejected. If the first mission in mid-1171 had been sent back empty-handed, so to speak, without

knowledge of the appointment of Cardinals Albert and Theodwin
and their commission to investigate the miracles, they might easily
have concluded that the initial request had failed.

It appears that the cardinals followed their instructions to the
letter. Their own mandate for the solemn re-opening of the great
church (which was conducted on Becket's birthday, 21 December
1171) survives;[52] and in the stream of canonization letters, issued
throughout March and April 1173, Alexander referred to the written evidence about the miracles presented by his legates and
others.[53] In their own letter, moreover, the cardinals were instructed
to ensure that the relevant notifications were transmitted to the two
kings, to Canterbury and to the English Church.[54] The survival of
a version of the third text, with the stirring opening, *Redolet Anglia*
(England is perfumed), addressed to William of Sens and his suffragans, suggests that canonization letters were sent to every province
of the Latin Church.[55] What had started as the piety of a few
Canterbury locals was being proclaimed through the most advanced
system of international communication then known. Even before
that, in 1172, Herbert of Bosham warned Abbot Peter of Saint-Rémi
of Reims about a Canterbury servant, who was selling large quan-
tities of Becket's blood and claimed to have the cap in which the archbishop had died.[56] By the middle of 1174, there were not one, but
two books of miracles: Benedict's, which was arranged more or less
chronologically, and a second, compiled from July 1172 by William,
another Canterbury monk, who organized his material by category.
Allowing for the considerable overlap between the two works, more
than 400 signs of the martyr's efficacy were recorded.

In the light of so much activity, the fact that no English bishop
seems to have added his voice to those of his continental colleagues and
the Canterbury monks appears shocking – does that prove shameful
disinterest? There were only three of Becket's suffragans in England
at the time of his death, and they were distributed around their
dioceses (Exeter, Coventry-Lichfield-Chester and Winchester) for
the Christmas season. All three had publicly expressed their opposition to Henry's 1169 decrees and had refused to join Gilbert Foliot's
third appeal, so they are likely to have been outraged at the assassination. The remaining three bishops from the Canterbury province
(London, Salisbury and Worcester), together with the archbishop of
York, were all in Normandy; three of the four (London, Salisbury and
York) were under papal censure; and Roger of Worcester was drawn
into the royal embassy that was sent to the Curia to exculpate the
king. The episcopal presence in England was so attenuated as to be

almost non-existent, and it was reduced still further with the death of Henry of Winchester on 9 August 1171. It is not known when or how the news was conveyed to the three bishops, but it is likely that John of Salisbury made contact with Exeter, at least, for he had written to the bishop throughout the exile, and Bartholomew was a friend.[57] The activities of Richard of Coventry-Lichfield have not been recorded, but Bartholomew of Exeter was very active. He received William de Tracy's confession and may have sent him to the pope; he requested papal instructions on the penitential treatment of the guilty parties;[58] he presided at the re-opening of Canterbury on Becket's birthday (21 December); and he must have been consulted on the dossier of miracles that was submitted to the cardinals.

The immediate reaction of the royal administration was to throw a *cordon sanitaire* around Canterbury, both to control the way in which the news got out and to suppress any popular reaction to the assault on the archbishop.[59] All the preventative measures that had been set up to thwart Becket's escape remained in place, so that the country was effectively sealed off from the continent. The news reached the king, at Argentan in Normandy, probably in the first week in January. According to Herbert of Bosham, he grieved for 40 days;[60] Diceto says that he laid aside his royal state, Newburgh that he fasted for some days.[61] These images are unlikely to be accurate. Although he arranged for Arnulf of Lisieux to send a defensive letter, which stressed his extraordinary demonstrations of grief, his innocence, except in so far as 'he was believed to have less affection for [Becket]', his willingness to submit to the Church's judgment, and 'humbly accept its decision',[62] his own letter to the pope put all the blame on Becket. Although he (Henry) had observed every detail of the peace (of Fréteval) as laid down by the pope, the archbishop had returned to England 'bearing not the joy of peace but fire and sword ... raising questions against my kingdom and my crown' and excommunicating 'my servants' on all sides. 'Not willing to accept such impudence, the excommunicates and others from England fell upon him and (I say it with grief) killed him.' This is not the letter of a grief-stricken man. The only expression of regret is a minimal *pro forma* 'I say it with grief', inserted in parentheses, although he allowed that his recent anger may have been a cause of the wrongdoing. In respect of the deed itself, however, he was more concerned for his reputation than for his conscience.[63] This letter had been described as 'a masterpiece of distortion and suppression',[64] wholly devoid even of surprise at the bloody murder of an archbishop in his own cathedral by four barons who had travelled directly from the king's own court.

The assertion that the murder was carried out by excommunicates and others is, at the least, deliberately misleading. Henry's first reaction was to blame the victim and distance himself as far as possible from the crime, hoping, no doubt, that his envoys would be able to get to the Curia with his version of events before the alternative could be presented.[65] The embassy consisted of two bishops (Roger of Worcester and Giles of Évreux), one abbot (Richard de Blosseville of the Cistercian monastery of Le Valasse in Normandy), two archdeacons (Reginald FitzJocelin of Salisbury and R., probably Robert of Lisieux), one dean (Robert of Neufbourg, dean of Évreux), an unnamed templar and two royal clerks (Richard Barre and Master Henry of Northampton). He could not, of course, risk employing any of those who had been suspended or excommunicated in the wake of his son's coronation. The two clerks were skilled canon lawyers and the two archdeacons had conducted business in the papal Curia before. They were too late, however. A messenger from Canterbury had managed to bring the news of Becket's murder, with the names of the malefactors, to Herbert of Bosham, Alexander Llewelyn and Gunther of Winchester, probably at Sens, some time in January; and Herbert was able to organize an appropriate response. Archbishop William of Sens summoned a council of his province, where, on 25 January, he promulgated an interdict on Henry II's continental lands (confirmed by Alexander III on 14 May);[66] and King Louis, Count Theobald of Blois, Archbishop William and others issued fierce denunciations of the broken faith of the English king, which reached the Curia in Frascati (Tusculum) before the end of February.[67] Travelling in relays, Henry's envoys were some days behind, and when the first of them (Richard Barre) reached the papal court around 3 March, the protests of Becket's clerks and of the French court were ringing in everyone's ears, and he was not even admitted to the pope's presence.

As they reported to their master, Henry's envoys had to work hard to protect him from excommunication and his kingdom from interdict.[68] That they did so is a reflection, not of Pope Alexander's view of the martyr, but of the commanding power of Henry Plantagenet. Even so, the king was subjected to personal interdict and submitted to papal judgment to be delivered by papal legates; and, on Maundy Thursday 1171, a general excommunication was imposed on all who had participated in the murder or who had supported them in any way.[69] The king certainly tried to wriggle out of responsibility, but the widespread, if not universal, revulsion at the deed for which he was held morally responsible, forced him to recognize a degree of culpability he had initially denied, and to concede, in stages, the two most contentious clauses of the Constitutions, on appeals and clerical immunity. Few during his lifetime dared to point the finger directly at him, but accounts of the reign contained coded signals that, for example, the great rebellion of 1173–74 was God's punishment. It was probably in deference to that opinion (whether he shared it or not), that he performed a penitential pilgrimage to the tomb in June 1174, which marked his reconciliation with the martyr. More than that, with one exception, he made a point of visiting the shrine on every return to England from the continent. Even if these actions were motivated purely by political calculation (which I think unlikely),[70] they are remarkable demonstrations of the power of Becket's cult within four years of his murder.

Professor Barlow comments on the deafening silence in respect of the king's responsibility. It was not quite that, although there seems to have been a compulsion to avoid directly implicating the king. Henry did not die until July 1189, and direct accusation would have been dangerous. Nevertheless, William of Canterbury devoted three pages to the king's self-exculpation, which suggests a degree of sensitivity on his part.[71] Even more significantly, William FitzStephen recorded that a member of the royal household later confessed to a priest, Richard de Halliwella, that he had with his own hands sealed the document ordering the archbishop's death which was sent into England, that it had been written by a tearful Nigel de Sackville, and that before the murder, Reginald of Warenne (brother of William de Warenne, earl of Surrey) had asked the Augustinian canons of Southwark Minster[72] to pray for him, for a terrible thing would soon happen in England.[73] Whether these are fictions or exaggerated rumours (and the latter seems likely),[74] their inclusion in FitzStephen's Life suggests more than a suspicion of King Henry's culpability. The chroniclers, on the whole, were careful, but Roger of Howden inserted the full texts of the French denunciations without counterbalance or comment, and Diceto slipped in the greater part of one of William of Sens' letters.[75] Even more tellingly, Jordan Fantosme, the royalist cleric who wrote a minor verse epic on the defeat of the Scots during the great rebellion against Henry II in 1173–74, put into Henry's mouth a confession of guilt:

> St Thomas, said the king, guard my realm for me!
> To you I declare myself guilty of that for which others
> have the blame.[76]

And the third of the Lansdowne fragments expresses considerable scepticism about the king's innocence: although he had not ordered the murder, he had not forbidden it; his 'grief' may have been assumed, and

> We would be inclined to excuse the king for this crime if
> he had not received the murderers in his kingdom, if he
> had not allowed them to pass through his towns and
> castella, if he had not allowed them to hunt in his woods,
> if he had not defended them because he knew that they
> had done it for love of him.[77]

This anonymous author was writing, probably in 1173, before the king's pilgrimage to Canterbury, in the belief that Henry had let the murders get away scot-free. But he did not know the whole story.

In an atmosphere of general execration, the murderers themselves began to manifest remorse for what they had done, by making donations to religious houses; William de Tracy confessed his guilt to Bartholomew, bishop of Exeter and, perhaps on his instruction, went to accept penance from the pope at the end of 1171; in the course of 1172–73, the remaining three accepted penance from the pope, and all four died on a penitential crusade to the Holy Land.[78] Their willingness to expiate their guilt was paralleled by the king's; but he went further in punishing FitzUrse, de Tracy, de Morville and Brito than has hitherto been recognized. Professor Vincent has demonstrated that Henry exacted a heavy penalty from all four. Without, it seems, issuing any judgment, the king systematically prevented their male heirs from inheriting their estates.[79] In this action he was anticipating the agreement he would make with the papal legate Hugh Pierleone in 1175–76, that the murderers of clerks would, in addition to any other secular penalty, suffer permanent disinheritance.[80] One can only speculate on the reasons for this punitive action. Knowledge of it does not seem to have passed into the written records of the time, which suggests a degree of secrecy on the king's part. Herbert of Bosham, indeed, reported that all of them had abandoned their lands and died on penitential pilgrimage, William de Tracy at Cosenza in Sicily, and the others in the Holy Land, but he attributed their actions to repentance, without any intervention by the king.[81] Roger of Howden said much the same, adding the embellishment that Becket's murderers were buried outside the gates of the Temple in Jerusalem, with the inscription, 'Here lie the wretches who martyred the blessed (*Beatum*) Thomas, archbishop of Canterbury';[82] but there is no suggestion of royal action, and the penance was imposed by the pope. Yet there is one, regrettably anonymous account which, while it does not mention their disinheritance, records that William de Tracy went to seek penance from the pope, while the other three sought the king's advice (probably late 1171). He told them that he could no longer protect them, because he had to purge himself. They then made the journey to the Curia, where Alexander imposed a 14-year penance in the Holy Land.[83] King Henry duly made his public purgation in the presence of papal legates in May 1172, not once, but twice, at Avranches and Caen. Despite all his original denials, the king had been forced to acknowledge some responsibility for his own role, while, surreptitiously, he withdrew his protection and imposed secular penalties on the murderers, who were, simultaneously, compelled to undertake a penitential crusade, which cost them their lives.[84]

11

The image constructed and deconstructed, 1171–1900

More was written about Becket by his contemporaries and near contemporaries than about any other medieval character. Why so much? And what are we to make of it? The answer to the first question is surely to be found in the extraordinary circumstances of Becket's career and death, and in his good fortune to be surrounded by a gifted household at a time when historical writing in England had reached an apogee not reached again in the middle ages. For the circumstances, his former career as King Henry's chancellor and his mode of office – the splendid court, the demonstrative embassies, the chivalric participation in military campaigns, all of which are stumbling blocks to seeing him as a potential saint – made him an international figure before his royally organized election as archbishop of Canterbury. Relatively humble as his origins were, particularly in the context of a nobility-dominated society, he was personally known to Pope Alexander III and the Curia, as well as to King Louis of France and a scattering of influential ecclesiastics across Europe. His exile accentuated his renown – especially as it paralleled Alexander's exile from Italy – and made him an even more international figure. The controversy with Henry II had never been an issue merely of domestic politics in any case; and its conduct, by letter, ambassador and papal legate was pursued in the most public way possible. All this heightened the drama of his murder in Canterbury Cathedral. His murder, therefore, when it came, was not just another regrettable murder of a bishop unknown outside his own region,[1] it was the brutal slaying of a well-known – and, to many, heroic – figure in a place not only sacred but extremely public, and in the presence of numerous unimpeachable witnesses.

Medieval men and women were not very different from their modern counterparts in their appetite for the gory details of a violent death. Most of those who were alive when it happened can remember exactly what they were doing when they heard the news of president John F. Kennedy's assassination, and their initial disbelief that such an event could have happened. The same, though to a lesser extent, is true of the death of Diana, Princess of Wales. Television newscasts beamed the dreadful images around the world in the blinking of an eye, and 'the world' was for a moment united in its shock. It was much the same in the case of Thomas Becket's murder. Twelfth-century Europe lacked modern electronic media, but it shared a common religious culture and remarkably effective networks of communication linking the various regions. Not only the Latin Church itself, with its international religious orders and a lively traffic between the papal Curia and the most distant regions, but commercial networks embracing Scandinavia, Germany and the Baltic, France, Spain, Italy and the Mediterranean bound the Latin West together. Although geographically on the periphery of Europe, England had been part of its political, religious and commercial history since its inclusion in the Roman Empire in the first century AD. At the time of Becket's death, moreover, England's king was the Angevin Henry II, whose territories stretched 'from the northern ocean to the Pyrenees', and included the whole of the western seaboard of France. Once the news got out of England, by whatever route, it spread rapidly.

Moreover, there was also a spectrum of participants and observers able to write what they knew, a monastic community, Christ Church Canterbury, ready (after some very short initial hesitation) to embrace the cause of the murdered archbishop, and, after his canonization in February 1173, a Latin Church eager to receive the liturgical materials necessary for the celebration of his feast throughout Europe. Their readiness to embrace the new saint is a factor in the establishment of his reputation.

The murder was not a piece of ordinary violence. It was not an everyday occurrence for an archbishop of Canterbury to be cut down in his own cathedral, and the surprise and shock the event created were genuine enough. While the king sought to reduce the diplomatic fallout, Becket's household, associates and admirers made the best of the opportunity to exploit his death and call for vengeance and vindication. The circumstances of his murder provided enough

material to build a picture of martyrdom: in the north transept of
Canterbury Cathedral, on the fifth day of Christmas (29 December),
as the monks were beginning the service of vespers in the cathedral.
His associates, in any case, were already convinced of the rightness of
his cause, the falsity of the king and the disloyalty of the opposing
bishops – convictions reinforced by the place and manner of his
death. Men and women of the time were familiar with the passions
of the early martyrs, whose stories could be reduced to a recurrent
pattern of devotion to God, pressure to abandon faith, resolute
resistance to the point of death and glorification. For the early
Christian martyrs, the enemy was the Roman State. In the case of
Becket, it was an expansionist secular power, manipulated by ambition and the Devil. Underlying both images was belief in God's providence, which ensured that the man (or woman) of faith would
prevail, even through death. After all, Christ's own sacrifice provided the primary image of martyrdom. It did not take much manipu-
lation of Becket's story to see the confrontation with Henry II and
the murder in the cathedral as the working out of a divine plan.[2]

The image constructed

Among the first written formulations of the iconic image was the letter drafted by the Old Testament scholar, Herbert of Bosham, for
Archbishop William of Sens.[3] It condemned the machinations of
'that most infamous man, not so much king of the English as enemy
of the angels',[4] whose actions imitated those of Ahab and Herod,
both kings, murderers respectively of Naboth, the Holy Innocents
and John the Baptist; it named the four murderers, denounced the
actions of the archbishop of York and the bishops of London and
Salisbury, 'not bishops, but apostates, who murdered their brother
Joseph.' Thomas is Christ's unique champion, God's anointed,
resisting the demands of the knights for absolution of the bishops
and, through God's dispensation, 'freely offering himself as a peace
offering to God.' A short letter from Louis VII amplified the message. 'Evil has risen up in God's sanctuary, driven its sword into
Christ's ward, and shamefully snuffed out the lantern of the church
of Canterbury.' Thomas is 'the martyr of Canterbury', whose 'blood
cries out … for vengeance, not for itself but for the whole Church',
at whose tomb 'God's grace is revealed through miracles.' Count
Theobald of Blois emphasized Henry II's bad faith and insisted that
Henry had given Thomas full power to punish the bishops who had
participated in the young king's coronation. Thomas is a fearless

man of God, filled with the Holy Spirit, an innocent lamb, slaughtered by 'creatures of the court', who put themselves forward as agents of the English king, whose blood cries to Rome for vengeance.[5]

These are the outraged reactions of associates and protectors: two call him martyr and all emphasize the sacrilegious aspects of the murder, and stress, variously, the complicity of the three bishops, the king's broken faith and the illegality of the coronation of the younger Henry (14 June 1170) as immediate circumstances. These were the images carried to the papal court by two of Becket's clerks; from a third, John of Salisbury, came a more extended circular letter, addressed to recipients in France, which lays out the fully developed theme. Thomas is 'the glorious martyr', a paragon of clerical virtue: primate of Britain, legate of the apostolic see, an incorruptible judge who accepted no bribes and made no exception of persons, a defender of ecclesiastical liberty, a hammer of the wicked, and a comforter of the poor and grief stricken. Already the circumstantial reality is passing into the universal image of the man 'who struggled unto death to defend God's law and overthrow the abuses of ancient tyrants'; and John, who was with the archbishop almost until the moment the assailants struck, emphasizes the martyr's willing acceptance of his fate:

> Gladly do I accept death, as long as the Church receives
> peace and freedom through the shedding of my blood.
> ... I commend myself and the Church's cause to God and
> St Mary, to the holy patrons of this church, and to St Denis.

He uses all the resources of his rhetorical repertoire to spell out the full horror of the sacrilege: in the metropolitan church, in the sacred Christmas season, the butchers not only 'profaned the church with the blood and murder of a priest [and] cut off the crown of his head, which had been dedicated to God with the unction of sacred chrism', but 'scraped out the brain of the already dead man with their murderous swords and scattered it with blood and bones all over the paved floor.' Throughout the whole event, the martyr stood unbroken in spirit, uttering neither word nor sigh, and making no effort at defence. Fearing further sacrilege, the 'holy men' took his body to the crypt and placed it in a marble coffin before the altar of St John the Baptist and St Augustine, Apostle of the English, where

> to the glory of Almighty God occurred many great
> miracles so that the crowds of people who flooded in
> should see in others and experience themselves the power

and mercy of Him who is marvellous and glorious in his saints. ...

Both in the place of his passion and before the high altar, where he spent the night before burial, and at the place of burial, the paralyzed are cured, the blind see, the deaf hear, the mute speak, the crippled walk, the fevered are relieved, the possessed are freed from the devil, and the sick are cured from diverse illnesses.

The letter ends with the question of whether it is right to honour Thomas as a martyr without consulting the pope – who would already have been consulted if the English ports had not been shut. For himself, John declares, 'it is better to stand by the will of God and revere as a martyr the man whom He has already honoured as a martyr.'

What John of Salisbury set out, probably after Easter 1171, was a description of Becket's martyrdom, which conformed in essentials to the pattern familiar from early Christian martyrologies, and the image was confirmed by a list of miracle types familiar to those who read the gospels: the lame walked, the dumb spoke, the blind were given sight. This letter was followed up with a short Life and Passion, written perhaps in 1171–72, which sets a slightly more detailed account in the context of salvation history. 'The Ancient Enemy is continually assaulting Holy Church', begins John, but

God's son, who redeemed it with his own blood, defended and promoted her to true freedom by the blood of his members – the glorious chorus of Apostles and the purple-clad army of the martyrs ... by whose blood the living stones were bound together to build Christ's body...

Pre-ordained by God's providence, Thomas put off the old life of chancellor as soon as he was consecrated, adopted a hair shirt and monastic habit, preached, gave what time he could to prayer and reading, said mass with great devotion, avoided all bribes, fed the poor and venerated the religious. 'Seeing that so great a man would greatly benefit God's Church, the Ancient Enemy ... chose many powerful creators of discord through whom he scattered the seeds of hatred in the hearts of the king and court.' Thomas thus becomes the victim of a devilish conspiracy; then, misled by bishops fearful for themselves, he eventually conceded at Clarendon and gave a verbal assent to the king's request, for which he did penance until absolved by the pope. At Northampton, he submitted first to an unjust sentence, but then appealed to the pope when charges relating to the Chancery were laid against him, against all law and right. At Pontigny, he prayed for the king and kingdom until the king caused him to be expelled by the Cistercian abbots, although he received a vision of his future glory before he left the monastery, after which he was received by 'the most Christian king of France'. Through the action of the venerable Archbishop William of Sens, Henry was threatened with anathema and the kingdom with interdict; meanwhile Roger of York presumed to crown the king's son in another's province, contrary to the right and dignity of the church of Canterbury. Compelled by canonical severity, the king agreed to restore the peace of the English church, and Thomas returned to be received like an angel of God. But when Thomas published the sentences of the pope, suspending Archbishop Roger of York and the bishops who had supported him, and re-imposing excommunication on London and Salisbury, the king was enraged. The Life concludes much as the letter.

What John produced was not the biography of an archbishop but the unabashed hagiography of a saint. And the same image, extended and interwoven with various accounts of Becket's life, was amplified by a stream of biographers. For Edward Grim, for example, who had stood by him in the cathedral and who wrote in 1172–73, Thomas was a providentially chosen instrument of divine power: 'The eminent martyr St Thomas comes forth into the world, a new knight of Christ, miracle of holiness, pattern of justice, incentive to patience, model of virtue, and invincible defender of truth'. Listeners and readers are invited 'to study his life, contemplate his character, admire the man.' Thomas was chosen before the making of the world; his parents Gilbert and Matilda were like the biblical Zachariah and Elizabeth, parents of John the Baptist. Becket, therefore, is 'St Thomas ... the holy man ... the holy archbishop ... the saint', and finally 'the holy martyr'. The adjective or noun *Sanctus* (holy/saint), occurs more frequently in Grim's *Vita* than in any other contemporary Life (about 73 times), supplemented by other phrases, such as 'the noble martyr', 'the man of God' and 'The Lord's champion'.

Ultimately, though, it was the murder that made the martyr; and from the murder the enduring image emerged of resistance to force, courageous endurance in the face of violence, and steadfast faith, all validated by the cures attributed to his intercession after death. As Alexander said in the bull sent to the English clergy and people in March 1173,

> England is perfumed by the fragrance and virtue of the
> manifestations (*signa*) which Almighty God is working
> through the merits of the holy and venerable Thomas,
> formerly archbishop of Canterbury; and the whole
> Christian religion everywhere rejoices that He who is
> marvellous and glorious in the saints has made famous
> after his death his saint whose laudable life shone with the
> great renown of merits and was finally crowned by the
> martyrdom of a glorious struggle. (*MTB*, vii, no. 785)

Having been convinced by Cardinals Albert and Theodwin of the
veracity of the many miracles being performed through Becket's
merits, the pope had no hesitation in solemnly canonizing the saint,
and ordering the annual celebration of the 'birthday' of the glorious
martyr, who 'in life suffered exile for Christ and by the steadfastness
of his courage endured in death the martyrdom of his passion.'
Alexander's letter repeated verbatim the phrase, 'marvellous and
glorious in [his] saints', used by John of Salisbury both in his circular letter and in his Passion, suggesting that copies of one or both
had been transmitted to the Curia by early 1173.

If Alexander's canonization, announced in a stream of letters to
the episcopate of the Latin Church, consolidated the picture of
Thomas, martyred for defence of the Church, the liturgy constructed
for his first feast day (29 December 1173) transformed the image
into an object of cult. Composed by the monk Benedict (later abbot
of Peterborough), who had been given the task of recording the miracles worked at the tomb, it was an amazing feat of compression and
powerful image-making. Taking John of Salisbury's Life as its basis,
Benedict constructed a liturgical office in which the sequence of
chants echoed the readings to powerful effect. The following is a
translation of Lections IV–VI, as copied into a manuscript in the
imperial monastery of Stavelot in the last quarter of the twelfth century. Lections I–III are a summary of Becket's resistance to the
unjust royal decrees, but are wholly unspecific as to their content;
Lection IV takes up the story in 1166.

> IV.   Learning of his steadfast constancy, the king, having
> sent threatening letters to the General Chapter of the
> Cistercian Order by certain abbots, procured his removal
> from Pontigny. For St Thomas, fearing that the holy men
> might suffer loss on his account, freely withdrew. But
> before he left the monastery, he was comforted by a
> divine revelation: it was revealed to him from on high that

he would return to his church with honour and pass to God by the palm of martyrdom. When he had been removed from Pontigny, Louis, the king of France, received him with the greatest honour, and treated him kindly until peace was restored. Often indeed, though fruitlessly, was he pressed not to accord any humane treatment to the traitor to the king of England. The mad fury and to pious ears the horrid cruelty went further. For although the Catholic Church prays for heretics and schismatics and the faithless Jews, it was forbidden for anyone to help him with the support of prayers.

V.   On the fifth day of the Lord's Nativity there came to Canterbury four men of the court, men certainly distinguished by birth, but notorious for their misdeeds. Having entered, they attacked the bishop with insulting words; they assailed him with violent abuse, and finally directed serious threats against him. The man of God responded moderately to each point, as reason required, adding that many outrages had been inflicted on himself and on God's Church since the re-establishment of peace. There being no one to correct errors, he neither wished nor could he do anything other than exercise the duty of pastoral care in the future. The foolish hearted men were therefore thrown into confusion, and they immediately went out speaking the utmost wickedness. When they had left, the pontiff went into the Church to render the evening praise to Christ. The devil's henchmen, in mail, followed by a crowd of armed men, pursued him from behind with drawn swords. Entry to the church having been closed off by the monks, God's priest, soon to be Christ's sacrificial victim, unlocked the door to his enemies as he reached it, saying, 'The church must not be locked up like a fortress.' As the knights and others burst in after him, with furious voices some shouted, 'Where is the traitor?', others, 'Where is the archbishop?'; Christ's fearless confessor went forward to meet them. To those threatening him with death, he said, 'I shall willingly accept death in defence of God's Church, but in the name of God I command you not to injure any of my followers', imitating Christ who said during his passion, 'If you seek me, allow the others to depart.'

VI.   The ravening wolves threw themselves upon the
pious pastor, degenerate sons against their own father,
most pitiless executioners against the Lord's anointed:
they cut off the consecrated crown of his head with their
bloody swords, and, casting the Lord's anointed onto the
ground, they most callously scattered his brains and blood
upon the pavement – a thing most terrible, even to say.
Thus did the chaff overwhelm the grain of corn, thus
was slain the vine-keeper in the vineyard, the leader in
the camp, the shepherd in the fold, the labourer on the
threshing-floor; thus the just man, murdered by the
unjust, exchanged a house of clay for a heavenly palace.
According to the statement of those standing closest to
him – which they could scarcely hear because of the
confusion and clamour – the last words of the martyr were
these, 'To God and blessed Mary and St Denis and the holy
patrons of this church, I commend myself and the Church's
cause.' Moreover, in all the torments which God's unbeaten
champion endured, he did not emit a cry, he did not utter a
sigh, he did not oppose arm or clothing to the one who
struck; rather, until all was completed, he held steady the
bowed head which he had exposed to the swords, and,
prostrated as if in prayer, he fell asleep in the Lord.

This is how the murder had been described in the readings at the
Canterbury Matins from 1173, copies of which were taken to the
furthest reaches of Christendom – from Iceland and Scandinavia to
Italy and Sicily. It was this image – and numerous adaptations – that
the eighth Henry ordered to be expunged from the service books of
the English Church in November 1538. The transmission of this picture did not depend on words alone. Visual reality was given to the
image in reliquary caskets, manufactured in Limoges (of which 45
survive to this day), which concentrated on the moment of the murder. With varying degrees of accuracy, they depicted in vivid colour
the moment at which three royal knights struck down the unarmed
and unprotected archbishop, while a fourth held back the citizenry;
and the same scene is the subject of an early miniature (*c.* 1200),
inserted into a later Psalter in the British Library (Harl. MS 5102,
fol. 32r). Having been martyred, Becket became an icon. By the late
1180s his image as an iconic saint raising a hand in blessing was
added to the array of saintly patrons in the apse of the high altar at
Monreale in Norman Sicily.[6]

Becket's *was* a constructed image – but all historical images are. Thomas was fortunate in his entourage, and one might argue that their posthumous admiration was self-justification for their own self-sacrificing loyalty, while for Alexander III, the propagation of 'his' saint consolidated the triumph of his cause against Frederick I and his anti-popes. Benedict of Peterborough, indeed, writing in 1174, specifically associated the evidence of divine approbation manifested in Becket's miracles with justification of Pope Alexander's cause.[7]

Among the 400 or so miracles recorded in two large volumes at Canterbury, there was one extraordinary event that astonished contemporaries and scandalized John Foxe in the sixteenth century.[8] This was the restoration of the virility and sight of Ailward of Weston (Bedfordshire) who, having been publicly castrated and blinded, was restored after invoking St Thomas of Canterbury. So exceptional was it that it was signalled in the third responsory of the third nocturn of the matins that Benedict composed for the first celebration of Becket's feast in December 1173:

> Thomas blazes forth with singular miracles:
> Male members gives he to the castrated;
> Sight he bestows on those deprived of eyes.

What scandalized John Foxe in Elizabethan England had been notified to Canterbury, not by the ecclesiastical authorities, but by the burgesses of Bedford, who claimed to have examined the victim. Exactly what happened will never be known; but Ailward himself, and his lay supporters, believed that there had been a miraculous cure.[9] Not only was the story recorded twice in Benedict's Book of Miracles,[10] and depicted in one of the Miracle Windows later set in the ambulatory around Becket's splendid tomb in the Trinity Chapel of Canterbury Cathedral, where it can still be seen, but also its notification to a Cistercian monastery in Germany provoked a copycat miracle. A monk at Himmerod, who had castrated himself, was restored to vigour after praying before the relic of St Thomas, which a German baron, Ludwig of Deudesfeld, and his wife, Ida, had brought back from Canterbury in 1173–74. Placed in a newly founded chapel, it became the centre of an important local cult that grew up, and resulted in the foundation of the Cistercian nunnery of S. Thomas an der Kyll. Like the initial castration miracle, the cure of the monk Sefrid of Himmerod was attested by witnesses, in this case, three Cistercian abbots, of Himmerod itself, Trois-Fontaines and Hautefontaine.[11]

What brought Ludwig and Ida to Canterbury in the first place cannot be established, but news of Becket's murder and the miraculous events recorded at his tomb would have travelled fast along the well-established trade routes between London and the Rhineland. The couple may, in fact, have come to pray for children, like the later Arnold 'of Grevingge' (=Groningge), a merchant from Cologne, and his wife, Oda (*c.* 1180). Their story was not recorded at Canterbury; but one of their grandsons, Arnold Fitz Thedmar, who became alderman of the German counter in London in 1251 and alderman of Billingsgate in 1274, told the story of his grandparents' pilgrimage and the subsequent establishment of his own parents in London. After their Canterbury pilgrimage, Arnold and Oda were blessed with two children. Their son, appropriately called Thomas, died on the fourth crusade in 1203–4; their daughter, Juliana, married Thedmar of Bremen, who established his business in London, where the family prospered, and where their son Arnold proudly recorded his own miraculous origins.[12]

Men and women thronged to Becket's tomb in the hope of spiritual refreshment and physical or psychological healing. Their demand for tangible tokens of their pilgrimage created a veritable industry for the manufacture of *ampulae*, badges, and small figurines, made usually of tin, which the pilgrim could pin to his hat, suspend round his neck, or attach to his staff or knapsack. Especially prized in the early days (late twelfth and thirteenth centuries) were small metal flasks resembling scent bottles (*ampulae*), some bearing the legend, 'Thomas is the best healer of the virtuous sick'. Fashioned in various shapes and sizes, they contained Canterbury water, a descendant of the blood relics scraped up from the floor on the night of Becket's murder.[13] These seem to have been superseded, from the early fourteenth century, by a host of pilgrim badges, whose diversity suggests a flourishing trade. At least ten different images were produced: the mitred head (denoting 'St Thomas's crown', the portion of Becket's skull hacked off during the murder and preserved in a separate reliquary); the shrine itself, the martyrdom, William Brito's sword (whose point had broken off with the force of the blow); gloves (depicting Becket's episcopal gloves, kept as a relic at Canterbury); Canterbury bells and stars, known as 'Thomas's bells/stars'; Thomas in a boat or on horseback (depicting his return to Canterbury – there was a special feast-day commemorating his *Regressio* (Return) on 2 December); and the letter T (for Thomas). The rich retrievals from excavations in the city of London alone suggest that many thousands of these devotional souvenirs were sold every year.[14] They functioned as personal mementoes, sacred objects, and even as passports. Pilgrims were a recognized category of privileged persons, allowed free and secure passage in the regions through which they passed, and the wearing of a badge was a sign of their *bona fides*.

Virtually all the surviving badges or *ampulae* are mass-produced objects, late in date and of little intrinsic value, but they represent the popular end of a market that embraced the highest in medieval society. The earliest *ampula*, in fact, was the pendant made for Queen Margaret of Sicily and presented to her, in all probability, on the occasion of the marriage of her son, King William II, to Henry II's daughter, Joanna, in 1177. Fashioned in gold, the tiny reliquary is inscribed with a list of the relics enclosed within: fragments of blood, bone and clothing;[15] three hundred years later (*c*. 1480), King Louis XI of France informed the Canterbury monks that he would appreciate the present of a badge, which he would wear on his hat![16]

Margaret and Louis XI were unable to visit the shrine in their own persons, but many notables did. Within seven years of Becket's death (1177), Count Philip of Flanders had made the first of three visits to the tomb;[17] within ten years (1179), King Louis VII of France made a spectacular pilgrimage to pray for the life of his only son and heir, Philip II,[18] and among his gifts to the shrine and the monastic community were a magnificent ruby, the *régale* of France, and an annual shipment of French wine.[19] With the single exception of 1188, when there was an interdict on the cathedral, Henry II made a detour to pay his respects to the martyr every time he returned to England from the continent after 1174; and Richard I went to pray at the shrine in 1190, before departing for the Holy Land and the third crusade; while another crusader, Hubert Walter, bishop of Salisbury, later archbishop of Canterbury (1191–1205), justiciar and chancellor, led 500 soldiers under the banner of St Thomas before the walls of Acre in 1191.[20] Through all that time, Becket's body remained in the crypt, where it had first been placed, although a splendid new chapel was constructed to receive it between 1174 and 1186.[21] Various political and ecclesiastical problems prevented the solemn translation of the relics until 1220, however; but then, the archbishop of Sens and an unnamed Hungarian archbishop joined Archbishop Stephen Langton, the young Henry III and magnates of Church and State to celebrate the translation of Becket's remains to the Trinity chapel of Canterbury Cathedral, following which a second Becket feast was added to the Church's calendar.[22]

Becket's cult was not simply a Canterbury phenomenon. By the time of his translation, St Thomas the Martyr was not only England's leading saint, but he had also become the most popular after St Olaf in Norway and Iceland, and he was venerated with varying degrees of solemnity throughout the Latin Church. Monasteries, priories and collegiate churches were founded in his honour in England, France, Germany, Hungary, Ireland, Norway, Poland, Scotland and the Norman kingdom of Sicily; churches and altars were dedicated to him;[23] liturgical music was composed in his honour;[24] and a reliquary enshrining some of his brains and blood was placed in the chapel at the heart of the templar fortress of Tomar, in Portugal (*c.* 1176).[25] His name appeared more than that of any other English saint in calendars and liturgical books;[26] his relics were enshrined in Limoges caskets;[27] his image was emblazoned in stained glass,[28] carved in statues and capitals, illustrated in friezes, manuscripts, mosaics and wall paintings;[29] confraternities were formed under his patronage; and hospitals were founded in his name.[30]

But for Peter the Chanter, who taught generations of clerical students at Paris, including Stephen Langton and Pope Innocent III, as well as for Absalon of Saint-Victor,[31] he was principally a moral and ethical exemplar, the image of a good pastor. He did not build up wealth for himself when he was chancellor or archbishop; he did not aggrandize his family or his *familia*; he did not allow his staff to charge for their legal and scribal services. This aspect of his brief career as archbishop appealed especially to the reformist theologians at Paris in the two or three decades following his death. There, together with Lukács of Esztergom, he became an exemplar of clerical probity in the teaching of Peter the Chanter, Robert of Courson and Stephen Langton, one of his successors as archbishop of Canterbury.[32] Langton's own dispute with King John of England was seen by him and by Pope Innocent III as a continuation of that of St Thomas.[33] The twin images, of martyr, symbolizing the Church in struggle, and good pastor, symbolizing the ideals of that Church, echoed down the ages in the sermons preached annually on his feast day.[34]

The image deconstructed and rebuilt

If, during the middle ages, the image of Becket was sanitized and simplified to become the miracle-working saint and the pattern of exemplary priesthood, the Henrician Reformation in England, with its formal rejection first of papal authority, then of independent priesthood, then of monasticism, then of the cult of saints, progressively stripped away many of the elements that had comprised the construction of the exemplary Becket. His appeal to Pope Alexander III became treason, his defence of clerical immunity was unlawful protection of criminals, his monastic affiliations confirmed his attachment to foreign and hostile powers, and his status as martyr and saint were at the same time spurious and manifestations of his un-Englishness.

The attack was mounted by the royal administration itself, as part of its policy of isolating the English Church from the power structures of Catholic Europe. Henry VIII's strategy had been masterly: first proclaim his own headship of the English Church, then compel the bishops to acknowledge it (1531–32), thus cutting off their only defence against a crown that could now through Parliament not only stigmatize but criminalize contacts and actions that had been lawful for more than 900 years. The wholesale destruction of monasticism (1535–39), although dressed up as 'reform', constituted a significant stage in the transfer of power and resources to the crown, as well as the elimination of a potential source of opposition; while the destruction of saints' shrines was the removal of one of the foci of popular religious belief and practice. Eamon Duffy has shown how the whole religious landscape, both intellectual and physical, was changed in a couple of generations.[35] No English shrine was more potent in its political and ecclesiological symbolism than that of Thomas Becket. Three years before its destruction, Thomas More's last letter, written on the eve of his own execution for treason, expressed the power of Becket's name. Addressing his daughter, Margaret Roper, he said,

> I cumber you much, good Margaret, much, but I would
> be sorry if it [his own execution] should be any longer
> than tomorrow (6 July, 1535), for it is St Thomas' Even
> and the Utas [octave] of St Peter, and therefore tomorrow
> long I to go to God – it were a day very meet and
> convenient for me.[36]

Two decrees in particular established the new environment in 1533–34. The first, the Act of Supremacy (24 Henry VIII, c. 1), proclaimed Henry to be 'the only supreme head in earth of the Church of England, called *Anglicana Ecclesia*'; the second, the Act in Restraint of Appeals, (c. 12), proclaimed the imperial character and overall supremacy of the English crown:

> Wheras divers sundry and authentick Histories and
> Chronicles it is manifestly declared and expressed that

this realm of England is an Empire ... governed by one
supreme Head and King, having Dignity and Royal Estate
of the Imperial Crown of the same: Unto whom a Body
politick ... divided in terms and by names of Spirituality
and Temporality, been bounden and owen to bear next
to God a natural and humble obedience: He being also
institute and furnished, by the goodness and sufferance
of Almighty God, with plenary whole and entire Power,
Pre-eminence, Authority, Prerogative, and Jurisdiction,
to render and yield Justice and final determination to all
manner of folk, residants or subjects within this his
Realm, in all Causes, Matters, Debates and Contentions ...
without restraint or provocation to any foreign Princes or
Potentates of the World....

Simultaneously, oaths denying papal authority were imposed
throughout the country, refusal of which was accounted high treason,
punishable by death. The practical dualism of the middle ages was
swept away. Thenceforth was the English Church absorbed into
the political ordering of the state, the king its supreme head, and
all papal authority permanently abolished from England. Appeals
would go to an ecclesiastical commission appointed by the crown;
papal taxes would be paid to the crown; all clerical officers would be
obliged to take the Oath of Supremacy, affirming their acceptance of
the new order. There could be no place for St Thomas of Canterbury
in this new world; and a royal proclamation, issued from Westminster
in November 1538,[37] re-drew Becket's image in brutal and uncompromising fashion. Instead of the steadfast defender of the Church,
Becket was 'really a rebel who fled to France and to the bishop of
Rome to procure the abrogation of wholesome laws' who 'shall no
longer be named a saint.' It was not enough, however, merely to
un-canonize him, as it were; the decree went on to declare that 'his
pictures throughout the realm are to be plucked down and his festivals shall no longer be kept, and the services in his name shall be
razed out of all books.'

At this early stage in what became the Reformation, there had
been no change in the liturgy or theology of the English Church. The
language of both remained Latin; the calendars still glowed with the
'red-letter days' of numerous medieval saints; mass was still said or
sung in accordance with the ancient rubrics. Becket became the first
casualty of what was essentially a political campaign. Here was
an archbishop of Canterbury who had withstood an English king,

appealed to foreign powers (France and the papacy) and had his cause canonized. It was necessary, therefore, not to attack the cult of saints as such – that would come later – but to destroy the reputation of this particular one, so that he could not be held up as a model for the English bishops, clergy and people.

Henry's decree attacked Becket's reputation at three crucial points: the cause, the character and the canonization of both. Now proclaimed not only an un-saint but also a pseudo-saint by royal decree, Becket's name was deleted from the prayer books, his feasts removed from the calendars and his shrine broken up for the benefit of the crown. What had once been one of the particular glories of the tomb, the ruby given by Louis VII in 1179, was made into a thumb ring for Henry VIII. A more complete reversal of image could scarcely be imagined. England's most widely celebrated saint was consigned to the rubbish bin, together with all that he had come to represent in popular religion, ecclesiology and law. However much the reformed *ecclesia Anglicana* preserved of its medieval heritage, it did not include the cult of St Thomas of Canterbury, and every mark of his liturgical existence was scrupulously removed, in a manner reminiscent of the way in which men who usurped the office of Pharaoh in Ancient Egypt, systematically deleted the cartouches of their dead predecessors from public monuments, in order to confirm their own legitimacy. Inconvenient history was literally expunged from the record.

This political rewriting of historical tradition set the pattern for much of the subsequent writing on Becket in Protestant circles. No longer the hero of an English Church in union with Rome, Becket became a particularly expressive example of all that had been rejected in the Henrician and post-Henrician Reformation. Even more: in the feverish atmosphere of the time, Becket symbolized treasonable subservience to the papacy, 'the Babilonical bawdy Romysche church and religion ... vile painted lecherous whore, Rose of Rome' (these are the colourful words of Bishop Stephen Gardiner of Winchester (1531–51, 1553–55) in his *De vera obediencia* (Latin, 1536; English translation, 1553). John Foxe's (1517–87) *Acts and Monuments* (Latin, 1554; English translation, 1563), generally known as the 'Book of Martyrs', continued the theme: 'This *Becket* ... did not (as some affirm) dye a Martyr, but a stubborn man against his King; who had preferred him from an Archdeacon, to Lord Chancellor of *England*, and after to be Archbishop of *Canterbury*.' 'If the cause make a martyr (as is said), I see not why we should esteem *Thomas Becket* to die a Martyr, more than any other whom the Princes Sword doth here temporally punish for their temporal deserts. To die for the Church I grant is a glorious matter', but since the Church 'is a Spiritual and not a Temporal Church', to 'contend with Princes for ... temporal Possessions, Liberties, Exemptions, Privileges, Dignities, Patrimonies, and Superiorities ... is no matter (to my mind) material to make a Martyr, but rather a Rebellion against them to whom we owe subjection.'[38]

Whatever personal merits he had were vitiated by his allegiance to Rome ('So superstitious he was to the Obedience of the Pope, that he forgot his Obedience to his natural and most beneficial King') and by a suspicion of hypocrisy. It was Foxe who first constructed the image of Becket the character actor, which surfaces from time to time in modern historiography (Lord Lyttelton, Lady Stenton, Zachary Brooke, Frank Barlow) and was given dramatic form in Eliot's *Murder in the Cathedral*. Recommended by Theobald 'to bridle the young King, that he should not be fierce against the Clergy ... he left playing the Arch-deacon, and began to play the Chancellor ... He played also the good Souldier under the King in *Gascoigne*'.[39] Moreover, his claims to sanctity rested upon forgery and falsehood. Foxe expressed the opinion that was to predominate in Protestant circles for a long time: 'If thrue, [the miracles are] not wrought by God, but by the contrary Spirit; or else feigned and forged of idle Monks, and religious bellies, for the exaltation of their Churches, and profit of their pouches.' To record them would be to write 'a Legend of lies'. The one example which particularly attracted his fierce denunciation was the cure of Ailward of Weston:[40]

> This one Miracle (gentle Reader) so shameless and
> impudent, I thought here to express, that by this one
> though mightst judge of all the residue of his Miracles ...
> and the filthy wickedness of all these lying Monks and
> Cloisterers, which count it a light sport to deceive the
> simple souls of Christs Church with trifling lies and
> dreaming fables.[41]

Equally, the liturgical cult of 'Saint' Thomas was an affront to true religion. Particularly offensive to pious Protestant ears was the invocation of the fourth antiphon from the Sarum office of Lauds, which Foxe presented in its Latin and English forms as an example of the genre:

> Tu per Thome sanguinem, quem pro te impendit
> Fac nos Christe scandere, quo Thomas ascendit.

That is:

For the bloud of Thomas,
Which he for thee did shed,
Grant us, O Christ, to climb,
Where Thomas did ascend.

And his conclusion was uncompromising. Such a prayer was nothing less than 'blaspemous, and derogateth from the praise of him to whom only all praise and honour is due.'[42]

For English Catholics, in contrast, St Thomas the Martyr became an icon of their claims to represent the authentic continuation of the ancient English Church and its thousand years of history as part of the Latin Church in communion with the successors of St Gregory the Great (who had sent the Roman mission of St Augustine). The English College (Collegio Inglese) in Rome, founded in 1579 as a seminary for the training of English Catholic priests, on the site of an earlier hospice for English pilgrims to Rome, made St Thomas one of its chief patrons, its chapel dedicated to him, and its chief altarpiece, a crucifixion by Durante Alberti, depicted St Thomas as the chief supporter on the right side of the crucified Christ. Before this picture prayed many of the English recusant priests, before their departure for an uncertain fate in England, through the late sixteenth and seventeenth centuries. The college, the chapel and the picture are still there. It was alleged by anti-Catholic propagandists that every Spanish ship sailing to the Indies from Seville, Sanlúcar, and Cadiz carried a collecting-box bearing the image of St Thomas with the inscription, *Sancte Thoma Cantuariensis, ora pro nobis* ('St Thomas of Canterbury, pray for us'), to gather financial support for St Gregory's College in Seville, another of the seminaries for English Catholic priests, founded in 1592.[43] Here was yet another transformation: Becket the patron of English Catholics, the protector of underground priests, the icon of 'old Catholicism'.

The defence of Becket's reputation thus became a matter of confessional identity. Typical of this approach was *Tres Thomae* ('The Three Thomases'), first published at Douai, a seminary and centre of English Catholic scholarship,[44] in 1588, the year of the Spanish Armada (and again in Cologne in 1612), in which Thomas Stapleton linked Becket with Thomas the Apostle and Thomas More, and set out to rebut the charges made by the 'English heretics', by presenting 'the true cause of the martyr Thomas, archbishop of Canterbury'. To the claims that Becket was a traitor defending worldly claims, rightly executed for his crimes, Stapleton opposed the counter-image of a courageous defender of ecclesiastical law. But his emphasis was also coloured by the contemporary religious situation. His Thomas died for the judicial authority of the Church and the Holy See. The same image was invoked by Pope Pius VI at the height of the French Revolution, which transformed France from a Catholic to a secular state. His letter of admonition to the French bishops, issued on 10 March 1791, condemned both the approbation given by 30 of their number (a very small minority) to the new Civil Constitution of the Clergy (August 1790) and the oath imposed on the French clergy. In it, he compared the actions of the French national assembly with those of Henry II, and cited Bossuet's comparison of Thomas Becket and Thomas Cranmer, the one defending the Church, the other betraying it, while Talleyrand, then bishop of Autun, was depicted as playing Cranmer's role.[45]

If Catholics could see St Thomas as a Catholic icon, to Anglicans he was a *Roman* Catholic idol, a representative of the papal and clerical power that they rejoiced in having defeated in the days of the eighth Henry, and which many seemed to fear might be reinstated if any concessions were made to the remnant of fully practising Catholics (called recusants, because they refused to take the Oaths of Supremacy) still surviving. Belief that the Catholics/papists, in league with the Jesuit Order and the papacy, were plotting the overthrow of Protestant England was widespread, and popular paranoia was fed by anti-Catholic tracts, mostly anonymous, which continued to appear throughout the seventeenth century. Typical of this firebrand writing was a little booklet printed in London in 1679 with the title, *The Ungrateful Behaviour of the Papists, Priests, and Jesuits, Towards the Imperial and Indulgent Crown of England Towards them, From the Days of Queen Mary unto this present Age*; its second segment, *The Real Merits of the Papists*, contains an extraordinarily creative rewriting of English history, which purports to demonstrate the involvement of 'papists' in every rebellion and plot against the English crown from Henry II onwards.

Even John Locke's rational and urbane plea for mutual toleration between different religious groups, first composed in Latin in 1685–86, excluded Catholics from those deserving such consideration, not because of their beliefs,[46] but because of their alleged political aspirations:

> Those ... who upon pretence of religion do challenge any
> manner of authority over such as are not associated with

them in their ecclesiastical communion, I say these have
no right to be tolerated by the magistrate. ... That Church
can have no right to be tolerated which is constituted
upon such a bottom that all those who enter into it do
thereby *ipso facto* deliver themselves up to the protection
and service of another prince.[47]

The 'other prince', of course, was the pope; and Thomas Becket had
made much of his allegiance to that 'foreign' authority.

Yet the position of the established Church was by then no longer
as self-evidently justified as it had appeared. The disconcerting experi-
ences of the civil war, in which Puritanism played no small part, the
execution of the lawful 'supreme head' and king (Charles I) in
1649, the successive governments of a Puritan Parliamentary
Commonwealth, a suspected crypto-Catholic (Charles II, 1660–85),
and finally of a professed Catholic (James II, 1685–88), whose
forcible substitution by the Protestant William of Orange and Mary
Stuart (1688) caused considerable unease among believers in legitimacy – all these events, and the backward and forward swing of
the pendulum between the 'Laudian' and 'anti-Laudian'[48] wings of
the Church, proved unsettling for the leaders of Anglican opinion.
The debate about the nature of the Church of England, its claims to
apostolicity and catholicity, and its compatibility with the royal
supremacy, were issues not only between Anglicans and their
opponents, but also increasingly within Anglicanism itself.

One line of argument, advanced by William Wake, later archbishop
of Canterbury (1716–37), in the non-juring crisis,[49] vehemently
defended the royal supremacy.[50] This was countered by Francis
Atterbury (1662–1732), later bishop of Rochester (1713–32), who
used medieval records to prove the independence of the English
Church within the realm, even to the extent of citing a pope
(Innocent III) and a papal council (Fourth Lateran, 1215) among his
authorities.[51] His contemporary, White Kennett (1660–1728),
responded with a spirited defence of the Reformation settlement and
an interpretation of Atterbury's sources, which confirmed the royal
supremacy.[52] Against such a background, Becket's opposition to
Henry II and appeal to papal authority remained anathema.

A full-blown re-statement of the Protestant view of a medieval
Church sunk 'in the most corrupt and dark ages of Popery, when the
pure light of the gospel was almost extinguished, and the ministers
of it were become a mere faction, combined together under a foreign
head, against the civil power' was presented in Lord George Lyttelton's

monumental *History of the Life of King Henry the Second*.[53]
Lyttelton saw the twelfth century through the prism of the eighteenth,
so that Henry II's council became 'the High Court of Parliament'.[54]
From this standpoint, virtually every aspect of Becket's position was
repugnant, from his defence of the canon law in Gratian's *Decretum*
(which 'continued ... to raise and support in them [the clergy] a
spirit of independence pernicious to society, and principles incom-
patible with the obedience they owed the laws of their country'), to
his appeal to the pope at Northampton, which drew the comment,

> to deny the authority of the highest court in the kingdom,
> and, in a cause purely civil, to appeal from these to an
> ecclesiastical and foreign tribunal, when such an appeal,
> even in spiritual causes, had been so lately forbidden
> by one of the statutes enacted at Clarendon, was the
> highest act of contumacy that can be conceived: it was
> not only an infringement of that particular law, but a
> rebellion against all the laws of the land and the whole
> legislature.

Alexander III's disapprobation of ten of the Constitutions of
Clarendon was roundly condemned:

> That the Pope and his consistory should then sit in
> judgment upon the laws and statutes of England was a
> most insolent violation of the independence, the freedom,
> and the dignity of the crown; and the abetting of such an
> act was without question highly criminal in a subject of
> that kingdom.[55]

Lyttelton's highly critical treatment of Thomas as archbishop was
underpinned by his discovery of Gilbert Foliot's *Multiplicem*, in a
manuscript in the Cotton Library (Claudius B. ii), which he printed
in an appendix and exploited to considerable effect in his denunciation of the character and stand of Thomas Becket.[56]

From first to last, Becket is a wily, dangerous opponent of the laws
and institutions of England, lawfully indicted on civil charges (financial), lawfully condemned and unlawfully calling in the insolent
judgment of a foreign power (the papacy) against his lawful sover-
eign. Having created the gratifying image of an orderly parliamentary state on the model of post-1688 England, with its High Court
of Parliament, its legislature and its established laws and statutes,
confronted by a corrupt and un-Christian medieval Church and a

predatory papacy, the Becket controversy took on the appearance of a dangerous conspiracy against a generally good and constitutional monarch. In the background was the spectre of a potentially hostile Catholic Europe:

> Even the rudest form of our government has always been animated by the spirit of freedom. May that spirit continue to inspire and support it in the more perfect state to which it has gradually been brought by the wisdom of many ages, and more particularly by the revolution of the year 1688, when the bounds of the royal prerogative were better marked out, and the privileges of the people more clearly defined and established. ...
>
> Where the papist religion remains established, the principles of Becket will also remain.[57]

This was too much for English Catholics, still labouring under anti-Catholic legislation. Joseph Berington in 1790 responded with a reversal of Lyttelton's interpretation, which made Henry the aggressor and Thomas the protector of the Church against the ecclesiastical policies of the Normans. *Multiplicem* he branded a forgery.[58] Fifteen years later, Father John Lingard (1771–1851) laid the foundations of a reassessment of the Anglo-Saxon and medieval worlds in two monumental works. His *Antiquities of the Anglo-Saxon Church* aimed to demonstrate the extent to which the ancestral races of the 'English' had received and practised the 'Romish' practices, which the Reformation and three centuries of Anglican writing had condemned. Even a cursory perusal of the headings in the 'Contents' pages of the third edition must have sent shock waves down the spines of many of his English contemporaries: 'Papal Supremacy', 'The Pope head of the church', 'Celibacy of the clergy', 'Sacrifice of the Mass', 'The Latin language', 'Penance', 'Sacrament of Extreme Unction', 'Prayer for the dead', 'Intercession of the saints', 'Relics of foreign saints, Relics of native saints', 'Belief in miracles' and 'Anglo-Saxon pilgrimages'.[59] Here was being redrawn the spiritual map within which the restoration of Thomas Becket as saint and martyr could be made. The recently unspeakable characteristics of his world were described with sensitivity and respect, and assigned to the golden age of the pre-Conquest world, long before the time of 'Hildebrand and his school'. Not surprisingly, Lingard's second great work of historical scholarship, the many-volumed and much republished *History of England*, which first appeared in the

years 1819–30, provided an extremely positive interpretation of
Thomas Becket. For Lingard, Henry II is the villain: 'pride and passion, caution and duplicity formed the distinguishable traits of his
character'; and the controversy is the product not of the impertinent
rebellion of an arrogant archbishop but a consequence of the development of Christianity since the days of Constantine. Far from canon
law being an instrument of clerical oppression,

> The proceedings of the former [ecclesiastical courts] were
> guided by fixed and inviolable principles, the result of the
> wisdom of the ages ... The clerical judges were men of
> talent and education: the uniformity and equity of their
> decisions were preferred to the caprice and violence which
> seemed to sway the royal and baronial judiciaries.

Lingard then produced a critique of the Constitutions of Clarendon,
which denied their claim to ancient authority on the grounds that
none of the obnoxious clauses was older than the Conquest. The
hostile witness of Foliot's *Multiplicem* is dismissed; and Becket's
erratic behaviour at Clarendon is explained as

> the hesitation of a mind oscillating between the decision
> of his own judgment and opinions and the apprehensions
> of others. His conviction seems to have remained
> unchanged; he yielded, to avoid the charge of having by
> his obstinacy drawn destruction on the heads of his
> fellow-bishops.[60]

It was Lingard's mastery of the sources, both of the Old English and
the medieval English Church, that enabled him to set Becket in his
medieval context and thus re-evaluate the man and his cause.

Two different emphases in Lingard's exposition found fuller
expression in works of the next generation. Augustin Thierry amplified the Saxon vs Norman implications of Lingard's work, and made
Thomas into a Saxon hero who resisted the tyranny of Norman
rule,[61] and Richard Hurrell Froude (1803–36) reverted to the image
of the clerical hero, defending the Church from lay aggression.[62] At
the same time, Robert Southey's *The Book of the Church* (London,
1824) set an equally positive interpretation of Becket into the context of general church history, in a work that was to pass through
six further editions in the nineteenth century, in addition to being
summarized for the use of Sunday schools. On a different level, in
Baltimore, William Eusebius Andrews attacked the icon of Elizabethan

Protestantism, in order 'to refute and expose the greatest mass of falsehood and calumny ever issued against the social and religious principles of our Catholic fellow-men'.[63]

Outside the world of historical debate, but not wholly unaffected by it, the entire ecclesiastical landscape was transformed by two movements: the campaign for Catholic Emancipation (*c.* 1778–1829) and the Oxford Movement (*c.* 1833–45). The first grew out of the necessity of finding a solution to the problem of governing Ireland, where the majority of the native population had remained resolutely Catholic, and whose resistance to English government included demands for religious freedom. Political independence was not conceded, but the religious question was largely resolved in 1829 with the lifting of many (but not all) of the legal restrictions placed on the practice of Catholicism, not only in Ireland, but throughout the British Isles. The second, led by John Henry Newman (1801–90), Edward Bouverie Pusey (1800–82) and John Keble (1792–1866), and associated with Samuel Wilberforce (1805–73), bishop successively of Oxford and Winchester, and others, sought to prove the 'catholicity' of the Church of England through revived study of the early Church. Each movement brought profit and loss to the popular reputation of English Catholics. The Emancipation Bill was rejected by the House of Lords in 1825 and occasioned fierce debate. John Cross prefaced his denunciation of the bill with a summary of Christian history, which saw the papacy as an unscriptural usurpation, whose 'supremacy' disrupted the tranquillity of 'this kingdom … arising from a *double allegiance*'. 'Through the succeeding reign of *Henry the Second*, the contract between the ecclesiastical and the civil power was contested, and the peace of the kingdom again distracted, by the disloyalty of the primate *Becket*, and by his turbulent resistance of the Regal, and entire subjection to the *Papal* authority'. For Cross, the Reformation and the Revolution of 1688 'are the title-deeds, by which the king holds his crown. With that title, they have transmitted to us a Constitution the admiration of the civilized world, and an Empire comprising a rich inheritance'. The Bill amounted to 'national suicide', which would undermine the Constitution based on the Reformation, the Revolution and the Acts of Union, and preserved by the Coronation Oath and the Oath of Supremacy.[64]

Emancipation itself, though granted grudgingly and incompletely for the settlement of the Irish question,[65] combined with the government subsidy (1845) to Maynooth, the Catholic Seminary in Ireland, displeased Anglicans and Methodists, who feared a resurgence of popery; and Pope Pius IX's restoration of a Catholic hierarchy to

England in 1850 (with 12 dioceses and a cardinal archbishop of
Westminster at its head!) only added fuel to that particular fire.
If the Maynooth subsidy was 'Protestantism betrayed', Pope Pius's
action was 'papal aggression'; and the disestablishment of the
Church of Ireland in 1867 sent shock waves through the Anglican
establishment in England. What had been established by an Act of
Parliament (the Anglican Church) could just as easily be *dis*established by the same institution; and the political and religious configu-
ration of that assembly had ceased to be reassuringly high church and
Tory. Equally, as members and supporters of the Oxford Movement
sought to give the Thirty-Nine Articles a 'Catholic' interpretation,
and reclaim for Anglicanism some of the authority of the medieval
English Church – and with it some of the 'popish' practices abandoned
at the Reformation (cult of saints, the mass, auricular confession, the
sign of the cross, celibacy, monastic institutions for men and women) –
in the 1840s and 1850s, the royal supremacy became an obstacle.
Edward Bouverie Pusey even wrote a study on the royal supremacy
(1850) that argued, on the basis of a historical survey reaching back to
Christian Roman times, that the crown's authority in matters ecclesiastical (including both theological and disciplinary matters) was 'limited
by the laws of the Church, of which kings are members', that appeals
against bishops lay to 'other Bishops, or the Primate, or a General
Council', not to a 'Civil Court', and that 'the principle that Ecclesiastical
offences could only be tried by Ecclesiastical Courts, was formally
admitted into the Theodosian Code.'

Here was a very distinguished high Anglican, Regius Professor of
Hebrew at Oxford, proclaiming as essential elements of the freedom
of the early Christian Church principles for which Thomas Becket was
said to have died, with this difference: that the papacy does not feature
in his list of authorities to whom appeal may be had. His King Henry
VIII, who 'knew of no law of God or man but his own passions',

> meant doubtless to remove any constraint from his own
> will, and circumvented the Clergy to accomplish it. We
> have to consider principles to which the Church has
> expressed her assent, not the acts of a lawless king (whose
> memory is held in abhorrence in the whole world), even if
> in the guise of law.[66]

Pusey remained an influential Anglican, but he proclaimed many
of the beliefs and practices associated with the medieval Church:
monasticism, private penance, the Real Presence of Christ in the
Eucharist, and so on.

If Catholics could be gratified at this growing recognition of some of their practices and beliefs, more evangelical Anglicans could feel that the Protestant credentials of their religion were being undermined by a creeping Romanism and they were alarmed at the leakage of converts to Catholicism. Some of the leading lights of the Oxford Movement converted (Frederick Oakley (1844), Frederick William Faber, rector of Elton (Northants) (1845), John Henry Newman (1845), William George Ward (1845), Henry Edward Manning (1851)); so did Augustus Welby Pugin (*c.* 1835), one of the principal architects of the Gothic revival in architecture, noblemen (John Patrick Crighton-Stuart, marquess of Bute (1868), George Frederick Robinson, marquess of Ripon (1874)), and three of the four sons of the renowned humanitarian William Wilberforce, no less. Moreover, from the 1850s, Catholic religious institutions (monasteries and convents) were being founded and gained legal recognition as voluntary associations in 1871. Catholicism was thus legitimized and many of its hitherto condemned manifestations were again publicly displayed throughout England (though not without strong popular opposition): the cult of saints, the Latin mass, a celibate clergy, monasticism and the spiritual authority of the pope. And even after the collapse of the Oxford Movement (through the defection of its leading lights to the Roman Church and the confusion of its survivors), aspects of its programme of restoring ancient theology and ancient liturgy flourished among high churchmen who fostered liturgical regeneration (the Ritual Movement) on the basis of the rubrics of the *Book of Common Prayer*. As supporters of the revival found, the *Book of Common Prayer*, which had been magnificently translated by Cranmer from the medieval Sarum liturgies, contained many of the desired solemnities and practices that offered high church Anglicans some of the consolations of formal religion that attracted many to Rome. Even the revival of the Gothic style in architecture, which was applied not only to churches but also to major secular buildings (the law courts, the Houses of Parliament, and St Pancras Station in London, for example) assisted in the reassessment and re-evaluation of all things medieval.

The results of this renewed interest – even passion – were not always either accurate or reassuring, but they broke down the alienation between medieval and 'modern' that had been occasioned by the fact and the rhetoric of the Reformation. Sir Walter Scott's highly coloured novels and Alfred Lord Tennyson's (1809–92) *Idylls of the King* (1859) and *The Lady of Shallot* (1851) were hugely popular. At the same time, the tireless industry of the Reverend John A. Giles

(1808–84) produced a stream of medieval Latin works and translations, covering pre-Conquest history (Gildas, Nennius, Bede, St Boniface, Aldhelm, Alfred, etc.) and the twelfth and thirteenth centuries (Geoffrey of Monmouth, William of Malmesbury, the Peterborough Chronicle, Richard of Devizes, Roger of Wendover, Matthew Paris). Undistinguished as his editions proved to be, they helped to transform the historical landscape, by making available a host of works hitherto available only in manuscript or in rare early editions. Among this enormous output, 15 volumes, published between 1844 and 1848, were devoted to Thomas Becket and four of his contemporaries – Arnulf of Lisieux, Gilbert Foliot, Herbert of Bosham and John of Salisbury – and 12 of these were included in the Patres Ecclesiae Anglicanae (Fathers of the English Church) series, published in Oxford. Becket's Lives, Letters and Miracles were thus made available in a respectable English imprint by an Anglican cleric, and associated with the venerable heritage of the English Church. In addition, Giles made an English compendium from the Latin letters of the Becket controversy, which he published in two volumes with the title *The Life and Letters of Archbishop Thomas of Canterbury*. Although later judged a 'useless work' by Freeman,[67] his was perhaps the most sympathetic study on Becket to appear since the Reformation. Giles shared the growing Romantic view of the middle ages. The images that emerge from his *Life and Letters* are of a brutal Henry confronting a courageous if not quite saintly Becket. Whatever he is, though, Becket is a clerical hero and a hero of the *English* Church.

Canon John C. Robertson's learned but critical biography of Becket, challenged both the Saxonizing view of Thierry (1835) and the clerical hero depicted by R.H. Froude (1838–39), but he looked at the Becket dispute with a value system based on the contemporary constitution of the English Church, whose bishops were appointed by the crown, paid homage to the queen, and sat in the House of Lords. In his view, Becket should not have given up the chancellorship or opposed Clarendon; the king's demands were warranted by the advice of learned canonists and jurists; Becket's case had no real foundation; 'the immediate cause for which he fell was but a quarrel as to the privileges of Canterbury and York'; and it was 'his defiant behaviour and intolerable language' that 'excited [the murderers] to uncontrollable fury.' 'The great fortune of Becket's reputation was the manner of his end.' 'Was it for a Christian prelate, not only to oppose the king in a reasonable claim, but to render his opposite move offensive by continual displays of that pride for which his enemies loudly reproach him?'[68]

But the heroic and justified image drew influential partisans. In the context of Catholic revival, Becket became once more a defender of ecclesiastical law against the illicit *customs* introduced by the Norman kings. The first edition of the Jesuit John Morris's *Life and Martyrdom of Saint Thomas Becket* appeared in the same year as Robertson's critical Life.[69] This was written more like a hagiography than a critical history: Becket is 'St Thomas' and 'Our Saint' throughout. Cardinal Manning – a former leader of the Oxford Movement – in an 'Inaugural Address to the Academia of the Catholic Religion' at the opening of the 1868–69 session, discussed at length the Constitutions of Clarendon, citing Becket's letters (from the edition by Giles), and argued that St Thomas died for the lawful freedom of the Church, specifically the right of appeal, access to Rome, free elections and independent tribunals. He concluded, 'It is therefore beyond a doubt that the conflict of S. Thomas was precisely in behalf of the true and legitimate union of Church and State', in which Becket, in his view, had a 'prophetic instinct' about the consequences of Henry II's proposals, if they were not resisted,[70] and was deservedly honoured as a 'Martyr for the liberties of England'.[71] Meanwhile, Edward A. Freeman, a distinguished (if controversial) historian of Anglo-Saxon England and the Norman Conquest, criticized Robertson's interpretation, principally on the grounds that it was anachronistic, since it viewed the Becket controversy through the eyes of the nineteenth century; and he argued that contemporary dealings with Rome should not be taken into account in evaluating Becket's career. This was an important statement in the immediate context in which Freeman was writing, for 'no popery' and 'papal aggression' were given a new lease of life in the fierce debates surrounding the proclamation of papal infallibility in the First Vatican Council (1870). Freeman, it should be noted, was a defender of the greater antiquity and civilization of the Anglo-Saxons, for whom the Norman Conquest and all that followed was an unmitigated disaster. His Becket, therefore, like Thierry's, wears a distinctly English mantle in confronting Henry II, who is described as 'a mere foreigner, a Frenchman living in France, devoting his energies to French objects, and holding England almost as a province of Anjou'.[72]

So, the contempt and disdain with which the medieval Church was generally viewed in England was being moderated by foreign travel (especially in Italy and Rome), by historical research, by restoration movements within Anglicanism itself, by Romanticism, by the Gothic Revival, by the spin-off from the Oxford Movement, and by the Catholic revival. The congeries of national attitudes that had cast Becket in the guise of traitor, ecclesiastical zealot, power-hungry adversary of constitutional legitimacy, opponent of the High Court of Parliament, supporter of popery and canon law, was much muted by the end of the nineteenth century, although it did not disappear entirely.

12

Conclusion

Historical opinion is still broadly split between those who interpret the Becket controversy in exclusively secular terms and those who see it from the Church's perspective. One of the most uncompromising presentations of the former view was made by Egbert Türk in his 1977 study on Henry II's court. In many ways, this is an excellent analysis of the realities of life at a court that was full of ambitious place-seekers, ready always to do one another down; but its reduction of Thomas to the role of a turncoat Curialist who bit the hand that fed him, does less than justice to the man and to the cause that he came, reluctantly, to serve. Although he pays scant attention to Becket's archiepiscopal career, Türk blames the crisis on Becket's 'provocation' and refusal to 'compromise'.[1] The moral dilemma that confronted conscientious clergy in royal service is written off as old-fashioned 'Gregorianism', out of place and irrelevant to the dynamic world of royal government. Becket's repudiation of royal service was, therefore, wrongheaded, the cause perverse, and the murder a 'violent death, wished for and provoked by the primate', which 'could thus be seen both as an act of savage justice and as an extreme case of the settling of accounts between curialists.'[2] A similar view pervades the long section devoted to Becket in Warren's *Henry II*. Where Henry's 'interference' in ecclesiastical affairs is 'well-meaning', Becket's actions were 'grand gestures', in which 'he seemed to be deliberately picking a quarrel', or 'melodrama'; on the matter of sheriffs' aid, he was 'obtuse and cantankerous' and 'quite improper'; intellectually, he was 'a theological dinosaur', clinging to an outmoded 'Gregorianism', and, at the end, 'He brought a violent death upon himself because he could not bring himself to admit that his reading of the situation had been mistaken, his sufferings largely self-inflicted, and his obstinacy misguided.'[3] As early as 1943, in contrast, Raymonde Foreville presented a sympathetic interpretation of the Church's position in the context of Henry II's wide-ranging policy of aggressive recuperation. Her monumental study was received coolly in England, but it remains one of the most scholarly and penetrating analyses of the subject. David Knowles frankly acknowledged the problems of Becket's dual life, but concluded that there was justice in his cause and dignity in his end, and Charles Duggan revealed the broad validity of his canonical position and emphasized the importance of his defence of ecclesiastical freedom.[4] Professor Barlow's probing and critical *Thomas Becket* judged his archiepiscopate 'disastrous for all concerned' in the short term, yet concluded,

> We can see that after Thomas's death things were never quite the same again, whether in the English church or in Latin Christendom at large. He had, through his stand against Henry and his martyrdom, brought the archaic English customs to the notice of the pope and cardinals and all canon lawyers and had succeeded in getting them scrutinized, debated, and in part abolished or reformed.[5]

Could these benefits have been achieved by other means? Historians point to the generally harmonious relationships between Henry II and the two archbishops that succeeded him, Richard of Dover (1174–84) and Baldwin of Forde (1184–90). If they could do it, why couldn't Thomas Becket? For Warren, Türk and Barlow,[6] the answer is that the archiepiscopate went to his head, that he was too arrogant to make the necessary accommodation. Yet Becket's position was very different from theirs. Richard and Baldwin were monks; neither had been a Curialist; neither was called upon to combine secular office with the primacy. Moreover, Becket's opposition, murder and canonization had for ever changed the context in which they and their successors were operating, as Barlow conceded.[7] The concessions Henry made in 1172 (at Avranches) and 1175–76 (to Cardinal Hugh Pierleone), regarding appeals to Rome, clerical immunity and the punishment of the secular murderers of clerics, are unlikely to have been made if the king had not been constrained, first by the consequences of Becket's murder, then by the great rebellion of 1173–74. Only after those two serious crises, which some contemporaries saw as cause and effect, was he willing to negotiate with the Church, and in a manner inconceivable during Becket's lifetime. Professor Warren compared Thomas unfavourably with his friend, John *aux Bellesmains*, bishop of Poitiers: but Poitou had never been subjected to the same degree of comital control which the

Norman rulers had imposed in their Anglo-Norman realm, and Henry did not push the matter to extremes, as he did in England.[8]

Any judgements on Thomas must take into account the attitude and behaviour of what Christopher Brooke called 'his mercurial master', of whom Arnulf of Lisieux wrote a very perceptive assessment in 1165, at the beginning of Becket's exile:

> He is great, and greater than many, because he has neither superior who can frighten him nor subject who can resist, nor is he attacked from outside by foreign assaults, which might cause him to tame his innate ferocity at home; but all who have causes for contention against him join together in perilous leagues of empty peace rather than run to a trial of strength, because he exceeds them in the abundance of his riches, the multitude of his forces, and the extent of his power.

Henry had been accustomed to the exercise of power from the age of 16, when he was recognized as duke of Normandy in 1149. Two years later, in 1151, he became count of Anjou (with Maine and Touraine) on the death of his father, Geoffrey. This young man then married Eleanor of Aquitaine, the former wife of Louis VII of France, through whom he acquired the duchy of Aquitaine in 1152, a duchy that embraced the county of Poitou and claimed jurisdiction over Toulouse and the Auvergne. Even without its claims to these territories, it constituted about one-quarter of modern France. To these lordships he added the right of succession to the English kingdom in 1153, when he was acknowledged as King Stephen's heir, and he entered into that great inheritance in October 1154, on Stephen's death. As the English bishops pointed out in 1166, his lordships 'stretched from the Northern Ocean to the Pyrenees'.[9] This accumulation of dominions, which historians have labelled the 'Angevin Empire', made him potentially one of the richest and most powerful of the European kings. Moreover, in England and Normandy he inherited the nucleus of a highly efficient administrative system, which he was able to mould into the core of a bureaucratic state. Although rightly associated with laying the foundations of English common law in the series of new devices and processes that were created in his reign, that law was his law and its processes served his purposes. He ruled by force and will (*vis et voluntas*), and used his goodwill (*benevolentia*) and ill-will (*malevolentia*) as instruments of control. 'Besides the rule of law there was always another rule *per voluntatem*.'[10] This Henry was no male Victoria!

Running through the records of the reign, moreover, there is an unedifying thread of slipperiness, chicanery and broken faith. Henry made lavish promises, which he probably had no intention of keeping; he stridently advanced claims he must have known were fraudulent;[11] and his dealings with Louis VII of France were not entirely honest. The best-known example, which poisoned relations between the two kings for the rest of Louis' life, was the Vexin affair. What was intended to be an enduring peace between the two monarchs was sealed in 1158 by the betrothal of Henry's eldest son, Henry, to Louis' daughter, Margaret, who was duly handed over for education in Henry's court. A key element in the agreement, however, was the assignation of the Norman Vexin as Margaret's dowry. This little territory, with its two castles (Gisors and Neuflé), occupied a highly strategic position, commanding the main route between Normandy and Paris. Since the betrothed were infants (Henry was three; Margaret even younger), King Louis naturally believed that the formalization of the marriage, which would entail his transfer of the Vexin to Henry's lordship, would not take place for many years. But in 1160, Henry persuaded the two papal legates who were negotiating the recognition of Pope Alexander III to solemnize the marriage, and so stole a march on King Louis, to his great consternation.[12] Louis later (1168) declared that Henry was 'clearly a transgressor of every obligation undertaken by oath; and it would be foolish to trust his bare word.'[13] The Becket letters are full of charges of duplicity and sharp practice, and Gerald of Wales called him 'a seller and delayer of justice, changeable and twisting in his words, a ready breaker, not only of his word, but of his faith and oath'.[14] Even men who served him most loyally, and praised his kingship, admitted that his government was vulnerable to serious criticism. His treasurer Richard FitzNeal, for example, who wrote the *Dialogue of the Exchequer* at the end of the reign, acknowledged that not all his money was obtained lawfully;[15] and that the forest laws were not called 'just' without qualification, but 'just according to the forest law'.[16]

Much is made of the close friendship between Henry and Thomas of London, both by contemporaries and by later commentators. There is no doubt that they were friends, but, as the incident of the beggar's cloak shows, it was a very unequal relationship.[17] Twelfth-century courts functioned on a system of clientage and expectation. Their members were expected to give their lords exclusive service, in return for maintenance and promotion. In such a context, Becket's resignation of the Chancery was an act of unforgivable arrogance and disloyalty;[18] and from this 'gran rifiuto' flowed the whole sorry sequence of events. But historians have to ask whether Henry would have accepted any form of opposition from the man he regarded as his servant, even if he had retained the office of chancellor?

Although even sympathetic writers, like Knowles, found fault with his behaviour in the first nine months of his archiepiscopate – and Warren and Barlow thought him needlessly provocative – was he doing more than any new appointment to an office would have done: insist that customary duties be performed; that wrongly obtained land be restored; that homage be paid to the new lord? On sheriffs' aid he stood for the established custom; on clerical immunity he did no more than was already being done in high-profile cases; and his opposition to the king's proposals at Westminster had the full backing of the episcopate. Thereafter he was subject to fierce pressure to find a compromise. The papal crisis was at its most acute, and many of the English bishops were, frankly, terrified of the king's anger. It has been argued that Henry's *ira* was only a public demonstration – a 'staged emotion' that enabled the baronage to submit without loss of face.[19] Its consequences, however, were real enough: as Becket's family and household discovered in 1164; as the Welsh hostages experienced in their fearful mutilation in 1165. Henry's rage worked, not because of its ritualistic dimensions but because its observers knew that real force and a willingness to use that force lay behind it. The English Church was 'his' Church, its bishops and abbots 'his' bishops and abbots, who held their estates from him by military service, suit of court, and homage and fealty. What he wanted from Thomas the archbishop was obedience and collaboration – anything else was a form of treachery.

Becket's mistake was to allow himself to be persuaded to make an oral concession at Woodstock in December 1163, following which he was backed into a corner at Clarendon. But at that moment, despite Foliot's assertion in *Multiplicem*, he stood almost alone: he had been pressed by all sides, including leading bishops and special papal envoys, to make some kind of accommodation in order to avoid a breach with the most powerful king in the West. His acceptance at Woodstock was an attempt at conciliation in accordance with the forceful advice he had been given. Men he respected, like the two templars, joined with the papal emissary, Philip of l'Aumône, to assure him that the king wanted only an oral commitment to 'the customs', to save his royal honour; when that was given, the king raised the stakes by demanding a public repetition of the agreement – which was given at the royal council at Clarendon, again in deference

to his honour; and then the written constitutions were sprung, fully
fledged, with all the formal protocol of a binding recognition already
in place. There is no evidence that the contents of the Clarendon
constitutions were discussed with the bishops before being presented
as a binding formulation of the customs of the realm. If Gilbert
Foliot's description of the threatening language and demeanour of
the barons is accurate –

> when the princes and all the great nobles of the realm
> had already broken out into a very great rage, they came
> shouting and clanking into the room where we were
> sitting and, throwing off their cloaks and thrusting out
> their arms, they addressed us in these words. 'Pay heed,
> you who scorn the laws of the realm and do not accept
> the king's commands. These are not our hands that you
> see here, nor our arms, nor these in fact our bodies: they
> belong to our lord the king, and they are most ready to
> be directed at this very moment in accordance with his
> every pleasure, to avenge every wrong committed against
> him, to carry out his will, whatever it is. Whatever he
> commands will be wholly just to us, simply because it
> comes from his will. Withdraw your resolution; bend
> your wills to his command, so that, while it is possible,
> you may avoid the danger which could not be avoided
> just now.' (*CTB*, i, no. 109)

and he was seeking to defend the king, not attack him – then
Becket's perplexing behaviour (accepting the Constitutions and then
refusing his seal) was a tactical manoeuvre.

Was it weakness or desperation? Probably the latter. Two of his
clerks were already in exile; his friend the bishop of Poitiers was
contemplating flight to Pontigny, where their mutual friend, Cardinal
Henry of Pisa, was negotiating for both of them; the papal Curia was
living on charity in France; and the emperor, Frederick I, seemed to be
tightening his hold on Italy. Becket's instruction to the bishops to make
the required acknowledgment of the customs was a temporary ploy to
protect them from the king's wrath. If all of them had to flee, then
Henry would have been able to take the territorial endowment of all 16
sees into his own hands (as King John did in the early thirteenth century). It is highly probable, in fact, that the desperate stratagem was not
his idea. Gilbert Foliot, who was not seeking to excuse his action, said
that he had explained his capitulation with the words, 'It is my lord's
will that I should forswear myself; I submit for the present and incur

the guilt of perjury, to do penance in the future as far as I can.'[20] This allusion to 'my lord's will' implies that the pope – or rather, Philip of l'Aumône, who was speaking in his name – had suggested the device of a formal submission to force and fear, which could be withdrawn at a later date. In canon law, an oath or promise, or contract made under duress ('force and/or fear') was not binding. It would be on such grounds, among others, that King John obtained Pope Innocent III's absolution from his oath to observe Magna Carta; and in February 1164, Pope Alexander declared unlawful the bishops' promise to observe the Constitutions.

Such an explanation would reconcile all the divergent accounts: the discomfiture of the bishops, the pressure of the envoys and Becket's sudden *volte-face*. The concession was intended to be a tactical retreat, but it became a strategic error of the first order. No doubt the bishops were surprised, even the fearful ones; and they were left with a formal promise – even if not sealed – to observe the 16 constitutions; and the king had a public commitment to which he could hold them. The fact that Henry failed to persuade the Curia to agree to the whole schedule, and that Becket was absolved by Pope Alexander, did not cut any ice. He would have been pleased indeed to have been able to use papal authority to compel the archbishop to assent to the schedule; but if he could not secure that, he could go forward on the basis of the original promise, as, indeed, he did.[21] Becket nevertheless remained a living obstacle to their implementation, and his attempts to flee were thwarted.

The state trial at Northampton was the king's response; and Becket's conduct must be read in the context of the king's actions. Was he lawfully charged? Was he lawfully convicted of any serious offence? Northampton was the king's court; it was presided over by him and its processes were directed by him. Thomas was led into an ever deeper legal trap from which he could not escape. Was he victim or villain? Certainly, many voices were raised against him; but by then his disgrace was common knowledge. Most, if not all, of the bishops were terrified and wanted a quick resolution. Becket's condemnation, submission or resignation would have got them all out of a very tight spot. Professor Warren argued that, despite the irregularity of the Northampton 'trial', Becket should have 'borne with composure the king's manifest persecution ... exposed patiently the hollowness of the accusations, and ... suffered perhaps imprisonment on such flimsy charges'; that 'would have been true martyrdom'. Ignoring the consequences that would have followed from such capitulation, Warren saw Becket's resistance as entirely self-absorbed,

aimed at 'preserving his dignity'.[22] This was, largely, the theme of
the sarcastic *Multiplicem*. In that 'letter', Foliot argued that Thomas
could have achieved much by humility and conciliation – implying
that it was his own arrogance and pride that had exasperated his
'good king'. That argument needs to be pondered carefully. Is there
any evidence that Henry II would have modified his ecclesiastical
policy if Becket had 'humbled himself', either at Clarendon or at
Northampton? In the light of the king's tenacity through the six-year
exile, one must doubt whether the archbishop's sacrifice would have
brought a satisfactory resolution for the Church. The Council of
Clarendon was called to witness the bishops' submission; that of
Northampton was staged, both to destroy the obstacle (Becket) and
as a warning to other bishops that they would not be safe from the
king's *ira* if they followed the same path.

Although most commentators see Thomas as obstructive in the
negotiations at Planches–Argentan (1167), Montmirail–Saint-Léger-
en-Ivelines (early 1169) and Montmartre (late 1169), one should ask,
perhaps, obstructive of what? It is clear that at Planches–Argentan,
Henry and the hostile bishops expected Cardinals William and Otto
to preside over a replication of the Northampton trial, and they were
extremely disappointed to find that the cardinals' judicial status had
been withdrawn, since events in Rome made it unnecessary for
Alexander III to sacrifice Thomas on the altar of expediency. Becket
could have accepted their formal mediation or even judgment, but
did he have any reason to trust William of Pavia, whom everyone
believed was the king's choice? As at Northampton, Henry wanted
'judgment', meaning condemnation, not a negotiated agreement that
would have seen Becket restored to office and honour in England.
He wanted 'to be free of him'.

In the series of negotiations at Montmirail–Saint-Léger and
Montmartre, where the papal commissioners strove to find a formula that would satisfy both sides, the outcome turned on the inclusion or exclusion of saving phrases, *saving my* order, *saving God's
honour*, etc. Was Becket's insistence on such formulae obstructive pedantry? As he pointed out, the phrase *saving my order* was
included in the oath of homage as defined in the Constitutions themselves; it was a regular part of any oath taken by clerics; and Pope
Alexander had instructed him to use both phrases in any agreement
with the king. Henry, for his part, wanted an end to the Becket crisis, which was damaging to his international reputation, but he had
no intention of modifying or abandoning the Constitutions, and
Thomas was not prepared to bind himself unreservedly to their

observance. He knew well enough that the innocent-sounding 'dignities of the realm' were nothing other than the 'customs of the realm' – that is, the Constitutions of Clarendon – in a very thin disguise. The word 'dignities', indeed, was used as a synonym for 'customs' in the preamble of the Clarendon chirograph. Far from refusing fair offers of reconciliation, Becket can be seen in a desperate struggle to avoid repeating the mistakes of Woodstock, Clarendon and Northampton, where each concession was the springboard for more demands. Professor Barlow argued that the whole sorry business could have been avoided, if Henry and Thomas had been prepared to accept the compromise that was adopted at Fréteval; but the Fréteval peace studiously avoided the central issue, and solved nothing. The Constitutions of Clarendon remained flagrantly in place and they were waved in Becket's face as a kind of *praemunire* at every turn.

Did Thomas blow the peace of Fréteval? The answer will depend on how solid that peace actually was. There had been no kiss of peace; Becket's clerks found open hostility and obstruction when they attempted to take possession of his estates in November 1170; he himself was faced with an armed force when he landed – only the intervention of John of Oxford prevented his baggage being searched and a foreign clerk being made to take an oath of fealty to Henry II; and he was denied access to the court of the young king. As far as one can judge, the archbishop of York and the bishops of London and Salisbury had become implacably hostile. Roger of Pont l'Évêque was a willing participant in the coronation, which advanced the claims of his see; Gilbert Foliot had been Henry's tool and Jocelin de Bohun had urged concession since the days of Clarendon. All three would have known that some censure would come their way for their infringement of Canterbury's rights in the coronation, to say nothing of London and Salisbury's persistent resistance throughout the years of the exile; but they – like the clerks whom the king had intruded into Canterbury's churches, and the de Brocs who had done well out of the exile – were in no hurry to see a return to normality.

It is possible that if Becket had not issued the papal letters against York, London and Salisbury, they would not have run with their complaints to the king in Normandy, he would not have made his outburst, and the nefarious four would not have set out on their fateful path; but there were numerous indications that Becket had not been, and never would be, admitted to Henry's grace and favour. If the bishops had not been censured, some other 'provocation' would have triggered a similar explosion of rage and exasperation. The Constitutions of Clarendon and the 1169 decrees remained in place; the archbishop was effectively confined to Canterbury; and Henry had issued writs summoning English clergy to his presence in Normandy, to elect five new bishops. Five of the six 'elections' made in 1173–74 – Richard of Ilchester to Winchester; John of Oxford to Norwich; Geoffrey Ridel to Ely; Reginald FitzJocelin to Bath and Wells; the king's illegitimate son, Geoffrey, to Lincoln – show that the episcopate would have been flooded with Curialists already committed to the king's programme, and any opposition on Becket's part would have caused a similar crisis. As it was, by the time that Henry got his mostly compliant bishops, the context had been changed significantly. The king had been forced to a public avowal of some degree of responsibility for the murder; he accepted penances from two papal legates; he conceded freedom of appeals to Rome; and he and his son, the young King Henry, swore allegiance to Pope Alexander and his legitimate successors.

Did Thomas provoke his murderers? The four knights who executed what they thought was the king's will had not originally intended to kill, but they had assembled a considerable force, and when the archbishop refused to surrender himself, they put on their armour, broke into his house and pursued him with drawn swords into the cathedral. Should Thomas of Canterbury have gone meekly with them at the first interview, or allowed himself to be hauled ignominiously out of his own cathedral, or run away and tried to hide himself in the crypt? No doubt they were angry at being baulked of their prize in the archbishop's palace, and angry also when he reminded them of their homage and FitzUrse of his less than honourable role on the fringes of the royal household.[23] But did that anger justify their extreme violence? The ferocity of their attack and their deliberate desecration of the body suggests otherwise.

It would be easy to reduce the dispute to the refusal of two 'stubborn' men to compromise, or even, as Türk argued, as the revenge of the court for his defection,[24] but these interpretations diminish the importance of the matters at issue. Both men were 'stubborn' because there were high stakes. The Constitutions purported to be ancient custom, but they contained some very skilful formulations, which set new boundaries to the competence of church courts, and laid down an appellate procedure, which could have isolated the English Church from the rest of the Latin West. The argument that the king would not in practice have proceeded to the full extent of the new definitions ignores the tendency of Henry's legal reforms. Whether intentionally or not, and some historians are tending to the former,[25] the 'common law' drew more and more jurisdiction into the king's courts. There is no reason to believe that the Church's jurisdiction would have fared any better. Henry II was embarked on a programme not only of recuperation but of expansion, and there was little to stand in his way.[26] Compromise is possible only when both sides are prepared to give something to the other, and there is no evidence that Henry was prepared to concede anything to the man he had made archbishop of Canterbury.

Would the dispute have proceeded differently if another man had been archbishop? Almost certainly – but not necessarily any better from the point of view of the English Church. Would Gilbert Foliot have been a better choice? He had the social and religious status; he had the diplomatic skills; but would he have had the courage to resist Henry's demands? The apparent willingness with which he was prepared to act as the king's cat's-paw against Becket, suggests that he would have been a collaborator rather than an opponent. He and his extended family had too much to lose.[27]

Certainly the biographers were writing as much hagiography as biography; but if the pre-birth premonitions and the titles of saint and holy man are stripped out, there remain remarkably detailed and not always adulatory accounts of the key events in Becket's life. The writers confronted the duality of Becket's life, not with embarrassment, but as a matter of fact. He did lead a secular life as archdeacon-chancellor: he rode and fought and hunted with the king; he imposed royal taxes on the Church (and the rest of the nobility) for the king's campaigns; he enjoyed the wealth and the splendour. But he did change his manner of life, as the full weight of the new responsibility bore down upon him, and not only superficially. He did renounce the power and the status of the Chancery; he did commit himself to the service of the English Church, and his bitter exile could readily be seen as preparation for the final sacrifice. As one of the Matins Responsories declared:

> For six years this stone is chipped away,
> thus polished, thus squared up,
> Yielding less the more it is struck.

> The furnace tests the gold, nor is it consumed;
> The strong house is not shaken by the wind:
> Yielding less the more it is struck.

Thomas of London was much more than the shallow and flashy cleric described by some critics.[28] He was a man of faith. His early devotion to the Virgin, his public charity and private penances all point to his religious commitment; and it was a commitment that the brutal changes in his fortunes seem to have deepened rather than lessened. He admired the saintly Anselm, whose relics he translated in April, and whose canonization he sought in May 1163;[29] he promoted the cult of the Holy Trinity; he celebrated mass with particular devotion; and although his personal library contained both Gratian's *Decretum* and a full set of Justinian's Roman Law, its principal components were designed to aid contemplation and preaching.[30] There is a clue to deeper currents of spirituality in his invocation of St Denis in his dying moments. Thomas had been present with Archbishop Theobald at the consecration in 1144 of the splendid new abbey church of Saint-Denis. Built in the newest 'Gothic' style by Abbot Suger, it not only celebrated the proto-martyr of 'France', but expressed the mystical theology of the *Celestial Hierarchy* of [Pseudo-]Denis the Areogapite, with whom the Apostle of Paris had been (wrongly) identified. The work was known to the Becket circle, for John of Salisbury had persuaded his friend, John Saracen, to make a new translation,[31] and Herbert of Bosham wrote a short commentary on the concept of theophany – the mystical experience of the divine described by Denis. It was this word, *theophania*, that Herbert used in the context of Becket's celebration of mass, which was characterized by special devotion.[32] The moral courage with which Thomas faced his murderers was very different from the physical valour he had shown in Toulouse and the Vexin, and drew on deeper roots. To assess Becket's career as archbishop without giving full weight to the spiritual and intellectual milieu in which his outlook had been formed is to ignore the beliefs that shaped his attitudes and behaviour. Equally, to reduce them to a caricature of 'Gregorianism' or 'narrow clericalism' is to deny the broad streams of reformist teaching coming out of the schools in Paris and Laon, which sought to raise the level of clerical behaviour and so make the clerical order worthy both of its claimed inheritance from the Old Testament priesthood and of the privileges it claimed as mediator between God and man. Such teachers, from Hugh of St Victor to Peter the Chanter (d. 1197), agonized over the morality of clerks being caught up in the often brutal business of contemporary rule; and they felt free to lecture kings and princes on their misdoings.[33]

Had Thomas been no more than an ambitious place-man, there would have been no difficulty in his holding the crozier in one hand

and the Great Seal in the other. The bishops might have thought ill of the arrangement, but they would have accepted the fait accompli; some chroniclers, especially the monastic, might have written sharp comments in their histories – but Becket's position as chancellor-archbishop would have been protected by the power of his master, just as it had been when he was chancellor-archdeacon. Nobles who held his origins in contempt would still have sent their sons to his court, as the king himself had done. For a brief few months, indeed, he seems to have toyed with the possibility of holding both offices, but as the magnitude of the responsibilities of the archbishopric imposed itself upon him – as he, one by one, received priestly ordin-ation and episcopal consecration, took his place in Augustine's chair and received the *pallium* – he made the choice that cost him his career and, eventually, his life.

Martyrdom exists only where there is both force and choice. Christian martyrs could have saved their lives by publicly subscrib-ing to the Roman religion or sacrificing to the emperor. Thomas Becket, also, probably could have saved his life by surrendering to the quartet that stormed into the cathedral, but such surrender would have given the lie to his whole archiepiscopal career. Once Becket had been consecrated bishop and received the *pallium*, which symbolized his authority as head of the province of Canterbury, he ceased to be Thomas of London and became, literally, another person, successor to Augustine, Dunstan, Lanfranc, Anselm and Theobald. From that moment he was called upon to 'stand like a wall before the house of Israel' – to defend the material and spiritual rights of the Church. If bishops didn't, who would? Warren and Türk saw him as an incarnation of 'Gregorian ideas', but Thomas was drawing inspiration from a source far older. In 252, Cyprian, the martyr bishop of Carthage, wrote these stirring words to Cornelius, martyr bishop of Rome:

> If, dearly beloved brother, things have really reached this point that men can be cowed by the insolence of the wicked and that what evildoers cannot achieve by lawful means they can get by uncontrolled violence, then we must despair of the strength of our episcopal authority and of that noble and God-given power which had been granted to us for governing the Church. No more can we persevere as Christians; indeed, no longer can we even be Christians if it has come to this, that we can be terrorized by the menaces and machinations of such a lawless

rabble ... No, dearly beloved brother: we must preserve
unshakable strength of faith, and a courage that is
unyielding and unassailable in order to withstand all the
battering and assaults from the waves that come in
roaring against us, beating them off with all the firmness
of some massive opposing rock.[34]

Thomas owned a copy of Cyprian's letters – it was in the extensive
library he left to the cathedral priory[35] – and this particular text was
in his memory in 1170. In an attempt to persuade Bishop Roger of
Worcester to try to prevent the young king's coronation, he quoted
to him one sentence from this letter, which summed up the martyr-
bishop's assessment of the dignity and responsibility of the episcopal
office. It was short and to the point: 'If a bishop is afraid, he is
finished!'[36] Cyprian was speaking of the state-encouraged anti-
Christian riots in the wake of the Decian persecution of 249–51; but
the words, 'If ... what evildoers cannot achieve by lawful means they
can get by uncontrolled violence, then we must despair of the
strength of our episcopal authority and of that noble and God-given
power which had been granted to us for governing the Church', must
have resonated in Becket's mind as he faced the 'menaces and machinations of [the] lawless rabble' with 'unshakable strength of faith, and
a courage that is unyielding.'

At a time when the Latin Church was striving to free its institutions
from the privatization and politicization that had become endemic,
Becket's courageous articulation of this ideal had a powerful appeal.
This in part explains the enthusiasm with which his cult was embraced
in Iceland and the Scandinavian countries, for example, as well as in
Poland and Hungary. Here was a new martyr who spoke to the contemporary Church. Here also was a man whose transformation from
lordly chancellor to oppressed and penniless exile was known across
Europe, so that the news of his atrocious murder, when it came, was
interpreted in the light of all that had preceded it. Thomas of London,
Thomas the Chancellor and Thomas the Archbishop was already an
international figure, known personally to Pope Alexander, the Curia,
archbishops, bishops and lesser clerics across Europe, and by repute
to many more. Cistercians and Benedictines had given him shelter;
canons regular had educated him – all could claim him in some way as
their own. Individual friends, acquaintances, supporters and protectors could all rejoice in the reflected glory of having known Thomas
the Archbishop, and embrace the cult of 'their' saint. As Robert,
an English canon regular from St Frideswide's in Oxford, said in a

sermon, which must have been delivered before his own death in 1174, 'we have seen and known him, and many of us were his friends.'[37]

Many who had not known him and who were not his friends were equally impressed by the drama. The story of the 'new martyr' made compulsive reading and listening, and attracted some unexpected devotees. One remarkable incident, recorded in an early thirteenth-century Icelandic saga, exemplifies the extraordinary extent of the popularity enjoyed by St Thomas outside England. In telling the story of its hero, the *Hrafns Saga Sveinbjarnarsonar* recounts how, at the spring gathering of Iceland's notables in 1192–93, the hero (Hrafn) and his companions saw a walrus swimming near the shore. Leaping into their boat, they struggled to trap the valuable prize, but the creature evaded all their efforts, and began to escape back into the sea. At this point, the saga relates, Hrafn vowed that he would give the ivory tusks to St Thomas, the martyred archbishop, at Canterbury, if they succeeded in bringing the walrus ashore. And so it happened. Hrafn and his party captured the walrus and then departed to Norway, where they spent the winter. During the next spring (1194) they sailed west to England, where Hrafn 'presented the ivory to St Thomas and commended himself to the monks in the Minster'.[38] Nor can this tale be written off as a piece of romantic fiction. Whatever the accuracy of the specifics of *Hrafns Saga*, at least 11 churches were dedicated to the English St Thomas on the island,[39] and a later, mid-thirteenth-century, saga relates that one nobleman was listening to a 'Thomas Saga' at Hrafnagil in 1258 on the night that he died.[40] Indeed, one of the longest compositions in Old Icelandic is the *Thómas Saga Erkibyskups*, which was based on a range of Latin originals, including the lost Life by Robert of Cricklade, prior of St Frideswide's in Oxford, who died in 1174.[41] St Thomas could be everybody's saint.[42]

In addition to the heroic Becket, however, there is the wonder-working Becket: the saint and martyr, to whose tomb the sick and the sorrowful came for healing and relief; to whose protection sailors and crusaders prayed for safe passage. This aspect of the cult of Becket has provided easy targets for attack and embarrassment for a rationalist age. John Foxe alleged monastic duplicity and medieval gullibility, but it is hard to claim that all the miracles were fakes or frauds. Twelfth-century men and women believed in miracles; and miracles, particularly miracles of healing, when well attested, deserve to be accorded more serious consideration than they normally receive. Medieval people were no less ready to challenge 'tall stories' than their modern successors; but they were more ready to accept supernatural explanations where natural ones were not immediately evident. At the same time, miracles of healing or finding should not be dismissed as the fancy of the foolish or the trickery of dishonest monks seeking a source of renewable income. Medical professionals are increasingly recognizing the 'placebo effect' of medicines and pseudo-medicines. In a very wide variety of conditions, double-blind trials of new drugs and treatments have demonstrated that a statistically significant proportion of those afflicted experience measurable improvement in their condition following the administration of 'dummy' drugs. This is far more than what Abbot dismissed as the relief of 'hysterical conditions' in the Becket miracles. A recent article by Anne Feinmann in *The Times* (3 September 2002, T2, p. 12) noted the placebo effect in such serious cases as angina, stomach ulcers, migraine and depression. Patients who thought that they were receiving painkillers, or blood pressure-lowering medications, or even ultrasound treatments, responded to inert dummy drugs or procedures. So significant is the placebo effect that the clinical evaluation of new drugs has to allow for it. The men and women whose wounds healed, whose arthritic or rheumatic pains decreased, whose sight was restored, were not necessarily fooling themselves or others. If a twenty-first-century patient can be relieved or even cured because he *believes in* and *trusts* the person administering the treatment, it is not all that surprising that a twelfth-century sufferer, who equally *believed in* the power of prayer and *trusted* that God would cure his ailment following his performance of pilgrimage and its attendant rituals, actually found relief at the martyr's tomb, and triumphantly broadcast news of the event to friends and neighbours.[43]

If one picture is worth a thousand words, the depiction of Becket's murder – with the armour-clad knights brandishing their swords above the unprotected head of the priest – created an unforgettable image, which expressed the tension between religious and secular forces. No commentary was required to interpret the dramatic scene transmitted across Europe in manuscripts or on the reliquaries manufactured in Limoges. Detached from the specifics of his dispute with Henry II, that image became a powerful symbol of ecclesiastical steadfastness in the face of secular excess. In a sense, the image was the message; and the meaning of the message was not lost on Henry VIII, who destroyed the shrine and caused the hated name to be erased from the service books of the English Church; nor was it lost on the controversialists of the post-Reformation era, Catholic,

Anglican and Protestant, who responded to the message with praise or censure according to its application to their own outlook.

Many secular heroes are made by single events: Richard I at Acre, Henry V at Agincourt, Nelson at Trafalgar, Wellington at Waterloo, Montgomery at El Alamein. For martyrs, it is the fact of their death in defence of their beliefs that justifies their claim. In Becket's case, the cause for which he died was ultimately bypassed by history; but it had numerous analogues that could be recognized in very different historical settings. Even in this generation, the murder of Archbishop Oscar Romero of San Salvador in 1988, or of Father Jerzy Popiełuszko in Poland, called up the image of St Thomas of Canterbury, murdered for opposition to a powerful king. Becket's example, of resistance to an aggressive 'public power' and courage in the face of extreme violence, could be appreciated by men and women across the ages.

Notes

Introduction

1. Guernes (English translation by J. Shirley, *Garnier's Becket* (London, 1975)). Cf. Ian Short, 'An early draft of Guernes' *Vie de Saint Thomas Becket*', *Medium Aevum*, 46 (1977), 20–34.

2. Written between mid-1175 and August 1176, for he refers to *Prior* Benedict (1175–77) and does not give John of Salisbury (bishop of Chartres from August 1176) his episcopal title.

3. The attachment to Anon. II (80) of the short preamble which asserts that the author witnessed the murder ('me presente'), is doubtful, since the same text is also attached to another (fragmentary) Life (cf. *MTB*, iv, 80 n.).

4. *MTB*, i–iv (listed individually in 'Abbreviations'); cf. translated extracts in Staunton; FitzStephen is translated in George Greenaway, *The Life and Death of Thomas Becket*, Folio Society (London, 1961). For the intriguing, but not entirely convincing, theory that Alan of Lille and Alan of Tewkesbury were one and the same person, see Françoise Hudry, *Alain de Lille(?), Lettres familières (1167–1170)* (Paris, 2003). If Madame Hudry's thesis is confirmed, Alan of Tewkesbury becomes a primary witness for events down to 1166.

5. *CTB*.

6. JS, *Letters*, i–ii; *The Letters of Peter of Celle*, ed. and trans. Julian Haseldine, OMT (Oxford, 2001).

7. *Multiplicem*: *CTB*, no. 109.

8. *CTB*, ii, no. 252; cf. *Letters of Peter of Celle*, no. 92.

9. Respectively by Benedict 'of Peterborough' and William of Canterbury, *MTB*, ii, 21–281 and i, 137–546. For an excellent

analysis of the miracles, see R. Foreville, 'Les "Miracula S. Thomae Cantuariensis"', in *Actes du 97e Congrès National des Sociétés Savants, Nantes 1972, Section de Philologie et d'histoire jusqua'à 1610* (Paris, 1979), 443–68, at 444.

10. *Thomas Becket*, ed. Foreville; A.J. Duggan, 'The Cult of St Thomas Becket in the Thirteenth Century', in *St Thomas Cantilupe*, ed. Meryl Jancey (Hereford, 1982), 21–44. See also Chapter 11.

11. See Chapter 11.

12. Edwin A. Abbott, *St. Thomas of Canterbury. His Death and Miracles*, 2 vols (London, 1898).

Chapter 1 The social climber

1. Barlow, *Becket*, 14–15.

2. There was far from unanimity about Becket's age on his death and hence about his date of birth, with suggestions ranging from 1115 to 1123. In choosing 1120 as the probable date, I follow Raymonde Foreville, 'Tradition et comput dans la chronologie de Thomas Becket', *Bulletin philosophique et historique* (Paris, 1957), 7–20, esp. 20; and Barlow, *Becket*, 10, 281.

3. EG, 356–9; WF, 13–14; Anon. I, 3–5; Anon. II (calls his mother Rosea), 81–2.

4. Anon. I, 7–8 (trans. Staunton, 44).

5. JS, 307.

6. From *Florebat olim studium* (*Carmina Burana*, 6, vv. 5–8, 13–20), trans. David Parlett, *Selections from the Carmina Burana: A Verse Translation* (London, 1986; repr. 1988). For discussion of the world of the schools at the end of the twelfth century, see Anne J. Duggan, 'The World of the *Carmina Burana*', in *The Carmina Burana: Four Essays*, ed. Martin Jones, King's College London Medieval Studies, 18 (London, 2000), 1–23.

7. Anon. I, 6–7.

8. F. Barlow, *Thomas Becket and his Clerks*, William Urry Memorial Lecture (Canterbury, 1987), 8.

9. *Draco Normannicus*, ed. R. Howlett, *Chronicles of the Reigns of Stephen, Henry II, and Richard I*, 4 vols, RS 82 (London, 1884–89), ii (1885), 744.

10. *The Becket Conflict and the Schools* (Oxford, 1973), 112.

11. EG, 361; cf. Anon. I, 8 (trans. Staunton, 45).

12. WF, 15; cf. EG, 361; WC, 4; Anon. I, 9 (trans. Staunton, 45); Anon. II, 83; HB, 167.

13. *Adrian IV. The English Pope (1154–1159). Studies and Texts*, ed. B. Bolton and A.J. Duggan (Aldershot, 2003), esp. Chapters 2–4 and 9.

14. William of Newburgh, i, 110.

15. *Thómas Saga*, i, 28. The translation given here is by Haki Antonson, in Staunton, 42. Compare Anon. I, 4–6 (trans. Staunton, 43).

16. WF, 17.

17. *Dictionnaire de droit canonique*, vi (Paris, 1957), 1111–12; R. Weigand, 'Die Dekret-Abbreviatio Omnebenes und ihre Glossen', in *Recht als Heilsdienst. Mathias Kaiser zum 65. Geburtstag gewidmet*, ed. W. Schulz (Paderborn, 1989), 271–87.

18. Brixius, *Die Mitglieder*, 57–8, 112–13; Zenker, *Die Mitglieder*, 25–9.

19. Klaus Ganzer, *Die Entwicklung des auswärtigen Kardinalats im hohen Mittelalter*, Bibliothek des deutschen historischen Instituts in Rom, 26 (Tübingen, 1963), 134–6; *CTB*, ii, 1377.

20. *PL*, ccxi, 338 no. 38. Cf. Charles Vulliez, 'Études sur la correspondence et la carrière d'Étienne d'Orléans dit de Tournai' (d. 1203) in *L'Abbaye parisienne de Saint-Victor au moyen âge*, ed. Jean Longère (Paris, 1991), 195–231.

21. Brixius, *Die Mitglieder*, 43, 90, 134, 139, 140.

22. Brixius, *Die Mitglieder*, 52, 104; Helene Tillmann, 'Ricerche sull'origine dei membri del collegio cardinalizio nel XII secolo', ii/1, *Rivista di storia della Chiesa in Italia*, 26 (1972), 313–53, at 350–3.

23. Brixius, *Die Mitglieder*, 58, 113; F. Geisthardt, *Der Kämmerer Boso* (Berlin, 1936); cf. *Dictionnaire d'histoire et de géographie ecclésiastiques*, ix [1937], 1319–20, which states, erroneously, that he was English, and a nephew of Adrian IV.

24. Brixius, *Die Mitglieder*, 54–5, 108; John of Salisbury, *Historia Pontificalis*, ed. and trans. Marjorie Chibnall (London, 1956; revised repr. Oxford, 1986), 21–3.

25. Anon. I, 11–12 (trans. Staunton, 47–8), said that Theobald engaged the help of Bishops Philip of Bayeux and Arnulf of Lisieux; WF, 17–18 (trans. Staunton, 48) named Bishop Henry of Winchester; cf. WC, 4–5.

26. WF, 18 (cf. trans. Staunton, 48).

27. WF, 29.

28. T.A.M. Bishop, *Scriptores Regis* (Oxford, 1961), 9–11.

29. Richard FitzNeale, *Dialogus de Scaccario*, trans. Charles Johnson, NMT (London, 1950), xxiii, 72–3.

30. J.E.A. Jolliffe, *Angevin Kingship* (London, 1963).

31. Eyton, 2–23.

32. Ibid., 26–32.

33. Ibid., 34–8.

34. Ibid., 41, 44, 46–7, 49–50, 52–3, 55–6.

35. WF, 20–2; cf. Anon. I, 11.

36. WF, 29–33.

37. WF, 31.

38. F.R.H. Du Boulay, *The Lordship of Canterbury* (London, 1966), 76.

39. WF, 33–4 (cf. trans. Staunton, 57). Eye, Berkhampstead and the Tower of London would have supplied some of the knights; contingents from vacant bishoprics would have supplied more; and individual homages more. It is possible, too, that 80 or so knights from Canterbury estates and a further 10 from the diocese of Rochester, swelled the contingent (Du Boulay, *Lordship of Canterbury*, 63, 75–7, 84–5). Equally, the chancellor could, like the king, have employed mercenaries, as he did in the Vexin campaign.

40. WF, 34–5 (trans. Staunton, 57–8).

41. JS, *Letters*, i, no. 128, esp. pp. 221 and 222.

42. WF, 22. Pope Eugenius III, for example, wore a rough linen tunic next to his skin and slept on straw, covered with purple cloth (Ernald, *Vita S. Bernardi*, ii. 8, n. 50).

43. WF, 23–4.

44. WF, 21; cf. EG, 365; WC, 5–6; Anon. I, 13–14.

45. Warren, *Henry II*, 455.

46. EG, 363–4; WF, 17–35; HB, 176.

47. WF, 34–5.

48. For the position of Thomas, the *curialis*, see Egbert Türk, *Nugae curialium: le regne d'Henri II Plantegenêt 1145–1189, et l'éthique politique*. Hautes études médiévales et modernes, 28 (Geneva, 1977), 11–25.

49. JS, 306; Anon. I, 18; Anon. II, 86; cf. EG, 365–67; WC, 7–8.

50. *CTB*, ii, xxx, Appendix, *s.v.*; Eyton, 54–5.

51. HB, 181 (trans. Staunton, 60).

52. EG, 366–7; cf. WC, 7–10; WF, 35–36; Anon. I, 14–18; HB, 183–5.

53. Gervase, 169–70.

54. HB, 182; Anon. II, 85.

55. EG, 367; WF, 36. In the most detailed account of Becket's consecration, from the pen of an anonymous author (Lansdowne, Fragment II: *MTB*, iv. 154–5), the release was reiterated in Canterbury Cathedral, by the young Henry, Earl Robert of Leicester, and many other officials and earls, just before his episcopal consecration.

56. Diceto, i, 306–7.

57. EG, 367; WF, 36; Anon. I, 17.

58. *CTB*, i, no. 109.

59. EG, 368. Anon. I (21) attributes similar advice to Christ, who appeared to one of his household.

60. Diceto, i, 307.

61. Gervase, i, 172.

62. Based on the recorded oath of Hubert Walter in November 1193: *English Episcopal Acta*, iii: *Canterbury 1193–1205*, ed. C.R. Cheney and E. John (Oxford, 1986), 1; cf. *The* epistolae vagantes *of Pope Gregory VII*, OMT (Oxford, 1972), 152–3.

63. Barlow, *Becket*, 28; idem, *Becket and his Clerks*; cf. review by Anne J. Duggan, *Journal of Ecclesiastical History*, 40 (1989), 453.

64. *CTB*, i, no. 8 (before 28 April 1163).

65. JS, *Letters*, i, 144; Foreville, *L'Église et la royauté*, 122–61.

66. *English Lawsuits*, i, no. 360.

67. Du Boulay, *Lordship of Canterbury*, 52–113, esp. 63, 75–7.

68. Diceto, i, 307–8.

69. Henry Mayr-Harting, 'Hilary, Bishop of Chichester (1147–69) and Henry II', *EHR*, 78 (1963), 224; A. Saltman, *Theobald, Archbishop of Canterbury* (London, 1956), 44–5.

70. WF, 43–4.

71. Warren, *Henry II*, 456.

72. William of Malmesbury, *Historia Novella*, ed. and trans. K.R. Potter, NMT (London, 1955), esp. 37–40; J. Kealey, *Roger of Salisbury, Viceroy of England* (Berkeley, 1972).

73. *CTB*, ii, 1383–4; Stefan Weinfurter, 'Colonia (Köln)' in *Series Episcoporum Ecclesiae Catholicae occidentalis*, Series v/i, *Archiepiscopatus Coloniensis*, ed. Stefan Weinfurter and Odilo Engels (Stuttgart, 1982), 3–42.

74. *CTB*, ii, 1366–7.

75. Smalley, *Becket Conflict*, 115, 'Becket's conversion was predictable, given his temperament and circumstances … it is not play-acting to take ideas seriously.' This conclusion is supported by consideration of Becket's library, much of it acquired during the exile, which reflected his commitment to his episcopal office, see ibid., 135–7, esp. 137, 'He specialized in works suitable for devotional reading and aids to teaching.' See now, M. Staunton, 'Thomas Becket's Conversion', *Anglo-Norman Studies*, 21 (1999), 193–210, esp. 211.

Chapter 2 The controversial archbishop

1. *CTB*, i, no. 45.

2. Warren, *Henry II*, 453–9, esp. 453, 'It almost seems that he was deliberately picking a quarrel with the king'; 455–6, 'He filled the early months of his archiepiscopate with grand gestures; that some of these gestures proved offensive to the king seems almost incidental.'

3. Barlow, *Becket*, 89.

4. Diceto, i, 308.

5. Diceto, i, 311; WF, 43; Gervase, i, 174; HB, 252. See Du Boulay, *Lordship of Canterbury*, 85–6. Warren (*Henry II*, 457) saw this was another 'dramatic gesture' to curry favour with the monks, the bishops and the pope. He should not have 'antagonised' so powerful a man, and 'it would have been more proper and it might have been more effective if he had brought an action for recovery in the royal court'. How Warren can conclude that it was 'improper' for a new archbishop to summon a vassal to pay the homage due for a castle and appurtenances is hard to fathom.

6. Diceto, i, 311; HB, 251; Gervase, i, 174.

7. Diceto, i, 311. The lands in question had been granted to Canterbury by King Stephen, and their lordship was recovered in 1202 (Du Boulay, *Lordship of Canterbury*, 357–8).

8. *CTB*, ii, 1373; cf. Du Boulay, *Lordship of Canterbury*, 367–8.

9. JL 10124, 10128. Foreville, *L'Église et la royauté*, 89–90, 93; *Heads of Religious Houses*, 36; cf. Gervase, i, 76–7, 163–5; E. John, 'The Litigation of an Exempt Abbey, St Augustine's Canterbury, 1182–1237', *Bulletin of the John Rylands Library*, 39 (1956–57), 390–415.

10. *PU England*, ii, no. 118 (14 Nov. 1164); *MTB*, v, no. 102 (10 July 1165); *PU England*, ii, no. 122 (7 May 1166/67). After Becket's murder, Clarembald was deposed by papal judges delegate in 1173–4: JS, *Letters*, ii, no. 422.

11. *Historians of the Church of York and its Archbishops*, ed. J. Raine, RS 71, 3 vols (London, 1879–94), iii, no. 53 (Anagni, 21 January 1161); cf. *MTB*, v, no. 13 (Montpellier, 13 July 1162).

12. Ignoring that the matter had been raised by Roger, Warren (*Henry II*, 456) puts Becket's defence among the 'gestures' by which he sought to vindicate his appointment.

13. Another of Warren's 'gestures' (*Henry II*, 457–8).

14. Warren, *Henry II*, 458, 'public gesture'.

15. *English Episcopal Acta*, ii (Canterbury), nos 84–5.

16. Cf. Türk, *Nugae Curialium*, 18–21.

17. WC, 12.

18. Warren, *Henry II*, 458–9.

19. WC, 12; cf. EG, 373–4; Guernes, vv. 751–70 (trans. Shirley, 20–1); Anon. I, 23–4. For Henry's fiscal preoccupations in this period, see Graeme J. White, *Restoration and Reform 1153–1165. Recovery from Civil War in England* (Cambridge, 2000), 130–60, 218.

20. Barlow, *Becket*, 88–9.

21. WF, 45–6; *English Lawsuits*, ii, nos 409–10.

22. EG, 374–6; WC, 12–13; WF, 45; Guernes, vv. 771–825 (trans. Shirley, 22–3); Anon. I, 24–5; HB, 265–6; Diceto, i, 313; *English Lawsuits*, ii, no. 411. There are some discrepancies in the accounts of the case: most say the deprivation was for two years, but one (WF) says for one year; one (WC) says that the canon was flogged; one (Diceto) that he was also exiled for the time of his deprivation.

23. EG, 374–6; WC, 12–13.

24. White, *Restoration and Reform*, 181–2.

25. JS, *Letters*, i, no. 16; *English Lawsuits*, ii, no. 520, esp. pp. 572–3.

26. See Newburgh, 142–3, who thought that Thomas was wrong, despite his laudable zeal; but he does not discuss the canon law.

27. HB, 266, 'utriusque iuris se habere peritiam ostentantium'.

28. HB, 266–5; cf. WC, 12–15; Anon. I, 25–9.

29. Anon. I, 29–31; cf. EG, 377–8; WC, 14; Guernes, vv. 851–80 (trans. Shirley, 24–5); HB, 276–7.

30. *CTB*, i, 80–3.

31. Diceto, i, 312; cf. *CTB*, i, 80–1.

32. *CTB*, i, 80–3.

33. Barlow, *Becket*, 97.

34. Chapter 4, at nn. 28–38.

35. Barlow, *Becket*, 97.

36. *CTB*, i, no. 18.

37. WC, 14–15; EG, 378–9; Anon. I, 30–3 (Woodstock); cf. Guernes, vv. 881–965 (trans. Shirley, 25–7); HB, 276–7 (Oxford).

38. WC, 16–17; EG, 281–2; Anon. I, 34–5; HB, 279 (confuses Winchester with Norwich).

39. WF, 48.

40. *Councils and Synods*, 1/ii, 852–93, no. 159; W. Stubbs, *Select Charters*, 9th edn (Oxford, 1913; repr. 1960), 163–7; *English Historical Documents*, ii (1042–1189), ed. D.C. Douglas and G.W. Greenaway (London, 1953), 718–22.

41. WC, 15–23; cf. EG, 379–83; WF, 47–9; JS, 312; Guernes, vv. 1010–30 (trans. Shirley, 28–9); Anon. I, 33–7; HB, 278–89 (with commentary on the clauses). The statement in the printed version of WF (48), that the bishops sealed the document, is a later interpolation. The phrase 'et sigillorum suorum impressione' is not in the earliest manuscripts of the Life.

42. *CTB*, i, 511.

43. *Becket*, 87.

44. *CTB*, i, 511.

45. Anon. I, 37–8; Guernes, vv. 1036–45 (trans. Shirley, 29).

46. *CTB*, i, 78–9.

47. *CTB*, i, no. 28.

48. *CTB*, i, no. 106.

49. For the preservation of the title 'Codex' in preference to the generally used Anglicization of 'Code', see *Justinian's Institutes*, trans. Birks and McLeod, 9a.

50. See the listings in *GFL*, 552. For Foliot's legal expertise, with speculation that he may have been an early student in Bologna, see Dom Adrian Morey and C.N.L. Brooke, *Gilbert Foliot and his Letters* (Cambridge, 1965), pp. 59–69.

51. Ethelred, VIII, 26–7; Cnut, 43; cf. 41 (repeating Ethelred, VIII, 26): *English Historical Documents*, i, 412, 425.

52. Stubbs, *Charters*, 99–100; *English Historical Documents*, ii, 604–5.

53. Stubbs, *Charters*, 143.

54. *Policraticus sive de nugis curialium*, ed. C.C.J. Webb, 2 vols (Oxford, 1909), ii, 364.

55. *English Lawsuits*, ii, no. 413.

56. White, *Reform and Restoration*, 196, 197–8.

57. Paul Brand, '*Multis vigiliis excogitatam et inventam*: Henry II and the Creation of the English Common Law', *Haskins Society Journal*, 2 (1990), 197–222, repr. in idem, *The Making of the Common Law* (London, 1992), 77–102.

58. 'Henry II and the Criminous Clerks', *EHR*, 7 (1892); repr. in *Roman Canon Law in the Church of England* (London, 1898), 132–47.

59. Charles Duggan, 'The Becket Dispute and the Criminous Clerks', *BIHR*, 35 (1962), 1–28; R.M. Fraher, 'The Becket Dispute and Two Decretist Traditions: the Bolognese masters revisited and some new Anglo-Norman texts', *Journal of Medieval History*, 4 (1978), 347–68. Cf. Smalley, *Becket Conflict* (1973), 124; Barlow (*Becket*, 102–4) preferred Fraher's view.

60. C. 11, qu. 1, c. 15: rubric.

61. C. 11, qu. 1, c. 16.

62. C. 11, qu. 1, *dictum post* c. 30.

63. Paul was suspected of Arianism, and the bishop of Milan had consecrated him against papal instructions. Narses, in fact, took no action, since he did not wish to inflame an already disturbed situation in the region.

64. *Iuliani epitome latina Novellarum Iustiniani*, ed. G. Haenel (Leipzig, 1873), 77.1 (c. 298, pp. 102–3). For the original version, see *Corpus Iuris Civilis*, iii, ed. R. Schoell and G. Kroll (repr. Berlin, 1912), Novel 83.1 (p. 410) = *Authenticum* 84.1. On the *Epitome*, see Wolfgang Kaiser, *Die Epitome Iuliani. Studien zum römischen Recht im frühen Mittelalter und zum byzantinischen Rechtsunterricht* (Frankfurt, 2004).

65. Fraher, 'The Becket Dispute', 350b–51a wrongly calls this a *palea* (an addition) inserted after the canon; but it is part of the Justinian *novel*, and should be interpreted in that context.

66. The original title of Gratian's *Decretum* was *Concordia discordantium canonum*: 'Concordance of Discordant Canons'.

67. Fraher, 'The Becket Dispute', 351b–55a.

68. Cited in Fraher, 367a, nn. 5 and 6.

69. *Rufinus von Bologna, Summa decretorum*, ed. H. Singer (Paderborn, 1902; repr. 1963), 306–12, esp. 308–9; cf. Fraher, 352a–54a. His contrast between Roman and canon law was based in fact on Gratian's Causa 11, questio 1, c. 45, which is identified as an (imperial) constitution: Item constitutione 74. c. 1 (actually, *Epitome Iuliani*, 77.298.1); cf. *Authenticum*, 123.

70. *Stephan von Tournai, Summa decreti*, ed. J.F. von Schulte (Giessen, 1891), 211–12; cf. Fraher, 354a–55a.

71. *Summa magistri Rolandi mit Anhang Incerti auctoris queastiones*, ed. F. Thaner (Innsbruck, 1874), 293; cited Fraher, 352a.

72. WC, 28–9; EG, 388; HB, 281.

73. Ed. Webb, ii, 364.

74. Smalley, *Becket Conflict*, 126–8.

75. Above, at n. 70.

76. *Decretales ineditae*, no. 35. Since Alexander was acknowledged only in mid-1160, the letter should probably be dated late 1160–64. The subdeacon claimed that he was innocent.

77. *Liber Extra* (*Decretals of Gregory IX*), 2. l. 10.

78. Duggan, 'Criminous Clerks', 27.

79. But see his condemnation of Clauses 7 (excommunication of tenants-in-chief) and 12 (elections): HB, 282–4.

80. Cf. Smalley, *Becket Conflict*, 122.

81. Barlow, *Becket*, 104, 105.

82. F.R.H. Du Boulay, in *The English Church and the Papacy in the Middle Ages*, ed. C.H. Lawrence, revised edn (London, 1999), 241.

83. *Becket Conflict*, 182; cf. 133. For her brilliant assessment of Foliot, who 'threw the mantle of piety over compromise', see ibid., 167–86.

Chapter 3 The trial

1. D. Crouch, *William Marshal, Court, Career and Chivalry in the Angevin Empire 1147–1219* (London and New York, 1990).

2. WF, 53–70; HB, 296–312 (both translated, together with Howden, i, 225–8, who used Anon. I and other written sources, in *English Lawsuits*, ii, no. 421); EG, 390–8; WC, 30–40; Anon. I, 41–52; Guernes, 1380–1945 (trans. Shirley, 38–9). Cf. Knowles, *Colleagues*, 66–89; Barlow, *Becket*, 108–14.

3. WF, 50–3.

4. Barlow, *Becket*, 108–10; Du Boulay, *Lordship of Canterbury*, 25, 361; Mary Cheney, 'The Litigation between John Marshal and Archbishop Thomas Becket in 1164: a pointer to the origins of Novel Disseisin', *Law and Social Change in British History*, ed. J.A. Guy and H.G. Beale (London, 1984), 10–26.

5. WF, 53.

6. WF, 54; cf. HB (299–301), who places these events on 'the third day, Saturday'.

7. Ganzer, *Die Entwicklung des auswärtigen Kardinalats*, 121–3, correcting Brixius, *Die Mitglieder*, 64, 122.

8. Another ambiguous term. Van Caenegem, *English Lawsuits*, ii, 437, translates it as 'one accountable to him'; Greenaway, p. 81, as 'auditor of accounts'. In the late Roman Empire, *rationales* were top-level administrators (procurators), principally, but not exclusively, concerned with financial and fiscal matters (Berger, *s.vv.* 'procurator', 'rationalis'), no doubt the meaning intended here. The chancellor was the king's 'procurator ecclesiastical'.

9. Bishop Hilary's fear that Becket might be held guilty of extortion puts a much more sinister gloss on the king's intentions than Foliot's insistence on the civil nature of the case against Becket; so also, of course, does FitzStephen's assertion that Becket was sued on an *actio tutelae*, which condemned the unsuccessful defendant to *infamia* – loss of reputation, with various civil disabilities. An *infamis* could not hold public office, for example. In Becket's case, it could have been argued that deposition from the archiepiscopate would be a logical consequence of an adverse verdict in the case brought against him by the king.

10. *Digest*, 44.11.1: 'Lex Iulia repetundarum pertinet ad eas pecunias, quas quis in magistratu potestate curatione, legatione uel quo alio officio munere ministerioue publico cepit'; 44.11.3: 'Lege Iulia repetundarum tenetur, qui, cum aliquam potestatem haberet, pecuniam ob iudicandum uel non iudicandum decernendumue acceperit.'

11. *Digest*, 48.11.4: 'uel quo magis aut minus quid ex officio suo faceret.'
12. *Digest*, 48.11.7, §3: 'uel exilio puniuntur uel etiam durius, prout admiserint'. For John of Salisbury's use of this material in 1159, see n. 17 below.
13. London, BL MS Cotton Claudius B. ii, fol. 26ra, bottom margin: 'Hec ex mandato regis digessit Iohannes Oxeneford ...'.
14. *GFL*, no. 106. The work was carried out by one Ambrose, described as 'your [Robert de Chesney's] Ambrose', perhaps the civilian *Master* Ambrose, who later represented the monastery of St Albans in its disputes with the bishop of Lincoln.
15. *GFL*, 129, n. 2; 130, at nn. 1–3.
16. Ibid., 151, at nn. 3–6; 152, at n. 1.
17. *Policraticus*, v. 16, headed *De crimine repetundarum* ..., which is largely directed against (secular) judges who accept bribes.
18. JS, *Letters*, i, 160, n. 17.
19. *Glanvill*, Prol. (ed. Hall, 1), 'Regiam potestatem non solum armis contra rebelles et gentes sibi regnoque insurgentes oportet esse decoratam, sed et legibus ad subditos et populos pacificos regendos decet esse ornatam'; cf. Justinian's *Institutes*, prol. 1 (trans. Birks and McLeod, 32–3), 'Imperatoriam maiestatem non solum armis decoratam, sed etiam legibus oportet esse armatam, ut utrumque tempus et bellorum et pacis recte possit gubernari ...'.
20. *Glanvill*, x. 3 (ed. Hall, 117), 'ex causa mutui, aut ex uenditionis causa, aut ex commodato, aut ex locato, aut ex deposito, aut ex alia iusta debendi causa'; cf. *Institutes*, 4.6.28.
21. WF, 54; cf. *Institutes*, 1.21.3; Adolf Berger, *Encyclopedic Dictionary of Roman Law*, Transactions of the American Philosophical Society, New Series, 43/ii (Philadelphia, 1953; repr. 1991), 747–8 (for guardianship).
22. AT, 326–8.
23. WF, 56; cf. EG, 392–3; WC, 32; HB, 301.
24. A view shared by Barlow, *Becket*, 112.
25. HB, 301–4; cf. EG, 394–5, who says that the bishop of Winchester advised resignation; it is more likely that Lincoln was intended. The Latin forms *Wintoniensis* and *Lincolniensis*, especially if abbreviated to *Wint'* and *Linc'*, could easily be confused by an inattentive copyist.

26. WF, 56; HB, 304; cf. Knowles, *Episcopal Colleagues*, 77.

27. Guernes, vv. 1556–9 (trans. Shirley, 42).

28. WF, 57.

29. Martin Aurell, 'Le meurtre de Thomas Becket: les gestes d'une martyre', in *Bischofsmord*, 187–210, at 191–6.

30. WF, 58.

31. EG, 394.

32. WF, 57–9; cf. EG, 394.

33. WF, 62.

34. WF, 65.

35. Gerald of Wales, *Opera*, viii, 160, 301, 309.

36. WF, 64–5. Warren (*Henry II*, 433) carefully avoids describing the nature of the 'persecution', which he seems almost to excuse!

37. Barlow (*Becket*, 111–12) is disinclined to believe that these and other threats were anything more than 'mimetic violence', citing Arnulf of Lisieux's assertion in early 1165 (*CTB*, i, 189), 'He hoped to bend your obedience by terror, and the more serious he thought your fear to be, the more he decided to hold back from serious injury.' Arnulf's testimony is tainted, however. Not only was he the man who had advised the king on how to split the episcopal opposition after Westminster, he was himself too afraid of the king's displeasure to express publicly any support for Becket.

38. WF, 65–6.

39. WF, 67.

40. *CTB*, i, no. 28.

41. Warren, *Henry II*, 488; Barlow, *Becket*, 112.

42. Barlow's conviction (*Becket*, 112) that the 'trumped-up' charges were 'civil', ignores the escalating tendency of the sequence of charges and the threat of imprisonment, or worse.

43. EG, 398–9; cf. WF, 68; HB, 310; WC, 39–40; Anon. I, 51–2.

44. WF, 68–9.

Chapter 4 Flight and exile

1. Foliot: *CTB*, i, 525–7; Warren, *Henry II*, 488–9; Barlow, *Becket*, 96.

2. WF, 70–1; EG, 399–401; WC, 42–3; Anon. I, 54–8; AT, 335–6; HB, 323–6; Guernes, vv. 1991–2100 (trans. Shirley, 53–7).

3. Anon. I, 60–1, names the archbishop of York and four bishops (London, Chichester, Exeter and Worcester); three royal clerks (Richard of Ilchester, John of Oxford and Guy Rufus, dean of Waltham); Earl William de Albini II of Arundel (who had married Adeliza of Louvain, widow of Henry I), Reginald of St-Valery, and the Chamberlain, Henry FitzGerold. He also says (57) that Richard de Lucy was sent to Flanders. Cf. WF, 72; WC, 44–5; EG, 402.

4. Paul Latimer, 'Henry II's campaign against the Welsh in 1165', *Welsh History Review*, 14 (1989), 523–52, at 531; *Recueil des historiens*, xvi, 117, no. 358 (complaint about the outrage to Louis VII).

5. Guernes, vv. 1542–5 (Shirley, 42); EG, 393.

6. Anon. I, 58–60, names Gilbert Foliot, Richard of Ilchester and the earl of Arundel, who met Louis at Compiègne; cf. WC, 44–5; EG, 401–2 (Soissons); HB, 332.

7. Chapter 3, end.

8. HB, 332–4.

9. Ives, seigneur de Nesle, count of Soissons 1141–78.

10. *PL*, cc, no. 223; JL 10973.

11. *CTB*, i, 119.

12. For example, Barlow, *Becket*, 96. The suggestion (ibid., 97) that the mere making of such provisions helped to bring about those worst fears is highly questionable.

13. Hilary had served in the papal court in the 1140s under Eugenius III.

14. Among the meanings of the verb *parco* were 'spare', 'refrain' and 'restrain'.

15. AT, 337–41; WC, 45–6; EG, 402–3; WF, 72–4, 75; HB, 335–8.

16. HB, 334–5.

17. WF, 99–101.

18. HB, 339–40.

19. HB, 340–57; AT, 341–4.

20. Anon. I, 61–2; cf. HB, 341–3. For Warren (*Henry II*, 490–1), this was 'melodrama'.

21. WF, 76.

22. AT, 343–4; cf. HB, 343.

23. Cardinal priest of S. Clemente 1145–58, cardinal bishop of Porto and S. Rufina 1158–76, d. 18 June 1176: Brixius, *Die Mitglieder*, 53, 105, 135, 136.

24. Cardinal deacon of SS. Sergio e Baccho 1150–58, cardinal priest of S. Anastasia 1158–83: Brixius, 55–6, 110–11; Zenker, 73–7. Evidence of strong support for Henry II is provided in *MTB*, vi, 380–2, no. 396.

25. Cardinal priest of S. Pietro in Vincoli 1158–76, cardinal bishop of Porto 1176–78: Brixius, *Die Mitglieder*, 40, 118–19. For the suggestion that he had formerly been a Cistercian monk, and cardinal deacon of S. Maria in Via Lata, see *Italia Pontificia*, vi/1, 189 n. to no. 2. Cf. *CTB*, i, 96–9 (mid-1164). 'Naples, Porto [Bernard of Lucca], and Pavia are attacking you [Thomas] in every way'.

26. Cardinal priest of SS. Giovanni e Paolo 1151–80/1, papal vicar in Rome from Oct. or Sept. 1167: Brixius, *Die Mitglieder*, 55, 109. Cf. JS, *Letters*, ii, 447, n. 20.

27. From a noble Roman family, Peter was cardinal deacon of S. Eustachio 1158–65/66, cardinal priest of S. Lorenzo in Damaso, 1165/6–1174, d. 14 Sept. 1174: Brixius, *Die Mitglieder*, 59, 116, n. 143; cf. Tillmann, 'Ricerche', ii/2, 365–6.

28. Chapter 1, n. 21.

29. Cardinal bishop of Albano (1158–?1178): Brixius, *Die Mitglieder*, 60, 118, n. 146; Zenker, *Die Mitglieder*, 39; JS, *Letters*, ii, 432–3 and n. 1. Probably English and a canon regular from Saint-Ruf.

30. Cardinal priest of S. Marcello 1165–66, cardinal bishop of Sabina 1166–1200, archbishop of Salzburg 1177–83, archbishop of Mainz 1184–1200: *CTB*, ii, 1366–7. Cf. *CTB*, i, 242–5, no. 62; *CTB*, 246–7, no. 63.

31. Chapter 1, n. 18.

32. Chapter 1, n. 24.

33. A member of the anti-imperialist Grassi family of Bologna, Hildebrand was cardinal deacon of S. Eustachio 1152–56, cardinal priest of SS. XII Apostoli 1156–78: Brixius, *Die Mitglieder*, 55, 109; corrected by Zenker, *Die Mitglieder*, 107–9.

34. Chapter 1, n. 23.

35. Chapter 1, n. 22.

36. Cardinal deacon of S. Giorgio in Velabro 1162–73, cardinal priest of S. Cecilia 1173–76, cardinal bishop of Palestrina 1176–78; d. 17 Jan. 1178: Brixius, *Die Mitglieder*, 64, 122–3, 135, 136, 142.

37. Cardinal deacon of S. Nicola in Carcere Tulliano 1153–75, d. 7 March 1175: Brixius, *Die Mitglieder*, 56, 111–12. Becket likened him to 'an angel from heaven' when he arrived in France as papal legate in autumn 1167 (*CTB*, i, 624–7), and his support for Becket was demonstrated at Argentan, in the following December, when Becket was told (*CTB*, i, 692–4) that 'Lord Otto is secretly informing the Lord Pope that he will be neither the agent nor the abettor of your deposition, although the king seems to want nothing else but your head on a platter.'

38. *Recueil des historiens*, xvi, 107–8, no. 334. See now, Anne J. Duggan, 'Thomas Becket's Italian Network', *Pope, Church and City: Essays in Honour of Brenda M. Bolton*, ed. Frances Andrews, Christoph Egger and Constance M. Rousseau (Leiden, 2004), 177–201.

39. These included some of the most distinguished religious foundations in the country, then at the height of their popularity: Buckfast, Fountains, Furness, Kirkstall, Meaux, Rievaulx, Tintern, Woburn.

40. JS, 313–14; WF, 75–6; Anon. I, 64–5.

41. *Interdict Documents*, ed. P.M. Barnes and W.R. Powell, Pipe Roll Society NS 34 (London, 1958).

42. Although they were not as destructive: Du Boulay, *Lordship of Canterbury*, 204, found evidence that the necessary stock was being maintained.

43. *English Lawsuits*, i, no. 134, esp. p. 97, based on the account 'De injusta vexatione Willelmi episcopi primi' in Symeon of Durham, *Historia ecclesiae Dunhelmensis: Symeonis Monachi Opera Omnia*, ed. T. Arnold, 2 vols, RS 75 (London, 1882–5), i, 170–95, at p. 181. Cf. G.B. Adams, *Councils and Courts in Anglo-Norman England* (1926; repr. New York, 1965), 43–69.

44. *CTB*, i, nos 41, 48, 51.

45. *CTB*, i, no. 54.

46. *CTB*, i, no. 50.

47. *CTB*, i, no. 41.

48. *CTB*, i, 261; cf. i, 225.

Chapter 5 Defiance? The Vézelay excommunications

1. *CTB*, i, nos 62–3.

2. *CTB*, i, no. 70 (8 April); *MTB*, v, no. 173 (24 April).

3. *CTB*, i, no. 71 (2 May), 279–81.

4. *MTB*, v, no. 182.

5. Warren, *Henry II*, 513.

6. Smalley, *Becket Conflict*, 29–38, esp. 29–31.

7. Jennifer O'Reilly, 'The Double Martyrdom of Thomas Becket: hagiography or history', *Studies in Medieval and Renaissance History*, 7 (1985), 185–247, at 190–7, esp. 194. 'Like the device of Gospel parallelism, it could be used to show that not only do the saints imitate Christ, but that Christ is crucified in his saints.'

8. J.A. Froude, *Life and Times of Thomas Becket* (London, 1878; new impression 1917), 92, 'insolent and absurd'; Warren, *Henry II*, 513, 'narrow clericalism, dogmatic and basically unspiritual, despite the trappings of pious sentiment'.

9. *CTB*, i, 375.

10. *MTB*, v, no. 188.

11. *CTB*, i, nos 79–81, 84–5.

12. *MTB*, v, nos 97 and 100 (cf. *Admonter Briefsammlung*, 151–2); confirmed by anonymous reports of the council: *MTB*, v, nos 98–9.

13. *MTB*, v, no. 101.

14. Jocelin de Balliol (Bailleul) had been a leading member of Henry II's administration from at least 1152/4 (cf. J.H. Round, *Calendar of Documents Preserved in France Illustrative of the History of Great Britain and Ireland*, i (London, 1899), 135, no. 403), and remained in the inner circle after he became king of England, witnessing royal charters with Thomas the Chancellor (cf. Round, *Calendar*, i. 44, 135, 171, 360, 491, nos 129, 405, 480, 1019, 1352).

15. Keeper of the Canterbury estates after Becket's flight (*PR 11 Henry II* (1164–65)–*PR 16 Henry II* (1169–70)). He and his nephew occupied Saltwood castle and the archbishop's palace at Canterbury during the exile, and they remained implacably hostile: they refused to surrender the estates after the peace of Fréteval; opposed Becket's landing in Dec. 1170; and welcomed

the murderers to Saltwood castle on the eve of the murder in the cathedral (Du Boulay, *Lordship of Canterbury*, 238, 247, n. 3; Barlow, *Becket*, p. 125).

16. He had been granted substantial lands, to the value of £12 a year, in Tarring and Newington (*PRR* 12 Henry II, 115, 13 Henry II, 201, 14 Henry II, 53, 15 Henry II, 165, 16 Henry II, 161, 17 Henry II, 142). Du Boulay has found a John Seyntcler and his brother Thomas holding Canterbury lands in Wimbledon and Wrotham in 1418–19 (*Lordship of Canterbury*, 383, 392), and it is possible that their ancestor established his claim during Becket's exile. The family name may be traced to one of the two Saint-Clairs in Normandy: Saint-Clair-en-Auge (Calvados, arr. Pont l'Évêque) or Saint-Clair-sur-l'Elle (Manche, arr. Saint-Lô).

17. Henry II's master Forester. He may similarly have profited from the archbishop's exile, for Thomas, son of Thomas FitzBernard, held Canterbury estates (in Eythorne, Sibton in Lyminge, and Sundridge) in 1171 for the service of three knights, and the family had established its court in Sibton by 1250 (Du Boulay, *Lordship of Canterbury*, 331, 356, 369, 375).

18. *CTB*, i, no. 78.

19. M. Richter, *Canterbury Professions*, Canterbury and York Society, 67 (Torquay, 1973), xviii–xix.

20. *CTB*, i, nos 76, 77, 86.

21. *CTB*, i, no. 78.

22. WC, 58 (trans. Staunton, 146).

23. JS, *Letters*, ii, 142–3. For the notification, see *CTB*, i, no. 93.

24. *CTB*, i, no. 82.

25. Innocent (401–17) refused to recognize Chrysostom's two successors and broke off communion with the Eastern bishops, who removed his name from the diptychs; the resulting schism was not resolved until after Innocent's death in 417.

26. In 390 Theodosius had had 7000 Thessalonians massacred in reprisal for the murder of imperial officers during a riot. Under threat of excommunication by Ambrose, archbishop of Milan, the emperor did public penance for the outrage (*NCE*, i (1967), 374). The whole passage beginning 'There are indeed two things', is a slight adaptation of Gratian, D. 96 c. 10, and is ultimately derived, through Gregory VII (JL 5201) from the famous letter of Gelasius I (494) to the Emperor Anastasius.

27. Smalley, *Becket Conflict*, 37–8.

28. *CTB*, i, no. 87, with *MTB*, v, no. 178.

29. *CTB*, i, no. 88, with *MTB*, v, no. 173 (24 April 1166).

30. *CTB*, i, no. 90.

31. The question of York's legation is confused (*English Episcopal Acta*, 20, *York 1154–1181*, ed. Marie Lovatt (Oxford, 2000), lvi–lvii), but Alexander III addressed him as legate of the apostolic see on 30 Sept. 1164 (*PU England*, iii, no. 151).

32. *CTB*, no. 100; 2 Kings (2 Sam.) 16: 20–23, 17: 1–23 (Achitophel); 1 Kings (1 Sam.) 22: 18–19 (Doeg).

33. *CTB*, i, no. 104.

34. *CTB*, i, no. 94.

35. *CTB*, i, no. 99.

36. *CTB*, i, no. 100.

37. *CTB*, i, no. 101.

38. The story first appeared in the apocryphal 'acts of St Peter' and was transmitted by St Ambrose in *Sermo contra Auxentium de basilicis non tradendis*, c. 13 (*PL*, xvi, 1011).

39. *MTB*, v, no. 213.

40. Friedrich Opll, *Friedrich Barbarossa* (Darmstadt, 1990), 95.

41. *CTB*, i, nos 115–18.

Chapter 6 God's honour and the Church's liberty

1. *MTB*, vi, no. 258.

2. *MTB*, vi, no. 257.

3. *CTB*, i, nos 115–16.

4. CTB, i, nos 96–9. 'Naples, Porto, and Pavia are attacking you [Thomas] in every way'; W. Janssen, *Die päpstlichen Legaten in Frankreich vom Schisma Anaklets II. bis zum Tode Coelestins III. (1130–1198)* (Cologne, 1961), 74–5; *Papsturkunden in Frankreich*, NS 5, ed. J. Ramackers, Abhandlungen der Akademie der Wissenschaften zu Göttingen, phil.-hist. Klasse, 3rd Ser., 35 (Göttingen, 1956), nos 114–16. He was cardinal priest of S. Pietro in Vincoli 1158–76 and cardinal bishop of Porto 1176–78: Brixius, *Die Mitglieder*, 40, 118–19.

5. Opll, *Friedrich Barbarossa*, 95–7.

6. *CTB*, i, no. 123.

7. *CTB*, i, no. 121.

8. *MTB*, vi, no. 292; M.G. Cheney, *Roger, Bishop of Worcester 1164–1179* (Oxford, 1980), 34.

9. *MTB*, vi, 171.

10. *MTB*, vi, no. 293. Herbert of Bosham drafted letters of protest for Count Henry of Troyes and Matthew, precentor of Sens: *MTB*, vi, nos 280–1.

11. *CTB*, i, nos 124–6.

12. *CTB*, i, no. 127.

13. *CTB*, i, no. 130.

14. *CTB*, i, no. 131.

15. *CTB*, i, no. 136; cf. ibid., nos 135 and 138.

16. *CTB*, i, no. 132.

17. *CTB*, i, no. 134.

18. *MTB*, vi, nos 307 and 324.

19. *CTB*, i, no. 137.

20. *MTB*, iii, 528–9; see Chapter 1, n. 19.

21. *GC*, ii [1720], 50–4.

22. *CTB*, i, 578–9.

23. Opll, *Friedrich Barbarossa*, 98. Peter Herde, 'Die Katastrophe vor Rom im Aug. 1167: eine historisch-epidemiologische Studie zum vierten Italienzug Friedrichs I. Barbarossa', *Sitzungsberichte der wissenschaftlichen Gesellschaft an der Johann Wolfgang Goethe-Universität Frankfurt am Main*, 27/iv (1991), 139–66.

24. *CTB*, i, nos 140–1.

25. *CTB*, i, no. 139.

26. *CTB*, i, no. 142; cf. no. 143, to Otto.

27. *CTB*, i, no. 144.

28. *Decretum*, C. 3 qu. 2 c. 8.

29. Linda Fowler, 'Recusatio iudicis in civilian and canonist thought', *Studia Gratiana*, 15 (1972), 719–85; cf. R.H. Helmholz, 'Canonists and standards of impartiality for papal judges delegate', *Canon Law and the Law of England* (London and Ronceverte, 1987), 21–39.

30. *CTB*, i, nos 123 (cf. n. 4), 140, at n. 12.

31. *CTB*, i, no. 144; cf. JS, *Letters*, ii, no. 230.

32. *CTB*, i, no. 150, late November 1167 (correcting the date of *c.* 11 December assigned to nos 150–153 in *CTB*, i).
33. *CTB*, i, nos 151–3.
34. *MTB*, v, no. 257.
35. I.J. Churchill, *Canterbury Administration*, 2 vols (London, 1933), i, 63–79, esp. 63 nn. 2 and 6; cf. Du Boulay, *Lordship of Canterbury*, 194–5 and Map 3. The Deanery took its title from St Mary of the Arches, and embraced a further 13 churches. Hilary of Chichester had made a similar challenge at the beginning of the exile (*CTB*, i, no. 42 at n. 15).
36. *CTB*, i, no. 149.
37. *CTB*, i, no. 148, *c.* 9 December 1167.
38. *CTB*, i, no. 157.
39. *CTB*, i, no. 154 (which is better dated late December 1167).

Chapter 7 God's honour and my order

1. Chapter 4 at n. 4.
2. *MTB*, vi, no. 400.
3. *MTB*, vi, nos 412–13.
4. *MTB*, vi, no. 415.
5. *MTB*, vi, no. 401.
6. *MTB*, vi, no. 395; cf. no. 258.
7. *CTB*, i, nos 158–9.
8. JS, *Letters*, ii, 406.
9. *MTB*, vi, 485–6.
10. *MTB*, vi, no. 424 (25 May 1168) was probably also issued in multiple copies, although only one version survives.
11. *MTB*, vi, no. 404.
12. *MTB*, vi, no. 423 (22 May 1168). The three surviving mandates (*MTB*, vi, nos 404, 423, 424) overlap. Helene Tillmann (*Legaten in England*, 63–96) argued that two pairs of commissioners were appointed, in the manner of judges delegate, to enable one to act if the other could not or would not.
13. *MTB*, vi, no. 395.
14. *CTB*, i, nos 171–4.
15. *MTB*, vi, nos 435 (to the pope), 439 (to Cardinals Hubald of Ostia and Hyacinth of S. Maria in Cosmedin).

16. *MTB*, vi, nos 446, 437, 440.

17. *CTB*, ii, no. 438. Matthew's own attitude can be gauged from the earlier letter that Herbert of Bosham had drafted for him in Feb. 1167 (*MTB*, vi, no. 281).

18. *CTB*, i, 170: after 2 June 1168.

19. Knowles, *Becket*, 106.

20. *CTB*, ii, no. 179.

21. *MTB*, vi, no. 436 (undated; probably 9 October 1168).

22. *CTB*, i, no. 150 at n. 28.

23. *MTB*, vi, no. 460 (9 October 1168).

24. *Gesta regis Henrici secundi*, i, 6–7. Cf. J. Martin and L.E.M. Walker, 'At the Feet of St Stephen Muret. Henry II and the Order of Grandmont *redivivus*', *Journal of Medieval History*, 16 (1990), 1–12 at 7.

25. *MTB*, vi, no. 404.

26. HB, 418–29; JS, *Letters*, ii, no. 288.

27. JS, *Letters*, ii, 640–1.

28. *CTB*, ii, no. 182; cf. *MTB*, vi, no. 424. See also *CTB*, ii, nos 183–5. For the biographers' accounts, see WC, 73–5; WF, 96–7; Anon. II, 113–14; HB, 418–29.

29. *JohnS*, ii. 644–5; *MTB*, vi, 537.

30. *CTB*, ii, no. 187.

31. *CTB*, ii, nos 188–9.

32. *CTB*, ii, nos 192–3. Foliot's appeal was made in front of the altar in St Paul's on 18 March (*MTB*, vi, 619).

33. *GFL*, nos 159–61; *CTB*, i, nos 98, 111; ii, 1399–1400.

34. Witness to *Early Charters of St Paul's*, no. 160.

35. *CTB*, ii, nos 194 and 195.

36. Formerly a member of Theobald's familia, with Becket and John of Salisbury, canon of St Paul's 1163x73–1183/4, archdeacon of Gloucester 1177–84, and bishop of Worcester 1186–90 (*Fasti*, i. 64, where he is designated Master).

37. Witness to *Early Charters of St Paul's*, no. 160.

38. Archdeacon of London from before 4 May 1162 (possibly before August 1158) to *c.* 29 September 1189: *Fasti*, i, 9.

39. Cf. *CTB*, ii, no. 195; WF, 89–91.

40. St Bartholomew's, Smithfield and Holy Trinity, Aldgate, were houses of Augustinian canons regular; St Martin in the Fields

was a college of secular canons. FitzStephen recorded that
Ralph, an earlier prior of Holy Trinity, Aldgate, administered
the discipline to Becket when he was chancellor (WF, 22).

41. Above, 118–19.
42. *MTB*, vi, no. 506; cf. no. 517.
43. *MTB*, vi, nos 518–29.
44. *MTB*, vi, no. 476.
45. *CTB*, ii, nos 204–5.
46. JS, *Letters*, ii. 654–5; *MTB*, vi, no. 506.
47. Also the intruded rector of Charlwood, Surrey, in the Deanery of Croydon: WF, 82.
48. *CTB*, ii, nos 209–12.
49. *CTB*, ii, no. 208 (19 June 1169).

Chapter 8 God's honour, king's honour, Becket's honour

1. *PL*, ccxi, 338, no. 38.
2. JL, ii, 146; Brixius, *Die Mitglieder*, 61, 141.
3. JS, *Letters*, ii, 650–1, n. 1.
4. *CTB*, ii, no. 215, at 938–9. On amicitia as a formal relationship, see *Friendship in Medieval Europe*, ed. J. Haseldine (Stroud, 1999).
5. Brixius, *Die Mitglieder*, 66–7.
6. JS, *Letters*, ii, 650–1.
7. *CTB*, ii, nos 216–22.
8. Vivian (*MTB*, vii, no. 563); Anonymous, *CTB*, ii, no. 227; cf. Henry II's version, addressed to Alexander III (*MTB*, vii, no. 564).
9. *MTB*, vi, no. 492: Benevento 10 May.
10. *MTB*, vii, nos 565, 567 and 564.
11. *CTB*, ii, Appendix, *s.v.*
12. *CTB*, ii, nos 229–30.
13. *MTB*, vi, no. 340 (misplaced by Canon Robertson).
14. *MTB*, vii, 80.
15. *CTB*, ii, nos 231–2.
16. L. Falkenstein, 'Étienne de La Chapelle als Vertrauter Ludwigs VII. und Delegat Alexanders III', *Archivum Historiae Pontificiae*, 26 (1988), 375–92, at 383.

17. *CTB*, ii, nos 233–6.
18. *CTB*, ii, no. 235.
19. *Councils and Synods, with other Documents Relating to the English Church*, I/i–ii, ed. D. Whitelock, M. Brett, and C.N.L. Brooke (Oxford, 1981), 1/ii, 926–39. For an exaggerated rumour of these royal decrees, see *CTB*, ii, no. 238.
20. *CTB*, ii, no. 244.
21. *CTB*, ii, no. 260.
22. *CTB*, ii, no. 243.
23. Cf. the full version, transmitted by Master Vivian to the Pope: *MTB*, vii, 168.
24. Cf. *CTB*, ii, no. 244. For Vivian's report, see *MTB*, vii, no. 607. Cf. also, *CTB*, ii, nos 237, 239–43. The allusion to the Sillé case was telling, for Robert had been included in the peace between the kings at Montmirail, but was subsequently captured by one of Henry's men, and died in prison.
25. Martin Aurell, 'Le meurtre de Thomas Becket', 196–200.
26. *CTB*, ii, nos 243, 245, 247–51.
27. *CTB*, ii, no. 244.
28. *CTB*, ii, nos 254–9.

Chapter 9 A hollow peace: Fréteval and after

1. *MTB*, vii, nos 623–5.
2. *MTB*, vii, no. 626.
3. *MTB*, vii, nos 627 and 656.
4. *MTB*, vii, nos 629–30, 634.
5. *MTB*, vii, no. 631.
6. *MTB*, vii, no. 647 and *CTB*, ii, no. 266.
7. JS, *Letters*, ii, 694–95; *CTB*, ii, no. 270.
8. *CTB*, ii, no. 270.
9. *CTB*, ii, nos 275–6.
10. *CTB*, ii, nos 277; cf. nos 278–81.
11. *CTB*, ii, no. 274.
12. *CTB*, ii, nos 283–5.
13. *CTB*, ii, no. 286; the papal mandate is *MTB*, vii, no. 633: 26 February 1170.

14. *CTB*, ii, no. 289.

15. New interdict letters (*CTB*, ii, nos 290–5) may have been drafted at this time.

16. *CTB*, ii, no. 296.

17. *CTB*, ii, no. 297.

18. He obtained *MTB*, vii, no. 700 (16 September; addressed to London, Salisbury, Exeter, Chester, Rochester, St Asaph and Landaff), which suspended all the bishops who had participated in the coronation where, it was alleged, the coronation oath was changed to include maintenance of the 'customs of the realm', restored the excommunication of London and Salisbury, and subjected Rochester and Geoffrey Ridel to Becket's authority; 701 (16 September), suspending Roger of York and Hugh of Durham.

19. *CTB*, ii, no. 298.

20. *CTB*, ii, 1251.

21. *MTB*, vii, no. 669.

22. Cf. *MTB*, vi, no. 310 (trans. in Warren, *Henry II*, 501). For the date, see Anne Heslin (= Duggan), 'The Coronation of the Young King in 1170', *SCH*, 2 (1968), 165–78.

23. *CTB*, ii, no. 300.

24. *MTB*, vii, 199.

25. Martin Aurell, 'Le meurtre de Thomas Becket', 196–200.

26. *CTB*, ii, no. 300.

27. Waren, *Henry II*, 507–8; Newburgh, 160–1; cf. Anon. II's reference to such opinions (which he does not share), 123–4: see n. 28.

28. Anon. II, 125–6.

29. *CTB*, ii, nos 300–5; cf. ibid., nos 310, 312–15.

30. *MTB*, vii, no. 687.

31. Cf. Du Boulay, *Lordship of Canterbury*, 107–8, 366–8, 80–1.

32. So ill, in fact, that he made arrangements for his possible death (*Gesta regis Henrici secundi*, i, 6–7).

33. HB, 468.

34. Not October: Howden's account (*Gesta Regis Henrici Secundi*, i, 7–9), is seriously garbled and must be abandoned; see Barlow, *Becket*, 214, 313–14, n. 34.

35. HB, 468–70; cf. WF, 114–15.

36. HB, 470–71; cf. WF, 115–16.

37. *CTB*, ii, no. 299.

38. *CTB*, ii, no. 300, n. 19.
39. He was expecting to leave Sens on 1 November, for John of Salisbury sent notification of the date to the monks at Canterbury (JS, *Letters*, ii, 712–13).
40. William FitzAdeline had accounted for the scutage of the Canterbury knights in 1161 (Du Boulay, *Lordship of Canterbury*, 6, n. 1); Ralph FitzStephen was a sheriff.
41. Earl Reginald of Cornwall (1141–75), an illegitimate son of Henry I; William of Saint-Jean, from the Avranchin, one of the leading royal officers in Normandy and farmer of the vicomté of Coutances (*c.* 1160–1203) (Haskins, *Norman Institutions*, 340); a Robert de Sancto Johanne held one fee in Crayford in 1253 (Du Boulay, *Lordship of Canterbury*, 338).
42. *MTB*, vii, nos 700–1, issued from Ferentino on 16 September. They had been intercepted by an unidentified courier in the immediate aftermath of the coronation. The replacements were issued from Tusculum (Frascati) on 24 November (*MTB*, vii, nos 720–1).
43. WC, 86.
44. *CTB*, nos 310, 312–15.
45. *MTB*, vii, nos 689 and 697.
46. *MTB*, vii, no. 710.
47. *MTB*, vii, no. 711.
48. *MTB*, vii, no. 715.
49. *MTB*, vii, nos 700–1.
50. WF, 119–20; cf. HB, 478–80.
51. Possibly Master Edward (Evrardus) Grim, Becket's biographer.
52. *CTB*, ii, nos 321, 327–9.
53. *Thomas Becket*, 227.
54. *English Episcopal Acta*, 20: York 1154–1181, ed. Marie Lovatt (Oxford, 2000), xxiii–lvii, esp. xlvii–xlviii.
55. *CTB*, ii, no. 326.

Chapter 10 Murder in the cathedral

1. William FitzStephen at Northampton (1164): WF, 58; an unknown cleric in discussion with Robert of Hereford: WF, 60; John of Salisbury: *CTB*, i, 473–5 (1166).
2. WF, 83.
3. WF, 130.

4. WF, 121–2; WC, 105–6 (says Winchester); cf. HB, 481–2.

5. WC, 107–12.

6. WF, 122–3; cf. HB, 482–3.

7. WF, 125.

8. WF, 123–4; WC, 112–13; cf. HB, 484. EG, 427 attributes the command to envoys from the older king, who said that Becket had been the first to break the *federa pacis*.

9. WC, 114–15. Cf. Barlow, *Becket*, 231. For the identification of W. *medicus*, see William Urry, *Thomas Becket. His Last Days*, ed. Peter A. Rowe (Stroud, 1999), 60–1.

10. WC, 114–18.

11. WC, 114–19.

12. WC, 119–20; WF, 130.

13. Above, 77.

14. WF, 128–9.

15. *MTB*, vii, nos 730, 731, 732; *Letters of Arnulf of Lisieux*, ed. Frank Barlow, nos 54b, 59, 60. The 'authority' may have been *MTB*, vi, no. 310, obtained during the Canterbury vacancy in 1161 (Chapter 9, n. 22).

16. Saltman, *Theobald*, 26–7.

17. EG, 429; WF, 128; WC, 127–9; Anon. I, 69–70; cf. HB, 487.

18. HB, 535–8; cf. Lansdowne Fragments, *MTB*, iv, 158–64.

19. Nicholas Vincent, 'The Murderers of Thomas Becket', in *Bischofsmord*, 211–72, esp. 244.

20. WF, 129–30, 131–3; cf. EG, 429–32; WC, 129–30; Anon. I, 70–2; HB, 488–9.

21. WF, 134–5; cf. EG, 432–3; Anon. I, 72–3.

22. BP, *Passio*, 9.

23. WF, 135–7; WC, 130–1; cf. EG, 433–4; WC, 130; Anon. I, 74.

24. WF, 141.

25. WC, 133–4.

26. WF, 140.

27. JS, 320; cf. EG, 437; WC, 133; WF, 140–1; Guernes, vv. 5576–80 (trans. Shirley, 148); Anon. I, 77 (adding St Alphege); HB, 499.

28. EG, 436–7 and Anon. I, 77, name FitzUrse; WC (132), WF (141), Guernes, vv. 5581–91 and HB (498) name de Tracy. WC (134), and Guernes, vv. 5596–6000 (trans. Shirley, 148),

said that de Tracy boasted at Saltwood that he had cut off John of Salisbury's arm; HB wrote in his *Liber Melorum* (Book of Melodies), *MTB*, iii, 537, that de Tracy confessed that he had struck the first blow.

29. Vincent, 'Murderers of Thomas Becket', 226.
30. WF, 138–43; EG, 434–8; WC, 132–5; Anon. I, 75–7; cf. HB, 492–9, 506. Cf. Knowles, *Historian and Character*, 126–7; Barlow, 244–7, esp. the judicious comment (246), 'The recorders constructed a story out of confused recollections of imperfectly observed events and from what the participants are alleged to have said later. These factors make a completely certain reconstruction of the happenings in every detail impossible'. For Hugh of Horsey, possibly a clerk in the service of Hugh de Morville, see Vincent, 'Murderers of Thomas Becket', 226.
31. *Becket*, 247; cf. Warren, *Henry II*, 510, who avoids recording the bloody details.
32. Martin Aurell, 'Le meurtre de Thomas Becket', 200–10.
33. WF, 140–1.
34. BP, *Passio*, 15–16.
35. BP, *Miracula*, 16; WF, 148; cf. Barlow, 249, 'distributed as worthless alms'.
36. WF, 144–9; EG, 441–3; cf. HB, 518–22.
37. P. Kidson, 'Gervase, Becket and William of Sens', *Speculum*, 68 (1993), 969–91; D. Webb, *Pilgrimage in Medieval England* (London, 2000), 18–20; B. Nilson, *Cathedral Shrines of Medieval England* (Woodbridge, 1998), 128–34.
38. EG, 440; WC, 148.
39. BP, *Miracula*, 22–4; EG, 440–3; WF, 146–50.
40. WF, 150.
41. BP, *Miracula*, 37; EG, 440.
42. BP, *Passio*, 16, *Miracula*, 53.
43. BP, *Passio*, 16, *Miracula*, 49–53.
44. BP, *Miracula*, 42, 52–3, 54.
45. BP, *Miracula*, 35, 57, 60–1.
46. BP, *Miracula*, 37 (Sussex), 39 (Gloucester), 40 (Berkshire), 44 (Hoyland), 46 (Warbleton), 47 (Surrey), 48 (Worth), 54 (Bourne), 41 (Canterbury), 42 (London priest at Canterbury), 54 (Canterbury), 55 (Canterbury), 56 (Canterbury); WF, 150 (Canterbury x 2).

47. BP, *Miracula*, 43.

48. A view first voiced by J.C. Russell, 'The Canonization of Opposition to the King in Angevin England', *Anniversary Essays in Mediaeval History Presented to C.H. Haskins*, ed. C.H. Taylor (Boston, 1922), 279–90.

49. BP, *Miracula*, 47, 50, 57, 61, 76–7, 144, 217; cf. Robertson's discussion of the miracles, *MTB*, ii, xxvii–xl.

50. *Decretales ineditae*, no. 36.

51. WC, *Miracula*, 321; cf. Barlow, *Becket*, 268; Anon. II, 143. This evidence also challenges Peter Draper's assertion that the monks 'took more than two years to dispatch a monk to Rome' with a petition for canonization: 'Interpretations of the Rebuilding of Canterbury Cathedral, 1174–86. Archaeological and Historical Evidence', *Journal of the Society of Architectural Historians*, 56 (1997), 184–203 at 196.

52. *MTB*, vii, no. 788.

53. *MTB*, vii, nos 783–5.

54. *MTB*, vii, no. 783.

55. *Petri abbatis Cellensis … epistolarum libri ix*, ed. J. Sirmond (Nivelliana: Paris, 1603), no. 54; cf. the different canonization letter sent to the bishop of Aversa (*MTB*, vii, no. 786).

56. *MTB*, vii, no. 770.

57. JS, *Letters*, ii, nos 150, 168, 171, 288, 302, 309, 312, 319, 321–2. There is one letter to Henry of Winchester: no. 260.

58. *MTB*, vii, no. 780.

59. BP, *Miracula*, 43; WF, 151.

60. *Liber melorum*, *MTB*, iii, 542.

61. Diceto, i, 345; Newburgh, i, 163.

62. *MTB*, vii, no. 738.

63. *MTB*, vii, no. 739; the same point was made by William of Newburgh, i, 163–4.

64. Anne J. Duggan, 'Diplomacy, Status, and Conscience: Henry II's penance for Becket's murder', *Forschungen zur Reichs-, Papst- und Landesgeschichte. Peter Herde zum 65. Geburtstag von Freunden, Schülern und Kollegen dargebracht*, eds Karl Borchardt and Enno Bünz, 2 vols (Stuttgart, 1998), i, 265–90 at 267.

65. *MTB*, vii, 476.

66. *MTB*, vii, 444; no. 755.

67. *MTB*, vii, nos 734–6 and 743 (Meaux).

68. *MTB*, vii, no. 750; cf. no. 751.

69. *MTB*, vii, 474, 477.

70. Anne J. Duggan, 'Diplomacy, Status, and Conscience', 266, 288–90.

71. WC, 124–6.

72. D. Knowles and R. Neville Hadcock, *Medieval Religious Houses in England and Wales* (London, 1971), 174; cf. *Heads*, 184, for Prior Waleran (Valerian), *c.* 1154/5–1190.

73. WF, 114.

74. The document written by Nigel de Sackville, sealed by the unidentified official, and seen by Reginald of Warenne could have been the warrant for Becket's arrest, issued from Bur-le-Roi on 26 December.

75. *Chronica*, ii, 18–25: from Louis VII, William of Sens (two), and Theobald of Blois; Diceto, 347–8.

76. *Jordan Fantosme's Chronicle*, ed. and trans. R.C. Johnston (Oxford, 1981), vv. 1905–8; *Chronique de la Guerre entre les Anglois et les Ecossais en 1173 et 1174, par Jordan Fantosme*, ed. R.G. Howlett, in *Chronicles of the Reigns of Stephen, Henry II and Richard I*, RS 82 (London, 1884–89), iii (1886), vv. 1605–6.

77. *MTB*, iv, 150–1; cf. the fourth fragment, ibid., 161–4; cf. Gervase, i, 238.

78. Vincent, 'Murderers of Thomas Becket', 252–4, 262–3; HB, 535–58; cf. Lansdowne Fragments, *MTB*, iv, 158–64.

79. Vincent, 'Murderers of Thomas Becket', 256–62, concluding, 262, 'Far from taking no action, Henry II in effect stepped in to claim the lordship of all four estates, allowing only daughters, sisters and cousins to succeed, and then only to a limited share of the murderers' former lands'.

80. Diceto, i, 410.

81. HB, *Liber Melorum*, *MTB*, iii, 535–8; cf. Barlow, *Becket*, 258, 'this may be wishful thinking'.

82. Howden, *Chronica*, ii, 17. From him the story passed to William of Newburgh, i, 164 (without the inscription).

83. *MTB*, iv, 161–4.

84. Duggan, 'Diplomacy, Status, and Conscience'.

Chapter 11 The image constructed and deconstructed, 1171–1900

1. Myriam Soria, 'Les evêques assassinés dans le royaume de France (XIe–XIIe siècles), *Bischofsmord im Mittelalter. Murder of Bishops*, ed. Natalie Fryde and Dirk Reitz (Göttingen, 2003), 97–120.

2. Smalley, *Becket Conflict*, 190–215.

3. *MTB*, no. 735. Ahab's wife, Hiezabel (Jezebel), had compassed Naboth's death by causing false witnesses to testify against him, but she acted for Ahab's advantage.

4. A play on *Angli* (English) and *angeli* (angels), which echoed Pope Gregory I's exclamation that the English slaves offered for sale in the marketplace looked more like angels than Angles.

5. *MTB*, nos 734 and 736.

6. Raymonde Foreville, 'Mort et survie de saint Thomas Becket', *Cahiers de Civilisation Médiévale*, 14 (1971), 21–38, esp. 26–31; *Thomas Becket*, ed. eadem; eadem, 'La diffusion du culte de Thomas Becket dans la France de l'Ouest avant la fin du XIIe siècle', *Cahiers de civilisation médiévale*, 19 (1976), 347–69: repr. in eadem, *Thomas Becket dans la tradition historique et hagiographique* (London, 1981), no. 9.

7. BP, *Miracula*, 24–5.

8. Below, at n. 40.

9. For a discussion of an analogous case, see Paul Hyams, 'The Strange Case of Thomas of Eldersfield', *History Today* (June 1986), 9–15, esp. 14–15.

10. BP, *Miracula*, 26, 173–82; cf. WC, *Miracula*, 156–8.

11. WC, *Miracula*, 517–20. S.K. Langenbahn, 'Die wiederentdeck-ten Himmeroder *Miracula S. Thomae Cantuariensis (1175)*. Zugänge zur frühesten narrativen Quelle zur Geschichte von St. Thomas/Eifel', *Kurtrierisches Jahrbuch*, 41 (Trier, 2001), 121–64, esp. 149–52; cf. B. Caspar, 'Thomas Becket und das Kloster St. Thomas an der Kyll', ibid., 2 (1962), 74–81.

12. *De antiquis legibus liber* and *Cronica maiorum et vicecomitum Londoniarum* (attributed to Arnold Fitz Thedmar), ed. T. Stapleton, Camden Series, 34 (London, 1846), 238–9; cf. esp. 238, which, translated, reads: 'These (Arnold of "Grevingge" and Oda), vowed to go [to Canterbury], having heard reports of the

many great miracles which God had performed in England for St Thomas, archbishop of Canterbury, who had at that time recently been martyred by wicked men ... .' For Arnold's career, see N. Fryde, 'Arnold Fitz Thedmar und die Entstehung der Grossen Deutschen Hanse', *Hansische Geschichtsblatter*, 107 (1989), 27–42, with an extensive family tree of 'Arnold Fitz Thedmar and his clan' (ibid., 42); cf. B.J.M. Lappenberg, *Urkundliche Geschichte des Hansischen Stahlhofes zu London* (Hamburg, 1851; repr. Osnabrück, 1967), 15.

13. P.A. Sigal, 'Naissance et premier développement d'un vinage exceptionnel: l'eau de saint Thomas', *Cahiers de Civilisation Mediévale*, 44 (2001), 35–44.

14. B.W. Spencer, 'Medieval Pilgrim Badges', in *Rotterdam Papers. A Contribution to Medieval Archaeology*, ed. J.G.N. Renaud (Rotterdam, 1968), 137–53, esp. 139, 140–1, 143, 144, Figs 1d, 3b–c, 5, and Plates V and VI. See the splendid illustrated catalogue of London in Brian Spencer, *Pilgrim Souvenirs and Secular Badges: Medieval Finds from Excavations in London* (London, 1998), 37–133.

15. P.A. Newton, 'Some New Material for the Study of the Iconography of St Thomas Becket', in *Thomas Becket, Actes du colloque international de Sédières 19–24 Août 1973*, ed. R. Foreville (Paris, 1975), 255–63. This precious object is now in the Metropolitan Museum in New York.

16. Spencer, 'Medieval Pilgrim Badges', 143.

17. Eyton, 212–13, 228, 257.

18. Howden, ii, 192–3; Eyton, 228. His choice of shrine was particularly significant, since he had made pilgrimages to Jerusalem, Constantinople and Compostela (A. Graboïs, 'Louis VII pèlerin', *Revue d'Histoire de l'église de France*, 74 (1988), 5–22 at 17–20).

19. Howden, ii, 193; Andrew of Marchiennes, *MTB*, iv, 265, no. 9.

20. C.R. Cheney, *Hubert Walter* (London, 1967), 35.

21. Draper, 'Interpretations of the Rebuilding of Canterbury Cathedral', which challenges the arguments of Peter Kidson, 'Gervase, Becket, and William of Sens', *Speculum*, 68 (1993), 969–91, and M.F. Hearn, 'Canterbury Cathedral and the Cult of Becket', *Art Bulletin*, 76 (1994), 19–54.

22. A.J. Duggan, 'The Cult of St Thomas Becket in the Thirteenth Century', in *St Thomas Cantilupe*, ed. Meryl Jancey (Hereford,

1982), 21–44; cf. R. Eales, 'The Political Setting of the Becket Translation of 1220', *SCH*, 30, *Martyrs and Martyrologies*, ed. D. Wood (Oxford, 1993), 127–39.

23. A great deal of work remains to be done on dedications to St Thomas of Canterbury, but see M. Barth, 'Zum Kult des hl. Thomas Becket in deutschen Sprachgebiet, in Skandinavien und Italien', *Freiburger Diozesan-Archiv*, 80 (1960), 97–166; R. Foreville, 'Le culte de Saint Thomas Becket en Normandy'; eadem, 'Le culte de Saint Thomas Becket en France'; H. Martin, 'Le culte de Saint Thomas Becket dans les diocèses de la province de Tours'; J. Becquet, 'Les sanctuaires dédiés à Saint Thomas de Cantorbéry en Limousin': all in *Thomas Becket*, ed. Foreville, 135–52, 153–8, 159–61, 163–87; R. Foreville, 'La diffusion du culte de Thomas Becket dans la France de l'Ouest avant la fin du XIIe siècle', *Cahiers de civilisation médiévale*, 19 (1976), 347–69: repr. in eadem, *Thomas Becket dans la tradition historique et hagiographique* (London, 1981), no. 9; 'The Cult of St Thomas Becket in the Thirteenth Century', in *St Thomas Cantilupe*, ed. Meryl Jancey (Hereford, 1982), 21–44.

24. D. Stevens, 'Music in Honour of St Thomas of Canterbury', *The Musical Quarterly*, 56 (1970), 311–38; idem, 'Thomas Becket et la musique médiévale', in *Thomas Becket*, ed. Foreville, 277–84; A. Hughes, 'Chants in the rhymed office of St Thomas of Canterbury', *Early Music*, 16 (1988), 185–201; K.B. Slocum, *Liturgies in Honour of Thomas Becket* (Toronto, 2004).

25. A.J. Duggan, 'Aspects of Anglo-Portuguese Relations in the Twelfth Century. Manuscripts, relics, decretals, and the cult of St Thomas Becket at Lorvão, Alcobaça, and Tomar', *Portuguese Studies*, 14 (1998), 1–19.

26. See, for example, Hermann Grotefend, *Zeitrechnung des deutschen Mittelalters und der Neuzeit* (Hanover, 1892; repr. Aalen, 1970), ii, 1–2.

27. About 45 reliquary caskets in Limoges enamel still survive, from an estimated 100: see S. Caudron, 'Les châsses de Thomas Becket en émail de Limoges', in *Thomas Becket*, ed. Foreville, 223–41.

28. For Canterbury, see M.H. Caviness, *The Early Stained Glass of Canterbury Cathedral circa 1175–1220* (Princeton, 1977), 146–55, Appendix, Fig. 2, and Plates 92–3, 115, 159, 164, 167, 169, 171–5, 185–91, 194, 197a–h, 199, 205–6, 208–11; for France, see esp. Catherine Brisac, 'Thomas Becket dans le vitrail français au début du xiiie siècle', in *Thomas Becket*,

ed. Foreville, 221–31; cf. L. Grodecki and C. Brisac, *Le vitrail gothique au XXXe siècle* (Fribourg, 1984), 59, 84.

29. T. Borenius, *St Thomas Becket in Art* (London, 1932); M.-M. Gauthier, 'Le meutre dans la cathédrale, thème iconographique médiévale', and J.C. Dickenson, 'Some Medieval English Representations of St Thomas Becket in France': in *Thomas Becket*, ed. Foreville, 247–53 and 265–71, and Plates I–XVIII.

30. Among the many hospitals founded in England under the patronage of St Thomas the Martyr, one may list the following (in addition to St Thomas's in Southwark (London): Scarborough, New Romney (SS. Stephen and St Thomas), Peterborough and York (W. Dugdale, *Monasticon Anglicanum*, revised edn by J. Caley, H. Ellis and B. Bandinel, 6 vols, in 8 (London, 1817–30; repr. 1846), vi/2, 639, 640, 771, 782). For France, see Foreville, *Thomas Becket*, 138, 145, 147, 151, 152, 175.

31. In Sermon no. 44 (*PL*, ccxi, 253), St Thomas is named with St Victor of Marseilles and St Martin of Tours: see J. Châtillon, 'Thomas Becket et les Victorins', in *Thomas Becket*, ed. Foreville, 97.

32. *MTB*, iv, 265, no. 10; cf. John W. Baldwin, *Merchants, Princes and Merchants: the social views of Peter the Chanter and his circle* (Princeton, 1970), i, 181; ii, 121 n. 46; Smalley, *Becket Conflict*, 201–4.

33. F.M. Powicke, *Stephen Langton* (Oxford, 1928), 23–48; Smalley, *Becket Conflict*, 204–5.

34. Phyllis B. Roberts, *Thomas Becket in the Medieval Latin Preaching Tradition: An Inventory of Sermons about St Thomas Becket c. 1170–c. 1400*, Instrumenta Patristica, 25 (The Hague, 1992).

35. *The Stripping of the Altars* (New Haven, 1992).

36. Germain Marc'Hadour, 'La confrontation Becket-Henri II comme paradigme historique', *Cahiers de Civilisation Médiévale X^e–XIIe Siècles*, 37 (1994), 101–10; *The Correspondence of Sir Thomas More*, ed. E.F. Rogers (Princeton, 1947), 564 (cited in Marc'Hadour, 103).

37. *Letters and Papers, Foreign and Domestic, on the Reign of Henry VIII*, ed. J.S. Brewer, J. Gairdner and R.H. Brodie (London, 1862–1910), 13/ii, 848; cf. Duffy, *Stripping of the Altars*, 412; cf. Plates 131 and 132.

38. Cf. one of the many later printings: *Acts and Monuments of Matters most Special and Memorable, happening in the Church*, 9th edn, 3 vols (London: printed for the Company of Stationers, 1684), i, 231–2.

39. *Acts and Monuments*, i, 253.

40. Above, at n. 8.

41. *Acts and Monuments*, i, 255.

42. Ibid., i, 256.

43. Martin Murphy, *St Gregory's College, Seville, 1592–1767* (Southampton, 1992), 23–4.

44. Founded 1568 by William (Cardinal: 1587) Allen (1532–94).

45. Jean Chaunu, *Pie VI et les évêques français: droits de l'Église et droits de l'homme* (Paris, 1989), 136–7, no. 8.

46. John Locke, *A Letter Concerning Toleration*, in *The Second Treatise of Civil Government* and *A Letter Concerning Toleration*, ed. J.W. Gough (Oxford, 1946), 150, 'If a Roman Catholic believe that to be really the body of Christ which another man calls bread, he does no injury thereby to his neighbour.'

47. Locke, *Letter Concerning Toleration*, 155.

48. William Laud, successively dean of Gloucester (1616), bishop of St David's (1621), of Bath and Wells (1626), and London (1629–33), archbishop of Canterbury (1633–45), who argued for the 'catholicity' of the Church of England, had sought to restore some of the liturgical practices of the pre-Reformation Church and to impose liturgical uniformity. His opposition to Puritans led to his impeachment in 1641 and execution in 1645, although he died repudiating the charge of 'popery' and affirming his allegiance to the Protestant Church of England.

49. Provoked by the deprivation (1688–89) of 9 bishops and 400 clergy, who refused to take the oaths of allegiance and supremacy to William III and Mary, on the grounds that such oaths would mean breaking the oaths they had already taken to James II.

50. *The Authority of Christian Princes over their Ecclesiastical Synods …* (London: R. Sare, 1697); *A Vindication of the Realm and Church of England …* (London: J. Morphew, 1717).

51. *The Rights, Powers, and Priviledges of an English Convocation, Stated and Vindicated* (London: T. Bennet, 1700).

52. *Ecclesiastical Synods and Parliamentary Convocations in the Church of England* (London: A. and J. Churchill, 1701).

53. i, pp. vii–viii. Citations are to the sixth edition, 10 vols (London, 1854).

54. Lyttelton, iv, 41.

55. Lyttelton, iv, 60, 84.

56. Lyttelton, iv, 419–40, 127–8.

57. Lyttelton, i, p. viii; iv, 2.

58. *History of the Reign of Henry the Second, and of Richard and John, his Sons* ... (Robinson: Birmingham, 1790), esp. 78, 103–23, 664, 667.

59. John Lingard, *Antiquities of the Anglo-Saxon Church*, 1st edn (Newcastle, 1806), 3rd edn (London, 1845): I, xi–xii (cf. 113–16, 173–7); I, xiv (cf. 287–92); I, xv (cf. 307–8); I, xv (cf. 329–32); II, vi (cf. 45–6); II, vi (cf. 57–8); II, vii (cf. 83–4); II, vii (cf. 95–9); II, vii (cf. 101–2); II, vii (cf. 117–19).

60. *History of England from the First Invasion of the Romans to the Accession of William and Mary in 1688:* citations are to the 6th edn, 10 vols (London, 1854), ii, 55, 61–4, 66, 67–8, 309.

61. *Histoire de la Conquête de l'Angleterre par les Normands* (Paris, 1839).

62. *Remains of the late Reverend Richard Hurrell Froude*, published posthumously (London, 1838).

63. *A Critical and Historical Review of Fox's Book of Martyrs, Shewing The Inaccuracies, Falsehoods, and Misrepresentations in that Work of Deception* (Baltimore, 1824–26), 4.

64. *The Papal Supremacy* (London, 1827), 18, 19, 69, 70, 122.

65. The test acts were not repealed, so that Catholics were debarred from the universities and public life.

66. E.B. Pusey, 'The Royal Supremacy', 15.

67. Edward A. Freeman, 'St Thomas of Canterbury and his Biographers', in *Historical Essays*, First Series (London, 1871), 85.

68. *Thomas Becket* (London, 1859), 79, 81, 87, 290, 291, 313, 315. Robertson was later the distinguished editor of the seven-volume *Materials for the History of Thomas Becket* (1875–85).

69. Followed in 1885 by a second and much enlarged edition.

70. *Miscellanies*, 2 vols (1877), i, 257–91, esp. 272–82.

71. *Miscellanies*, ii, 104.

72. 'St Thomas of Canterbury and his Biographers', esp. 80–4.

Chapter 12 Conclusion

1. Türk, *Nugae Curialium*, 8, 22–3.

2. Ibid., 23, 'Cette mort violente, souhaitée et provoquée par le primat, peut donc être considerée aussi bien comme un acte de justice sauvage que comme le cas extrême d'un règlement de comptes entre "curiales".'

3. Warren, *Henry II*, 447–517, esp. 400, 453, 455–6, 459, 490, 514. The 'theological dinosaur' taunt seems particularly ill-chosen in the light of Miss Smalley's demonstration of his dependence on the latest opinions coming out of Paris: *Becket Conflict*, 18–38, 115–35.

4. Charles Duggan, 'The Becket Dispute'; idem, 'The Significance of the Becket Dispute in the History of the English Church', *Ampleforth Journal*, 75 (1970), 365–75, esp. 375; both repr. with the same pagination in idem, *Canon Law in Medieval England* (London, 1982), nos 1 and 10.

5. *Becket*, 271, 274.

6. Warren, *Henry II*, 456; Türk, *Nugae Curialium*, 6; Barlow, *Becket*, 89.

7. *Becket*, 274.

8. Warren, *Henry II*, 515–16.

9. *CTB*, i, 377.

10. Jolliffe, *Angevin Kingship*, 57.

11. J. Gillingham, *The Angevin Empire* (London, 1984), 28.

12. Ibid.; cf. Howden, i, 218, *sub anno* 1161.

13. JS, *Letters*, ii, 569.

14. *Opera*, viii, 158.

15. *Dialogus de Scaccario*, trans. Charles Johnson, revised by F.E.L. Carter and D.E. Greenway, OMT (Oxford, 1983), 1: 'this wealth is not invariably theirs by the strict process of law, but proceeds ... sometimes from the secret devices of their own hearts and sometimes even from their mere arbitrary power.' See also his comments on proffers for favour and/or justice: ibid., 120.

16. *Dialogus*, 60.

17. Above, Chapter 1, at nn. 47–8; cf. Türk's perceptive comments on Becket's dependence on the king, *Nugae Curialium*, 14–15.

18. Türk, *Nugae Curialium*, 6.

19. T.R. Reuter, '*Velle sibi fieri in forma hac*. Symbolic Acts in the Becket Dispute', forthcoming; cf. G. Althoff, '*Ira regis*: prolegomena to a history of royal anger', in *Anger's Past. The Social Uses of an Emotion in the Middle Ages*, ed. B.H. Rosenwein (Ithaca NY, 1998), 59–74.

20. *CTB*, i, 511.

21. WC, 25–26; Guernes, vv. 1120–30 (trans. Shirley, 31); Anon. I, 39.

22. *Henry II*, 488–9.

23. It is thought that he had charge of the prostitutes that followed the court.

24. Türk, *Nugae Curialium*, 23.

25. Paul Brand, '*Multis vigiliis excogitatam et inventam*: Henry II and the Creation of the English Common Law', *Haskins Society Journal*, 2 (1990), 197–222; repr. in idem, *The Making of the Common Law* (London, 1992), 77–102; White, *Reform and Restoration*, 196, 197–8.

26. Smalley, *Becket Conflict*, 119–20; M. Howell, *Regalian Right in Medieval England* (London, 1962), 29–33.

27. Smalley, *Becket Conflict*, 186, 'he compromised too much and too long for his reputation'.

28. Cf. H.G. Richardson and G.O. Sayles, *The Governance of Mediaeval England from the Conquest to Magna Carta* (Edinburgh, 1963), 267, 'Henry's greatest mistake was in choosing and trusting the flashy, shallow and egoistic Thomas Becket'; ibid., 294, 'We must regard Becket not as a martyr, but perhaps as the fatuous fool that Gilbert Foliot in his anger called him.'

29. Ursula Nilgen, 'Thomas Becket as a Patron of the Arts. The Wall Painting of St Anselm's Chapel at Canterbury', *Art History*, 3 (1980), 357–74, esp. 361–3, and Plates 1–7.

30. 'St Thomas's books' are listed in the inventory made in the fourteenth century by Henry of Eastry, prior of Canterbury (M.R. James, *The Ancient Libraries of Canterbury and Dover* (Cambridge, 1903), 82–5); cf. Smalley, *Becket Conflict*, 135–7.

31. JS, *Letters*, ii, 92–3, 269–71, n. 1, 424–5, 809.

32. HB, 217; cf. Raymonde Foreville, 'Thomas Becket', *Dictionnaire de Spiritualité*, xv (1991), 774–80.

33. John W. Baldwin, *Merchants, Princes and Merchants: the social views of Peter the Chanter and his circle* (Princeton, 1970), esp. i, 161–204.

34. *The* Letters *of St. Cyprian of Carthage*, 4 vols, trans. G.W. Clarke, Ancient Christian Writers, 43–4, 46–7 (New York, 1984–89), iii, 69. For the Latin text, see *Sancti Cypriani episcopi epistularium*, ed. G.F. Diercks, *CCSL*, iii B–C (Turnhout, 1994), no. 59 (formerly 55).

35. James, *Ancient Libraries*, 84, no. 834.

36. *CTB*, ii, no. 286, at n. 6.

37. 'Homilies on Ezechiel', vi (Hereford, Cathedral Library, MS O. 3. x, fol. 91ra, '... Veniamus ad beatissimum pontificem et martyrem Thomam, quem vidimus, quem cognovimus. cuius familiares plerique sumus ...', quoted in Smalley, *Becket Conflict*, 199, n. 44.

38. *Hrafns Saga Sveinbjarnarsonar*, ed. Gudrún P. Helgadóttir (Oxford, 1987), 3, vv. 6–39. I am most grateful to Professor Foote for translating the relevant section into English for me. See also Magnússon's valuable comments in *Thómas Saga*, ii, xii–xiii.

39. As, Engey, Gnúpr, Hamar, Holme, Hruni, Hvam, Hvanneyri, Ostrardal, Ströns, Varmlökr (Sigvard Skov, *Thomas Becket og Norden*, Kirkehistoriske Samlinger, Raekke 6/iii (Copenhagen, 1939–41), 401–36); cf. *Thómas Saga*, ii, xxviii–xxxii.

40. *Hrafns Saga*, lxxi.

41. For the context, see *Thómas Saga*, ii, vi–lx; for Robert of Cricklade, ibid., xcii–xciv.

42. As much as anything, this celebrity distinguished him from Albert of Liège, who was murdered in broadly similar circumstances in 1192 on the orders of Emperor Henry VI, but whose cult failed to take off. He did not receive official recognition until the seventeenth century.

43. Mostly, of course, the monks Benedict and William recorded only the success stories, which creates a false impression of automatic cure; but their more than 400 examples of recovery represented a very small proportion of the many thousands of pilgrims who poured through the cathedral's doors between Easter 1171 and 1175.

Further reading

Primary sources

Central to any further study of Thomas Becket must be the three categories of primary materials already discussed in the Introduction:
the various collections of correspondence and letters; the four volumes of contemporary and near contemporary Lives; the two volumes of Miracles, by Benedict 'of Peterborough' and William of
Canterbury; Guernes, the *Thómas Saga*, and the liturgical commem-
orations. To these should be added the notices, some very brief, some
extended, in contemporary chronicles, especially Roger of Howden's
Chronica (i, 218–81, ii, 4–39); Ralph de Diceto's *Ymagines
Historiarum* (*Opera*, i, 306–50); William of Newburgh's *Historia
rerum anglicarum* (i, 139–43, 160–5); and references in the works of
Gerald of Wales and Gervase of Canterbury. Diceto's version
formed the basis of the account transmitted through the thirteenth-
century St Albans tradition in the chronicles of Roger of Wendover
(*Flores historiarum*, ed. H.G. Hewlett, 3 vols, RS 84 (London,
1886–89), i, 20–91) and Matthew Paris (*Matthaei Parisiensis,
monachi sancti Albani, Historia Anglorum*, ed. F. Madden, 3 vols,
RS 44 (London, 1866–69), i, 320–73; idem, *Chronica majora*, ed.
H.R. Luard, 2 vols, RS 57 (London, 1875), ii, 218–86). For discussions of the date and relationship between the biographies, see
the fundamental work of E. Walberg, *La tradition hagiographique
de Saint Thomas Becket avant la fin du XIIᵉ siècle* (Paris, 1929),
with corrections in Barlow, *Becket* (4–9) and Staunton, *Lives*
(4–11). For hagiography as a genre, see esp. T.J. Heffernan, *Sacred
Biography: saints and their biographers in the Middle Ages*
(London, 1988); T. Noble and T. Head, *Soldiers of Christ: Saints
and Saints' Lives from Late Antiquity to the Early Middle Ages*
(London, 1995); A. Vauchez, *La Sainteté en Occident aux derniers
siècles du moyen age* (Rome, 1981); trans. J. Birrell, *Sainthood in the

Later Middle Ages (Cambridge, 1997); and for Becket's biographers, H. Vollrath, '"Gewissensmoral" und Konfliktverständnis: Thomas Becket in der Darstellung seiner Biographen', *Historisches Jahrbuch*, 109 (1989), 24–54.

Becket's life and reputation

The post-medieval historiographical tradition begins with John Foxe's 'Book of Martyrs' (*Acts and Monuments of Matters most Special and Memorable, happening in the Church*, 9th edn, 3 vols (London, 1684), vol. 1) and George Lyttelton's *History of the Life of King Henry the Second* (Birmingham, 1790): both presenting a strongly hostile view, which was continued by J.C. Robertson's *Thomas Becket* (London, 1859). For the twentieth century, R. Foreville's *L'Église et la royauté en Angleterre sous Henri II Plantagenêt* (Paris, 1943) remains the most comprehensive and sympathetic interpretation of the controversy and its broad context, although it has been superseded in some details. Full weight is given to the ethical and theological dimensions of the controversy in David Knowles' *Thomas Becket* (Cambridge, 1973) and especially in Beryl Smalley's brilliant *The Becket Conflict and the Schools* (Oxford, 1973); and there is an excellent summary in Charles Duggan, 'The Significance of the Becket Dispute in the History of the English Church', *Ampleforth Journal*, 75 (1970), 365–75; repr. in idem, *Canon Law in Medieval England*. Among many other studies, there is a long biography by Richard Winston, *Becket* (London, 1967), which makes extensive use of the primary sources, but the most authoritative, though not always sympathetic, modern biography is Barlow's, *Thomas Becket* (London, 1986), which should be compared with his much earlier summation in *The Feudal Kingdom of England* (London, 1955), 290–9; while L.B. Radford's *Thomas of London before his Consecration* (Cambridge, 1894) is still useful for Becket's early years.

King Henry II

For Becket's powerful adversary, the best study is Warren's *Henry II*; but its interpretations must be read in the context of E. Amt, *The Accession of Henry II in England: Royal Government Restored, 1149–1156* (Woodbridge, 1993); G. White, *Restoration and Reform 1153–65. Recovery from Civil War in England* (Cambridge, 2000); M. Chibnall, *Anglo-Norman England, 1066–1166* (Oxford, 1986);

R. Bartlett, *England under the Normans and Angevins, 1075–1225* (Oxford, 2000); J.E.A. Jolliffe, *Angevin Kingship*, 2nd edn (London, 1963). For the Angevin 'empire', J. Gillingham, *The Angevin Empire* (London, 1984); R. Benjamin, 'The Angevin Empire', in *England in Europe, 1066–1453*, ed. Nigel Saul (London, 1994), 65–75. For the court, *La cour Plantagenêt (1154–1204)*, ed. M. Aurell (Poitiers, 2000); for the *curiales*, R.V. Turner, *Men Raised from the Dust: Administrative service and upward mobility in Angevin England* (Philadelphia, 1988); M.T. Clanchy, 'Moderni in Education and Government in England', *Speculum*, 50 (1975), 671–88; *Law and Government in Medieval England and Normandy: Essays in Honour of Sir James Holt*, ed. G. Garnett and J. Hudson (Cambridge, 1994); R.V. Turner, 'Changing Perceptions of the New Administrative class in Anglo–Norman and Angevin England: the curiales and their conservative critics', *Journal of British Studies*, 29 (1990), 93–117: cf. E. Türk, *Nugae curialium: le regne d'Henri II Plantagenêt 1145–1189, et l'éthique politique*, Hautes études médiévales et modernes, 28 (Geneva, 1977). For Henry's reaction to the murder, Nicholas Vincent, 'The Murderers of Thomas Becket', in *Bischofsmord*, 211–72; A.J. Duggan, 'Diplomacy, Status, and Conscience: Henry II's penance for Becket's murder', *Forschungen zur Reichs-, Papst- und Landesgeschichte. Peter Herde zum 65. Geburtstag von Freunden, Schülern und Kollegen dargebracht*, ed. Karl Borchardt and Enno Bünz, 2 vols (Stuttgart, 1998), i, 265–90.

The conflict of law

For an introduction to the complexities of the jurisdictional conflict, see Charles Duggan, 'The Becket Dispute and the Criminous Clerks', *BIHR*, 35 (1962), 1–28 (with numerous citations of earlier work): repr. in *Canon Law in Medieval England* (1982), which contains many other relevant studies; R.M. Fraher, 'The Becket Dispute and Two Decretist Traditions: the Bolognese masters revisited and some new Anglo-Norman texts', *Journal of Medieval History*, 4 (1978), 347–68; and, for the classic defence of Henry II's position, now largely superseded, F.W. Maitland, *Roman Canon Law in the Church of England* (Cambridge, 1898), esp. 132–47. For a broader canonical perspective, see S. Kuttner, 'The Renewal of Jurisprudence', and K.W. Nörr, 'Institutional Foundation of the New Jurisprudence', in *Renaissance and Renewal in the Twelfth Century*, ed. R.L. Benson and Giles Constable, with C.D. Lanham (Oxford, 1982), 299–323, and 324–38; J.A. Brundage, *Medieval Canon Law* (London, 1995);

B.C. Brasington, 'Non imitanda sed veneranda: the Dilemma of Sacred Precedent in Twelfth-Century Canon Law', *Viator*, 23 (1992), 135–65. S. Kuttner and E. Rathbone, 'Anglo-Norman Canonists of the Twelfth Century', *Traditio*, 7 (1949–51), 286–8 (repr. in S. Kuttner, *Gratian and the Schools of Law 1140–1234*, Variorum Reprints (London, 1983), no. VIII, with important additional comments on Vacarius as a formal teacher of Roman law in 'Retractationes', 286–8; F. de Zulueta and P. Stein, *The Teaching of Roman Law in England around 1200*, Selden Society, Supplementary Series 8 (London, 1990); P. Stein, *Roman Law in European History* (Cambridge, 1999; repr. 2001); Charles Duggan, *Twelfth-Century Decretal Collections and their Importance in English History* (London, 1963), esp. first and last chapters; idem, *Decretals and the Creation of New Law in the Twelfth Century: Judges, Judgements, Equity and Law*, Variorum (Aldershot, 1998); *Papal Decretals Relating to the Diocese of Lincoln in the Twelfth Century*, ed. and trans. W. Holtzmann and E.W. Kemp, Lincoln Record Society, 47 (Hereford, 1954). The complex history of the so-called Pseudo-Isidorean collection has been magisterially presented in H. Fuhrmann, *Einfluss und Verbreitung der pseudoisidorischen Fälschungen*, 3 vols, Schriften der Monumenta Germaniae Historica, 24 (Munich, 1972–74).

English Law

Parallel with this extensive work on canon (and Roman) law, the history of English law is being systematically studied. For the most important work in the last 20 years or so, see P. Brand, '*Multis vigiliis excogitatam et inventam*: Henry II and the creation of the English Common Law', *Haskins Society Journal*, 2 (1990), 197–222, repr. in idem, *The Making of the Common Law* (London and Rio Grande, 1992), 77–102; Mike Macnair, 'Vicinage and the Antecedants of the Jury', *Law and History Review*, 17 (1999), 537–90; J. Hudson, *Land, Law and Lordship in Anglo-Norman England* (Oxford, 1994); R.C. Van Caenegem, *The Birth of the English Common Law*, 2nd edn (Cambridge, 1988); P. Wormald, *The Making of English Law: King Alfred to the Twelfth Century, i, Legislation and its Limits* (Oxford, 1999; repr. 2001); R.V. Turner, 'Henry II's Aims in Reforming England's Land Law: feudal or royalist?', in idem, *Administrators and the Common Law in Angevin England* (London, 1994), 1–15; idem, *The English Judiciary in the Age of Glanvill and Bracton, c. 1176–1239* (Cambridge, 1985); idem, 'The Reputation of Royal Judges under the Angevin Kings',

Albion, 11 (1979). For the issues involved in Becket's summons to Northampton, see M.G. Cheney, 'The Litigation between John Marshal and Archbishop Thomas Becket in 1164: a pointer to the origins of Novel Disseisin', *Law and Social Change in British History*, ed. J.A. Guy and H.G. Beale (London, 1984), 9–26; eadem, 'A decree of King Henry II on defect of justice', in *Tradition and Change. Essays in Honour of Majorie Chibnall presented by her friends on the occasion of her seventieth birthday*, ed. D.E. Greenway, C. Holdsworth and J. Sayers (Cambridge, 1985), 183–93. R.C. Van Caenegem's *English Lawsuits from William I to Richard I*, 2 vols, Selden Society 106–7 (London, 1990–91), provides an excellent Latin edition, with English translation, of cases tried in England between the Conquest and the death of Richard I. For a recent review of canonical influences on English common law, with particular reference to the Court of Chancery, see J. Martínez-Torrón, *Anglo-American Law and Canon Law. Canonical Roots of the Common Law Tradition*, Comparative Studies on Continental and Anglo-American Legal History, 18 (Berlin, 1998).

The English Church and the papacy in the twelfth century

For the broader church and England's relations with it, see I.S. Robinson, *The Papacy 1073–1198: Continuity and Innovation* (Cambridge, 1990); *Adrian IV. The English Pope (1154–1159). Studies and Texts*, ed. B. Bolton and A.J. Duggan (Aldershot, 2003); *Rolando Bandinelli Papa Alessandro III*, ed. F. Liotta (Siena, 1986); R. Somerville, *Pope Alexander III and the Council of Tours* (Los Angeles, 1977); M. Pacaut, *Alexandre III* (Paris, 1956); K. Pennington, *Popes and Bishops: the papal monarchy in the twelfth and thirteenth centuries* (Philadelphia, 1984); M. Brett, *The English Church under Henry I* (Cambridge, 1975); Z.N. Brooke, *The English Church and the Papacy from the Conquest to the Reign of John* (Cambridge, 1931); C.R. Cheney, *From Becket to Langton: English Church Government, 1170–1213* (Cambridge, 1956); C. Duggan, 'From the Conquest to the Death of John', in *The English Church and the Papacy in the Middle Ages*, ed. H. Lawrence (London, 1965; 2nd edn, 1999). For the bishops, see M.D. Knowles, *The Episcopal Colleagues of Archbishop Thomas Becket* (Cambridge, 1951); A. Morey and C.N.L. Brooke, *Gilbert Foliot and his Letters* (Cambridge, 1965); M.G. Cheney, *Roger, Bishop of Worcester 1164–1179* (Oxford, 1980).

Cult

For the cult there is a rapidly growing bibliography: A.J. Duggan, 'The Cult of St Thomas Becket in the Thirteenth Century', in *St Thomas Cantilupe*, ed. M. Jancey (Hereford, 1982), 21–44; eadem, 'Aspects of Anglo-Portuguese Relations in the Twelfth Century. Manuscripts, relics, decretals, and the cult of St Thomas Becket at Lorvão, Alcobaça, and Tomar', *Portuguese Studies*, 14 (1998), 1–19; Medard Barth, 'Zum Kult des hl. Thomas Becket in deutschen Sprachgebiet, in Skandinavien und Italien', *Freiburger Diözesan-Archiv*, 80 (1960), 97–166; U. Nilgen, 'Thomas Becket und Braunschweig', in *Die Welfenschatz und sein Umkreis*, ed. J. Ehlers and D. Koetz-Zabern (Mainz, 1998), 219–42; R. Foreville, 'Le culte de Saint Thomas Becket en Normandy'; eadem, 'Le cult de Saint Thomas Becket en France'; Henri Martin, 'Le culte de Saint Thomas Becket dans les diocèses de la province de Tours'; Jean Becquet, 'Les sanctuaires dédiés à Saint Thomas de Cantorbéry en Limousin': all in *Thomas Becket*, ed. Foreville, 135–52, 153–8, 159–61, 163–87; R. Foreville's numerous studies, reprinted in *Thomas Becket dans la tradition historique et hagiographique* (London, 1981); U. Nilgen, 'La "tunicella" di Tommaso Becket in S. Maria Maggiore a Roma. Culto e arte intorno a un santo "politico"', *Arte Medievale*, 2nd Series, 9 (1995), 105–20; S. Piussi, 'Il culto di Thomas Becket ad Aquileia, Venezia e Zara', *Antiquità Altoadriatiche*, 26/2 (Udine, 1985), 381–400; G. Barbetta, 'Sull'introduxione del culto di S. Tommaso Becket', *Studi Storici Veronesi Luigi Simeoni*, 20–21 (1970–72), 107–38. For the periodical renewal of St Thomas's cult at Canterbury, see R. Foreville, *Le Jubilé de saint Thomas Becket du XIIIe au XVe siècle (1220–1470)* (Paris, 1958); and for the historical transformations of his image, see now K.B. Slocum, 'The Making, Un-Making, and Re-Making of the Cult of St Thomas Becket', *Hagiographica*, 7 (2000), 3–16. Equally interesting for the transmission of Becket's name and reputation through the later middle ages are the sermons preached annually on his feast day, of which Phyllis B. Roberts has compiled an important inventory: *Medieval Latin Preaching Tradition: An Inventory of Sermons about St Thomas Becket c. 1170–c. 1400*, Instrumenta Patristica, 25 (The Hague, 1992).

The liturgical Becket

For the Becket liturgies, see A.J. Duggan, 'A Becket Office at Stavelot: London, British Library, Additional MS 16964', *Omnia disce.* Medieval Studies in Memory of Leonard Boyle, O.P. (Aldershot, 2004), Ch. 12; S. Reames, 'Liturgical Offices for the Cult of St Thomas Becket', in *Medieval Hagiography: an anthology*, ed. T. Head (New York, 2000); D. Stevens, 'Music in Honour of St Thomas of Canterbury', *The Musical Quarterly*, 56 (1970), 311–38; idem, 'Thomas Becket et la musique médiévale', in *Thomas Becket*, ed. Foreville, 277–84; A. Hughes, 'Chants in the Rhymed Office of St Thomas of Canterbury', *Early Music*, 16 (1988), 185–201; and K.B. Slocum's somewhat disappointing *Liturgies in Honour of Thomas Becket* (Toronto, 2004); cf. eadem, 'The Remaking of a Saint: Stephen Langton and the Liturgical Office for Becket's Translation', *Hagiographica*, 7 (2000), 17–34. For a recent collection of studies on the liturgical offices of the medieval Church, see *The Divine Office in the Latin Middle Ages*, ed. M.E. Fassler and R.E. Baltzer (Oxford, 2000).

Canterbury, miracles, and pilgrimage

For debates about the rebuilding of the cathedral, see P. Draper, 'Interpretations of the Rebuilding of Canterbury Cathedral, 1174–1186. Archaeological and Historical Evidence', *Journal of the Society of Architectural Historians*, 56 (1997), 184–203, which challenges P. Kidson, 'Gervase, Becket, and William of Sens', *Speculum*, 68 (1993), 969–91 and M.F. Hearn, 'Canterbury Cathedral and the Cult of Becket', *Art Bulletin*, 76 (1994), 19–54. The most recent study on Canterbury as a pilgrimage centre is in B. Nilson, *Cathedral Shrines of Medieval England* (Woodbridge, 1998); cf. A. Loxton, *Pilgrimage to Canterbury* (London, 1978). The most complete analysis of the Miracles remains R. Foreville, 'Les "Miracula S. Thomae Cantuariensis"', in *Actes du 97e Congrès National des Sociétés Savants, Nantes 1972, Section de Philologie et d'histoire jusqua'à 1610* (Paris, 1979), 443–68, which includes statistical tables of the different categories of cure, and maps illustrating the geographical extent of the beneficiaries. For the broader context, see R.C. Finucane, *Miracles and Pilgrims: Popular Beliefs in Medieval England* (London, 1977; repr. New York, 1995); D. Webb, *Pilgrimage in Medieval England* (London, 2000); eadem, *Pilgrims and Pilgrimage in the Medieval West* (London, 1999; repr. 2001); P.-A. Sigal, 'Reliques, pélerinage et miracles dans l'église médiévale (XIe–XIIIe siècles)', *Revue de l'église de France*, 76 (1990), 193–211; B. Ward, *Miracles and the Medieval mind: theory, record, and event, 1100–1215* (London, 1982); J. Sumption, *Pilgrimage: An Image of Medieval*

Religion (London, 1975). For the city and the archbishop's estates: W.G. Urry, *Canterbury under the Angevin Kings* (London, 1967); idem, 'The Normans in Canterbury', *Annales de Normandie*, 2 (1958), 131–2; F.R.H. Du Boulay, *The Lordship of Canterbury* (London, 1966). Still useful, though superseded by more recent work, H. Stanley, *Historical Memorials of Canterbury* (London, 1854; variously reprinted).

St Thomas in art

For artistic representations of St Thomas, the starting point is T. Borenius, *St Thomas Becket in Art* (London, 1932), but the subject has retained the interest of art historians and iconographers across Europe. Among the most recent studies, see G. Beltrame, *S. Tomaso Becket: nella storia, nel culto, nell'arte, in Europa* (Padua, 1989); S. Caudron, 'Les châsses de Thomas Becket en émail de Limoges', M.-M. Gauthier, 'Le meutre dans la cathédrale, thème iconographique médiévale'; P.A. Newton, 'Some New Material for the Study of the Iconography of St Thomas Becket'; J.C. Dickenson, 'Some Medieval English Representations of St Thomas Becket in France': all in *Thomas Becket,* ed. Foreville, 223–41, 247–53, 255–63, 265–71, and Plates I–XVIII; M.H. Caviness, *The Early Stained Glass of Canterbury Cathedral circa 1175–1220* (Princeton, 1977), 146–55; and C. Brisac, 'Thomas Becket dans le vitrail français au début du xiiie siècle', in *Thomas Becket*, ed. Foreville, 221–31.

Becket in literature

Another aspect of Becket's reputation, which had to be omitted from this book, is his treatment in imaginative literature, from the sixteenth century onwards. The best introduction to the whole genre is provided by an important Norwegian study by H. Nordahl and J.W. Dietrichson, *Menneske, Myte, Motiv: Erkebiskop Thomas Becket i historie og diktning* (*Man, Myth, Motif. Archbishop Thomas Becket in History and Literature*) (Oslo, 1980), which has a short but excellent English summary (313–19). More accessible, but less discursive, is J.-M. Grassin, 'Le mythe littéraire de Thomas Becket', in *Thomas Becket*, ed. Foreville, 285–97, which provides a helpful, though not exhaustive, list of plays, novels, operas and films written or produced between 1536–39 and 1970; and it is still worth reading P.A. Brown, *The Development of the Legend of Thomas Becket* (Philadelphia, 1930).

Chronology

1161
c. May   Vexin campaign
18 April   Death of Archbishop Theobald

1162
23 May   Elected archbishop of Canterbury
3 June   Consecrated archbishop of Canterbury
10 Aug.   Receives the *pallium*
                          Resigns the chancellorship

1163
6 Mar.   Gilbert Foliot, bishop of Hereford, elected
                          bishop of London
21 May   Thomas attends papal council at Tours
1 July   Council at Woodstock
13 Oct.   Translation of Edward the Confessor
                          Council at Westminster
Dec.   Interview with Henry II at Woodstock

1164
c. 25 Jan.   Council at Clarendon
19 April   Consecration of Reading Abbey church
6–13 Oct.   Council at Northampton
15 Oct.   Thomas flees from Northampton
29 Nov.   Reaches the papal Curia at Sens
Dec.   Takes up residence at the Cistercian
                          monastery of Pontigny

1165   Thomas remains at Pontigny for the whole year
19 April   At Pontoise
21–23 May   Imperial council at Würzburg

23 Nov. **1165**–   Alexander III in Rome (Lateran, S. Pietro,
10 July **1167**   S. Maria Nova)

1166
12 June   Vézelay: Thomas issues sentences
c. 11 Nov.   Thomas leaves Pontigny for Ste-Colombe, Sens

1167
18–19 Nov.   Conference at Planches, between Gisors and Trie

1168
1 July   Conference at La-Ferté-Bernard

1169

6 Jan.	Conference at Montmirail
7 Feb.	Second Conference of the Kings, at St-Léger
c. 13 April	Thomas at Clairvaux: issues sentences
24–31 Aug.	Domfront/Beauvoir-en-Lions
18 Nov.	Conference at Montmartre

1170

14 June	Westminster Abbey: coronation of the young King Henry
22 July	Reconciliation at Fréteval
1 Dec.	Thomas lands in England
2 Dec.	Thomas returns to Canterbury
29 Dec.	Thomas murdered in Canterbury Cathedral

1171

21 Dec.	Re-opening of Canterbury Cathedral

1172

21 May	'Compromise' of Avranches

1173

21 Feb.	Canonization of St Thomas (at Segni)
29 Dec.	First celebration of the feast of St Thomas at Canterbury

1174

July	Henry II's penance at the tomb

1220

6 July	Translation to new shrine

1534   Act of Supremacy

1538

Nov.	Proclamation that Thomas should no longer be regarded as a saint

1829   Catholic emancipation

1850   Restoration of Catholic hierarchy in England

Index